The Historicity of Experience

The Historicity
of Experience

Modernity, the Avant-Garde, and the Event

KRZYSZTOF ZIAREK

Northwestern

University Press

Evanston

Illinois

Northwestern University Press
Evanston, Illinois 60208-4210

ISBN 0-8101-1835-1 (cloth)
ISBN 0-8101-1836-x (paper)

Library of Congress Cataloging-in-Publication data are available
from the Library of Congress.

The paper used in this publication meets the minimum requirements
of the American National Standard for Information Sciences—
Permanence of Paper for Printed Library Materials, ANSI z39.48-1984.

Contents

Acknowledgments

I gratefully acknowledge here the support which this project received from various institutions and individuals. The initial stage of my research for *The Historicity of Experience* was funded by the National Endowment for the Humanities Fellowship for University Teachers. I also received a research stipend from the Institute for Scholarship in Liberal Arts at the University of Notre Dame, which made possible extended work on this book during the summer of 1996.

I am grateful to Marjorie Perloff and Jerry Bruns for their comments and support of this project. Tom Butler helped me a great deal with editing and preparing the manuscript for publication. I am especially indebted to Ewa Płonowska Ziarek for her incisive comments, encouragement, and understanding throughout the work on this book. Finally, I would like to thank my editors at Northwestern, Susan Harris, Theresa Biancheri, and Susan Betz, for their generous advice and help with bringing this study into print.

Only one part of this book, in a slightly different version, was published before in another publication: the first two sections of the chapter on Stein, which appeared in *Sagetrieb* 12, no. 3 (1993). Sections of chapters 1 and 3 were presented at the meetings of the Society for Phenomenology and Existential Philosophy and of the International Association for Philosophy and Literature.

The Historicity of Experience

Introduction

The Avant-Garde as a Critique of Experience

I

The Historicity of Experience rethinks modern experience by bringing together philosophical critiques of modernity and avant-garde poetry. My purpose in introducing the avant-garde into the philosophical discussion of modernity is not to provide a new global theory of the avant-garde or a cultural-historical account of the diverse avant-garde movements but, rather, to explore, through selective readings of avant-garde poetry, the key aspects of the radical critique of experience: technology, everydayness, temporality, and sexual difference. To that extent, *The Historicity of Experience* is less a book *about* the avant-garde then a critique of experience *through* the avant-garde. Reading the avant-garde in dialogue with the work of some of the major critics of modernity—Heidegger, Benjamin, Lyotard, and Irigaray—allows me to situate avant-garde poetry in the broader context of the ongoing polemics about modernity and to explore how avant-garde "experiments" bear critically upon the issue of modern experience and its technological organization.

In his famous Baudelaire essay on the crisis of experience brought about by technology, Walter Benjamin links the eclipse of the lyric to the changes in the structure of being in modernity. For Benjamin, the atrophy of a certain kind of experience—of full presence or the aura—makes Baudelaire a representative poet of the nineteenth century and possibly the last lyric

3

poet. This Benjaminian diagnosis of the crisis of experience and its impact on poetry is reexamined in many divergent discussions of modernity: in Heidegger, Adorno, Foucault, Lyotard, Irigaray, and others. In this book, I propose to read the explosion of the avant-gardes at the beginning of the twentieth century as yet another response to the crisis of the humanistic concept of experience, a reaction which leads to a reappraisal of the very nature of poetry and technology. I approach the avant-garde not only as a contestation of the humanistic concept of experience and of its mediating function between body and history, the personal and the cultural, but also as a radical redefinition of experience in the context of everydayness.

Against the position taken by Bürger and Huyssen that the avant-garde is nowadays merely of historical interest, my book asserts that we have not yet properly articulated the critical import of the avant-garde for modern art and its continuing pivotal role for the current debates about the end of modernity. This so far unremarked importance of the avant-garde, I argue, lies in its radical refiguration of experience and temporality as an event. Such a notion of experience is always open to the future and transformation, and, as such, irreducible to representations and significations given to it. This critique of experience breaks with the approaches adopted, for instance, by Felski, which still see experience in terms of consciousness and representation. What is also new in my approach is the claim that this avant-garde revision of experience through temporality has its correlate in the philosophical critiques of modernity. In order to fully flesh out the importance of the avant-garde aesthetics as a critique of experience, I develop the conception of experience as event through an engagement with thinkers such as Heidegger, Benjamin, Irigaray, and Lyotard. I concretize this new concept of modern experience in terms of a cluster of issues of pivotal importance to modernity—technology, everydayness, history, gender, and aesthetics—and show how avant-garde poetry produces revisions in these aspects of modern experience.

Since this refiguration of experience is inextricably connected with the critique of aesthetics, crucial to my approach is Heidegger's attempt to find a postaesthetic approach to the work of art. Heidegger's importance for thinking about the radical aesthetics of the avant-garde lies in his definition of art as the temporal event of unconcealment, which radically departs from the dominant conceptions of modernist art: art for art's sake, formalism, art as a sector of culture, artwork as a commodity. Through a reading of Heidegger on art and technology, I develop this nonaesthetic understanding of art's critical role in relation to history, everydayness, and modern technology. Such a liberation of the work of art from aesthetic categorizations is also, I argue, at the heart of the avant-garde. This postaesthetic understanding of the avant-garde poetry shows that, contrary to common misperceptions, the avant-garde does not exhaust itself in its negative or self-destructive impulse but reaches toward a new understanding of experience and temporality.

The configuration of four poets, Stein, Khlebnikov, Białoszewski, and Howe in the second part of *The Historicity of Experience* allows me to demonstrate the broad reach and the variety of forms that the avant-garde revision of experience and aesthetics take. The inclusion of the Eastern European poets in my study not only broadens the perspective beyond the Western avant-garde but also illustrates the fact that one can detect the common threads of this new understanding of the relation between art and experience even in such distinct articulations of the avant-garde as Futurism, language poetry, or the work of Stein. Showing that the avant-garde poetry, which is usually elided from the philosophical discussions of modernist aesthetics, should be at the very center of such critiques, *The Historicity of Experience* proposes a fundamental reconceptualization of the current approaches to the avant-garde, and claims that the avant-garde offers us the most radical concept of experience, temporality, and aesthetics. It is the radicality of this concept, together with its political, aesthetic, and ethical implications, that makes the avant-garde critical for contemporary theoretical reconsiderations of modernity.

In the first part of *The Historicity of Experience,* I critique dominant ideologies of experience and develop a radically different notion of experience in terms of a scission between its everyday technological representation and its poetic disclosure. My argument is that Heidegger, Benjamin, and Irigaray explore the "poetic" dimension of experience in order to revise and modify our understanding of the everyday by emphasizing its historical dimension and the role of alterity in its formation. I begin by looking at the work of art in relation to modern experience, history, and language in the context of the thought of Walter Benjamin and Martin Heidegger. Although many critics want to keep Benjamin and Heidegger apart, I believe that there are at least as many affinities between them as there are irreconcilable differences. It is those similarities between Heidegger and Benjamin, especially in their critique of experience and technology, that provide the starting point for my argument for breaking with the governing psychological or empirical models of experience and articulating a different, *poetic,* notion of experience.[1] Next, I consider Dadaism's interest in technology and Heidegger's conception of the two modalities of experience: *technē* and *poiēsis,* in order to propose the notion of a poetic figuration of experience in the work of art as a contestation of the technicization of the everyday. I argue that the possibility of the work of art, its contemporary significance, lies in the alternative configuration of experience: What such a "post-" or "non-aesthetic" art figures is the possibility of a poietic formation of experience. By developing Luce Irigaray's idea of a new poetics necessary to rethink sexual difference and the gender inequality in everyday cultural practices, I radicalize my critique of experience and explore how the issue of sexual difference complicates the poietic formation of experience.

By turning to avant-garde poetry in parts 2 and 3, I focus on those forms of poetic language which, using the resources of ordinary language, undo dominant ideas of experience and everydayness. Much of contemporary thought, from Wittgenstein to analytic philosophy, on the one hand, and Heidegger, Benjamin, Merleau-Ponty, on the other, also gravitates around the problematic of everydayness and ordinary language. However, if Wittgenstein's work concerns itself largely with the description and analysis of the practices of ordinary discourse and ways in which their complexity exceeds and modifies the parameters of logic and philosophical inquiry, Heidegger and post-Heideggerian thought, by contrast, explore the poetic reserve of language in order to "critique" the everyday and ordinary language and disclose a different configuration of everyday experience. I see that kind of effort to turn the everyday "against" itself, against its increasingly technologically and scientifically determined manifestations, as a decisive characteristic of avant-garde poetry. In fact, this is how I define the "avant-garde impulse" for the purposes of my study: The avant-garde signifies a project of rethinking and reinventing the everyday "poietically," which questions the representation of the everyday within ordinary language practices and common knowledge, on the one hand, and the techno-scientific logic of representation, on the other. Avant-garde poetry reformulates and redesigns the structures and vocabulary of everyday discourse in order to bring into light what I call the poietic dimension of the everyday.

The word *poietic* does not signify here an aestheticization of the ordinary, a simple flight from its "reality," but, instead, an attempt to rethink the everyday through a reinvention or a "recreation," as Gertrude Stein calls it, of poetic language. In view of the pervasive technicization of modern experience, avant-garde poetry—precisely because of its fascination and preoccupation with technology and its impact on ordinary life—provides the best venue for the questioning of the techno-scientific modes of perception and their influence upon language and the logic of representation. This particular approach to the avant-garde allows me to situate the problem historically—as an issue of the specifically modern representations of experience and its relation to art—and yet proceed beyond the divisions and limitations that characterize the field of avant-garde "isms." For this part of my analysis I choose poetry that is rarely considered together with Continental thought, anchoring my inquiry in the writings of Gertrude Stein; a Russian modernist poet, Velimir Khlebnikov; a contemporary Polish poet, Miron Białoszewski; and an American language poet, Susan Howe. I read their poetry in terms of a reinvention of the everyday through the problematic of technology, history, and sexual difference.

I became engaged in this project for two sets of reasons. On the one hand, I wanted to articulate a conception of the avant-garde work of art and poetry that would underscore the difficult and complex ways in which this poetics, against common misreadings, was not only connected to but, in fact, redefined the problematic of experience and history in their ordinary, technological, and gendered dimensions. My book shows the significance of Heidegger and post-Heideggerian thought for such a project, arguing that, by critiquing aesthetics, these approaches begin to redefine modern experience in view of the progressive technicization of the everyday. The second set of reasons has to do with the still prevalent perception of Eastern European poetry largely within the narrowly understood political optics. Although there have been studies linking the language developments in the twentieth-century American poetry with Western European literature, particularly that of France and Germany, not enough attention has as yet been given to their correlations with the avant-garde movements of Eastern Europe.[2] By bringing contemporary poetry into a dialogue with the critiques of representation in Continental philosophy, *The Historicity of Experience* hopes to demonstrate that the ongoing revision of language in the avant-gardes across linguistic and national boundaries should play a critical role in the theoretical debates about modern experience.

2

Already in the early 1980s Lyotard diagnosed as constitutive of the postmodern condition the call to put an end to artistic and linguistic experimentation, a demand that has since become even more pronounced in the debates about the significance of the avant-gardes. In "What is Postmodernism?" Lyotard describes postmodernism as a period of a "slackening" of aesthetic criteria and intellectual "experimentation," a time when anxiety about communication and the stability of representation gives rise to widespread practices of advocating various eclectic forms of realist aesthetics, supported by the need for communicational consensus and certainty of meaning. We are thus faced with a far-reaching demand to forget or suppress the impulse of the avant-garde and the critical thought that developed with it: "There is an irrefutable sign of this common disposition: it is that for all those writers nothing is more urgent than to liquidate the heritage of the avant-gardes."[3] Lyotard charts two different responses that prescribe "post" or "non"-avant-garde functions to art. The first one, of Habermasian provenance and Hegelian inspiration, postulates the completion of the project of modernity by restoring a unity to the splintered spheres of modern experience. In their capacity to provide links among cognitive, ethical, and political discourses, art and aesthetic experience become enlisted in the service of the notion of a totality of social life, restoring an organic unity of experience. The second response liquidates the impact of the avant-garde through "postmodern" eclecticism, an aesthetic which Lyotard calls "the degree zero of contemporary general culture" (PC, 76). Without openly presenting an anti-modernist or anti-avant-garde front, this aesthetic proclaims itself as an advance beyond modernist experimentation. In Lyotard's view, though, it is nothing more than a form of "extended" realism that accommodates all tendencies, and, in a surreptitious fashion, installs money as the arbiter of taste: "But this realism of the 'anything goes' is in fact that of money; in the absence of aesthetic criteria, it remains possible and useful to assess the value of works of art according to the profits they yield" (PC, 76).

Two interconnected judgments determine the critical, even negative, attitude toward the avant-garde. On the one hand, there exists a widespread opinion that the avant-garde, in spite of the fact that its various techniques have been incorporated into and helped shape contemporary popular culture, has failed both to transform the aesthetic sphere and to reintegrate art into social practice.[4] The problem with this judgment is that it often leaves uninterrogated the metaphysical assumptions about experience, which underlie not only aesthetics and the organization of modern social life but also the concept of the divide between art and life and the postulated goal of the transformation of the everyday. On the other hand, even when the "achievement" of the avant-garde is recognized, it is most often circumscribed, and, in a simultaneous gesture, deprived of importance or even relevance, by the familiar qualification of its practices as an aesthetic of the experimental and the new, an aesthetic representative of the ideology of high modernism. To say in the postmodern moment that something is experimental and new is as much as to foreclose any discussion of its cultural impact, since the social and cultural reality of postmodernism seems to be predicated on the idea of the new, of a constant improvement of products, services, and the quality of life. Already Adorno and Horkheimer suggested—an argument repeated by Jameson—that the uninterrogated appeal of the new, which in fact repeats the same in the guise of novelty,[5] marks the absorption of avant-garde aesthetics into the mode of mass production characteristic of "late" liberal capitalism. This is why it is crucial to distinguish, as Lyotard demonstrates, between the new as novelty and innovation, and the surprise or the unexpected opened by the event structure of experience: "The occurrence, the *Ereignis*, has nothing to do with the *petit frisson*, the cheap thrill, the profitable pathos, that accompanies an innovation."[6] The event undoes "the presumption of the mind with respect to time," figuring experience as open-ended and excessive in relation to its representation. This temporal excess or incompletion, a certain untimeliness which always accompanies occurrence, unworks the privatization and subjectivation of experience. What is each time "new" is the singularity with which the event exceeds the bounds of representational thinking, and remains, in its occurrence, without essence.

In the United States, the "misconceptions" about the avant-garde are reinforced by the picture of modernism constructed by New Criticism, which underscores the aesthetic self-sufficiency of the text, a deep divide between "high art" and "reality." In this conception of literary modernity, the avant-garde becomes inscribed into the overall framework of modernist literature and the prevalent autonomy aesthetics of high modernism. In this setting, any attempt to interrogate avant-garde aesthetics becomes immediately suspect, if not already convicted, of a desire to aestheticize, to impose an "aesthetic" structuring of perception upon the "real" experience of everyday social life. Such a charge, presupposing often the idea of a nondiscursive experience prior to or outside of language, deeply misrecognizes the "avant-garde" impulse in modern art and poststructuralist critiques of modernity: a rethinking of being in terms of an event, whose historicity undoes, together with subject and essence, the idea of private aesthetic experience. Avant-garde art explicitly distances itself from the concept of aesthetic experience as a separate, "higher" or "more essential" moment of experience; it has to be kept distinct, therefore, from the aesthetics of autonomy characteristic of high modernism.[7] It demands, instead, a rethinking of the very structure of experience apart from the notion of the subjective and the private, a radical rethinking that can happen only through a reinvention of language, a transformation of the principles of discourse and representation. My study suggests that avant-garde art activates and reinvents the interval between experience and language: If there is a "content" to avant-garde art, a space "proper" to its experimentation, it is precisely the complex interlacing of experience and language. Such a reconfiguration of this mutual bind in the aftermath of modernity, in the increasingly techno-scientific culture, forms the texture of avant-garde art.

Many discussions which do recognize the importance of the avant-garde and its difference from high modernism are, unfortunately, too often narrowly circumscribed in terms of overcoming the divide between art and life.[8] Such approaches adopt what seems to me an uninterrogated, causal notion of transformation and posit art apart from everyday experience, which makes it difficult to see that the avant-garde contests such a constitution of the everyday not from the outside but from within the discursive "production" of experience. These readings of avant-garde's contestation of the autonomy of aesthetics often reduce avant-garde poetics to shock techniques in various artistic media, techniques now already obsolete and comfortably inscribed within mass culture, which has reappropriated their shock value in order to reaffirm perception and culture, rather than to question it. This limited view predetermines the outcome of the discussion of the avant-garde as an issue of the past, a failed project, which can only be seen in terms of its historical relevance. Even Andreas Huyssen, who nuances the understanding of the avant-garde in relation to its influence on American postmodernism, remarks in *After the Great Divide* that "[n]ot only is the historical avantgarde a thing of the past, but it is also useless to try to revive it under any guise" (15). Such an apodictic judgment excludes a priori any real reconsideration of the avant-garde impulse as a vital moment in postwar art and prevents us from seeing how contemporary "avant-garde" art can have any relevance beyond the ripple effect of the innovative techniques and transformative ambitions within mass culture.[9] Instead of trying to understand why the avant-garde impulse persists and what constitutes its unrecognized significance for postmodernism, such a version of what Lyotard identifies as the demand to stop trying to be avant-garde declares the avant-garde dead and any attempt to rethink it as arbitrary and devoid of importance for contemporary culture.

It is obvious that I agree with Lyotard that, in order to radicalize the critique of modernity, it is indeed imperative to rethink the avant-garde.[10]

However, such an imperative will fail to produce much resonance unless we first change the parameters of the debate away from the predominant, but worn-out and no longer productive, oppositions: art/life, aesthetic experiments/external reality, aesthetic experience/action, and so on. Only then it will be possible to show the "falseness" or simplification of the divide writing/life in the context of the avant-garde and recognize that the reinventions of language produced by the avant-garde work not on an "aesthetic" level (if by that we mean a separate domain of experience, abstracted from the everyday) but on the level of the texturing of experience, and pertain to the issue of how modernity constitutes itself through a techno-scientific unfolding of being. By bringing the avant-garde into a dialogue with Continental thought, we can move the discussion beyond the vexed issue of integration/separation of art from what often goes under various names: everyday life, social practice, reality, experience, and so on. The binary optics adopted in most discussions of the avant-garde is organized by an either/or logic that fails to recognize the nuances of the differential relation between art and experience, which questions both sharp divides and false sublations. What is required to rephrase the questions usually addressed to avant-garde works is a rethinking of the very notion of experience in ways that allow us to see art as a site where experience materializes in its linguistic structures (I deliberately bring here into play the two senses of matter: materiality and signification, to underscore their nonbinary relation which structures experience), as a space that remains both integral to experience and yet "apart" from it, without ever being separated from it. To accomplish that, I bring together Continental thinkers—Benjamin, Heidegger, Lyotard, Irigaray— and suggest ways in which to rethink, first, experience in the historicity of its event, and, second, the work of art in the active sense of (un)working and retexturing experience. Though this may not be the entire answer to the question of the integration of art and life, such a rethinking of experience in terms of the event allows us to begin examining avant-garde art from the different location it takes up in experience: within its historical fold, which holds experience in view of its nonself-identical and disjointed structures of eventuation, and which keeps disarticulating the significations which experience assumes within cultural practices.

Against the premise that it is constructive only to discuss the "historical avant-garde," I underscore the continuing "transformative" import of the critique of experience in the avant-garde. For that purpose, I discuss both examples of the avant-garde eruption in the 1910s (Khlebnikov) and its continuation through high modernism (Stein) and the instances of its reactivation and transformation in Białoszewski and Howe, representatives, respectively, of Polish linguistic poetry in the 1960s and American language poetry. I reexamine the avant-garde poetics as a contestation of the modern practices in which the everyday is constituted as either technologically determined and instrumentalized experience or as its apparent opposite: essentially private, socially and aesthetically isolated, sphere. Avant-garde art is not simply about transforming the everyday through the interjection of provocative and innovative aesthetic and perceptual practices into the routine functioning of mass society. What strikes one in Tzara's Dada manifestoes is not so much the gap between art and everyday life but the sense that capitalism and bourgeois culture "extinguishes" life and being itself: "Liberty: **DADA DADA DADA;**—the roar of contorted pains, the interweaving of contraries and of all contradictions, freaks and irrelevancies: LIFE."[11] The predominant conception of rationality and instrumentalized experience "liquidates" being through the processes of homogenization and reification. The question, at least for Tzara, is not how to overcome the divide between art and experience but how to rethink and contest experience itself, how to address the historicity and inessentiality of each instant, its contradictoriness, which disappears in the increasingly technological schema of being, and, finally, how to critique culture and society through such a revised, "dada" concept of experience. The new, technologically influenced, art—the "art" of Dada rather than the auratic art of aesthetics—orients itself specifically toward exploring the critical potential of the inessentiality of experience, of its nonsubstantive happening. It directs this impetus against representational and linguistic constants, and their foundational role in constructing the sphere of aesthetic and private experience as well as the techno-scientific calculus of being.

To assess the critical implications of this revision of experience, we have to move beyond the optics of the art/life divide and the residues of Hegelian dialectics evident in it. Despite its efforts, this perspective cannot shake off the idea that art is something "added" to life, something "other" to everyday experience, which has to be incorporated back into it. As other to life, art needs justification and legitimation through its possible "pragmatic" value—its usefulness for transforming culture. This concept of art repeats the Hegelian scenario of diremption and healing, the scenario which underpins many contemporary accounts of art: it is stilled in the negative by Adorno,[12] or animated again, though certainly in different ways, by Habermas, Bürger, and Huyssen. I argue that to open up a different perspective, we need to rethink experience in terms of its historicity, that is, in relation to the ecstatic temporality opened up in the event of experience. To illustrate this revised understanding of experience, I discuss Heidegger's and Benjamin's writings on aesthetics and technology against the backdrop of Lyotard's reading of the avant-garde, and supplement and revise their approach through Irigaray's critique of the patriarchal morphology of experience.

While Benjamin wrote on the avant-garde and Irigaray postulates a kind of "avant-garde" poetics of thinking, Heidegger seems at first an unlikely candidate to provide a constructive understanding of the avant-garde. It is rarely remembered that Heidegger in fact wrote on Cézanne, Rimbaud, Klee, Chilida, but that itself is not enough to make his thought on art pertinent to the avant-garde. What makes Heidegger important for rethinking the avant-garde is his discussion of *technē* and *poiēsis,* especially his conception of the event as *poiēsis,* which I adapt in order to flesh out avant-garde's critique of experience. I rethink Heidegger's notion of *Ereignis* to draw together strands from Benjamin's idea of dialectical image, Irigaray's notion of proximity, and Lyotard's conception of the avant-garde as event. The event, then, becomes the prism for rethinking experience and history through technology, sexual difference, and ordinary language. Such a rereading has been made possible by recent nuanced interpretations of the Heideggerian corpus, by what Robert Bernasconi calls "Derrida's Heidegger," [13] or, more broadly, a poststructuralist Heidegger, as well as by the growing feminist engagement with Heidegger's texts, especially Irigaray's critique. This resituating of Heidegger within the ongoing critiques of metaphysics and modernity also opens up a new perspective upon experience in which it becomes important to examine the confluences between Heidegger and Benjamin. Where I move beyond these readings and the debate between "hermeneutical" Heidegger and "deconstructive" Heidegger, is in linking Heidegger's call from "The Way to Language" for a transformation of our relation to language, [14] at least to some extent against Heidegger's "intention," with the avant-garde. Such a connection becomes possible and fruitful when we rethink Heidegger's terms *poiēsis* and *Ereignis* through his critique of experience and technology.

The concept of event, which I develop through reading both Heideggerian critiques of modernity and avant-garde poetry, casts experience in terms of its emergence: that is, as the twofold structure of simultaneous coming into presence and withdrawal in which what is becomes measurable and representable only at the expense of suppressing historicity. I show that what Benjamin's dialectical image, Heidegger's *Ereignis* or "propriative event,"[15] and Irigaray's notion of proximity have in common are the critical effects of the event. The event here is not a temporal punctuality or an instant of presence but, instead, a dynamic and open-ended field of forces, whose historicity prevents experience from closing into representational constructs, psychic spaces, or lived instants. Historicity acts as a force of temporal dislocation: It (de)organizes the dynamic field of the event in such a way that its coming into presence never coincides with what is made present or opened up by it. Historicity both lets the event emerge into presence and withholds (full) presence from it, keeping the event disjointed and incomplete. Experience here is, then, neither an experience of presence nor an experience of absence (conceived as negation or lack) but an event "within which that opposition [between presence and absence] arises and which as such is not governed by it."[16] It counters the metaphysical understanding of experience in terms of presence, and should be placed, therefore, in quotation marks; such "experience" both opens up the spaces of experience, thought, and representation, and, through the working of historicity, makes their closure impossible. The effects of these disjunctions are not just a matter of negation or, as Lyotard suggests, of a negative presentation: that is, a "presentation" of the unpresentable, or the sublime. Their importance comes from how they trace the vectors of the most critical revisions within modern experience. Benjamin's dialectical image explodes historicism's notion of history, because it covers over the force of historicity, and renders the space of history representable as a series of consecutive presents. Irigaray's idea of wonder reconceptualizes utopia as the excess of the event, which, disarticulating the logic of identity, opens up the possibility of thinking sexual relations beyond the binary optics of sameness and difference. In Heidegger's discussions of *Ereignis,* historicity marks a difference between *poiēsis* and technology, a difference which reverberates within the everyday and the experience of language.

The notion of the event juxtaposes the technological modality of revealing which predominates in modernity with what might be called a "poietic" unfolding. I argue that, unlike *technē, poiēsis* retains the event in its historicity, underscoring its irreducibility to the order of representation. Historicity here is not an attribute of something that is seen as a product of specific historical circumstances or is thought in terms of an unstable and changing historical context. It refers to a structural indetermination intrinsic to "experience" as event, an irreducible excess or remainder which *poiēsis* marks in what it unfolds, or historiality which renders history structurally open to change. Reworking Heidegger's idea of *poiēsis* in the context of

Marxism and psychoanalysis, Castoriadis explores the creative potential of such indetermination for reimagining social and historical relations.[17] Linking *poiēsis* to the "creativity" of history itself, to the rupture and reinvention of social relations, Castoriadis, however, takes the aesthetic paradigm of historical transformation for granted.[18] I argue, instead, that the very idea of aesthetics also has to be called into question to understand *poiēsis* as the model of historical change. My analysis of the avant-garde allows us to pinpoint the obverse side of the problem Castoriadis diagnoses: I show that it is the reduction of art to the aesthetic paradigm, that is, the assimilation of art to an object of aesthetic experience, that obliterates historicity and temporality. The reason why we are disposed to forget historicity is the eclipse of the temporality of event not only in institutional structures but also in the instituting of art as aesthetic object. My understanding of the avant-garde is based, then, on the notion of art that tries, through a critique of aesthetics, to recover *poiēsis* and bring it to bear upon the denial of the temporality of experience. It is this specific critique of art and experience through *poiēsis* which makes avant-garde art postaesthetic.

As I show in chapters 1 and 2, rethinking experience as event does not lead either to the privatization of experience or to the aestheticization of social practice, but results in a rigorous questioning of the technological schematization of experience and its formative influence on the everyday. I explore Heidegger's idea that technology as manufacturing and processing into information becomes possible only because the actual in modernity is always already revealed as a standing-reserve of, in principle, calculable and measurable resources. In this perspective, technology is not manufacturing or production but a modality of the revealing of the actual which underlies modern techno-scientific reality. It organizes and constitutes reality in terms of its availability and transparency as resource.[19] Discussing the conception of technology in Benjamin, Lyotard, and Heidegger, it becomes clear that the global transformation of what is into information as well as the commodification of time and experience hinges upon the technological mode in which the modern world unfolds. As a result, experience loses the quality of an event irreducible to signification, becomes regulated, ordered, and compressed into information. What is particularly important for my study is that this technological structure of the actual dehistoricizes being, which, reduced to its existence as resource and turned into information, becomes a commodity in a rapidly expanding marketplace.[20] Knowledge undergoes a similar transformation: It becomes instrumentalized, reducible to processable informational data, and subjected to the process of commodification.[21] In the end, the actual finds itself structured without remainder according to what Lyotard calls in *The Postmodern Condition* the efficiency criterion.

As my readings of Benjamin, Heidegger, and Irigaray show, art is a site where technology, as a modality of revealing constitutive of the modern world, can be called into question and the reductive concepts of experience and knowledge reconsidered. Where this approach matters is precisely with regard to how it undermines the dehistoricized notion of experience, which forms the basis for structuring the world in terms of global availability as resource and information. The idea of the tension between technic and poietic unfolding opens up the possibility of seeing art as always already "integral" to experience, reworking it, as it were, from within, because of art's "figuring"[22] of the event structure of being. In "The Origin of the Work of Art," Heidegger discerns in art the potential to displace the ordinary experience of being and open thought to the possibility of questioning its technological determinations:

> We believe we are at home in the immediate circle of beings. Beings are familiar, reliable, ordinary. Nevertheless, the clearing is pervaded by a constant concealment in the double form of refusal and dissembling. At bottom, the ordinary is not ordinary; it is extraordinary. (*BW*, 179)

What the work of art brings into a figure *(Gestalt)* is the concealment at play in the distinction between the poietic and the technological, or, more precisely, the tendency of the technological to erase this difference and to cover over the role of the poietic in the formation of the everyday.

Although the problem of the everyday is usually associated with Heidegger's discussions of the topic in *Being and Time,* that issue is not confined to Heidegger's early work. Often not thematized as such, this reworking of the everyday constitutes a vital undercurrent of all of Heidegger's work: from the analyses of "The Origin of the Work of Art," to his discussion of the everydayness in "Letter on Humanism" in the context of Heraclitus, and, finally, to his late work on poetry, language, and technology. While it is true that those essays do not, at least on the surface, return to the problematic of everydayness which Heidegger developed in *Being and Time,* I would argue that Heidegger's reflections on "poetic dwelling," and thus also on language, rework the concept of everyday experience through the tension between poetry and technicity. To the extent that Heidegger's work identifies the everyday with the technological revealing—the analyses of average everydayness in *Being and Time* can be taken as forerunners of

Heidegger's later critique of technology—the displacement of the ordinary in art can be read in terms of the difference between the poietic and the technological and as a questioning of the dominant "technological" concepts of experience. In other words, the distinction between the technic and poietic modes of revealing, which runs through much of Heidegger's late work (for example, "Poetically Man Dwells," "The Thing,") corresponds, but also modifies and rearticulates, Heidegger's critique of everydayness in *Being and Time* in terms of authenticity and inauthenticity. In those late essays, the focus is no longer on *Dasein's* being authentic or inauthentic but, instead, on whether the human dwelling takes the shape of an ethos, in which beings are let be in their otherness. Yet these analyses still concern themselves with the issue of everydayness and the critique of its inauthentic modes.[23] Heidegger's reflections on ethos give a different slant to the problem of the everyday by exploring the possibility of transforming the technic mode of existence and opening up a dwelling in which relationality would be poietic.

Seeing art as folded into and constitutive of the work of experience offers the possibility of rethinking experience in terms of *poiēsis*. This approach negotiates art outside of the (metaphysical) constraints of the art/life opposition and, moving art beyond the narrowly conceived notion of aesthetics and private aesthetic experience, fundamentally questions how we conceive and produce being in the modern technological era. It interrogates the increasingly techno-scientific constitution of what it means to be, which equates being with the capacity to be scientifically measured, produced, or made available for consumption. Thinking the work performed by art in an active, historial (and not just historical) fashion, does not bridge but, instead, undermines the divide between art and experience, thought and practice. Art does not "passively" represent experience or "actively" transform it—both views posit art as external to the everyday and thus a priori limit, or even misconstrue, its work. I argue instead that, suspending the everyday modes of perception and action, art activates—that is, actively constitutes—experience by responding to and "figuring" (in the sense of *Gestalt*) the *poiēsis* of the event.

Since the event both instantiates and escapes presence, it calls into question the models of experience and knowledge based on the notions of substantive existence and representational constants. What Derrida calls the eventness *(événementialité)* of the event, signifies the inconspicuous, subjectless, and self-emptying historial structure through which experience unfolds into the signifying texture of the world. I argue that, even though the staging of this simple eventness renders art "weightless" and its work "inconspicuous"—that is, working without the support of concepts and representational structures—one cannot underestimate the critical import of this lightness and uselessness of art's figure. While technological revealing circumscribes and cancels historicity, art's figure reopens the question of eventness *as* historicity: not as a question of historicism and of rewriting history but as the task of calling into question the effects of rendering experience representable and commodified as resource.

The Historicity of Experience shows how avant-garde art infuses into its figure, and continuously (re)produces in it, the disjunctions which historicity marks in experience. The attentiveness in art to the historicity of being, inscribed at the fringes of techno-scientific legibility of experience, marks a space where the structure and the boundaries of modernity come into question. Contrary to the statements of those who, like Habermas, see the Heideggerian approach to art as esoteric and aestheticist, I argue that art taken as event is not a scene of subjective contemplation or aesthetic relishing of *poiēsis*. Instead, *poiēsis* marks a space of critique in its proper sense, that is, a space of a de-cision, of a differentiation and separation of the technological and the poetic. As such, it becomes a "thoughtful" action of turning the historicity of experience against the metaphysical substantialization of being within the technological organization of life, in order to call into question its effects on the constitution of the everyday. Since it cannot be represented, measured, or made available as a calculable and processable resource, the event is incommensurate with the technological standards of being, it does not register as "real."[24] As Foucault's *The Order of Things* suggests,[25] the notion of the event exposes the reductive concept of experience in positivist social sciences, which dehistoricize "reality" and limit it to empirical regularities and causal schema. It also takes to task the idea of historical experience as self-experience of society, for the event describes experience not in terms of a self but as a field and an occurrence, which exceeds the space of consciousness or the symbolic realm of social experience.[26]

Reconceiving "experience" as event has not only aesthetic but also social and even political implications. To articulate them, it is important to note that the event's historicity is never simply equivalent to avant-garde utopianism, to what Poggioli describes as the "prophetic and utopian phase, the arena of agitation and preparation for the announced revolution."[27] Such a moment of rupture, or a "futurist" manifestation, belongs, as Perloff shows, to various avant-gardes of the early twentieth century and produces "a short-lived but remarkable rapprochement between avant-garde aesthetic, radical politics, and popular culture" (*FM,* xvii). This futurist rupture continues to reappear in more disillusioned, ironic, or "cool," versions throughout the twentieth century (*FM,* xviii). The vital question for understanding the critique of experience in the avant-garde's critique is how one reads this, in Poggioli's words, "futurist moment": whether it is defined within the linear schema of history as a future moment of fulfillment of the avant-garde's dreams or whether the avant-garde rupture is perceived to be itself a refiguration of temporality. I agree with Kristeva and Lyotard that the avant-garde's time is always within the present, but as a specific noncoincidence of its works with the presence of meaning, as a "future anterior."[28] The avant-garde rupture dislocates the present and discloses it as an event whose historicity marks a structural incompletion, opening the now to the future. The futural dimension inheres in the present by virtue of a structural inscription, which renders the present disjointed, incapable of being self-identical. Any possibility of envisioning the future, utopian or otherwise, is contingent upon this futural inscription within the present.

The Historicity of Experience works, then, against the widespread sentiment that the avant-garde's innovation and novelty has degenerated into a tradition, into a repetition for its own sake, a form of aesthetic play; in other words, against the institutionalization of the avant-garde, when, as Ferry puts it, "[t]he break with tradition itself becomes a tradition."[29] In Ferry's reading, the avant-garde appears as determined above all by its proleptic and anticipatory character: It is untimely, in the sense of being in advance of its historical moment, incomprehensible to its contemporaries, and it fulfills itself—and annihilates itself at the same moment—when its challenge turns into tradition. I would argue that as long as it is caught in this futural dialectics, the understanding of the avant-garde as proleptic or visionary cancels the more complex radicality of its art. The proleptic reading of the avant-garde annuls precisely the "future anterior" effect of the avant-garde. It sees the avant-garde as a revolution in the aesthetic structures and categories of knowledge, with which a future will catch up, rather than seeing in it a questioning of the paradigm of knowledge, of the legibility of experience produced by modernity. This approach remains especially problematic with regard to understanding history, since reading the avant-garde as a prophetic vision of the future reduces the event to its dialectical notion and evacuates its historicity. As a result, history is read in terms of a linearly conceived progression, and historicity of being is reduced to the infinitely recuperable space of historicism. In the end, the proleptic reading domesticates the avant-garde by reinscribing it within the very schema of time, history, and experience it critiques.[30] The fact that we have become comfortable with the avant-garde is, then, not necessarily a sign that it has turned itself into a "tradition" or that it has failed to produce the future it promised, but that, perhaps, we *still do not read* the avant-garde.

The dialectical reading of the avant-garde prolepsis—a reading it is only fair to note is strongly encouraged by the futurist strand in the avant-garde itself—covers over the fact that what matters for the avant-garde, and matters in artistic but also political terms, is precisely that a certain "non-comprehensibility" of the event of experience becomes opposed to the progressivist scenario of history. There is a very important difference between incomprehensibility that offers the possibility of being comprehended at some point in the future, that is, recuperated with a change in the categories and practices of thought and knowing, and incomprehensibility as the flexible limit which historicity inscribes in representation. The latter is not due to some deficiency or fault of the present, or to the necessarily limited *historical* perspective available at any given point in time, but describes the historial limit of representation as emerging—always and already "now"—from the singular and irreducible event. This form of incomprehensibility is the result precisely of the inessentiality of experience (that is, its withdrawal from essence and presence), of its irrecuperable (never made fully present or representable) historicity. It is not a matter of incomprehension produced by the advanced, "avant-garde" nature of the aesthetic at play in avant-garde works but of a historial limit to comprehension produced always singularly as an effect of the event structure of experience.

The reduction of the event to the synchrony of meaning circumscribes also its political signification. If as Virilio suggests, the irreducibility of the event reflects the political dimension of experience,[31] then reading the event in dialectical terms forecloses the political significance of the avant-garde. The dialectical approach cancels the event as nonself-identical and reads the dislocations produced by the historicity of experience as, in principle, recuperable. Such a reading of the avant-garde, as Lukács makes clear, paradoxically renders it always already "anachronistic":[32] the avant-garde comes "true" only in the future which, retrospectively, validates the importance of its past rupture. In this scenario, the political import of the avant-garde is read against and, indeed, *in* the future, rather than in the historial limit it marks to representation and meaning. This position in advance disconnects the avant-garde from the present, from its contemporaneity, rendering almost a priori impossible the avant-garde's purported reintegration into the social praxis, into the everyday. It is important to note here that the conventional understanding of politics as orienting and underwriting artistic activity is reversed in the avant-garde: its politics rises from the implications of exposing the historial limit to the coherence of meaning, and spills outward from the inessentiality of experience, which language cannot quite register. As Kristeva suggests, Russian futurism did not lose contact with the historical situation as result of its challenge to the stability of linguistic structures but, in fact, became receptive to its revolutionary potential: "it paid strong attention to the explosion of the October revolution. It heard and understood the Revolution only because its present was dependent on a future" (*DL*, 32). Reading the event of the avant-garde in terms of Heidegger's *Ereignis* and Lyotard's event, that is, as a radical de-essentialization of happening, underscores this "other" political significance of the avant-garde: opened up and continuously renewed by the reworked language, which turns the inappropriable in experience against its "appropriations" into presence and meaning, this other politics "exceeds" avant-garde's explicit political statements in manifestoes, proclamations, or artistic provocations.

3

In my readings of the avant-garde poetry, I make the distinction between *technē* and *poiēsis* into one of the frames for investigating how the avant-garde reinvention of the everyday is contingent upon a double critique of aesthetics and technology. While the avant-garde is too often unproblematically identified with fascination and uncritical acceptance of technological progress, with the one-sided belief in the emancipatory function of the technological means of reproduction, I suggest that this issue is fraught with tension in avant-garde art. The avant-garde certainly recognizes, and often celebrates, the rapidly intensifying technological determination of modernity, but it also raises the question of the limits of the metaphysical and representational foundations of the modern. In *The Inhuman,* Lyotard articulates the importance of the avant-gardes specifically in terms of such a critique: "The avant-gardes get to work on the conditions of space and time. Attempts which have been going on for a century without having finished yet. This problematic makes it possible to resituate the real issue of the avant-gardes by putting them back in their real domain. They have been inflexible witnesses to the crisis of these foundations of which theories of communication and the new technologies are other aspects, much less lucid ones than the avant-gardes" (*IN* 115). If the real issue of the avant-garde is the _poiēsis_ of the event irreducible to the calculus of space and time, then the discussion of the "experience" of modernity and the problems it brings to the foreground has to be inflected through this prism.

The second frame for my study is Irigaray's critique of philosophical and psychoanalytic figures of sexual difference, which rethinks the difference between the sexes in terms of an event of proximity. Avant-garde writing has always played an important, perhaps even formative role in French feminism, especially in the work of Cixous (Joyce and Lispector) and Kristeva (*Revolution in Poetic Language* and *Desire in Language*).[33] Both Kristeva and Irigaray extend and revise Heidegger's approach to poetic language by inscribing it within the problematics of sexuality and desire, absent in Heidegger's considerations. Kristeva underscores the revolutionary potential marked in the manner in which poetic language in Heidegger "grounds" history and opens up the narrow notion of language code to bodily, subjective, and social inscriptions: "As to Heidegger, he retains currency, *in spite of everything,* because of his attentiveness to language and 'poetic language' as an opening up of beings; an openness that is checked but nonetheless occurs . . . and on which, as a consequence, 'History' is grounded" (*DL,* 25). She argues that poetic language, supplementing and transforming normative structures of language and sociability with a sub- or transsignification, eludes the order of the present and opens meaning to "an impossible time-to-come." Such a "future anterior" modality "proper" to poetic language, constitutes the nucleus of historicity, and makes poetry "the most appropriate *historical* discourse" (*DL,* 33). It is Irigaray, though, who rethinks in the most innovative way the proximity between the morphology of sexual difference and the morphology of language. She rewrites the discursive grammar of modernity through sexual difference, opening up to radical questioning the structures of being and experience. Motivated in part by a rethinking of Nietzsche's and Heidegger's critiques of aesthetics, Irigaray's poetics of sexual difference owes much of its impetus to a critical engagement with Heidegger's understanding of technology, being, and poetic thinking. Irigaray's book on Heidegger, *L'oubli de l'air,* which precedes her proclamation of a new poetics of sexual difference in *An Ethics of Sexual Difference,* ends with a rethinking of Heidegger's understanding of poetic language for a project of feminist ethics.[34] It reappraises Heidegger's idea of poetic language as a site where the boundaries of linguistic, social, and economic structures are transformed and dissolved by the fluid and ungraspable proximity to the other. Irigaray provides a critical bridge between

socialism in the early 1930s, and makes prominent the places where Heidegger compromises the radicality of his thought to inscribe it into the reflection on the historical importance of the fascist movement.[38] But it also allows us to nuance the reading of Heidegger and to underscore the fact that his conception of historicity works against the closure of linguistic and social structures. In my approach, Benjamin's notion of reproducibility as the structure of the work art becomes pivotal to thinking Heidegger's idea of art as "reproducing" the historicity of experience. Benjamin's preoccupation with danger and responsibility in relation to historical experience allows me, in turn, to focus precisely on those moments in Heidegger's reflection on art which, though most often unnoticed and unexplored, make it inseparable from the problematic of danger. As "Hölderlin and the Essence of Poetry" makes clear, Heidegger regards danger as intrinsic to the very structure of experience. Literally inscribed in the German word for experience, *Erfahrung,* danger marks the historial structure of experience, which always already collapses the open-ended event into the uniform and knowable spaces of representation. Juxtaposing Heidegger and Benjamin, I point to these two kinds of danger: one inscribed in the structure of experience and the other manifesting itself in specific historical circumstances.

The thought of Luce Irigaray, in turn, introduces the question of sexual difference into the apparently gender-neutral event of experience. Irigaray's critique of patriarchy is doubly important to my study: Irigaray not only rethinks experience *through* an ethics of sexual difference but ties this ethics explicitly to remaking and radicalizing Heidegger's idea of poetic thinking. In Irigaray's work, the irreducibility of the event to the order of representation becomes the mark of sexual difference, of the inflections of identity through the fluid proximity to the other (sex). The idea of the *poiēsis* of event as linking the question of the historicity of experience with sexual difference is explored further in the chapters on Stein and Howe.

The interworking frames I adopt in my study allow for a "positive" and yet noninstrumental reading of the reworking of experience in the avant-garde. This approach to the event contests the limits of experience marked in technological revealing, which recognizes as being only what can be comprehended and calculated as resource and information. It is in terms of the implications of this reworking for the understanding of history, technology, and sexual difference that I propose to rethink experience in modernity. Within this broader philosophical-aesthetic critique, it becomes possible to read the continuing significance of the avant-garde: avant-garde not merely as a historical event from the recent past but as postaesthetic works, as art "after" aesthetics, encoding a modality of thinking whose importance has not waned but, as Lyotard suggests, still increases.

The first three chapters of *The Historicity of Experience* lay out my approach to the question of the relation between experience and art at the end of modernity. The readings of Heidegger, Benjamin, and Irigaray develop the idea of *poiēsis* as a critique of the traditional understanding of experience. Chapter 1 explores art and *poiēsis* with a view to several critical issues — experience, reproducibility, danger — where, despite their many sharp differences, the writings of Heidegger and Benjamin converge. Elaborating the notion of *Erfahrung* in relation to Heidegger's and Benjamin's conceptions of language allows me to flesh out the cognitive and aesthetic implications of experience as event and to show how the work of art stages the historicity of the everyday. I rethink the work of art in modernity as "postaesthetic," that is, as an active, quasi-performative event, which contests the idea that art is an aesthetic object. Reading together Benjamin's remarks about reproducibility and Heidegger's "The Origin of the Work of Art," I argue that the work of art both is historical and itself stages or "makes" history, that is, it reproduces (in its reception) an irreducible and irrecuperable distance of its repetition as the "same" work. I suggest that such reproducibility inscribed in art constitutes the postaesthetic poetics of the modern artwork. The approach I develop here makes it possible to critique both the aesthetics of private experience and the practices of the totalization of experience that lead to the aestheticization of social and political relations.

In chapter 2, I develop Heidegger's notion of *poiēsis* as a critique of the technological organization of experience in modernity. Breaking with instrumental understanding of technology as a tool or a means at the disposal of human subjects, Heidegger explores the "ontological" status of technology in modernity: The importance, but also the danger, of technology lies not only in the augmentation of technical means of production and reproduction, or in the proliferation of mass produced objects and the increasing instrumentalization and commercialization of the everyday; rather, technology in Heidegger's sense of *Technik* pertains to the level of the structuration of experience itself, to what Heidegger calls "technological revealing." It is only when being — that is, what it means to be — has been always already determined as "technological," that is, disclosable, calculable, and available, that technology in the narrow sense of scientific progress, industrialization, technical means of production and communication, becomes thinkable. Amidst the technological understanding of being in terms of availability and resource, Heidegger looks for the possibility of opening up a reserve of a different modality of happening, which he explores under the rubric of *poiēsis*. This critical opening provides parameters for thinking the role of modern art, and its avant-garde impulse. I take up the understanding of the historicity of experience as event in the third chapter to propose a reading of Irigaray's critique of the patriarchal/metaphysical frame of experience through sexual difference. Irigaray's calls for a new poetics and ethics of sexual difference point toward the necessity of rethinking the morphology of experience and its articulation into socio-political relations with a view to the sexuation of experience. Rereading technology and commodification in terms of a desexualization of the space of experience and a canceling out of its materiality, Irigaray links historicity with the fluid texturing of sexual difference.

The remainder of the book is divided into two parts which explore the critique of experience in avant-garde poetics. Chapter 4 offers a reading of Gertrude Stein's work as paradigmatic of the avant-garde "poetics of event." Against the backdrop of Lyotard's writings on the avant-garde and Heidegger's notion of poetic naming, I examine Stein's interest in writing the English language into a state that would allow her to circumvent the fixity and conventionality of nouns and "name without using names." Such a fluid naming, focused on the indeterminacy of pronouns and connectives and the "activeness" of verb structures, underscores the inessential texture of experience, which never becomes substantive and must be described "without names." The two critical moments in the texturing and constructing of experience for Stein are everydayness and sexuality. Playing with the feminization of the ordinary, especially of the domestic space, Stein's idiosyncratic use of the English syntax opens up the routinized and familiar spheres of everyday experience and language to the unpredictable and shifting effects of historicity. Counteracting the generalizing effects of meaning, Stein's writing in *Tender Buttons* or "Patriarchal Poetry" underscores the inessentiality of experience, and connects this fluid texture to the rethinking of the significations of femininity and sexual difference. I focus my discussion, therefore, on how Stein's thinking about "how to write" depends upon figuring the ordinary and sexuality in terms of the event structure of experience.

The second modernist poet included in my discussion is a Russian cubofuturist, Velimir Khlebnikov, famous for his linguistic innovations and his theory of *zaum* (beyonsense), conceived as a poetic stratum of language which, although not irrational, reaches beyond the rationalist boundaries of signification. Although Mayakovsky is probably the best known Russian avant-garde poet, it was Khlebnikov's experimental poetry which, in spite of his relatively short life (1885–1922), most influenced the development of modernist aesthetics in Russian literature and helped shape a distinctively Russian voice in the avant-garde, a voice which is best known in the West through the abstract visual movements of suprematism and constructivism. Focusing my discussion of Khlebnikov on his late "supertale" *Zangezi*, I link his conception of *zaum* with historicity and read his poetic experimentation as recalibrating language to reflect the "essence-less" texture of experience. Creating new semantic planes and producing unexpected linguistic shifts through modifications of Russian inflectional system, Khlebnikov negotiates his idea of "revolutionary" poetry as well as his approach to time and technology through the optics of *zaum* as reflection of the unstable, constantly resignified, texture of experience.

The third part of *The Historicity of Experience* reappraises the questions of everydayness, history, and sexual difference by focusing on two poets whose work has not been discussed within the theoretical debates about modernity: Howe and Białoszewski, representatives of American and Polish poetic orientations which, although quite distinct in their respective poetics, are known under the same name: "language poetry." The Polish "language" or "linguistic" poetry *(poezja lingwistyczna)* is a phenomenon of the 1960s and 1970s, and the name is used usually to refer to a relatively small group of poets: Białoszewski, Karpowicz, Wirpsza, Barańczak. The American language poetry, or "L=A=N=G=U=A=G=E" poetry as it is often written, is a much larger movement, and numerous poets both on the East and the West coasts are associated with it. I focus my discussion on the two most important poets within those orientations, Miron Białoszewski and Susan Howe, whose poetries I find to be "postmodern" instances of avant-garde poetics.

Chapter 6 introduces to the English speaking audience Miron Białoszewski, the most important representative of Polish language poets, whose work radically brings poetry down from its elevated stance and rhetoric and into touch with the everyday and the ordinary by concerning itself both with the most banal and mundane objects, events, and conversations and with the ordinary and colloquial language. Białoszewski's poetic and prose writings only recently (he died in 1983) have become influential both in literary and critical circles in Poland, and, unfortunately, they are virtually unknown in the United States.[39] At a recent conference on Białoszewski at the Literary Studies Institute of the Polish Academy of Sciences, his writings have been

Part One : **Rethinking the Experience of Modernity**
Art, Technology, and Sexual Difference

1. Reproducing History

Benjamin and Heidegger

on the Work of Art in Modernity

In the perspective of Benjamin's work, the work of art in modernity—in the age of rapidly intensifying technical reproducibility—finds itself, paradoxically, both in the face of unprecedented danger and within view of previously unrecognized possibilities for radical cultural and political change of art's significance. The danger arising from the exponential increase in the means of technical reproduction as well as from the overall impact of technology upon experience remains twofold. On the one hand, art runs the risk of obsolescence, of becoming totally inconsequential, with its effects limited in scope and actuality to the isolated moment in which a work of art is seen, heard, or read. It is isolated in a double sense: within the punctual self-presence of its enactment, effectively separated from history and from other splintered zones of experience, and socially, to the extent that it remains identified with the absence of relevance and reference beyond that of the individual's "aesthetic" experience. Following the trajectory of the disciplining of the human sensorium,[1] art begins to operate like any other "lived moment"—without historical, cultural, or political "memory," it becomes a certain aesthetic *Erlebnis*. What's more, the functions of the work of art can be seen as limited to only being part of the sector of cultural activities and hence circumscribed by the reputed isolation of artistic activity, even though this sector is regulated discursively and institutionally much like the other "realms" of modern experience.[2]

The other moment of risk for art is when what is perceived as a growing isolation, even alienation, of art from everyday life and ordinary communicative practices can instigate the hypostasis of art into the model or design for the totality of experience. From being just an aesthetic form of *Erlebnis,* art becomes transformed not only into a model of experience but into the totalizing paradigm of experience as such, a metamorphosis signifying the aestheticization of all experience—aestheticized *Erlebnis* or experience *as* the aestheticization of life. This curious alliance of the lived moment—an isolated instant with no apparent connection to other "experiences"—with an aesthetic totality conceived as a myth or an archaic plentitude can assume the dangerous form of a totalitarian ideology, whose embodiment Benjamin saw in the practices of fascism. Promising redemption from the fragmenting and destabilizing effects of modern shock experience by taking recourse to a collective, mythical, "reality," fascism proffers in place of historical experience a perverse *Gesamtkunstwerk,* a living artwork of a nation or a state.[3] As it deploys the technological means of control and propaganda together with the mythical sense of identity, fascism draws upon a collusion between aesthetic and technological models of the totalization of experience. To the extent that in modernity art is regarded as merely a cultural activity, artworks become part and parcel of the overall scheme of orderability and calculation characteristic of modern society.[4] In effect, the practices of production, distribution, and consumption of art become indistinguishable from technological processes, making it possible, even desirable, not only to project the aesthetic patterning of experience *upon* the entirety of the already technologized social life but, in fact, to see this totality *as* itself aesthetic. In hope of rediscovering or impressing beauty and meaning upon the technological regime of everyday life, the aestheticization of politics mobilizes both technology and mythology to produce an aesthetic form of life.

This twin predicament in which modern art finds itself—fragmentation of experience and its mythological recuperation—reflects, beside the historical conditions of artistic production, the tensions that crisscross the spectrum of modern experience: from the fragmentation or splintering of everyday life, attempts at political and social totalization, to the problem of thinking experience historically. The consideration of art in modernity pivots, therefore, upon understanding how artworks figure experience in its historical/historial dimensions and also upon recognizing how art participates in the unfolding of history, in rendering, to paraphrase Benjamin, history legible, that is, readable *as* history. I follow Benjamin's and Heidegger's reflections on art precisely to the extent that they both make their rethinking of the work of art the venue for the revision of experience and history beyond the optics of fragmentation and totality. Although their works have very different trajectories, which, in the context of Benjamin's cursory remark in *Passagen-Werk,* may be regarded as incompatible, Benjamin and Heidegger come close in locating in the work of art the blueprint for an understanding of experience and history outside the parameters of enlightened modernity, that is, in very general terms, outside the metaphysics of the subject and the historicist-progressivist concept of history.

My interest is less in pointing out both major differences and similarities that exist between Benjamin and Heidegger[5] than in exploring the tension between their projects to articulate how their reflections on the work of art in modernity offer us ways to revise the concepts of experience and history. What is rarely underscored in this context is that both Heidegger and Benjamin come to associate the work of art in modernity with the refiguration of the metaphysical models of history and experience by way of their exploration of language, and, in particular, of the link between the concept of language as event and the notion of the work performed by art. What marks their departure from aesthetics is that, for Benjamin and Heidegger, art is not an object of aesthetic experience, but a certain work—in the active, verbal sense that Heidegger gives to this word in "The Origin of the Work of Art"[6]—precisely because it "works" experience and history, that is, renders them legible as such. Art ceases to be a work in an organic sense, a unified object accessible to and judged by the aesthetic gaze. Transferring the emphasis from the work as an object that is produced or created to work in the sense of the working of art, of setting into work that takes place in art, opens the door to the idea that art works by unworking its own articulations. For Heidegger, although the work is the *Gestalt* (the figure), this figure works historically, that is, it refigures itself because the *Gestalt* inscribes the historicity of the rift between the world and the earth. In other words, the work crosses into the unwork; the line between working and unworking becomes increasingly fine, like the corresponding play between concealment and unconcealment. The work of art *works* precisely when it draws attention to the dynamic field of the rift, its continued reemergence as itself "an openness opened by itself" (*BW,* 191), rather than a closed form associated with an aesthetic object. The transformation of the ties to the everyday which the work of art is supposed to effect is possible because the *Gestalt* figures precisely its own recasting—the reforming and the reworking that constitute the riftlike relation between the world and the earth. As the rift is brought into the figure, the openness it projects unworks the very fixity of the figure through which the rift "presents" itself.

This simultaneous figuring and unworking describes the logic of language, which Benjamin and Heidegger characterize in terms of a translationlike movement through which experience constitutes itself as always already linguistic. Because art works *like* and *as* language—it unfolds the world by transposing it into discourse—artworks stage being in its historial character, rendering legible the historicity of the discursive constitution of experience. To see art as working this way, and to recognize the critical potential of this work, it is necessary to move beyond aesthetic reflection into a post- or paraesthetic understanding of art.[7] It is a matter of understanding how modern art works in paraesthetic manner and of fleshing out the critical implications of the shift beyond aesthetics and aestheticism for the understanding of modern experience. For both Benjamin and Heidegger, critiquing aesthetics and reading art post- or nonaesthetically requires the exploration of art within the constellation of language, experience, and history. The prefixes "post" and/or "non" are less an indication of a new era in the history of thought about art than a reflection of the necessity of circumventing the series of exclusions—of the aesthetic from the cognitive and the practical—on which aesthetics is founded. This nonaesthetic approach to art traces the way in which experience and history are inscribed in the very work that art performs, apart from the aporias of beauty/truth, sensible/intelligible, thought/action—that structure aesthetic thinking. To think art nonaesthetically is to recognize its *work,* that is, to discern how its practices of unworking the boundaries of aesthetics refigure experience and history through the prism of their discursive constitution.

The importance of this critique can be seen in the fact that, in order for the hypostasis of art into a totalizing regime of experience to take place, art has to be thought in traditional aesthetic categories, that is, in accordance with the metaphysics of the subject and its categorizations of aesthetic experience. Paradoxically, then, the very metaphysics that has produced the doctrine of art as an object of disengaged contemplation triggers also the mechanism of its inversion—of the aestheticization of politics and life. On the one hand, the aesthetic understanding of the work renders art autonomous, reflecting, perhaps reinforcing, the splintering of the zones of experience in the way it assigns to art a separate, even alienated, sphere of aesthetic sensibility. On the other hand, aesthetics, precisely to the extent that it is underwritten by metaphysical conceptuality, holds out a promise of recuperation, of a beyond—a Romantic blue yonder as Benjamin refers to it—which, when reclaimed, would assure the restitution of the fullness of meaning. This nostalgia and the temptation of an archaic, mythical plane—the halo or aura drawn around the notion of the aesthetic—conceals the possibility of the transference, or projection, of the "total" aesthetic image upon other spheres of experience. In spite of, or maybe because of, the separation of the aesthetic, the auratic enchantment becomes the sign of compensation, the promise of much more than just aesthetic satisfaction. Notwithstanding his early optimism about technology, Benjamin's focus at the time of the rise of fascism on the possibilities of postauratic art reflects the fear that the dissipation of the work's aura as a result of mass reproduction and commodification may foster the transfer of the aura from the work of art to the totality of social life. We can, in fact, see the tensions between the punctuality of the moment and mythical recuperation at work in the paradoxes of the modernist artistic scene, of its extension from the avant-garde experimentalism to the aesthetics of high modernism. Apart from its reflection in the breadth of the aesthetic spectrum of modernism, this dual tendency is encoded in some of the most prominent modernist works. In Eliot's *Waste Land* or Joyce's *Ulysses,* the aesthetics of fragmentation inscribes, often in a teasing manner, the promise of an explanatory and unifying mythical code, a playful, but still nostalgic, evocation of a beyond. The trajectory of Pound's work, from "luminous details" to the project of gathering and reconfiguring them into the master narrative of the *Cantos,* is symptomatic of the fragmenting and unifying strains at work in modernist aesthetics.

As an offspring of metaphysics, aesthetics is implicated in the technological culture of modernity and its politics. This is why, although proceeding from different locations, both Heidegger and Benjamin undertake a critique of aesthetics, of the metaphysical categorization of art as a beautiful object, in order to expose, and perhaps avert, the twin danger implicit in the aesthetic framing of art. Taking into consideration the historical correlation between aesthetic categories and metaphysical underpinnings of technology, we can conclude that the dangers associated with the aestheticization of politics depend upon another "danger": the aestheticization of art. In fact, it could be argued that it is specifically the aesthetic conceptualization of art that, by creating and delimiting the sphere of the aesthetic, makes room for aestheticism and, in the same gesture, for its inversion into the aestheticization of lived experience. Aesthetics is not a term for a neutral, "objective," reflection upon art; rather, aesthetic reflection is already implied in the larger philosophical and cultural framework, whose outline has been shaped by metaphysical conceptuality. To think the work of art as an aesthetic object is, in a sense, to aestheticize art, to make the work of art legible, or, as I will suggest, illegible, precisely to the extent that it can be conceptualized, "forced," under aesthetic rubrics. For only when the work of art is rendered aesthetic through the same conceptual operations that have made possible and implemented the progressive technologization of modern culture can a certain inverted equivalency emerge between the work of art and the possibility of totalizing experience on the aesthetic model. In other words, the philosophical, but also cultural, aestheticizing of art becomes the prelude, the groundwork, as it were, for the inversion of the aesthetic paradigm into the comprehensive, even totalizing, design of experience. Perhaps the production of art as "aesthetic" creates a certain liability for culture which becomes visible in the period when modernity begins to increasingly understand itself through the technological paradigm it has generated. This is why it is in the critique or the "end" of aesthetics, which both Heidegger and Benjamin make central to their late writings, that the dangers facing modern art become most palpable. By pushing aesthetics to its double limit—the isolation of aestheticism and its inverse or "double": totalizing aestheticization of experience—modernity can rethink art and perhaps activate its radical cultural possibilities, covered over and neutralized by aesthetics. While for Heidegger, this questioning of aesthetics is designed to lead to the critique of the metaphysical roots of modernity, in particular its ways of schematizing and regimenting experience, for Benjamin, this critique is inseparable from the analysis of the specific historical situation of the 1920s and 1930s.

The locus for such a questioning of aesthetics, and, at the same time, the site where the twin "dangers" of art for art's sake and the aestheticization of politics become legible, is the avant-garde. In the ambiguous experience of the avant-garde art or, to be more exact, in the avant-garde's questioning of both aesthetic and everyday experience, modernity is brought face to face with the ghosts of metaphysics haunting its technological present and forced to confront the divide between mythical and historical forms of experience. Benjamin's identification of the avant-garde, Surrealism in particular, as the site where art, engaged critically with its own aesthetic provenance, comes close both to the paradigm of the aestheticization of experience and to a radical writing practice, opens the possibility of a post-aesthetic reading of art.[8] Benjamin not only discerns in Surrealism a critique of aesthetic practice but recognizes it as a contestation of everyday experience: "[A]nyone who has perceived that the writings of this circle are not literature but something else—demonstrations, watchwords, documents, bluffs, forgeries, if you will, but at any rate not literature—will also know, for the same reason, that the writings are concerned literally with experiences, not with theories and still less with phantasms."[9] Attempting to undo the notion of literature bequeathed to it by aesthetic cannons, Surrealism both promises liberation and revolution—a new, "nonaesthetic" writing practice—and runs the risk of leaving this change only a promise. To the extent that the surrealist practice of estrangement, of suffusing the ordinary with the marvelous, may become its own end, instead of being a strategic move in what Benjamin refers to as "the dialectics of intoxication," Surrealism, and the avant-garde in general, courts the danger of turning its work into yet another repetition of Romantic utopianism. (Re)producing the "literary absolute," this new "Romanticism" may unexpectedly find itself in complicity with the effort to generate a modernist *Gesamtkunstwerk* and its ominous reflections: totalitarian ideology and state. This possibility manifests itself in the idealization or deification of technology, often combined with the sympathy for fascist ideology, characteristic of some avant-garde "isms." One can invoke here the example of early Italian Futurism, and Marinetti in particular, whose fascination with technological progress, with the machine as the model for art and action, is well known.[10] On the other hand, the political ambiguities that crisscross the Russian avant-garde, cubo-futurism and its subsequent development into suprematism and constructivism, confound and render problematic the clear-cut distinction that Benjamin tries to maintain between the ("fascist") aestheticization of politics and the ("communist") politicization of art.[11]

The problematic status of this boundary between politicization and aestheticization testifies to the inadequacy of conceiving the political in art, or of art *as* political, on the model of dialectical opposition. Politicization of art cannot be just a reversal of the aestheticization of politics, or a reaction against the social and cultural isolationism of art for art's sake, that would redeem the situation by reintegrating art into social practice still conceived on the metaphysical models of presence and subjectivity. Before the "post-aesthetic" significations of art can be recognized, it is necessary to redefine art and literature outside of the province of aesthetics and its metaphysical categorizations of experience. This exigency becomes obvious in the context of the still dominant readings of modernist and avant-garde art in terms of self-reflexive textuality and epistemological aporias. Regarding the apparent autotelism of modernist art as the confirmation of its divorce from, or worse, indifference to, everyday life practice, these interpretations see modernism as largely a repetition, extension, or even intensification, of the aestheticist doctrine of the separateness of aesthetic experience. Because it takes aesthetics to its limits, the avant-garde practice, when interpreted according to aesthetic categories, risks being collapsed into the ideology of the autonomy of art. At the same time, the transformative possibilities inherent in the avant-garde can be activated only if we can show how such art unreads aesthetics, and, in the process, account for the risk of trivializing and isolating art and for the temptation to aestheticize experience, both characteristic of the situation of modern art.

In his essay on Surrealism, Benjamin appears to consider this risk worth taking. All the more so since for him at stake in the surrealist practice is the question of experience, the very possibility of historical experience and of the experience *of* history, which Benjamin considers threatened by the emergence of mythical forms of thinking within technology.[12] The danger that materializes itself in the modern work of art is the absence of historical experience and its replacement by either the punctual experience of shock without memory or the compensatory recuperation of everyday *Erlebnis* in the totality of myth. Heidegger's work is remarkably consonant with Benjamin's on this point, especially when it critiques, as in "The Origin of the Work of Art," the aesthetic and cultural optics within which modern art functions as part of subjective, lived, experience, rather than as the historical index of its times. For Heidegger, the "sheer aesthetic mindedness" (*BW,* 317) about art relegates it to the status of a sector of cultural activity, thereby assigning to oblivion the enigmatic *critical* mode of revealing or disclosure of the world that takes place in the work of art. Contrasted with the work performed by art is the technic modality of the unveiling of things in(to) their presence—what Heidegger qualifies as the "essence" of technology: the enframing *(Gestell)*—which calculates and orders the world in terms of its availability for use and processing; as a result, "reality" constitutes itself as a "standing-reserve" *(Bestand).* The experience of such a reality transpires no longer even as the perception of its objectivity—characteristic of eighteenth- and nineteenth-century culture and thought—but instead as the exercise of mastery over its readiness for use and appropriation. For Heidegger, the predominance of the calculative modes of thinking and the impact of technology upon experience render other paradigms of experience not only "irrational" but, in effect, "unreal." Because the standing-reserve disclosed through the activity of the enframing *(Gestell)* becomes identified with the real, that is, with the only "experience" that is quantifiable and thus "exists," the *Gestell* as a totalizing form of explanation begins to function not unlike myth, the all-encompassing and the all-deciphering narrative of modern culture. This technic quantification of reality inscribes in its very structure an unprecedented degree of control and manipulation of the world as resource (human and nonhuman, natural and social), and produces a constant threat of the erasure of alterity across the spectrum of experience: from the everyday and the aesthetic to the social and the political.

Within this overall ordering of reality, experience, I argue, assumes the punctual form of *Erlebnis,* of an instance of calculability and usage. At the same time, though, this instant finds itself already connected to the network of computations, it functions as an already calculable point within the rationalistic matrix which globalizes reality into the order of availability. Experience comes to be channeled into two interconnected orders, both of which erase history and historicity. The first order describes the punctual experience of the self-identical instant without historicity, whose self-presence becomes representable in terms of its calculation and availability. The second, higher and all embracing, order designates a mythlike totalization of experience on the model of ultimate computation—a kind of technological "absolute knowledge." Both founded on and enforcing the principle of representability, those interfacing orders of experience schematize being in terms of a calculable presence, computed and available at will to the self-styled subject of history—humankind. In both cases what is erased from the patterning of experience is its historicity; instead of constituting the modus of experience—of experience *as* history—history becomes constructed, as it were, post factum, as the linearity of progress or the uniform space of historicism. Both options offer the comfort of order and calculability, at the expense, however, of erasing the historicity of experience—of the event of its unfolding—whose excess of singularity marks its alterity against the scheme of computation.

For Heidegger art and, more specifically, its poetic medium or element, when read nonaesthetically, figures a modality of thought alternative to technology, a thinking that remains attentive specifically to the always singular historicity of the event. Hence it is in art that the danger that technology poses for experience by effacing its historicity manifests itself. The parallel problems of inconsequentiality and aestheticization visible in modern art reflect the risks that the technological comportment toward being implies for experience. I argue that at stake in technology's impact upon art—in both the obsolescence of the lyrical and the intensification of the reproducibility inherent in the work of art[13]—is the question of history, and, more specifically, of the historicity of the event versus history constructed as a story or a narrative. At issue is the difference between, on the one hand, the "excessive" folds of history as the quasi-transcendental condition of experience that mark in each moment of presence an alterity which needs to be remembered without ever being recuperated, and, on the other, history composed as the uniform and infinitely recuperable space of historicism. In other words, at stake here is the easily collapsible distinction between *Geschichte* and *Historie*,[14] which holds the key to the problem of otherness and difference, and its inscriptions in the space of history. Heidegger and Benjamin would agree that it is art that bridges the question of the effects of technology upon experience (being) and the possibility of history as *Geschichte*. Restaging and remarking the historicity of the historical space, art opens the possibility of critiquing historicism by regarding experience as an uncontainable, nontheorizable event, always excessive in relation to its historical or political descriptions. But art can produce this constellation of experience *(Erfahrung)* and history *(Geschichte)* only when it questions its own aesthetic framework, when it breaks with its position within the hierarchy of cultural activities and critiques the metaphysical provenance of modern thinking about art. In other word, such a critique is possible only in art that stands at the end of aesthetics and history, an art "after aesthetics," as I argue elsewhere.[15] At the end of "Some Motifs in Baudelaire," Benjamin credits Baudelaire's poetry with opening the venue for thinking experience in modernity historically, as *Erfahrung*, against the bearing of the punctuality of shock experience: "Having been betrayed by these last allies of his, Baudelaire battled the crowd—with the impotent rage of someone fighting the rain or the wind. This is the nature of something lived through [*Erlebnis*] to which Baudelaire has given the weight of an experience [*Erfahrung*]" (*I*, 193–94). Only art that, like Baudelaire's poet, discards its aura, can assume the task of both recognizing the traces of experience and history within the accumulation of instants—the splintered map of modernity—and of reserving the prerogative of interrupting any recuperative totalization that this fragmentation may provoke.

Experience as Event

Even though the risks confronting modern art are historically conditioned, idiomatic to modernity and its technological forms of reason, they reflect the inscription of danger within the very structure of experience, whose markings become legible historically as a result of the highlighting of the reproducibility inherent in the work of art through the rapid development of the means of technical reproduction. Both Heidegger and Benjamin base their discussion of art and experience on a "literal" inscription of danger in the matrix of experience. Like the Latin *periri* in *experiri,* to undergo, the German *Erfahrung* (experience) keeps in play the correlation between traversing and being on the way, on the one hand, and danger and peril, on the other.[16] The danger that interests Benjamin and Heidegger is not only an experience of danger, of finding oneself face to face with a perilous situation or event, but rather danger as the experiencing itself, as the modality intrinsic to historical being. In the Heideggerian parlance, danger exists both on the ontic level, in the form of threatening and perilous historical circumstances, and on the ontological level—as the very modality of experiencing, as the manner or the way in which one undergoes an experience.

Although "experience" *(Erfahrung)* is a term that is not too common in Heidegger's discourse and unusual in the Heidegger scholarship, it is tied in important ways to his understanding of thinking *(Denken),* and to the possibility of an event in which being unfolds in its very "essence"/occurrence *(Wesen).* The use of the term "experience" in the context of Heidegger's thought demands caution, as Heidegger is openly critical of the empiricist and psychological understanding of experience, especially of the term *Erlebnis,* or lived experience. However, when Heidegger does use the term *Erfahrung,* it is precisely to call into question, as Bernasconi suggests,[17] the metaphysical understanding of experience and to reconceptualize it in relation to his most important terms: *Ereignis,* language, technology, danger, and so on. For example, a series of poems from 1947 entitled "*Aus der Erfahrung des Denkens*" gives its title to the collection of Heidegger's short texts on poetry and art. This title suggests that thinking hinges on the modality of experiencing, on how the "experience" of thinking unfolds. More significant, Heidegger's two most important essays on language, "*Das Wesen der Sprache*" and "*Der Weg zur Sprache,*" open with the question of what it means to experience *(erfahren)* language as a way-making or an event.[18] Heidegger wants to "experience the way to language in terms of what transpires with the way while we are under way on it" *(BW,* 397), so that language may strike us in all its strangeness as a *way to language:* not as a means of representation or a space of signification but as a saying, which is itself the most proper manner of occurring or propriating ("*die eigenste Weise des Ereignens*"). But to "experience" language as "on the way to language," that is, as a manner of propriating, experience itself has to have the character of event that lets what is into is own—it has to be *ereignend*. It is that sense of being on the way, which at the same time brings forth and withdraws, propriates and dis- or de-propriates (*er-eignen* and *ent-eignen*), which Heidegger reinscribes in the word *Erfahrung*. Such "experience" is a nonsubjective correspondence *(Entsprechung)* with the "saying" character of being, with *das Ereignis* occurring (on) the way to language (where "occurring" has to have both transitive and intransitive character).

Ereignis or propriative event is the term Heidegger introduces into his discourse in mid-1930s as a way of rethinking the problematic of being beyond the ontico-ontological difference and outside of the metaphysical strictures and determinations of the word *being*. At its most simple, *Ereignis* refers to the very giving of what is, to the fact that such a giving takes place in terms of the givenness of time and being: "*Ereignis ereignet Sein und Zeit*"[19]/"*Ereignis* disposes/propriates being and time." As this giving, *Ereignis* reflects the empty subject of the German *es gibt* (there is). Even though *Ereignis* has no essence or ground, it names the very force thanks to which something unfolds and comes to be what it is. Heidegger transforms *Ereignis,* an ordinary word for event in German, into a linguistic and philosophical pun, exploiting the semantic possibilities inherent in the word, especially in its root *eigen:* own, proper. While *-eignis* refers to the complex play of both "owning," that is, coming to be what something properly is, and dispropriation or ungrounding, the prefix *er* underscores the occurrence, the temporal character of this event. *Ereignis* names then an occurring in which what comes to be is given into its own. But it is given into its own in a manner that also de-propriates, that is, in coming to be what it is, a being *(Seiende)* discloses the withdrawal of being *(Sein)* as the nonground *(Abgrund)* of its being. As a propriative event, *Ereignis* is the very movement, the way that decides or carries out this simultaneous propriation and de-propriation. In this sense, *Ereignis* is also a de-cision *(Entscheidung)*, a scission that carries out or disposes what is into its time and being: "*Er-eignis ist Austrag.*"[20] This de-cision is the way in which the nonground or the abyss, namely "being" in its no longer metaphysical sense, is disposed ("*Der Aus-trag trägt den Ab-grund,*" [*B,* 307]). It carries out and (ap)propriates differences "over" the abyss *(Abgrund),* over the absence of ground and essence, which characterizes the way it gives time and being.

Experience occurs as *Erfahrung,* and not *Erlebnis,* only as such an event *(Ereignis),* that is, as this disposing or carrying out, which unfolds the very site of differentiation and relationality. To experience would then mean to be on the way, in the very movement through which beings keep coming into their own, each time anew into the singularity of their differences. It would be tantamount to remaining or standing in the temporalization of the propriating and dispropriating folds of *Ereignis* which draw out *(austragen)* and dispose the vectors and valencies of relations. Drawing relations in the manner of propriation, the event releases and frees what is to be its own. The movement of saying to language, *Ereignis,* disposes relations as a bind that unbinds, that relates and propriates by way of freeing something to be properly what it is: "The Saying's way-making movement to language is the unbinding bond, the bond that binds by propriating" (*BW,* 419). The bind of relation here propriates, that is, frees and enables something to be what it is and to unfold into its own by way of relation to what is other. As such, *Ereignis* is the relation of all relations, the very scission or drawing out of relationality: "For propriation—owning, holding, keeping to itself—is the relation of all relations" (*BW,* 425). As the de-scission which carries out/disposes all relationality, *Ereignis* lets beings come into their own, to retain themselves only through differentiation and, at the same time, through the dispropriating ungrounding of time and being. For as it lets come into presence, *Ereignis* withdraws and retains itself; it remains unsaid. This dispropriating force with which *Ereignis* gives time and being by withholding itself constitutes the bind of relating, or, in other words, it draws out relations. In its withdrawal *Ereignis* releases and carries relations in the sense that it de-cides them, that is, draws them out by separating and holding beings in relation to one another. As *Austrag* or decision, *Ereignis* draws out relations and carries them in their abyssal, nongrounded occurrence. It thus draws relations into what is "proper" for them: the *Abgrund* of the scission of being and time. The emphasis in such experience falls upon the futural temporality of such a de-cision and the absence of ground which is "experienced" precisely as the movement of propriating. Thus, Heidegger's notion of *Ereignis* is an "instant" critique of subjectivist, empiricist, and essentialist ideas of experience. It ungrounds their assumptions, disclosing the propriating *(ereignend)* force of the dispropriating *(enteignend)* abyss *(Abgrund)* of being. To undergo such an experience, as "The Way to Language" suggests, is to experience the carrying out of the futural unfolding of being as an event ungrounded, "properly" drawn out and de-cisioned, in the dispropriating temporality of its giving.

In one of his Bremen lectures, entitled "Danger" *(Die Gefahr),* Heidegger, playing on the etymological association of the Old High German *fara* with *Gefahr* and *Erfahrung,* writes about the need for thinking to travel *(be-*

fahren) within the "zone of the dangerousness of danger" *("die Zone dieser Gefährlichkeit der Gefahr")* in order to experience the unfolding of being *("um das Wesen des Seyns zu erfahren").*[21] This typical instance of Heidegger's etymological and linguistic play demarcates the structural inscription of danger within the formation of experience. The danger in this case is the forgetting of being within the technological enframing (the *Gestell*) of modern reality, and the journey refers to the ways or paths on which thinking "experiences" the unfolding of being. For Heidegger, thinking happens at those moments when thought traverses the very dangerousness of danger, that is, the zone in which being unfolds technologically. It is in this zone of technological revealing, both through and against the enframing, that the occurrence of being *(das Wesen des Seyns)* can be "experienced." *Erfahrung* points here to the limit of experience in its ordinary sense, to that no doubt rare occasion when "experience" occurs as event, as *Ereignis*. Just as *Denken* is nonsubjective in Heidegger, I use the word "experience" against its modern empiricist and psychological baggage.[22] It is in this specific nonsubjective sense that a certain co-disposition[23] between the *Ereignis* and the "experience" of being can take place. It suggests that being is "experienced" in its "essence" *(Wesen)* only when experience itself occurs in a nontechnological, propriating manner as an event.

I read both Benjamin and Heidegger as linking the legibility of the perilousness of experience to technology: Benjamin to shock experience and Heidegger to the "essence" of technology, or technicity, understood as the *Gestell* (the enframing). Both look for ways of thinking this danger within the figuration of experience (or being) in the work of art, that is, in relation to the specificity of the work that art performs. Perhaps most indicative in this context is Benjamin's invocation of the writings of the avant-garde as a form of constant awakening to the "dangerous structure" of experience, the practice emblematized by the ringing of an alarm clock: "They [the Surrealists] exchange, to a man, the play of human features for the face of an alarm clock that in each minute rings for sixty seconds" (*R,* 192).

The motifs of awakening and unforgetting interwoven in Benjamin's and Heidegger's work remind us that the perilous turn of experience, taken with the rapid technologization of modern society, is not simply the punctuality and shock value of *Erlebnis* but, primarily, the disappearance or erasure of historicity and the event. It is not only auratic experience that is shattered by shock but the historicity at play in *Erfahrung*—the historical indexing of the present. With the effacement of historicity, and of experience as event, the present can all too easily be (mis)taken as presence—

self-identical and impermeable to alterity. Invested with authenticity and power, the present can either authorize itself as its own ground or transfer this authority onto a prehistoric, mythical origin, thereby making possible a totalization of experience at the expense of otherness and difference. In either case, the discursive and political effects of the erasure of alterity in the wake of the collapse of *Erfahrung* into *Erlebnis* become apparent. While the punctuality of shock experience clearly spells out the absence of historical memory, for Benjamin the most disquieting aspect of modernity lies in the political transformation of this absence into a need for the recuperation of the "wholeness" of experience through reference to prehistory or myth. In late Heidegger, it is the matrix of calculation and ordering that becomes the ultimate framework of reference, the technological horizon of intelligibility within which the differential modality of being becomes reducible to the calculus of availability.

Experience and its textual figurations constitute a steady undercurrent of Benjamin's writings and in the 1930s achieve a critical articulation in his conception of history and time designed to unmask the heightened presence of mythic consciousness in modern technological culture and combat its most pernicious manifestation—fascism. Benjamin's preoccupation with nineteenth-century culture, with the Paris arcades, with Baudelaire, Proust, and the avant-garde, functions as part of his project of articulating, through the changes in social and cultural conditions, the paradigm of modern(ist) experience. What interests me most is the relation that Benjamin sketches between the transformation of experience and the changes in art, in particular the decline of lyric poetry and the emergence of avant-garde literary practice: "If conditions for a positive reception of lyric poetry have become less favorable, it is reasonable to assume that only in rare instances is lyric poetry in rapport with the experience of its readers. This may be due to a change in the structure of their experience" (*I,* 156). The cultural, literary, and philosophical diagnoses of this transmutation in the conditions and, hence, also the structure of experience, which Benjamin locates somewhere in the nineteenth century, follow the trajectory of the difference, mutual exclusion but also, as I suggest, the interplay between two forms or patterns of experience that describe the tensions crisscrossing modernity: *Erfahrung* and *Erlebnis*. My remarks here will be limited to tracing this distinction between *Erlebnis* and *Erfahrung,* fleshing out the difference between the notions of history and temporality that are at work in these two forms, and, finally, examining the way this difference is traced in the work of art.

Although Benjamin refers in general to experience as *Erfahrung,* it is important for tracing the complexity and ambiguity of his reflection upon modernity to maintain a distinction between experience as a form of immediacy and self-presence *(Erlebnis)* and experience as a pattern of dislocation and temporal distance *(Erfahrung).* I employ *Erlebnis* as an umbrella term for all those instances in which experience is characterized by punctuality, self-coincidence, and closure. At the beginning of "Some Motifs in Baudelaire," Benjamin associates these forms of experience with the conception of lived experience in *Lebensphilosophie* and Bergson's notion of *durée,* indicating that their overarching characteristic lies in their immediacy and "lived," unreflected quality. In contrast, the *Erfahrung*-forms of experience are defined specifically by the inscription of an unsublatable temporal distance in their very mode of occurring; they take place as already dislocated and noncoincident. *Erfahrung* transpires as the opening of a distance, a dislocation into time, and an irruption of history. This degree of noncoincidence characterizes not only the work of memory and dreams, or the surrealist suffusion of the ordinary with the marvelous, that is, the sur-reality inflecting the everyday world, but also, and primarily, historical thinking. This is why in his polemics with *Matière et mémoire* Benjamin singles out the absence of "any historical determination of memory" as the most significant factor placing Bergson in the vicinity of *Lebensphilosophie* and its conception of "true" experience as *Erlebnis.*

Benjamin relates this understanding of experience as *Erlebnis* to the heightened, though often concealed, presence of the mythic elements and archaic consciousness in modern technological culture and to the political dangers rising from the totalization of experience implicit in this attitude:

> Since the end of the last century, philosophy has made a series of attempts to lay hold of the "true" experience *(der "wahren" Erfahrung)* as opposed to the kind that manifests itself in the standardized, denatured life of the civilized masses. It is customary to classify these efforts under the heading of a philosophy of life. Their point of departure, understandably enough, was not man's life in society. What they invoked was poetry, preferably nature, and, most recently, the age of myths. Dilthey's book *Das Erlebnis und die Dichtung* represents one of the earliest of these efforts which end with Klages and Jung; both made common cause with Fascism. *(I,* 156)

Regarding the mythic underpinnings of *Erlebnis* as possibly facilitating the embrace or at least complacency with fascist ideology, Benjamin posits the necessity of historicist and materialist analysis as an antidote to the mythologizing force of primal or archaic experience. The difference between the fulfillment implicit in *Erlebnis* and the distance operating in *Erfahrung* is replayed in the tensions running through Benjamin's work: mythology and history, dream and awakening, historicism and dialectical materialism, fascism and revolution.

The pivot of Benjamin's thought, this difference is more complex than it appears on the surface and often comes close to erasing the boundary between the *Erlebnis* and the *Erfahrung* patterns of experience. Even though Benjamin appears anxious to assure mutual exclusiveness of *Erlebnis* and *Erfahrung*, the forms of experience associated with *Erlebnis* often incorporate in their occurrence the distance and disjunction characteristic of *Erfahrung*, while the latter is sometimes given by Benjamin the valency of a "true" or "whole" experience, evocative of the metaphysical ideas of closure and self-identity. This ambivalence is due at least partly to the wide register of examples that Benjamin procures for those two patterns of experience, though it also reflects a structural ambiguity at work in *Erlebnis*. Even though, or perhaps because, *Erlebnis* designates the punctuality of shock experience, its correlate is the desire to reclaim fullness and closure of experience, an idealized plentitude which is most often placed at a distance, at a remove from the splintered experience of the present. Dislocated from the punctual present, this plentitude functions as either an archaic, mythic past, an origin that has degenerated into the alienated forms of modern life, or as a transcendental ideal, a future utopia—the "blue dream" of Romanticism. In this case of what might be called *Erlebnis* at a distance, the present functions merely as a distorted reflection of a "true" past or a harbinger of the plentitude to come. The experience of the present—regarded as alienated, fragmented, and incomplete—becomes totally inadequate with regard to the posited past or future fullness that haunts and exposes the lack and deficiencies of the present instant. In spite of the disjunction, this pattern of experience envisions the eventuation of the promised fullness, the realization of its closure, the recuperation of the alienated ideal. Whether it designates an archaic past or a future utopia, the dislocation in either case, unlike the structural dislocation operating in *Erfahrung*, may be redeemed and the promised immediacy restored. It has only the status of an appearance, an immediacy lurking beneath or just beyond everyday fragmentation and regimentation—the "natural" immediacy of common knowledge and the naturalness of the everyday. That is why Benjamin is so careful to prevent the dislocation in the *Jetztzeit* and in the surrealist writing practice from being collapsed into the paradigm of an ideal at a distance and read as another version of distanced fulfillment.

Heidegger's critique of *Lebensphilosophie* and the forms of lived experience, its ties to organicism and biologism, makes up a long story, in fact an undercurrent of the project of rethinking existence and being in terms of the event *(Ereignis).*[24] Though Heidegger is less explicit in linking this idea of a distanced origin with myth, the way he deploys the notion of *Erfahrung* in his writings is correlated with his critique of the uniformity and totalizing scope of the calculative thought dominating the technological present. As long as we think technology instrumentally, we fail, Heidegger believes, to understand, and to "experience," the extent to which enframing—the technological mode of disclosing the world—organizes modern reality. Regarding technology instrumentally prevents "the question as to whether we actually experience ourselves as the ones whose activities everywhere, public and private, are challenged forth by enframing [*vom Ge-stell herausgefordert ist*]" *(BW,* 329).[25] For Heidegger, it is the recognition of how experience is "enframed" within modernity that may permit a questioning, perhaps even an unfastening, a release—in the sense of *Gelassenheit*—of the technological frame of being: "[W]hen we once open ourselves expressly to the *essence* of technology we find ourselves unexpectedly taken into a freeing claim [*Anspruch*]" *(BW,* 330–31). To be able to read the claim of *Erfahrung* as a passage, a "perilous journey," and to question the uniformity and immobility of *Bestand*—of the world as a resource at hand—it is necessary to realize how technology has become the pattern of experience, the modality of the world's unfolding. This other, "freeing," claim Heidegger mentions is the work of art, in the double, objective and subjective sense of the genitive, that is, the historical *poiēsis* performed by art, which unfolds the legibility of history.

The lessons of Heidegger and Benjamin could be encapsulated into a call for attentiveness to the distances and disjunctions into which experience unfolds and for thinking and keeping in play the event character of experience, its disjoining eventuation or traversal into presence. The new legibility of experience in modernity signifies nothing other than the possibility of thinking experience nonmetaphysically, by attending, apart from the notions of subjectivity and presence, to the temporal translocation at work in experience, which encrypts the possibility of history. In Heidegger, this translocation is marked by the excess, the always already, characteristic of *Ereignis.* For Benjamin, it is the structure of *Erfahrung* as a historical experience, whose emblematic representation is given in the dialectical image and in the dislocation of the "now-time" *(Jetztzeit)*.

This "new" legibility of experience can be obtained only through a redefinition of language beyond its "technological" determinations as a means of communication and the circuitry for the flow of information. If Benjamin's earlier essays on technology, "The Work of Art in the Age of Mechanical Reproduction" and "A Short History of Photography," describe its potentially emancipatory effects, his later texts associate technology with the reduction of experience and its eventual encapsulation in information. It is this later Benjaminian attitude toward technology which strikes me as parallel to Heidegger's reflection on the *Gestell*. Benjamin is very specific in singling out information as one of the chief culprits in isolating experience into discrete moments: "The principles of journalistic information (freshness of the news, brevity, comprehensibility, and, above all, lack of connection between the individual news items) contribute as much to this as does the make-up of the pages and the paper's style. . . . Another reason for the isolation of information from experience is that the former does not enter 'tradition' " *(I,* 158–59). Equally important is the parallel recognition of the linguistic determination of experience, which, in turn, renders "experience" problematic as a metaphysical concept. In fact, the agreement about the always already discursive form of experience, widespread in contemporary debates, puts into question, even seems to disqualify, the very notion of experience. This is certainly the case if by experience one means some sort of a non- or prelinguistic sensation, an operation through which reality impresses itself upon consciousness, which is already at work to "imagine" and represent what it undergoes or "experiences." Such experience immediately assumes foundational functions, serving as a source or origin of meaning, a "signification" prior to signification and language, which can be handily invoked as an authorizing moment and a corrective to the "excesses" of language and the uncontrollable play of rhetoric. It would be advisable, therefore, to abandon the term "experience" altogether if it were not for the fact that much of contemporary thought is too often misread as limited "simply" to an analysis of language or textuality, with apparently no interest, and no bearing, upon "experience." I keep, therefore, the word "experience"— if only in quotation marks, requalified and critiqued—because it opens a space for demonstrating that the textuality at work in post-Heideggerian thought is a way of remapping "experience" outside the grid of the foundational dichotomies of subject and object, presence and absence, experience and language.

This refiguration of experience transposes the boundary between being and thought, existence and language, rendering "experience" indissociable from thought, indeed equivalent to a form of thinking: *Denken* or *Andenken* in Heidegger, *Eingedenken* in Benjamin. In both cases, for Benjamin as well as for Heidegger, *Erfahrung* acquires the texture of thinking, it bears the imprint of the dislocation and excess characteristic of thought overflowing its articulations, its representationality. Perhaps the best illustration of this pattern is the way in which "experience" in Heidegger's work is taken over and reworked through the notion of thinking *(Denken)*. Because of the metaphysical provenance of the concept of experience, of its virtual inseparability from the metaphysics of the subject, Heidegger's critique of the philosophy of life and its governing notion of *Erlebnis* institutes in place of experience and its subject the modality of "being-in-the-world" and the site of its "thereness," *Dasein*. In Heidegger's later writings, what marks and reinscribes the shifting perimeter of being-in-the-world is thinking *(Denken)*, a poetic thinking within, but also of, *Ereignis*—the infold.[26] In this context, experience is no longer opposed, prior to, or different from thinking; it is not an encounter with the world through the senses, which serves as the sensible basis for reflection and ratiocination. Instead, experience, refigured as event, is a form of thinking which acts upon reality and effects it, "lets it be," through the act of transposing it into language. Being-in-the-world has the form of thinking, whose most characteristic trait is attending to the always already completed transfer or translation of the world—its history—into language and discursive structures. For Heidegger being means participating in the linguistic event *(Ereignis)* which opens a world and history.

Redescribing experience as thinking, Heidegger disengages experience from the pattern of passive receptivity and from the reactive model of consciousness, according to which the world inscribes or impresses its outline upon the senses and, through them, upon thought. For Heidegger thinking is both a responding *(Entsprechen)* to the event of the world and an active transmission or transposition of this event into language. Always already profiled in language, thinking is this "constellation of the truth" *(BW,* 317) of the unconcealment of the world and history, the configuration of thinking *(Denken)* whose modality of the middle voice escapes the simple polarity of the active and the passive. Prior to the distinction between practice and theory, the thinking Heidegger has in mind outlines the comportment of *Dasein* toward the world; its constellation continuously reconfigures the patterns of engagement with what is, the modalities of being-in-the-world ("experiencing"), from which both theoretical reflection and action derive. "Thinking does not become action only because some effect issues from it or because it is applied. Thinking acts insofar as it thinks. Such action is presumably the simplest and at the same time the highest, because it concerns the relation of Being to man" (*BW,* 217). The middle voice of such thinking, both guided by the unfolding of history and actively participating in it by shaping its articulation into language, breaks with the metaphysical polarization into theory and practice by recognizing how the dynamic of experience is determined by language.

In Benjamin's work the question of passivity and activity is broached through the distinction between *Erlebnis* (the lived moment) and *Erfahrung* (experience). Even though *Erlebnis* cannot be described simply in terms of a passive reception of stimuli, consciousness fragmented by shock experience appears to be rendered passive, overwhelmed by the punctuality of the instant, and incapable of (historical) experience beyond the scope of the lived moment. Unlike *Erlebnis,* experience as *Erfahrung* requires the work of *Eingedenken,* the attentiveness of thought to the possibility of the past emerging within and dislocating the present from the closure and isolation of the "lived moment" and endowing it thus with the valency of historical experience *(Erfahrung)*. The Benjaminian modality of thinking as commemoration or remembrance *(Eingedenken)* functions as the opening of history, the inauguration of historical time and the possibility of historical experience. Brushing history against the grain, this form of remembrance unmasks history as injustice, as the evolution of the means of exploitation: "There is no document of civilization which is not at the same time a document of barbarism" (*I,* 256). To the extent that historical experience in Benjamin has the structure of *Eingedenken,* of the constellation of the past and the present, it marks the labor of the historian or the thinker to obtain "a unique experience with the past" (*I,* 262). However, the practice of *Eingedenken* cannot be confused with activity that would remain at the discretion of a subject, since the irruption of the past within the present, the maturation of the past's weak messianic force that makes possible the crystallization of the monad of *Jetztzeit,* can never be forced within the present. The activity of *Eingedenken* consists above all in preparation, in getting thought ready to register the flashing emergence of the unique experience with the past, an experience that not only marks the past with the force of the present but, in the same gesture, dislodges the *Erlebnis* of the present into the interval, the in-thinking of experience *(Erfahrung)*. *Eingedenken* functions as both the constellation of this in-thinking, the configuration of the past's infold into the present—the syncope of the now-time—and as the readiness to remember, to mark, this dislocation. For Benjamin, *Eingedenken,* blowing open the present and unmasking its injustices, repays a debt to the past by rendering legible the failure of the past to read itself historically.

Language, the Most Innocent and Most Dangerous of Possessions

> Writing poetry: "That most innocent of all occupations"
> —Hölderlin

Reading experience *(Erfahrung)* and thinking *(Denken)* in terms of the event of history, that is, as already indexed historically, hinges upon the etiology of "human speech," of language as a system of signs and an array of discursive practices. To understand how either Benjamin's or Heidegger's work is invested in the notion of experience *(Erfahrung)* as the site of the articulation of danger, it is important to recognize a certain homology that their writings elaborate between language and experience. In fact, for both thinkers, their conceptions of experience are correlates of their approach to language. The perilous nature of experience—the constant possibility of misreading being in essentialist terms—is conditioned by the proclivity of language to hide its own structure of translation and, in the process, to dissemble the discursive status of experience. In both the Heideggerian and the Benjaminian projects, the idiosyncratic conceptions of language become the site of interrogating experience and, more specifically, of elucidating the discursive constitution and working of experience. For Benjamin and Heidegger, "experience" *(Erfahrung)* is marked by an unbridgeable distance, a dislocation from presence, precisely to the extent that it occurs, as it were, "into" words or text, replaying the translational dynamic of the language event.

We should start by remarking that the Benjaminian as well as the Heideggerian approach to language differ quite distinctly from the Saussurean and the post-Saussurean models, which focus primarily on the relation between *langue* and *parole*. Like the Saussurean model itself, its critiques, putting in question the rigid demarcation between *langue* and *parole* through the concepts of textuality and discursive practice, often leave unexamined or devote less attention to the relation between language and its "other": reality, world, experience, and so on. This is the case, in particular, with the effects that the inscription of the relation of language and its outside has on the representational optics itself, or, to be more precise, on whether one opts for the representational paradigm at all. The recognition that reality and experience are constituted discursively, already as an interpretation, does not really modify the focus or the parameters of the inquiry which center upon the play of signification and its cultural determinations. Predictably, those inquiries return sooner or later to the question of representation and referentiality, reconfirming the double optics of the Saussurean model: the social and the referential.

If in Saussure the problem of reference, though implicit, remains largely unexamined, both Benjamin and Heidegger propose models of language that might be called translational or transpositional. Since for those thinkers language works on the principle of transition and translocation, it cannot be properly regarded as *either* representational *or* nonrepresentational. I read these approaches to language in terms of how they render the problem of representation *secondary:* They preempt, as it were, the issue of referentiality of language by extending the notion of language to the very event of manifestation, to phenomenality itself. To put it differently, they propose a transpositional model of language in lieu of the paradigm of representation grounded upon the metaphysics of the subject. Representation is a derived, though necessary, phenomenon, an effect of the metaphysical categorization of language as a means of representation and communication. Underlying the problem of representationality is what Heidegger would call a narrow understanding of language, which limits the event of language to the human system of signification. Such a demarcation of language of and against the "material" or "sensible" reality reflects one of the most fundamental metaphysical oppositions: between the sensible and the intelligible. This metaphysical divide predetermines and displaces reflection on language away from the question of its translational character to its representational function. Likewise, the question of reference can arise only when language is already regarded as separated, at least implicitly, from the "reality" or "experience" which it is, therefore, expected to describe and represent.

Against Saussure's view, which, characteristically, neither Benjamin nor Heidegger mention, their approaches can be seen as dissolving the double optics that frame the Saussurean model and substituting for them a dynamic design of language as a "way to language" (Heidegger) or "translatability" (Benjamin). The linguistic blueprint they elaborate demonstrates how the work of language consists in transposing "reality"—that is, the event of manifestation that itself already constitutes a form of saying—

into language (discourse, representation, conceptuality). In this view, the world is not only thought and experienced within language, that is, as always already transposed (translated) into language, but takes itself the form of a language event. The significance of the notion of translatability in the context of history and experience can be seen from the fact that for Benjamin translatability works as a structure of the work of art that liberates it from the mythical connection to reality. As Gasché explains, "[t]hanks to this structure the work of art raises itself above textual, weblike, and hence mythical interconnectedness to communicate that within it, language speaks, or that within it, a difference has been set forth."[27] The possibility of disentangling history and experience from the "danger" of reading in mythical terms is inscribed in the artwork's translatability, in its "linguistic intention," which draws attention to the distance and difference through which reality transposes itself into language. It is interesting to note here that in his 1942 summer course on Hölderlin's hymn "Der Ister," Heidegger, taking a position markedly different from his statements from 1933 to 1934, links the historical existence of a people precisely with the difference and otherness inscribed in translation. Noting that a historical people can never find its "essence" *(Wesen)* in their own language, Heidegger writes: "*Ein geschichtliches Volk* ist *nur aus der Zwiesprache seiner Sprache mit fremden Sprachen*" ("A historical people *is* only from the dialogue between its language and foreign languages").[28] Translation, especially the effects it has on one's own language, puts into question the "mythical" construction of identity, the connectedness constitutive of the sameness of essence.

Already in "On Language as Such and on the Language of Man," Benjamin describes the linguistic event in terms of translation: "The translation [*Übersetzung*] of the language of things into that of man" (*R,* 325). The title phrase "language as such" points beyond language conceived as a system of signs *(langue)* or discursive practice, and refers to the event (of language) which institutes language in its narrow sense as a signifying or representational system. The title designates not so much the play of signification (the human language or "naming") as the interval and the positioning of the "language of man" vis-à-vis the "language of things." "Language as such" is therefore a structuring that underlies and produces "human language," that underscores the possibility and the precariousness of the (mis)translation implied by the very dynamics of the event of language. Since for Benjamin the language of things is not fully uttered or expressed, it is not yet spoken (or written),[29] it finds itself in need of transcription into words; it must be translated into discourse. Not yet signifiable, the linguistic being *(sprach-*

liche Wesen) of things requires transcription: "To whom does the lamp communicate itself [*mitteilen*]? The mountain? The fox? But here the answer is: to man. This is not anthropomorphism. The truth of this answer is shown in knowledge and perhaps also in art" (*R,* 317). The Benjaminian notion of "language as such" indicates nothing other than the matrix of this transcription, itself unwritten and already erased by the results of the translatory operation: the orders of signification and representation. What communicates itself across languages, in the translatability marked within each language and each text, is the "language as such," that is, the translational event inaugurating discourse.

Considered in the context of Benjamin's work, Heidegger's idea of the way to language, of language that occurs "on the way" to words *(unterwegs zur Sprache),* prior to the systemic play of signs, can be taken to demonstrate how the translational conception of language inflects the metaphysical framework of linguistic and aesthetic speculation. Heidegger shows how this linguistic translation determines the dynamics of experience and how its self-erasure allows for the refraction of *Erfahrung* into the lived moment. Heidegger's various encounters with language through the prism of poetry oscillate constantly around the problem of the self-effacing character of the language event, the necessary disappearance of the translational "way-making" in the play of signification: "Such way-making brings language (the essence of language) as language (the saying) to language (to the re-sounding word)" (*BW,* 418). The Heideggerian insight into language pivots upon the recognition of the already linguistic character of phenomenality, on the idea that manifestation is a form of a "showing saying": "The saying is by no means the supplementary linguistic expression of what shines forth; rather all shining and fading depend on the saying that shows" (*BW,* 414). Here the saying *(Sage),* that is, phenomenality or the phenomenal condition of the world, understood as the play that eventuates into presence and absence (*Anwesen* and *Abwesen*), cannot be mistaken for the representation of the substantive being of a thing, because it delineates the thing's emergence within the nexus or the jointure that is called world or history. In other words, the saying transcribes the trajectory of the thing's propriation within the event *(Ereignis)* of language. *Sage* points beyond the essence, the idea, or the representation of a thing, and marks what I would call the thing's "phenomenal scription," that is, its tracing within the binary logic of presence and absence. "The saying that rests on propriation [*Ereignis*] is, as showing, the most proper mode of propriating. Propriation is telling [*sagend*]" (*BW,* 420). Beyond the play of signfication, the saying constitutes the very unfolding and occurrence, the drawing out and deciding of propriation—the event as *Ereignis*. As an event that brings what is into its own, that is, propriates, *Ereignis* occurs as saying, which means that its very unfolding composes a relationality that is "telling," that says itself beyond and "prior to" the space of signification. We might say that the *Sage* constitutes the linguistic coming into presence of the phenomenal, what Benjamin hints at with his notion of "linguistic being" *(sprachliche Wesen)*. An-archic, without the point of origin, this linguistic manifestation precedes the quantification of the phenomenal in terms of materiality and intelligibility. With his notion of the way-making of language, Heidegger proposes to see phenomenality as a linguistic event, which resonates in the phrase *"die Sprache spricht"*: language languages. It is out of this specific linguistic formation of the phenomenal that the distinction between the sensible and the intelligible arises.

The transposition through which language constitutes itself and effects its emergence as "human speech," as a set of discursive practices, remains for the most part covered by the play of signification. This is especially the case in the information age, where "being" or "reality" seem to be increasingly determined by their informational (and, more often than not, sensational) value, and where language becomes identified solely with its functionality, with its pragmatic dimension of an informational relay. The self-veiling language dynamics, no longer recognizable in the communicational and informational uses of language, is registered, however, by art, in particular in the poetic explorations of language which explicitly attend to the unfolding of language, its semantic and syntactical crystallizations. This is why Benjamin and Heidegger devote so much reflection to the working of art, to its "poietics," and to art's ability to retain and expose the traces of the translational character of experience.

What is rarely noted in this context is that both Benjamin and Heidegger inscribe their discussion of language and art in the problematic of the dangers facing history and thought at the end of modernity. The trajectories by which they arrive at this issue is markedly different: Benjamin works very closely with his immediate historical context, elaborating the constellation of the notion of history as injustice, the revolutionary possibilities of the avant-garde writing practice, and resistance to fascist ideology; Heidegger, distancing in the late 1930s his work from ideas close to the ideology of national socialism, projects his thought of the ontico-ontological difference against the broader scheme of the history of metaphysics, often anchoring his late remarks on art in the discussion of Hölderlin and poetry in the context of the dominance of technology and calculative thought.[30] What Heidegger's work shows is that the contestation of a specific risk or danger does not necessarily coincide with the questioning of the conceptuality or the framework that has produced the danger, and which, concealing the linguistic slip through which experience and history are constituted, itself becomes the possibility of danger, of restaging danger repeatedly. Benjamin's thought works in a different way, in a different direction, one might say: It extends its contestation of the specific historical circumstances of the rise of fascism to the reflections on the risks inscribed in the very paradigm of enlightened modernity. Benjamin's most poignant image linking language and danger is the alarm clock at the end of his essay on Surrealism: "They [the Surrealists] exchange, to a man, the play of human features [*ihr Mienenspiel*] for the face of an alarm clock that in each minute rings [*anschlägt*] for sixty seconds" (R, 192). If, as Benjamin's notions of translatability and *Intention auf die Sprache* attest, the work of poetry and art consists in attending to the event of language, to the linguistic intention inscribed in and sustaining each text, then art in the age of heightened reproducibility can be defined through its continual problematization of the textual makeup of "experience." This art, its avant-garde language, functions on the model of the alarm clock of Surrealism, ringing for sixty seconds in each minute. This Benjaminian image suggests that every sentence, even every word, has to be alarmed, ready to set off, to displace its own meaning the moment it is put down on the page. It points to a language that always alarms itself, undoing conventions, both literary and everyday, checking over its language games for the traces of what exceeds their practice and remains other. Not only to avoid forgetting or erasing these marks but, primarily, to amplify their disruptive force and turn writing against language into a gesture of exposing the textual, though also cultural and political, effects of the discursive inscription of experience. Modern art has language confront its own "alarming" face and never quite allows it to fall asleep or become lulled by its own playfulness. Perhaps that is indeed the practice of the avant-garde and the reason why this practice, when considered in the wide range of its implications, remains disquieting even beyond the specificity of its historical and cultural locations.

What underlies Benjamin's essay on Surrealism is a seldom underscored connection in his thought between, on the one hand, language and translatability inscribed in the work of art and, on the other, the need for a conception of history as a constant "state of emergency," which could inflect thinking into *Eingedenken* and thus keep the present open to the possibility of the emergence of the past and the dislocation produced by the release of its "weak" Messianic force: "The tradition of the oppressed teaches us that the 'state of emergency' in which we live is not the exception but the rule. We must attain to a conception of history that is in keeping with this insight" (*I*, 257). In this view, *Eingedenken* is not only a thinking *of* a danger, of the perilous historical situation of emerging totalitarian ideologies, but also a thinking *in* danger of failing to be historical, of forgetting its own historicity. This thinking takes place as a constellation of danger(s): of experience and history but also of the work of art and language. If danger is inscribed in experience as historicity "beyond" history, this inscription is a result of the fact that experience is always already an interpretation, itself in need of continuous rereading. In other words, it has to do with language, with experience and history being possible only as their own interpretation, that is, as having their occurrence already circumscribed by signification. Writing poetry, "that most innocent of all occupations," as Hölderlin remarks, seemingly divorced from the world of everyday praxis, from politics and the dangers of history, suddenly becomes a perilous and risky enterprise, a politically charged undertaking, since language turns out to be "the most dangerous of possessions." It becomes a matter of examining the political meaning of legibility, of the very grounds upon which politics becomes legible.[31]

Benjamin's alarm clock certainly rings differently than the "ringing of stillness" *(Geläut der Stille)* with which Heidegger's later texts describe poetic language and thought. It strikes *(anschlägt)* rather than gently pealing or chiming, evoking the ghosts of the past, the faces of the oppressed, and the barbarism of history rather than the stillness or silence that interweaves linguistic articulations. As "Theses on the Philosophy of History" suggests, this ringing becomes a reminder that history is a series of injustices, from which even the works of art and poetry are not immune: "[f]or without exception the cultural treasures [the historical materialist] surveys have an origin which he cannot contemplate without horror. They owe their existence not only to the efforts of the great minds and talents who have created them, but also to the anonymous toil of their contemporaries" (*I*, 256). While Heidegger's texts may be read as allowing one to entertain the illusion that the "ringing of stillness" signifies aesthetic quietism (although I do not think that this position is ultimately tenable), Benjamin's forceful pronunciations are directed at preventing the disruptive and critical impetus of this silence within the language of modern art from being misread as an expression of either cognitive skepticism or aesthetic formalism.[32]

Critics like Habermas often hastily misread Heidegger's pronouncements on language and poetry as an escape to "the luminous heights of an esoteric, special discourse, which absolves itself of the restrictions of discursive speech generally and is immunized by vagueness against any specific objections."[33] Yet, the linguistic stillness which is taken to unequivocally pervade, even paralyze, Heidegger's late work is clearly more complex, as it marks a revision of the very idea of action in terms of a response of listening, which breaks free of the metaphysical trappings of experience. As Fynsk suggests, Habermas's "narrative," according to which Heidegger abandons political thinking and revolutionary activism after his disastrous engagement with national socialism and retreats into quietism, is incorrect. In the context of Heidegger's numerous remarks about the danger at work in language, in metaphysical conceptuality, and in modern technology, it is impossible to read this stillness simply as a mark of indifference and not, as may well be the case, the sign of how language itself downplays, masks, or effaces, the danger at work in its articulations. As is evidenced by Heidegger's texts on language, "[t]he move from resoluteness to *Gelassenheit* involves a difficult rethinking of the will, but the 'rigors' of the hermeneutic circle remain constant in Heidegger's questioning" (*HTH*, 245). Heidegger's comments on language and its dangers, and his continued rethinking of action beyond its metaphysical determinations—from "Letter on Humanism" to *On the Way to Language*—make untenable Habermas's position, which hears nothing else in the *Geläut* than Romantic esotericism or the indifference of the aestheticist autotelism of art. Is the ringing in Benjamin and Heidegger—one of a technological gadget as an image of radical writing practice, the other of the "telling" silence of the poetic text— so unequivocally different? The everyday character of the object whose image Benjamin uses to describe the practice of the avant-garde indeed provides a corrective to the overbearing rhetoric of later Heidegger, directing us back to the connection between artistic and everyday practice; but it also serves as a reminder that Heidegger's own project involves above all the inquiry into the everydayness of being and that his involvement with art and poetic language should be considered in this light. The tension between Benjamin and Heidegger directs our attention to the question of the articulation of the danger inherent in the event of language: Can this danger ring silently? But maybe this question needs to be reversed: Perhaps silence *is* a way that the danger (of language) can ring in writing, since "amplified" articulations of danger, and Benjamin is well aware of that, run the risk of collapsing into activism, into manifestoes and propagandistic writing, so characteristic of some avant-gardisms. After all, since Benjamin's alarm clock is only an image, it always rings silently. On the opposite side of the spectrum of answers to this question lies quietistic indifference, which, when ascribed to Heidegger, leads to reducing his work on poetry to merely a theory of language, burying under this label its radical importance for experience and history.

Notwithstanding the problems with Heidegger's analysis, the stillness he explores through poetic text is quite "telling," with specific implications for the modern, "technological," conceptualization of experience and history. Commenting in the second section of "Hölderlin and the Essence of Poetry" on a Hölderlin fragment that includes the lines: "and therefore has language, most dangerous of possessions [*der Güter Gefährlichstes*] been given to man," [34] Heidegger considers language the initial possibility of danger, its "ontological," as it were, condition: "It is the danger of all dangers, because it creates [*schafft*] initially the possibility of a danger. Danger is the threat to being [of obscuring being and hence history and experience] through beings. . . . It is language which first creates the manifest conditions for menace and confusion to existence, and thus the possibility of the loss of existence, that is to say—danger" (*EB*, 275). Since it is through and as language that world and history unfold, language shapes the disclosure and determines the historical dispositions of what is and its existence. It is, therefore, both a danger and a good *(ein Gut)*, the synchrony of manifestation and deception, unconcealment and concealment, insight and error. Playing on the double valency of *Gut* (like the English "good" and "goods" or "possessions"), Heidegger renders language both a treasure (another meaning of *Gut*) and a trap, a good with an inherent propensity for metamorphosing into a tool for the erasure of alterity and the fulfillment of the totalizing ambitions of thought, an instrument, we could say, of enlightenment and of its double—cultural imperialism. Language is a play, innocent and dangerous at the same time, of its disclosive abilities and the constant possibility of endangering what it discloses. This approach entails the recognition that language is not a neutral medium of communication but a mapping of the world, an unfolding of legibility, which, to the extent that it obfuscates the historicity of its articulation, poses a threat to its own practices of disclosure. The implication of this erasure of historicity—that is, of a continuous crisis, of a ceaseless decision, that marks language—is not unlike Benjamin's historical rule of the "state of emergency."

As the initial possibility of danger, both the disclosure and the dissembling of historicity, language is characterized above all by the predilection for endangering itself, for obscuring its mechanism and appearing most innocent precisely at the moment when it poses most danger. "But language is not only the danger of dangers, but necessarily conceals in itself a continual danger for itself" ("*birgt in sich selbst für sich selbst notwendig eine fortwährende Gefahr*") (*EB*, 275).[35] This incessant danger inscribed in the event of language achieves its historical determination in modernity in the instrumentalization of language as information. The reduction of language to the transparency of communicational tool, so idiomatic to modernity and its technological determination of reason, changes the valency of *Gut* from that of a good to that of a *Werkzeug*—a tool or an instrument. This commodification of language, as either a tool or a piece of information, dissembles and hides the fact that language affords the possibility of world and history: "Only where there is language, is there world, that is, the perpetually altering circuit of decision and production, of action and responsibility, but also of commotion and arbitrariness, of decay and confusion" (*EB*, 276). For Heidegger, it is "the sphere of the action of poetry" (*EB*, 277) to resist this collapsing of language into an instrument of communication, to allow language to "language"[36] as the event that disposes the possibilities for being ("*dasjenige Ereignis, das über die höchste Möglichkeit des Menschenseins verfügt*" [*EHD*, 38]). It is the business of poetry, therefore, to remain attentive to the "good" character of language, to the danger that incessantly traverses the event of language, and, in particular, to make sure that the danger *(Gefahr)* inherent in the experience *(Erfahrung)* with language does not disappear under the apparently innocent surface of linguistic transactions. The unequivocal ascription of innocence, of the intention of mere "aesthetic play," to writing already loses sight of the *Gefahr* inscribed in *Erfahrung* and trivializes the workings of art beyond recognition.

To the extent that the work of art is structured by such a linguistic event, it has a performative function within history, one of disclosing the "ontological" condition of danger and the singular forms it assumes in concrete historical circumstances. Heidegger's focus on the precarious conditions of the eventuation of being *(Ereignis)*, on the constant slippage between *Sein* and *Seiende*, may account for the (mis)reading of his analyses as an ontologization of danger, as an escape or a dissolution of any responsibility through a gesture that makes danger "intrinsic" to language. It is certainly true that Heidegger, in a sharp distinction from Benjamin and his continuous inscription of the current historical context, sets his reflections in a broader historico-philosophical framework of modern technology and extends them to the "ontological" level of the historical determinations of the "essence" of modern technology as the enframing, the *Gestell*. Benjamin's texts work on a double impulse: The philosophical and cultural reflection is ceaselessly intertwined with the interpretation of the details of the historical situation, which gives a unique performative dimension to Benjamin's thought, an awareness of the quasi-interventionist character of his writing practice. It would be a mistake, however, not to see Heidegger's thought as itself performing a displacement of the conceptual and historical framework of modernity, although the general scope of his statements often renders their performative edge less distinct, even creating the appearance of indifference to historical detail. As Rebecca Comay remarks, noting Heidegger's problem, the ontic memory emphasized by Benjamin "would not be inconsistent with the remembrance of the ontico-ontological difference: indeed the very finitude of that difference should have, strictly speaking, required precisely such attention to the specific differences that are the stuff of history. Such attentiveness would have easily redeemed Heidegger's notion of 'historicity' from the sneering charge of 'abstractness' which both Adorno and Benjamin—not without some justice, but without real cause—were to insist on levelling."[37]

In *The Middle Voice of Ecological Conscience*, John Llewellyn demonstrates that Heidegger's work can be read through the optics of "ontological responsibility," as specifically underscoring the demands of "responsible" thinking, which the recognition of the differential working of history dictates. Indeed, Heidegger's ontological qualification of danger is consistent, if not coextensive, with a thinking that incessantly questions and reappraises its historical articulations, that works through the tension between the "initial possibility of danger" and its specific historical and ontic determinations; in other words, with a thinking that checks and corrects the way its own structures conceal or efface thought's "most own" dangerous mechanism. We have to remember that, for Heidegger, the historical specificity of modern thought trying to separate itself and question its philosophical (metaphysical) provenance consists precisely in the recognition of the difference or play between the ontic articulations and the concealed ontological dimension of history. The recognition of this forgotten tension, figured by the term "historicity," is to provide a corrective to the by-and-large calculative modes of thought by undercutting their totalizing practices in view of specific differences at play in history. Heidegger's insistence on keeping in play the ontico-ontological difference, on underscoring its finitude, attempts to prevent the subsumption of differences into a comprehensive narrative of history. The remembrance, the *Andenken*, of the ontological condition of danger, that is, of the constant erasure of the ontico-ontological difference, does not efface the specificity of historical articulations or the singularity of dangers posed by history. On the contrary, it "guarantees," as it were, this singularity by historicizing it, by inscribing it in the very event of history; that is, by rendering historicity into the condition of the singularity of experience. By exposing the danger at work in language, this thinking tries to ensure historical specificity against recuperation or completion. What is very important and often completely overlooked in this Heideggerian view is that the ontic particularity by itself *cannot prevent* thought from effacing the singularity of historical differences by means of description. It is the inscription of historicity, the mark of the finitude of the ontico-ontological difference, that defers the closure of thought and keeps it open, responsive, perhaps even responsible, to alterity. I would argue that it is precisely such "remembrance" of what Heidegger calls "the threat to being," that is, of the forgetfulness of being's historicity, that singularizes historical perils, or that, more specifically, allows thought not to lose sight of their distinctiveness. Heidegger's texts do not emphasize this point enough, or at least do not translate it into a detailed analysis of the historical circumstances of his own work. As one critic puts it, Heidegger's work in the 1930s and 1940s, through its critique of Nietzsche and metaphysics as the manifestation of the will to power, "gives us important and precise instruments for such a critique [of National Socialism], but he himself does not employ them in such function, for his task situates itself 'else-where.'"[38] It remains a question to what extent the "elsewhere" of Heidegger's task—the rethinking and critique of the metaphysical "essence" of thought in its historical manifestation as technology—stays within the perimeter of the philosophical enterprise, and thus within the metaphysical project which Heidegger contests, or extends into the problematic of its own historical context. Moreover, even this position will have to be submitted, though not here, to a further critique, because the recent appearance of Heidegger's unpublished texts from the years 1938 to 1940 demonstrate how central the critique of power is to Heidegger's project of the critique of metaphysics. *Besinnung* (from 1938 to 1939), *Die Geschichte des Seyns* (from 1939 to 1940), and *Metaphysik und Nihilismus* (its first part dates from 1938 to 1939), all published within the last two years, offer an extensive critique of power.[39] Even though they remain silent on the question of anti-Semitism, these texts develop Heidegger's "overcoming" of metaphysics in terms of the necessity of transforming relations away from power and manipulability *(Machenschaft)*. Central to this critique of power is Heidegger's reformulation of being as event *(Ereignis),* which provides the vantage point from which he critiques subjectivity, nationalism, and race, as well as the philosophical underpinnings of socialism, communism, and liberal democracy, showing how they remain part of modernity's drive toward the maximalization of power.[40]

In the context of Heidegger's remarks on language and history, what might be considered "dangerous" in the translatory linguistic event is its propensity to self-erasure and concealment: Language covers its own tracks, effaces the way it has made into words, and (re)presents itself as "present" in its significations. In effect, language tends to disguise the fact that its significations are produced through displacement; it conceals the otherness and the instability of meaning that are integral to its system of significations. Instituting the fiction of its own transparency, language disguises the danger of the obliteration of difference and otherness, which remains necessary for the possibility of any closure of meaning. The danger which Heidegger sees as inextricable from the "good" side of language is the tendency to erase the play of concealment and unconcealment, of the true and the untrue, as the "proper" element of language. This dissembling of presence and meaningfulness as the proper "work" of language spells out its own paradox, evident especially in how it conceals the fact that language, as a juncture of the manifestation of the world (phenomenality) and its linguistic saying, happens always as out-of-joint. As a translation without the original, language comes to be only a mistranslation, one which never coincides with itself, always distanced and without origin. Problematizing the notion of language as a system or interplay of signs, both Benjamin and Heidegger treat language as an event of translation which has already completed itself, that is, has reached words and produced itself as meaning. The temporal translocation, the Heideggerian *"immer schon,"* manifests itself in the effraction of the present, in the distance and dislocation which mark the play of signification in relation to its "originating" translatory event. This distanciation persists emphatically as a nonorigin, it remains beyond the margins of signification, beyond the retrievable continuum of the past. These markings of alterity—the continuous reopening within language of a distance or an infold without any point of origin—trace the historical indexing of language: They inaugurate history as the in-thinking, the memoration *(Eingedenken, Andenken)* not of a past which once took place but rather of the dehiscence which, spacing the past and the present, (re)opens history as an interval. In Benjamin's work, the translation in question refers to a transfer between the language of things (or the linguistic being of things) and the human languages, where the occurrence of this translocation describes what Benjamin calls first "the language as such" and later, in "The Task of the Translator," "pure language." For Heidegger, in turn, as *On the Way to Language* makes amply evident, the event of language takes the shape of an already breached way or path, a way-making *(Bewëgung)*, which language has traversed into words, utterances, and discursive practices.[41]

For Benjamin pure language indicates the way in which the world unfolds itself to us in any language. In each language, this unfolding takes place in a different way, but as it always "intends" words, it inevitably leads to translation into and through words. As the linguistic intention par excellence, pure language, for Benjamin, marks the contours of the unfolding of language: "In this pure language—which no longer means or expresses anything but is, as expressionless and creative Word, that which is meant in all languages—all information, all sense, and all intention finally encounter a stratum in which they are destined to be extinguished" (*I*, 80). Like Heidegger's event of disclosure, Benjaminian pure language indicates that "language and revelation are one" (82), that language is tantamount to the disclosive eventuation of the world. To put it differently, the manifestational saying, the linguistic phenomenalization of the world, constitutes the scaffolding of experience; it determines the patterns of experiencing and regulates the occurrence and organization of "experience." Pure language works beyond any specific system of signification, but, to the extent that it always marks a specific language, it describes how this language works. Language discloses the "world truth," that is, the ontological play of existence, not directly in words but rather in "*Intention auf die Sprache*," in the way in which words always resonate the function of language: the opening up of a world. It is in this pointing of words toward the "essence," toward the working of language, that the work of unconcealment lies. "Truth," if what is at stake here can still be called by that name, is never said, never put in words, but is instead transmitted as the linguistic intention, indicated by the word's turn toward "pure" language. What the interval between "pure" language and the signifying operations of each language demonstrates is the trajectory of experience, the manner according to which experience transpires as a text, a form of language, an occurrence whose shape is always already discursive. In both Heidegger's and Benjamin's work, the conception of language and its quasi-translative character hold the key to experience and its historical constitution. We have to write "quasi," since there is no "original," no prelinguistic, "lived" reality or experience *(Erlebnis)* that language "translates." Translation here is the hardly detectable movement, the hesitation, between the identity and the difference of the world and/as text, of the phenomenal and its signification, which, marking the discursive constitution of experience with the historicity of its "translation," keeps unworking the objectifying power of language.

Although Benjamin specifies that it is in translation rather than in the poet's work that "pure language"—the event of language's unfolding into words—is figured,[42] I would argue that much of the avant-garde writing, especially poetry, attempts to inscribe in language, as a form of an intralingual translation, the trajectory of the unfolding of the phenomenal. Literary texts themselves, poetry in particular, draw our attention to the "pure" language—its translative intention—because they expose the mechanism of signification within a given language. In avant-garde writing, even without the benefit of translation, most of the textual play intends specifically the working of the text's language. For at stake in the avant-garde poetry is nothing other than the "intralingual" translation, the way-making of language, which the linguistic innovations characteristic of avant-garde practice continuously put into play. On the one hand, we have the syntactical and typographical experiments of Dada and Italian and Russian futurism, in particular, Khlebnikov's explicit interest in figuring poetry as a multilingual translation of a "beyonsense" language *(zaum)*—that is, of a manifestation which takes the form of saying or scription—into the words of a specific language.[43] On the other, poets like Stein, Celan, or Białoszewski must be understood as performing variations of intralingual translation, a series of transpositions inside a language—English, German, or Polish— which inscribe in their texts the very movement of language's articulation into words and the ways in which this movement disarticulates the meaning it produces. What defines poetry for them is precisely writing in ways which foreground and register the translative modality of the language event, effaced in the largely propositional fashioning of discourse. Even though Heidegger was apparently not interested in avant-garde works, his conception of the way of language—its traversal *(Erfahrung)* from the manifestational saying *(Sage)* to discursive forms *(Verlautbarung)*—which is enacted within poetic language, appears particularly suited to the exploration of the avant-garde's predisposition for seeing language in terms of a translative event.[44] It is no surprise, therefore, that his work, especially the texts on poetry and language, have become a major factor in shaping contemporary American avant-garde poetic movements, from the work of George Oppen to the writings of the "language" poets. Avant-garde writing practices emphasize what both Benjamin and Heidegger regard as a main linguistic precept; above all, language intends itself: "all language communicates itself. Or more precisely: all language communicates itself *in* itself" (*R*, 316). However, neither the "*Intention auf die Sprache*" nor "*Die Sprache spricht*" signifies linguistic narcissism, the play of language for its own sake, so often mistakenly attributed to avant-garde writings. As soon as language is given its own space and is no longer confined to the compartment of a "means of communication" assigned to it within the technological cultures, language exhibits precisely the ways in which the world gains its being, and becomes "real," through language:

> Thus freed to its own open space, language can concern itself solely with itself alone. That resembles the talk one hears about egoistic solipsism. Yet language does not insist on itself, is not a self-mirroring that forgets everything else because it is so enamored of itself. As the saying, the essence of language is the propriating showing that in fact disregards itself in order to liberate what is shown into its own, into its appearance. (*BW,* 419–20)

Seeing language as the event in which the world constitutes itself certainly does not mean that language is a prison house, somehow separating us from the "true" reality and rendering the concerns of everyday life secondary and insignificant. On the contrary, because the world becomes present through language, language has the valency of determining the world's "being" rather than separating us from it.

This insight can be rephrased in the following way: The world is inseparable from language, its fabric is linguistic "before" it can be categorized in terms of materiality and intelligibility. The blueprint for the way of (the world into) language "decides" the world; it outlines—in the sense of *aufreissen* resonating throughout Heidegger's work—and breaks open and delimits the configurations of experience, the daily life practice, and sets the regimen for its ordinary and specialized idioms. This blueprint functions as the "negative" of the world: invisible, or unsaid, as Heidegger would put it, within the "positive," discursive constitution of experience, it subtends the play of signification, within which the world constitutes itself as "experienced." Developing or writing this blueprint, attending to the itinerary of language and its intention, reframes the question of "experience," and phrases it as a matter for and of language. This does not mean that language becomes the sole goal of such an inquiry, but, instead, that it constitutes the domain wherein world and experience, the real, come to pass. For the itinerary of language describes precisely the trajectory of "experience" and/as thinking; it renders legible the contours of our involvement with the world. The scope of the danger of language recognized by Hölderlin remains forgotten or hidden precisely when language is construed as separate from "reality" and its concern with its "intention" mistaken for an enclosure muffling the exigencies of everydayness. Such restrictive optics, however, is part of language, precisely the evidence of its "dangerous ways," of the propensity for dissembling its "intention" and effacing language as event. The manner in which the language event can be disregarded, become "invisible" to its own discursive articulations, underscores the role of the ideological and cultural formations in the shape that language takes, without, however, equating the event with its cultural appropriations. The unbounded disposition of the linguistic event, the changeable, even volatile, design of its saying, inscribes the risk of appropriation in the very moment of its articulation. Yet the language event of manifestation is never reducible to the manner in which language becomes bound, both *toward* words and *by* them, within the historical discursive strictures which regulate articulation.

The saying *(die Sage)* or the *"Intention"* precede the split between materiality and intelligibility, the split which dissembles the language event by figuring the difference between the sensible and the intelligible as the condition of signification, as the grounding of the distinction between the signifier and the signified. Tantamount in effect to the enigmatic play of phenomenality itself, the saying makes possible and regulates this "foundational" difference between the sensible and the intelligible, in effect producing the possibility of cognition, intentionality, and the order of representation: "We listen to language in such a way that we let it tell us its saying. . . . [W]e find ourselves caught up in a hearing that *lets itself be told,* a hearing that embraces all apprehending and representing [*das alles Vernehmen und Vorstellen*]" (*BW,* 411/*UZS,* 255). To the extent that the saying regulates representation, both makes possible and maps the representational divides which organize experience, the question of language becomes the question of "the world": of the everyday, of life practice, and of its discursive regimentation. To follow the trajectory of language, its translative "slip," is to reflect upon and contest everyday experience, and the figuration of practice in ordinary language. Reinscribing the event of language into its ostensibly homogeneous, fixed and static, "propositional" forms means rearticulating experience, redrawing the patterns which experiencing follows in route to presenting itself, to becoming present as experience. Turning language "back" to face its own way into words, to keep its articulations open to the trace of its translation, means undoing and rearticulating the practice of "experience" by exhibiting the features of its regulatory linguistic mechanism. For what describes the structure of experience, the dislocation that constitutes experiencing, is the "materialization" of language in its word-stage, that is, the process of language's coming into words, its "languaging," to recall Heidegger. "To experience" is to undergo the translocation into words, to traverse the world's, and history's, unfolding into their discursive map. "When we talk of 'undergoing' [*machen*] an experience, we mean specifically that the experience is not of our own making; to undergo here means that we endure it, suffer it, receive it as it strikes us and submit to it [*wir uns ihm fügen*]. It is this something itself that comes about, comes to pass, happens [*es schickt sich, es fügt sich*]" (*OWL*, 57). Heidegger's essays on language, "The Nature of Language" in particular, integrate experience *(Erfahrung)* with the event of language: "to experience" means to undergo—strictly speaking, to have already and always undergone—the transposition of the phenomenal into words. It signifies traveling *(er-fahren)* the way of language and incurring the risks that mark manifestation as the (b)reaching of words. In this context, experience becomes synonymous with the ever fading interval of its own route, with the collapsing of its event into its comprehensible and "compressed" outcome. The disappearance of the event structure of experience in the grammar of enunciation simultaneously marks the trail of history, the inauguration of historical "vision." What describes in the above fragment the course of experience, the ways in which it *happens*—sends, communicates, or transmits itself into words—is the German word *schicken,* used by Heidegger most often to refer to the dispositions of history. Heidegger's characteristic elaboration of terms which describe the intersections of language, experience, and history—*Ereignis, Geschichtlichkeit, Erfahrung*—attempts a revision of philosophical thought in view of how the dispositions of history mark the working of language. The way language works, having always already (e)lapsed into its enunciations, sketches the destinations of history, the appearances of historical experience as it makes itself known in its discursive forms: as texts, interpretations, significations. The historical importance of "undergoing an experience with language," its significance with respect to the production of history, consists in the performative effect of unworking the sedimentations of historical space. I argue that art, working on the principle of a language event, becomes the stage for the (re)production of the historicity of being, for the double movement of the appropriation and dispropriation of experience.

History in the Artwork

In every true work of art, there is a place where, for one who removes
there, it blows like a cool wind of a coming dawn. From this it follows that
art, which has often been considered refractory to every relation with
progress, can provide its true definition. Progress has its seat not in the
continuity of elapsing time but in its interferences—where the truly new
makes itself felt for the first time with the sobriety of dawn.

—Benjamin, *The Arcades Project*, N

Language provides, one wants to say, writes, the blueprint of experience.
The work of transposition which language performs in unfolding the world
constitutes the movement of experience. The excess of this linguistic event
over what is produced of it as "text"—images, words, representations—that
is, over what is accessible as opened and made present by this event, at the
same time posits the identity of being and language and marks its incompleteness. Experience both takes the form of a text—it happens already as
interpretation—and exceeds the contingency of this articulation. It is this
effraction that allows experience always to shock and dislocate, to bring
about a renegotiation of its textual "identity."[45] What never registers as part
of historical experience and remains excluded from its moment in history
inscribes in an event the possibility of revising and revisiting its image, of
rereading its historical "reality." As the withdrawal of "being" from "what
is," this excess or alterity, available only as the mark of its erasure, illustrates the workings of the linguistic event which inaugurates history. What
interests us here is the relation between this staging of history and the figuration of the linguistic event at the origin of the historical space within the
work of art. The attention that Benjamin and Heidegger (especially in his
later essays) give to the role of art and poetry in the "crisis" of modernity
not only foregrounds the link between art and history but locates in the
work of art the possibility of reconfiguring the paradigm of historical experience. In fact, both Heidegger and Benjamin underscore the historical
valency of the work performed by art, reading the linguistic event, or the
poetic provenance, of art in historical terms. The linguistic matrix of experience which I have traced through the work of Benjamin and Heidegger
brings us, therefore, closer to understanding the relation between art and
history.

At issue in showing the linguistic character of experience is the relation
between the place of the work of art in its specific historical context and the
way in which historicity registers in the work performed by art. I explore

this double inscription of history in art—as its historical context and as the paradigm of historical legibility at work in art—through the constellation of three terms: the event, the dialectical image, and reproducibility. As I argue, it is the understanding of history as event—event both circumscribed and ruptured by historicity that remains excessive in regard to conceptual grasp—that makes legible the tension encoded in Benjamin's dialectical image. On the other hand, the reproducibility which, for Benjamin, defines the work of art in modernity prevents the misreading of the event as simply punctual, a moment whose significance would be limited to the singularity of its occurrence. The reproducibility which marks the event figured in the work of art renders its particularity historial, projecting its significance against the moment of its repetition. As Derrida would say, reproducibility inscribes the singularity of the event in a series, it ensures, through repetition, the historical force of the (re)produced singularity. The constellation of terms I propose suggests that, at the end of modernity, the work of art becomes of historical importance precisely to the extent that it puts into play and unworks the concept of history operative both *in* and *as* modernity. In other words, its historical significance lies in its figuration of history outside of the model of historicism which, in its linear and progressivist scheme, reads the past as the consecutive stages in the making of modernity. One gets the sense from Heidegger's work that the historical specificity of modern art is defined by its ability to inaugurate history in ways which would resist modernity's technological interpretation of being and the uniformity of its historical space. Art can potentially enjoy such a role because the work it performs has itself the logic of the linguistic event at the "origin" of history. In fact, art's job could be described specifically in terms of foregrounding the heterogeneity at work in this linguistic event over and against the uniform picture that it becomes upon entering the present of representation. Contesting the role of the beautiful object outside of the space of theoretical and practical cognition that modernity has assigned to art through aesthetic theory becomes contingent upon the recognition of the work performed by art. For Heidegger, the time of such art is "now," that is, at the end of modernity and "after aesthetics," provided we can look at art postaesthetically and recognize its historical significance precisely in the way it refigures the historical space of modern technology. When Heidegger reminisces about the state of arts in ancient Greece, he actually seems to proleptically engage the opening that, as he hopes, postaesthetic art could make in the world almost uniformly governed by the offshoots of technological thinking: "The arts were not derived from the artistic. Artworks were not enjoyed aesthetically. Art was not a sector of cultural activity." [46] Positioning aesthetics negatively vis-à-vis the supposed state of Greek art, Heidegger's text in fact looks for alternative models of poetic production.

Rather than reading this moment in Heidegger's text historiographically, I take this passage in terms of Benjamin's dialectical image, in which the past of Greek art would achieve legibility only at the moment when modern aesthetics, modernity itself, reaches the time of reevaluation. To provide the context of my Benjaminian reading of this excerpt from Heidegger, let me quote here at length parts of *Konvolut N,* in which Benjamin explains the workings of the dialectical image:

> For the historical index of the images not only says that they belong to a particular time; it says, above all, that they attain to legibility only at a particular time. And, indeed, this acceding to "legibility" constitutes a specific critical point in the movement at their interior. . . . It is not that what is past casts its light on what is present, or what is present its light on what is past; rather, image is that wherein what has been [*das Gewesene*] comes together in a flash with the now [*der Jetzt*] to form a constellation. In other words: image is dialectics at a standstill. For while the relation of the present to the past is purely temporal, the relation of what-has-been to the now is dialectical: not temporal in nature but figural.[47]

The what-has-been of the Greek preaesthetic functioning of art becomes legible at the moment of the exhaustion of the aesthetic paradigm itself. This newly produced legibility, however, has a "dialectical" rather than empathic character, precisely to the extent that it becomes visible only against the image of the now—of the passage between modernity and its aftermath. It is not just the past and the present that become legible, but rather their constellation. Instead of the temporal valency of continuity, this legibility constitutes itself as a tension between two heterogeneous moments in which the recognition of the latency of the past critically dislocates the present from the possibility of closure.

What flashes in this Benjaminian constellation is legibility itself, the dangerous condition of reading, which also constitutes the opening of history: "The image that is read—which is to say, the image in the now of its recognizability—bears to the highest degree the imprint of the perilous critical moment [*gefährlichen Moments*] on which all reading is founded" (*AP,* 463). The tension that marks the dialectical images constitutes the legibility of history: it "makes" history—opens its distance—in the sense that it renders history legible precisely as tension, interval, gap. This tension is both the impetus and the moment (both meanings of *Moment*) that opens history as the space of what Benjamin refers to as its own recognizability, the moment when, as Fynsk explains, history becomes readable as history,[48] as the differentiating impulse and the spacing of difference. The legibility produced as the dialectical image is the interval, the translation between what has been and the now, which, always already outside and beyond origin, marks the articulation of the linear space of history. Rephrasing some of the previous statements, we might say that this legibility functions as a marker of relation—a sort of relationality itself—which renders events legible as history. The force that holds the constellation and thus "presents" history—that is, makes the relation between the has-been and the now readable as history—does not become properly present as a historical event. An obverse side of history, a story that is never told but makes telling possible, Benjaminian legibility or Heideggerian historicity marks each moment of presence as time out-of-joint, which prevents the closure of history into a narrative. It reminds us of the event character of the present, which is not reducible to the closure of presence or the continuum of linear progression. Although in the *Passagen-Werk* Benjamin summarily dismisses Heidegger's rethinking of history through the notion of historicity *(Geschichtlichkeit),* his own "materialist historiography" in fact figures excess and alterity in a way resembling the inscription of historicity in the present.[49] When a past moment is "blasted out" of the continuity of history,[50] what matters is not the image or the "truth" of the past but its excess over and above the present, its residue over the empathic thematization of the past within the present. In other words, what is recognized in the present is not the identity of the past but its difference and remainder, which force the present "out-of-joint." As the historical index of the dialectical image, this remainder functions not unlike Heidegger's notion of *Geschichtlichkeit,* marking a distance within the present that disallows the conflation of the now with presence. The remainder of the past incessantly disarticulates the present, rendering the itinerary of its "experience" historical in the sense of presenting experience as a paradoxical distance or displacement, as, at the same time, equivalent to and out-of-joint with its discursive articulations. The exchange that I stage between Benjamin and Heidegger is a two-way street: While Heidegger's understanding of history enables us to recognize the quasi-transcendental character, as Fynsk suggests, of Benjamin's "the historical index,"[51] Benjamin's insistence on the concreteness and "materiality" of the past that flashes, within the dialectical image, into a constellation with the now provides a venue for thinking historicity.

Benjamin's writings deploy the constellation of dialectical image as an alternative to both reading the present in terms of punctuality and to misrecognizing it in archaic, mythical images of unity. His work on the nineteenth century aims at producing its constellation with modernism, in which the readability acquired by the nineteenth century becomes the critical impetus that historicizes Benjamin's present and renders it legible. In the Baudelaire essay, it is the obsolescence of the lyrical that makes possible what Benjamin reads as the Baudelairean transformation of the punctuality of the lived moment into historical experience. The essay on Surrealism ends with remarks on the political significance of the image sphere, of the history-making images to which the profane illumination characteristic of surrealist writings initiates us (R, 192). These observations suggest a critical role of art, specifically avant-garde works, in the production of the history-making images, that is, images which, rather than representing historical reality, rework and realign the very space of experience. What is at stake in modern art is the historicizing legibility itself, the paradigm of a new, historical thinking capable of keeping in view the constellational character of historical space.

Benjamin's juxtaposition of modernism and the nineteenth century produces the effect of displacement not unlike the one sought by Heidegger through invoking the nonaesthetic character of Greek art.[52] Both approaches insist on the historical specificity of the moment in which such a displacement in the framework of enlightened modernity could be effected by a postaesthetic reading of art: the rapidly increasing technologization of life in the nineteenth and twentieth centuries. This moment, referred to by Heidegger as the culmination of metaphysics in calculative thought, is determined by technicity and its impact not only on the human sensorium but, perhaps more important, on the practices of experience. In "The Work of Art in the Age of Mechanical Reproduction" and "A Short History of Photography," Benjamin suggests that technological development of the means of mechanical reproduction can bring about a transformation in the notion of art. By placing the emphasis on reproduction, technology transforms the tradition in which the work of art functions in terms of its uniqueness; in effect, it undermines both the auratic character of art and the aesthetic values of originality and genius.[53] What is most significant about this change is the recognition, through the artifice of aesthetic conceptuality, of reproducibility as the structure of the artwork, or better yet, as the paradigm of the work that art performs. As Samuel Weber has shown, by *Reproduzierbarkeit* Benjamin means not mechanical reproduction but instead the structure of reproducibility in art brought out or intensified by the rapid development of the mechanisms of reproduction: It refers not "to the empirical fact of 'reproduction,' but to the possibility of *being reproduced, to reproducibility as a mode of being.* However clumsy even in German the noun *Reproduzierbarkeit* may be, it has the virtue of distinguishing between a structural attribute and an empirical fact." [54]

Although made more pronounced by historical circumstances, reproducibility determines the modality of art's existence: "In principle a work of art has always been reproducible" (*I,* 218). In effect, reproducibility defines and delimits the work performed by art. "In other words," as Eduardo Cadava explains, "technical reproduction is not an empirical feature of modernity, it is not an invention linked to the so-called modern era. Rather, it is a structural possibility within the work of art." [55] As they have made the structure of reproducibility visible, the new technologies proffered by science—photography, film, video, CD—affect also the very structure of artistic production. Benjamin's reflections on film explore the effects of working reproducibility directly into the structure of art: of linking the work performed by art, especially its historical force, to reproducibility. It is no longer a question of just reproducing individual works, but rather of recognizing that art operates through reproducibility: It works by reproducing itself as work.

For Heidegger, who searches in technology for an alternative to the calculative paradigm of rationality, the manner in which technological advancement highlights reproducibility as the mode of being of art would indirectly undermine technology's hegemonic hold on the modern world. At issue for Heidegger are always new modes of thinking that can emerge within the calculative matrix of technological rationality as alternative to it: "Thus the essential unfolding of technology harbors in itself what we least suspect, the possible rise of the saving power" (*BW,* 337). Perhaps what Heidegger calls, quoting Hölderlin, "the saving power" is nothing other than the emergence of reproducibility as the logic of the artwork, the logic which, I argue, when recognized in its linguistic, historical, and philosophical implications, prompts a revision not only of the notion of art but also of history. Taken as an excessive, ungraspable event, rather than as a succession of historical presents, history unfolds through distance and displacement, whose heterogeneity puts into question and unmasks the limits of conceiving history in terms of knowledge or narratives (of progress). The way that the event *(Ereignis)* both opens history and disarticulates the conceptualizations of historical reality assigns historical force and significance to the moments of rupture and epistemic uncertainty rather than to the narrative of intelligibility. My argument is that art's structure of reproducibility allows for such a repetition of the event figured in the work, which not only retains each time the singularity of the event but also gives this particularity a historical significance. Reproducing the event through historical distance, through the interval that makes history, art renders the event irreducible to the punctual presence of the moment, in terms of which events are often misread. Benjamin's repeated attacks on historicist empathy aim precisely at ascribing historical weight—one which would, in fact, keep unbalancing historical accounts as such—to the instants of the dislocating tension between the "then" and the "now."

To the extent that art "exists" by reproducing itself, by repeating its work, it operates on the model of the linguistic event, which continuously puts into play and restages the historical dislocation which makes art possible.[56] When it is interpreted, the work of art performs its own translation, a reproduction of its work, both *within* and *into* a different historical moment, which presents the work as a certain form of "dialectical" image. For Heidegger, the recognition of the nonaesthetic character of Greek art is contingent upon the possibility of inflecting the modern into the "postmodern," and, in turn, opens the possibility of thinking art after aesthetics. For Greek art to work "nonaesthetically" in the modern context, it has to rework the aesthetic framework of modernity; to be within the modern and rework it into a different historical moment—the postmodern (?). Derrida has analyzed at length this double historical optics and the modalities of reproducibility intrinsic to writing under the names of iteration and date. In "Shibboleth: For Paul Celan," for example, Derrida shows how the date, as the singularity of the historical moment inscribed in the text, becomes the paradoxical condition of the repetition, reproduction, or rereading of the work. Early in the text, he signals a distinction between the calendaric date and the form of dating which inscribes reproducibility into the organization of the poetic text: "[W]e will concern ourselves first of all with a dating which is registered *in* the body of the poem, *in* one of its parts, and under a form which accords with the traditional code (for example, 'the 13th of February'), and then with a nonconventional, noncalendrical form of dating, one which would merge entirely, without residue, with the general organization of the poetic text."[57] This double form of dating at work in the text—the insertion of a particular date into the dating structure of the work, the reproducibility of the date of writing in the moment(s) of reading—orchestrates the work's textuality. It both marks the singularity of the poem's creation and makes possible its repetition, its continued existence in reading.

What is repeated in the "afterlife" of the text is precisely the difference, each time particular, from the singularity of its date; in other words, what conditions the text's repetition is the possibility of its being different in what it is, that is, of reading differently in various contexts as the "same" work. This repetition as difference, which, in Derrida's words, "dates" the work, constitutes art, in its, as it were, "ontological" dimension as historial; historial, because the reproducibility which defines the work performed by art enacts or opens history. To the extent that reproducibility can be recognized as the modality of art's existence, art is, so to speak, history-in-the-making, that is, the existence of the work of art is always staged historically, as an irreducible and irrecuperable distance of its repetition as the "same" work. We could say that what the work of art does is precisely to restage not only its history of reading but also history *as* reading. Such reproducibility inscribed in art constitutes the "poetics" of the modern artwork, a poetics which resembles the dialectical image, the constellation of what has been and the now, (re)produced as the work's afterlife. As Benjamin remarks in *The Arcades Project* [N, 2, 3], "[h]istorical 'understanding' is to be grasped, in principle, as an afterlife of that which is understood; and what has been recognized in the analysis of the 'afterlife of works,' in the analysis of 'fame,' is therefore to be considered the foundation of history in general" (*AP,* 460). There is no simple past or present of the work of art available through empathic insight or interpretation on the model of historicism. Rather, the interval or the difference in the constellation of what has been and the now constitutes precisely the work that art performs. This differential constellation unfolds as a result of how art "performs" its figure—a postaesthetic art, to be sure, not an object but an event whose poetics must be thought of not in terms of a poetic theory but, rather, as the work's mode of being. The repetitive, reproducible character of the work's afterlife constitutes the basis of historical understanding. It enacts history, as it were, producing the (dis)union and the (con)fusion of the text and its (repeated) "copy." It is also the condition of the legibility of the work of art, the possibility of interpretation and meaning which can never be foreclosed, for its modality coincides with the movement of history itself.

Artwork understood in this sense is not only *made* historically, situated within historical space, but also *makes* history, producing a different possibility of reading in historical terms.[58] Read in a particular historical context, a work of art certainly "remakes" itself in this new setting, readjusts itself to it, but it also "stages" history by historicizing the difference between the reading and what remains unread. How this remainder or residue destabilizes the reading, opening it to what makes it possible and yet cannot find place within it, describes the historicizing character of reproducibility. As Heidegger remarks at the end of "The Origin of the Work of Art," "[a]rt . . . is essentially historical [*wesenhaft geschichtlich*]. This means not simply that art has a history in the extrinsic sense that in the course of time it, too, appears along with many other things, and in the process changes and passes away and offers changing aspects for historiology. Art is history in the essential sense that it grounds history" (*BW,* 202).[59] For Heidegger "grounding" does not mean that the work of art provides a foundation for history, a basis which would allow us to form and read historical narratives. Such a notion of the ground would be, in fact, ahistorical, and it would dehistoricize the unfolding of the world at work in art. Instead, the work of art "grounds" history specifically as an event, which, by keeping in play its historicity, incessantly ungrounds its "historical reality," together with its conceptual and discursive articulations. Paradoxically, the work of art "grounds," or, I prefer to write, unfolds, history as having no ground.[60] For Heidegger, history has no definable origin, no stable present, but eventuates in relation to its unpresentable historicity, the illegible remainder of which undermines the essentialist and historicist conceptualizations of history. Reproducing itself as an event, the work of art keeps opening history as the impossibility of its own narrative. It grants history legibility, but this legibility is contingent upon the illegible residue of historicity. In other words, history becomes readable as history—"experienced" historically—not in its accounts, or the supplements and revisions continuously added to them, but when the remainder of these accounts, the historicity of the event, bears upon and disarticulates the stories which are said to constitute history. Of course, this does not mean that revisions of history are not important; they are, in fact, critical, even though their significance does not necessarily extend to questioning the very idea of history.

I interpret Heidegger's idiosyncratic use of grounding as indicating that the work of art, by keeping in play its reproducibility, renders the articulations of the world it produces contingent: inherently questionable, made only to be remade, and their form nothing more than the historical context for this remaking. At the same time that the work is determined historically, that is, inflected each time by a particular historical setting, it also opens its world as historial—this world is never simply present or closed in its historical reality but unfolds from an irrecuperable past which, itself outside the expanse of historicism and cognition, keeps in question the historical and political space of the world it projects. It is less the world itself than its incessant remaking which constitutes the work (re)produced in art. To ground history, in this context, means to keep in play the unmeasurable historical distance—the interval of historicity—which reformulates the present without allowing it the luxury of fulfillment. History here points beyond the idea of singular moments which would keep adding themselves to a historical continuum according to the calculus of knowledge; rather, it refers to a series of uncontainable displacements which keep knowledge guessing as to the inadequacy of its formulations. History keeps itself not only *at* a distance from the present but also *as* an indeterminate interval which ungrounds the present, maintaining its historicity in play.

Let me illustrate this point by reference to Heidegger's notion of preserving *(Bewahren)* the work of art from "The Origin of the Work of Art." For Heidegger, the work of art after its creation returns to being at the moments when it is "preserved," that is, when it is allowed again to perform its work: "Just as a work cannot be without being created, but is essentially in need of creators, so what is created cannot itself come into being without those who preserve it" *(BW,* 191). That art is a work means that it is determined by moments of its reception, when it again works its art, so to speak, bringing the then of its creation into a constellation with the now of preservation. This is why preserving is not a recovery of a meaning encoded into the work at the moment of its creation but instead a displacement within the present, an opening of history, performed by the work's modality of being reproducible.

> To submit to this displacement means to transform our accustomed ties to world and earth and henceforth to restrain all usual doing and prizing, knowing and looking, in order to stay within the truth that is happening in the work. Only the restraint of this staying lets what is created be the work that it is. This letting the work be a work we call preserving the work. It is only for such preserving that the work yields itself in its createdness as actual, which now means, present in the manner of a work. *(BW,* 191)

As the German term *Bewahren* suggests, preserving means keeping or letting the work be "true" *(wahr)* to itself. For a work to be kept true to itself,

✓ it must cease to function as a beautiful object, categorized in terms of aesthetic pleasure and subjective experience, and, instead, be allowed to foreground the ways in which art provides historical legibility to the present. It would be a mistake to think that Heidegger's term *Bewahren* intends some transcendental or historical truth inscribed in art, because it points specifically to art's historial work, that is, to the way art underscores the historicity of the present. Let us recall here that historicity does not refer to historical
✓ contingency but to the dislocating effects of the event. Such an event exceeds the idea of an origin or a foundation, yet it is "originary" in the strict sense of how it incessantly reinvents and reinscribes itself in its discursive articulations. The "historical" work of art could be defined, then, as the trajectory of these repeated reenactments, which keep rewriting the discursive presence of history, revising its significance and questioning the knowledge it affords. The meaning the artwork projects when it is "preserved," that is, allowed to do its work, differs according to the historical circumstances of preservation. It differs not because the artwork is somehow an infinite font of meaning but, rather, because it works historically, projecting history as the necessary reinvention of its discursive manifestations.

This is why Heidegger is quite emphatic in differentiating between aesthetic enjoyment or pleasure and letting art perform its work: "When works are offered for sheer artistic enjoyment, this does not yet prove that they stand in preservation as works" (*BW,* 193). In fact, the art business, as Heidegger refers to it, interferes with the historial significance of art, with recognizing the history-making which takes place in the artwork. By contrast, "preserving" means letting the work find "a place from which it joins in shaping history" (193).[61] By reproducing itself through the difference of preservation, the work of art keeps rendering experience historical, remarking its historicity. Preservation "does not drag it [the work] into the sphere of mere lived experience [*den Umkreis des blossen Erlebens*], and does not degrade it to the role of a stimulator of such experience [*Erlebniserregers*]. Preserving the work does not reduce people to their private experiences, but brings them into affiliation with the truth happening in the work" (193).[62] Art (dis)places *(einrücken)* subjects within its historial work, transplanting them outside of the sphere of privacy and aesthetic perception. It inscribes the private within the differential matrix of history, transforming aesthetic experience into the experience of the historicity of being. The historicizing effects of the reproducibility make manifest that what conditions the attention to specific differences which make up histories is the dislocating movement of history which, in advance, "always already," affects its representations. "Preserving," or keeping art "working," means displacing the lived experience *(Erlebnis)* into its historical context, of reworking it into *Erfahrung* and its "historical truth"—the historial occurrence of being: "*das geschichtliche Ausstehen des Da-seins aus dem Bezug zur Unverborgenheit*" (55). This historial structure of reproducibility evident in preservation must be differentiated from the idea of aestheticized history, of a cultural *mythopoiēsis*. Reproducibility questions such an aesthetic construction of reality and connects art to the possibility of events unfolding in a historial manner, through the interruptions and discontinuities that "make" history.

To the extent that the history-making function of the work of art becomes legible in the context of the culmination of modernity in the technological practice, it remains a contemporary issue. Situated historically, at the specific juncture of modernity and "postmodernity," of aesthetics and its "after," the postaesthetic art stakes its claim to historical significance precisely on the possibility of refiguring history. As a turning point in modernity, such revision of history is entwined with the parallel critiques of aesthetics and calculative thinking. Both Heidegger and Benjamin saw the relation between history and technology in terms of a chance to alter the conceptual underpinnings of enlightened modernity, though at first in a radically different way. In the early 1930s, Heidegger voiced his support of national socialism, reading into it his own idea of the possibility of overcoming technicity, before he realized that, like Ernst Jünger's work, the fascist ideology proposed, in fact, a total mobilization of resources in a gesture that confirmed technicity as formative of relations in modernity, which transpire always in terms of power. Heidegger's later work on art and technology allows us to discern in the aestheticizing qualities of this gesture of "total mobilization" the confirmation of art's not infrequent compliance, even complacency, with the technological as a form of totalization. As we know now, in *Besinnung*, Heidegger submitted art to harsh criticism, claiming, in the context of references to kitsch and propaganda art, that art remained essentially complicit in the techno-metaphysical formation of being in terms of power (*B,* 30–31). He complained about the disappearance of the *work* of art and about the way in which art that was no longer "Kunst*werk*" (art*work*) paraded the "essence of power" in the guise of the beautiful. Such art represented the fulfillment of art's metaphysical essence, manifested as art's participation in the manipulative power over being, in the overpowering ordering of beings into universal availability. Art misread as an aesthetic alternative to technology, as an archaic image, to paraphrase Benjamin, in fact, provided the framework in which technological mobilization could be vindicated, proclaimed as more than just an exercise of calculative reason, namely, as an invocation of an archaic spirit of unity lost in the modern social and political life. Diametrically different from Heidegger's embrace of national socialism, Benjamin's critique of fascism and its use of the aesthetic focused on mobilizing art toward political ends by undermining the auratic character of art and, thus, disqualifying its ritual or cultic functions.[63] In Benjamin's thought, the dissipation of the aura becomes requisite for the renegotiation of art's historical importance, as the bearer of significations which put into question the paradigm of technological reason and its practices of calculation so ingrained in contemporary culture.

This demand, like the Surrealist alarm clock, continues to ring in contemporary debates about art and its postaesthetic possibilities. The issues raised in these polemics, from the question of aesthetic experience and philosophical quandaries about truth to political and cultural significance of otherness, revolve around the conditions that would allow for an "engaged" reading of art, that is, for what I call here a nonaesthetic concept of the work performed by art and its ties to "experience" and "history." Employing some of the notions operative in later Heidegger and in Benjamin's reflections on art at the "end" of modernity, I have proposed to begin examining the nonaesthetic work performed by modern art through reflection upon the relation among experience, language, and history. To be more precise, I argue that the performative linguistic *poiēsis* at work in art outlines the constellation of experience and history in terms of reinvention and reproduction. The constellation of the notions of the event, the dialectical image, and reproducibility in art works against both the punctuality of experience and the temptation of a totalizing, mytho-poetic recuperation of being. As it guards against the erasure of otherness in the totality of history by interrupting, to paraphrase Nancy, its myth of unity, such postaesthetic *work* also deploys the singularity of the event historically. Art presents its work as an event that, intrinsically reproducible, keeps reworking its singularity in a way that gives such singularity historial significance. The work's singularity is never isolated or punctual but, instead, inscribes history in its very structure of reproducibility. To say that art (re)stages history means that it brings about the recognition of how the discursive formulations of experience are liable to continuous reinvention and reinscription in light of their historicity, a historicity, which, figured as an irrecuperable past or an immemorial other, forces the present to reappraise itself in relation to its past and future. It compels the present to think of itself historically without lapsing into historicism. This recognition functions as the "historical index" of art, thanks to which art's reproduction of its work amounts to (re)staging history and putting in play the legibility of being in historical terms. The difference between the historical terms at work in this constellation and the truth-claims of historicism may well manifest the nonaesthetic and *historial,* rather than *historical,* significance of art.

Perhaps you will understand me better if I tell you that dada is a virgin microbe that insinuates itself with the insistence of air into all the spaces that reason hasn't been able to fill with words or conventions.

—Tristan Tzara, "Lecture on Dada"

2. Contestations of the Everyday

The Avant-Garde, Technology, and the Critique of Aesthetics

Art is a commodity: This seems like a truism in the age of digital technology, which makes the proliferation of various objects of consumption, be it art or popular culture, "instantaneous," with cultural artifacts available constantly, and almost literally, at our fingertips. But even though art has an exchange value and a market price, unlike objects, it has no "real" use value. It is *use-less*, because what art accomplishes, how it works, exceeds any quantification or calculative measure. Obviously, certain well-known cultural and educational uses can be ascribed to art, but the question remains as to what extent they describe what takes place in art. To say that art is use-less usually implies that art remains sectioned off from the "real" world, or that it becomes disconnected from experience, indifferent to it, or of no importance for it. But here "use-less" indicates that the category of use, and hence use value, is incompatible with the artwork (taken in the active, verbal sense of *work*), incapable of quantifying or measuring what takes place in art. As I argue in the previous chapter, the significance of art lies in the way in which it (re)figures experience, staging history—or the historicity which marks and disjoins historical time—by suspending the notion of a ground, origin, or principle of history. In this chapter, I suggest that the conceptuality implied in the notions of use and use value, the technological framework in which usefulness becomes thinkable as such, in fact renders the work performed by art invisible, relegating it to the sphere of irreality or

86

irrationality. As Heidegger puts it in his short note "*Das Wohnen des Men-schen*": "With regard to today's reality, which understands itself in terms of industrial or production society, and which itself produces itself and the resources it needs, the poet's words easily empty themselves for everyone into mere fantasy. In social terms, poetry is understood as the production of literature."[1] Because the work which reproduces itself in art exceeds the category of usefulness, it fails to register as "real," or to achieve the visibility, the character of actuality and presence—which is awarded to what can be calculated, known, and stored. This absence of measure constitutes both the "flaw" and a certain advantage of art.

When in "The Origin of the Work of Art" Heidegger takes issue with the institution of the museum and the art market, he specifically questions how the imposition of the use value upon art—making art "useful" for cultural, but also business, purposes: education, edification of the "soul," the culti-vation of taste, or even entertainment—obscures the work *of* art ("work" taken here again in the double meaning of the genitive, both as an artwork and as the work performed by art):

> Well, then, the works themselves stand and hang in collections and ex-hibitions. Yet are they here in themselves as the works they themselves are, or are they not rather here as objects of the art industry? Works made available for public and private art appreciation. Official agencies assume the care and maintenance of works. Connoisseurs and critics busy themselves with them. Art dealers supply the market. Art-historical study makes the works the objects of a science. Yet in all this busy activity do we encounter the work itself?[2]

This double question about the conditions of the existence of art in the modern world and about the character of the work which occurs in/as art echoes throughout Heidegger's texts on art and poetry, in particular in the implications which the poetic occurrence of art has for a postmetaphysical thought, whose possibility Heidegger's work both opens and qualifies. This question also delineates the tension between technology, or technic think-ing, which determines the framework for the institutionalization of art and legitimates the work of art as an object of the art industry, and the poetic work performed by art, which both escapes and contests the aesthetic cate-gories which encapsulate the artwork as an aesthetic object. Differentiating art from equipment, "The Origin of the Work of Art" discounts usefulness and availability—the instrumentalizing categories that reflect the workings of technic thought—as distorting the work of art. It thus echoes Kant's concern for the "disinterested" character of the judgment of the beautiful, though in a different, nonsubjective, tonality. Reading Heidegger's essay against Kant's *Critique of Judgment* renders sharper the implications of Heidegger's disavowal of the system of ideas which engender instrumentality—availability, resource, use, purpose, even, finally, the concept itself—when it comes to thinking the work of art. If Kant's insistence on the purposiveness without purpose as the determination of the beautiful grants autonomy or assigns a "proper" place to the judgment of taste, it still leaves the concept as the governing principle of thought. Art becomes an instance of symbolic *hypotyposis,* which presents concepts not schematically but analogically, allowing reflection to transfer from an object of intuition to a concept of practical reason, for which there is no suitable intuition.[3] Aesthetic reflection serves as an analogy of the intuition of the supersensible realm of freedom, while art becomes the symbol of morality. In Heidegger's case, however, the critique of the conceptuality of use extends to the concept as such, and marks a displacement of the concept-based notion of truth from its position as the center and the ground of thought in the name of the aletheic play of concealment and unconcealment. Heidegger disconnects art from usefulness to demonstrate the restricted scope and the derivative character—in relation to the aletheic unfolding—of the philosophico-scientific truth (dare we say "technological" truth?) and to emphasize the need to requalify truth as *alethēia,* an operation requisite for rethinking the *work* of art.

In contrast with Kant's reflection, where art symbolizes what it cannot "be," always at an "analogical" remove from truth, "The Origin of the Work of Art" attempts to break art free from the technic determinations of truth, and to show how the work of art unfolds history as the propriative event *(Ereignis),*[4] effaced and distorted within the representational paradigm of truth, based on the principle of correctness. Showing that art is useless, unthinkable in terms of use, does not lead to restoring a symbolic function for art within the technological economy of presence, but, conversely, becomes part of undermining the monopoly which the "technological" conceptuality of availability exercises within the modern world. We can, and obviously do, treat art in terms of usefulness, but at the price of reducing the work of art to an object, respectively of artistic creation, aesthetic experience, or art industry—an operation which, at least in Heidegger's eyes, obscures, even undoes, the work which occurs in art. In the process, the work *of* art—the unsettling effects of the displacement at the core of experience and history—is exchanged for the security and familiarity which comes with the idea that art can be grasped as an aesthetic object, a sector of cultural activity, an educational and cultural resource.

This complex set of relations between technology, its everyday use and impact on ordinary life, on the one hand, and the aesthetic treatment of art, on the other, comes under scrutiny in avant-garde art, especially in the "irreverent" play with both artistic conventions and everyday practices characteristic of Dadaist works and "provocations," whose best examples are Marcel Duchamp's ready-mades. From Italian futurism and Dadaism to Russian cubo-futurism and constructivism, the avant-garde shows its fascination with technology, machinism, mass production, and their growing influence on daily modern experience. The defining moment of the avant-garde, especially in its early stages, is the reimagining of art specifically through the intersection of technology and the everyday. As the avant-garde negotiates and describes the impact of technology on modern experience, it also begins, I argue, to figure the progressive (con)fusion of the everyday and the technological. It comes to understand itself through its continued engagement with everyday practice, specifically through considering the extent of the rationalization of the ordinary. On the one hand, such art becomes captivated by the structuring and regulative presence of technology in ordinary life, and, on the other, it sometimes contests the monopoly of the technological/scientific claim on experience.

Avant-garde art is an attempt to measure the extent to which the everyday coincides with the technological pattern of experience and, as I suggest, to open an alternative view of experience. My view is that the avant-garde keeps restaging the event of experience—and experience as event—in order to see if experience in the modern technological world indeed explains itself "fully" in terms dictated by the metaphysical project of rationalization. I am interested in how avant-garde works refuse to be confined within the notion of an "art object" and produce themselves as events, in which experience, no longer referable to a subject, is presented as interpretation, as a set of discursive operations, inseparable from the moment of its constitution in the "technological" terms of presence, usefulness, or availability. To that effect, I read the avant-garde artwork as the event which figures both how experience happens as "technological" and how this technologization reduces its very event—its excessive, *poietic* remainder—to the calculus of presence and availability. Restaging itself as event, the work of art reproduces the already accomplished technologization of experience, replaying the point when experience becomes dehistoricized, constituted in terms of what is present: available and measurable. By virtue of reproducing this moment, art also puts into play the invisible limit of this technologization, the boundary which remains unthought as long as experience remains deceptively transparent in its everydayness. In order to be able to read this limit, we need to rethink the work performed by art postaesthetically, in terms of historicity. Therefore, in my interpretation, art is "avant-garde" to the extent to which it keeps unworking the technologization of experience by showing how, in order to inscribe experience within the order of representation, it effaces historicity.

Another important preliminary point needs to be made concerning my use of the term "everyday." The turn to the everyday, to its commonplace and banal objects, to the event of the uneventful, characteristic of much of modern art, can sometimes take the form of the flight from the technological ambience of modern experience, and become an attempt to reclaim the ordinary which would somehow lie *outside* the domain of technocracy. This "romanticizing" of the ordinary, to use Cavell's phrase, would try to recover experience as immediate and common, as a sphere of familiarity, which would provide a guarantee of communication and understanding. More often, though, the turn to the banality of the everyday—from Duchamp's ready-mades to Warhol's Campbell's soup—discovers that the ordinary is already thoroughly technologized. I am interested in this latter, "critical" turn to the everyday, in how, exploring such art, we can begin to redefine the everyday beyond the opposition of the "artificiality" of technological practices and the constructed "immediacy" of the ordinary.

Marcel Duchamp's focus on ordinary objects is a deliberate denigration of art, a play on the high aesthetics stance, but it also initiates a reflection on the degree to which everyday life is dominated by the idea of usefulness and the actual objects of use. The ready-mades are obviously meant to shock the public, to offend its aesthetic taste, to finally ridicule aesthetics itself, as Duchamp suggests in a letter to Hans Richter, in which he distances his works from pop art and from what he regards as the neo-dadaist attempts to *aestheticize* the banal.[5] Indeed, if Duchamp's ready-mades can be regarded as works of art, it is only to the extent to which they precisely unwork art, undoing not just the artistic traditions and aesthetic cannons but, above all, the very principle of conceptualizing art as *aesthetic*. Though Duchamp himself was ready to end art, or at least to end *with* art, the provocation figured in the ready-mades describes precisely the limit of aesthetic art, and points toward, albeit only half-seriously, ways of refiguring art "after" aesthetics. In the context of Dadaism and early-twentieth-century art in general, this limit of aesthetics has to do with the question of technology and the impact of technologization and mass production upon everyday experience.

Just as much as they mock aesthetics, Duchamp's ready-mades also produce a parody, even a subversion, of the use value and functionality. For how else are we to approach "The Fountain," the urinal, which, when reversed, put on its head, so to speak, loses its use value? It is precisely the moment of the disappearance of its use value as a mass-produced object of everyday use that transforms the urinal into "art." The urinal becomes a work, which, unworking the notion that the urinal is simply a use object, reproduces the interruption of the use mentality, of the everyday functionality, which structures modern experience. The "fountain" is not equipment out of order, like the broken hammer in Heidegger's world, which draws attention to the equipment's falling out of use, its disuse or absence of usefulness. Instead, it is a work, a deliberate transposition of usefulness into the use-less, which makes us question how art works, and how, in order to think its "work," we need different parameters than the ones afforded by technic thought.

Fascinated by technology, Duchamp's works and the Dadaist visual art render visible the "operational center" of technic thought: technological rationality and its paradigm of representation, which orders the world by gradations of usefulness and availability. We can, then, read Dadaist art, often against itself, as an exposition, even an inversion, of the limits of the technological paradigm of thought. The great irony of Duchamp's ready-mades is that technology, the engine of the modern world and the font of profit, cannot quite negotiate the curve of its own product, the urinal. Technic thought "runs into the wall" in Duchamp's "Fountain," precisely because there is no wall, since the urinal is removed from its framework, from the tiles covering the wall and the plumbing to which it should be fastened in order to perform its intended function. Rendering mass-produced objects dysfunctional, the ready-mades play with functionality as the main determinant of modern experience and demonstrate to what extent aesthetics itself—the institutions of art and art market, and, finally, the understanding of art in terms of aesthetic experience—are implicated in the functionalist mentality. The technological thought can relate to Duchamp's work by reading it in functional terms, by assigning his work a function within a new, "modern" aesthetics of the banal which it inaugurates. It can only "buy" Duchamp's ready-mades as a "new aesthetic," as new artistic objects which, having offended the aesthetic taste, reform it, and, in the end, become again useful. Duchamp's challenge to art, his ridicule of aesthetics, is neutralized and his (un)work is recuperated on another level, within an enlarged scope of a new aesthetics. An imaginary wall of a refashioned aesthetics is added to "The Fountain," and reframes the ready-made, bringing it back into the culture it has disturbed. As a cultural artifact, "The Fountain" is again a urinal, an object; it is no longer a work but instead a commodity, an expensive art object, which is again use-ful, both as an illustration of what it means to be avant-garde and as an investment of capital for future profit. The imagined, and yet all too real, wall of aesthetic thought, working, through the art industry—as a subsidiary of the technological organization of society—covers the moment of conflict and hides the limit of the technic from view. Undisturbed, the aesthetic transactions go back to their smooth operations: we have a new aesthetic, perhaps more responsive to the technological conditions of modern life, more "contemporary" but, in the end, an aesthetic which represents just another step in the history of art. The avant-garde "dies," or becomes part of the art market it attacked, and the limit of thinking which Duchamp inscribes on the slippery edges of the urinal becomes invisible—white.

In his retrospective book on Dadaism, *Dada—Kunst und Antikunst,* Hans Richter claims that neither the urinal nor the bottle rack were "works of art," but instead jokes played on the notion of "high art" and aesthetics (*DAA,* 152). And the joke is precisely on those who take the ready-mades too seriously and approach them aesthetically in an endeavor to recuperate them into the fold of art. Neither art nor anti-art, the ready-mades are unartistic or postaesthetic. But precisely to the extent that the ready-mades are unartistic, they have to be taken seriously, as an earnest joke that, playing on the limit of art and aesthetics, brings to the surface the foundations of aesthetic experience. In addition to spatial reconfiguration, the transformation of the urinal into a ready-made involves also a renaming, a verbal manoeuver, which turns the urinal into "The Fountain." The verbal component of Duchamp's ready-mades is more than a title, as it in effect "makes" the work what it is, amplifying the resonance of its anti-aesthetic gesture. Even though the ready-mades are visual works, their existence is circumscribed verbally, much more decisively than is the case with titles conventionally affixed to paintings or sculptures. It is in its laconic title, "The Fountain," that the inverted urinal begins to suggest the inversion of art and aesthetics and thus comes to realize its performative potential: It is an anti-aesthetic event which provokes a redefinition of what "work" and "art" would mean in a postaesthetic perspective. What happens, what manifests itself in the transformation of the urinal into a ready-made is a relocation of the artistic "inspiration": away from the aesthetic feeling and aesthetically pleasing objects to the mundane and the banal. As Duchamp explains: "[T]he choice of these 'ready-mades' was never dictated by aesthetic delectation" (*DAA,* 89). Through its mockery of the aesthetic standards for the sources of artistic and poetic inspiration, "The Fountain" poses the question central to my study: How are we to conceive of the artistic and the poetic in the context of modern art? What is the ready-made urinal *the* fountain of—the poetic, the artistic, the ordinary? (One needs to keep in mind the definitive article in Duchamp's title, its both apodictic and parodic valency.)

In the previous chapter, I suggested that a postaesthetic approach to art involves a redefinition of the work in the context of the historicity of experience. Reproducing the historicity of its own event as a work, art manifests the historial occurrence of experience and its linguistic production as always already an interpretation. Duchamp's "Fountain" brings into focus two other aspects of this renegotiation of the work of art: the everyday and the technological. Using mass produced objects of everyday application—bicycle wheels, bottle racks, shovels, and so on—the ready-mades place the avant-garde revolt against aesthetics within the framework of rethinking the everyday, and place the emphasis on how, in ordinary life, technology affects experience, dehistoricizing and turning it into resource, measurable according to the criterion of efficiency. In the face of Duchamp's ready-mades we cannot escape asking the question about the relation between art and technology, and, especially, about the way this relation figures in the problematic of the everyday: its production, experience, and interpretation. Duchamp's ready-mades also introduce a change into the tonality of the discussion of the work of art which I proposed in the context of the thought of Benjamin and Heidegger. The irony and mockery of Duchamp's work, their impact upon aesthetic considerations within the avant-garde, recast the problematic introduced in the previous chapter without losing the seriousness of the inquiry. The urinal-fountain explicitly parodies the high pose and the grandiloquence of the aesthetic dream of origin and purity, "degrading" it to the sphere of the everyday, with its banal and even distasteful aspects. At the same time that it aligns itself with Heidegger's and Benjamin's critiques of the unified, pure origin or source of experience, its pervasive and sometimes violent irony serves here to diffuse both the grandiose tone lingering in Heidegger's thought and the remnants of nostalgia which envelops Benjamin's writings, and which can sometimes cloud the critical import of their projects.

The Ambiguous Provenance of Modern Art

"Since machinery is the soul of the modern world, and since the genius of machinery attains its highest expression in America, why is it not reasonable to believe that in America the art of the future will flower most brilliantly?"[6] This statement by Francis Picabia, one of the key figures in the Dadaist movement, underscores an important, one is tempted to say "essential," link between modern art and technology. I use the term "essential" in this context, because for Picabia the association of art with machinism is not just a matter of technology being the single most important factor determining modern life but an illustration of the technological "essence" of art. Apart from the proliferation of technology and mass-produced objects or the omnipresence of machinery, at issue is the question of reading modern being, or being in modernity, in technological terms. For Picabia, the machine both describes and determines the rhythm of everydayness, of ordinary life and social practice. It is, then, only logical — "reasonable" is Picabia's word — to expect that art should follow suit and adopt the spirit of machinism as the guiding principle of artistic creation. In fact, art appears to have no choice left, since being, reality in its entirety, has come to be defined by its machinistic "soul." The claim articulated here follows Futurism's visions of the reign of the machine, recalling Marinetti's 1912 "Technical Manifesto of Futurist Literature," where the poetic voice takes dictation from a propeller in a literary configuration which remakes the poet's subjectivity in the form of a new, modern and machinistic reality.[7] As the machine becomes the sign of modern life and its operation prescribes the rhythm of experience, it also dictates the functions of art: its machinistic poetics, as well as the models for interpreting and understanding works of art.

It is interesting to note, however, that in his praise of the machine Picabia resorts to Romantic diction: He employs the metaphor of the soul and the organic image of flowering to communicate the degree to which technology suffuses being in the modern world. He appears to need this spiritualizing and romanticizing in order to emphasize the preponderance of technology in the modern world and its defining presence in ordinary life. By designating the machine "the soul of the modern world," Picabia paints a picture in which technology becomes both the shorthand for the pattern of modern experience and the vehicle for a totalizing description of the world. In its characteristic exuberance and enthusiasm, Picabia's statement identifies the "brilliant" future of modern art with its dependence on technology, with art's total commitment to presenting the "soul of the modern world" as machinistic and technological. Itself machinelike, the art of the future is to be approached through some sort of a techno-poetics, in which there would be no substantive difference between the artistic and the technological, between the aesthetic experience and the technological everyday. This conflation of the aesthetic and the technological rendered in the image of America, represents in the end a virtual incorporation of art into technology, an involution of the poetic into the technic without a remainder. It would seem to confirm, in spite of Picabia's elation, a Heideggerian suspicion that art and technology have long co-existed in a "metaphysical" alliance and that, contrary to the appearances of the incompatibility of high aesthetics with technology, modern art's commitment to the machine finally brings into the open a deep-seated conformity between them. If we wanted to pursue this reading further, it would finally contest the Dadaists' belief that their revolution, at least in its enthusiastic espousal of technology, was anti-art and anti-aesthetic, and instead demonstrate something contrary: Namely, it would expose the apparently most anti-aesthetic statements about the machinist character of modern art as the confirmation of an inherent association between aesthetics and technological thought, hidden from view and often rendered unrecognizable by the historical diversity of artistic movements and phenomena.

If art's provenance is indeed identified with the technological, if there is no poetic remainder over and above the technological understanding of the world, then experience itself becomes analogous to and coextensive with technology: Experience of the modern world transpires on the model of technological relations of calculation, systematization, and instrumentalization. The problem is double: Experience has come to be shaped technologically, affected by the predominance of scientifically designed and produced objects which structure the world and regulate its everyday commerce, and, on the other hand, it has become increasingly difficult, perhaps impossible, to conceive experience in any other terms. To experience the world on a daily basis is to be in it and think it in a technological manner, through a relay of relations and connections which are increasingly fashioned on the model of calculation and scientific ordering. The standard of reality becomes technological: What cannot be measured, confirmed as existing in accordance with the scientific definition of being, does not exist, it is simply not real. In this context, it becomes difficult not to think about art depicted by Picabia as an instrument in the technological illumination and ordering of the world, as a subsidiary in the scientific mapping of experience into knowledge. Art's wager is to either slide into aestheticist lucu-brations without apparent connection to or importance for the "real" world or to stake its future upon technology and enlist itself, more or less directly, in the cause of a world-wide web of calculations. The work of art can be-come obsolete, assigned to the realm of private and subjective experiences or to mere fantasizing *(zu blossen Phantasterei)*, as Heidegger puts it, or, on the other hand, it can remain "real" by reproducing experience in terms of a technological revealing, which dehistoricizes the event and reduces it to the space of representation.

Yet the dilemma facing modern art is often misstated when we approach it in terms of aesthetic experience, since the debate almost automatically falls back upon the old and convenient opposition between aesthetic isola-tion and social integration. In fact, this manner of thinking about art forms an undercurrent of Picabia's remark. Even most radical anti-aesthetic state-ments do not necessarily leave behind the aesthetic framework and often reconfirm the aesthetic optics, realigning art, albeit unwittingly, with the techno-metaphysical project. This is why it is important to move the debate beyond the question of how art becomes anti-aesthetic and revolts against aesthetic traditions and prescriptions. I pose the problem of avant-garde art differently, in terms of how modern art positions itself vis-à-vis technology and its figuration of experience. As such its implications reach beyond art or the field of aesthetics and bear directly upon how we conceive of experience and its historicity.

Picabia's wager tells us as much about the state of modern art as it does about the state of modern experience: Both are caught between technology and unreality, both remain essentially determined by the technicized char-acter of being in modernity. Yet Picabia's way of posing the question does not take into consideration the way in which Duchamp's art or Tzara's mani-festoes render problematic the identification of the provenance of modern art with technology. Picabia's projection of a brilliant future art aligned with the machine opens up the question of the genesis of contemporary art, of the identification of its source with what might be called the technologi-cal organization of experience. But how are we in this context to think of technology, and, in particular, its (reductive?) relation to the historicity of experience? What forms does the technological experience of the world take and is its rhythm coextensive with the workings of art? How does the world experienced technologically appear in its "truth," and what relation does it bear to what transpires in/as the work of art? To articulate the significance of this confrontation of the avant-garde with technology within the broader scope of the philosophical critique of modernity, I propose to reconsider Heidegger's reconceptualization of being in modernity in terms of the tension between technicity *(Technik)* and art. With the exception of brief remarks about Klee or his comments on Cézanne and modern painting, Heidegger did not show much interest in avant-garde art. However, his critical rethinking of the relation between *poiēsis* and *technē* provides the best background for rethinking the avant-garde's own complex relationship to technology. This is the case because Heidegger proposes a unique reconceptualization of technicity beyond the idea of technology as industrialization or processes of production, and links such technicity with the problem of the determination of being in modernity. Heidegger's discussion of technicity and *poiēsis* allows us to recognize that the avant-garde, beyond its often discussed fascination with technology, becomes the scene of the questioning of whether modern art proceeds from the realm of the technological and fulfills itself, as Picabia suggests, in this affiliation, or whether it opens an alternative poietic event of experience. Foregrounding technology's saturation of ordinary life, avant-garde art repeatedly addresses itself to this space of decision, and even when it embraces technology as the essence of art, it renders visible the conditions and implications of such a decision. I would argue that this ambiguity in relation to technology is even more important than the other quandary about the avant-garde—the often misstated question of self-referentiality and autotelism, which produces the impasse and the continuing disagreement about the separation or integration of avant-garde art into the social practice. When we rethink the avant-garde through the problem of the technological formation of experience, the "formal" experiments of avant-garde art and literature appear in a different light: not as autotelic or aestheticist but as part of the refiguring of modern experience. They are part of the effort both to reinvent the language of art and to force thought to reappraise the work performed by art in terms other than those of aesthetics. Moving beyond the issues of aesthetic formalism and social separation, which have dominated the debates about the avant-gardes, I frame my discussion in terms of how experience sets itself to work in art, of how historicity becomes articulated in the "innovative" language of avant-garde poetry.

Heidegger's writings on technology, art, and poetic language from the 1950s and 1960s offer important insights into this question, in particular because they explore the possibility of a poietic remainder in the world structured in accordance with the techno-scientific formation of relations and develop the significance of such a residue for future thought. The overlapping of the problem of art with the question of experience and technology, which I signaled through Picabia's remark, constitutes the pivot of Heidegger's reflection on the provenance of art and its importance for the determination of thinking in his 1967 Athens lecture "*Die Herkunft der Kunst und die Bestimmung des Denkens*" ("The Provenance of Art and the Determination of Thinking"):

> Is there today, after two and a half millennia, an art which commands the same exigency as did the art of ancient Greece? And if not, from what region comes the exigency to which modern art, in all its domains, responds? . . . The modes by which we determine reality in a scientific world, and by the name "science," we understand natural science, mathematical physics, emphasize something that is only too well known.
>
> By this means one is easily prompted to explain that the region from which the requirement to which modern art responds is none other than the scientific world.
>
> We hesitate to give our ascent. We remain in indecision.[8]

In comparison with "The Origin of the Work of Art," dating from more than thirty years earlier, Heidegger's appraisal of art and its role in the modern world appears here more cautious and circumspect, even skeptical. Still, even though Heidegger assumes a position similar to Picabia's, noting that contemporary art appears to respond in the same modes of thinking by which science determines reality, he leaves open the possibility of another reading of art, one that in "The Question Concerning Technology" he describes as "poetic revealing" (*BW,* 340). Identifying the danger present in technology, beyond the threat of global annihilation or depletion of resources, with how the moderns think, or, rather, schematize experience and their relation to the world in accordance with the prevalent techno-scientific economy of being, Heidegger traces in art the possibility of responding to the demands of the modern world in a poietic way, in the mode of poetic thought. Contrary to many misreadings which arise precisely at this juncture of Heidegger's thought, such poetic thinking does not indicate a withdrawal from the world and its daily affairs into an aestheticized private realm but marks a possibility of letting experience happen as an event whose historicity inscribes the fluid yet irreducible significations of alterity within the very structure of experience. In this relation, thought becomes reconceived beyond the idea of representation or subjective reflection, and signifies a "correspondence" *(Entsprechen)* which, responding to being, lets the world unfold, *co-opens* it, so that representation and reflection become possible.

If Hegel's judgment pronounces the death of art, Heidegger prefers to leave this question undecided, perhaps even undecidable: a matter of continuous requestioning, an issue which has to be decided over and over again, perhaps with every instant a work of art reproduces its work, resetting to work the aletheic play of being. Contrary to Picabia's opinion, for Heidegger, if art follows the spreading technicism of contemporary culture, it already confirms its own death, its own irrelevance, rather than assure for itself a "brilliant future." Art remains alive precisely when it renders the technological economy of experience problematic, and, staging a break, marks an otherwise within the fold of calculative thought: "[b]ecause the essence of technology is nothing technological, essential reflection upon technology and decisive confrontation with it must happen in a realm that is, on the one hand, akin to the essence of technology and, on the other, fundamentally different from it. Such a realm is art" (*BW,* 340). Confronting technology, art has to wager its own existence on whether it can achieve a break from the technic formation of being, and open it up so that the critical force of history's "inessentiality" can disjoin and reformulate the representational framing of experience.

On the surface, this line of thinking appears to unduly privilege art as a site of radical critique and to "demonize" technology, casting it in the role of an adversary. Yet such a positioning of art, however strategic it may appear in the context of the debates about aesthetics, is the result of the historical development of art and the attendant critical discourses. Paradoxically, it is a certain aesthetic ideology, a version of aesthetics which perceives the work of art as a commodified object of private aesthetic experience, that sets up the situation in which art can become a counter-discourse. This aesthetics also prepares the ground for a backlash against the isolation of the aesthetic sphere, for an aestheticizing political appropriation of art into the symbol/ideal of a possible complete representation of social and political relations, which characterizes modernist political (mis)appropriations of art. I locate Heidegger's critique of aesthetics through the prism of the event between the privatization of the aesthetic and the aestheticization of the social/political sphere, that is, I see in it resources for preventing both "misreadings" by foregrounding as art's *Wesen,* that is, as its modality of being, the artwork's continuous reinscription of its own historicity.

Art assumes a "critical" function as a result of the efforts to contain its performative reinterpretation of experience in the private, "aesthetic," sphere of existence. What gives art its critical force is the circumscription of its work in aesthetic terms, which inscribes art into the metaphysical understanding of being: Aesthetic experience becomes conceived on the model of what might be called the "technic" parameters of being, or, when art exceeds such categorizations, its critical effects become effaced through a gesture which assigns art to the "insignificant" and "unreal" domain of the irrational, to the sphere of private affects and perceptions. This ideology of the aesthetic imprints upon art the same binary categories of thought and the protocols of conventional meaning through which metaphysics structures experience: subject/object, private/public, aesthetic/social-political, rational/irrational. Heidegger's assumption is that metaphysical conceptuality has quite successfully monopolized, through its technological ideal of systematized and calculable reality, various spheres of discourse: scientific, historical, political, philosophical, aesthetic. As he argues in the Nietzsche lectures, already since Plato art has been historically resistant to this "progressive" course of Western rationalization, and, if art is dead, as Hegel claims, it is because it is incapable of offering an alternative to the technological schematizations of experience. It is this Western, or as Nietzsche would have it, Socratic, ideology of art as explainable within the parameters of rationality that prepares the scene for the critique of aesthetics *as* aesthetics, that is, as the dominant way of conceptualizing art in modernity. Even if this fashion of perceiving and theorizing art is capable of transformation and modification, it does not venture beyond the aesthetic limits prescribed by Western rationality. My reading of Heidegger's critique of aesthetics underscores how art, performing the historicity of the event, revises the conventional understanding of the temporality of experience and history, which reduces the event to the measurement of time and the order of representation. This approach renders problematic the idea that art can be explained within the techno-metaphysical schema of experience, or, in a symmetrical gesture, disregarded as irrelevant *because* it seems unexplainable, without "meaning," within the prescribed conventions of signification. As "The Origin of the Work of Art" suggests, the inessential *work* of art inaugurates, through the historicity of the event, the possibility of displacing the metaphysical ground of customary relations to world and others. Because of the historical extensions between metaphysical conceptuality and aesthetics, this attempt to think of art otherwise than in aesthetic terms also opens to interrogation the practices of constituting experience and history in accordance with the techno-metaphysical schema of being.

The Two Grammars of Experience

In Heidegger's reflection on technology, we find the tension between two ways of revealing that compose the experience of being in modernity. Heidegger employs the Greek terms of *technē* and *poiēsis* to articulate and describe this tension. In the following section, I explain the stakes of this distinction for rethinking the place of technology and art in the present age and the importance that this approach holds for the recognition of the critical potential of avant-garde art. Even though Heidegger himself does not tie his reflections to discussion of modern or avant-garde art, he tries to explain in them the significance that art might still hold for the technological age. It is precisely this significance of art in relation to the technicization of the everyday that the avant-garde also struggles to articulate.

While many of Heidegger's statements reflect an underlying unease with the impact of techno-scientific thought on modern life and of the progressive immersion of Western culture in technicism, his thought becomes most interesting in its diagnosis of both the extent and the manner in which technology affects experience and thought on the ontological level of being-in-the-world. Heidegger critiques the instrumental notion of technology, the idea that technology is a means at the disposal or under the control of humans, who "create" technology and claim mastery over it. This does not mean, however, that technology is something foreign or added to a "natural" human mode of being but only that it has historically come to increasingly determine the constitution of experience and (human) being-in-the-world. Technology inheres in and regulates the modern experience of the world; it structures and determines the modes of representation through which the world takes shape and becomes present to thought, entering the domain of knowledge. If Heidegger repeatedly underscores the import of global technology, identifying the second half of the twentieth century as the era of the atomic bomb *(Atomzeitalter),* it is to draw attention to how the laws of science and the patterns of technological development emerge from the much older practices through which the power imbedded in modern technology historically has come to decide the shape of experience and thought: "The power concealed in modern technology determines the relation of man to that which exists." [9] In other words, Heidegger claims that modernity is defined by how what is, becomes constituted, experienced, and understood "technologically."

In *Überlieferte Sprache und technische Sprache,* Heidegger distances himself from the anthropological-instrumental concept of technology, according to which technology signifies a practical means, an instrument of implementing in daily life the findings of natural sciences. In order to flesh out his notion of technicity as distinct from the customary significations of modern technology, Heidegger reverses the commonly held idea about the relation between natural sciences and technology: natural science is not the source of technology but, conversely, technicity constitutes the foundational principle of modern science: "*Nicht die Naturwissenschaft ist die Grundlage der Technik, sondern die moderne Technik ist der tragende Grundzug der modernen Naturwissenschaft.*"[10] To see natural science as the origin of technology is to circumscribe technology in terms of a vast array of "man-made" technical products used daily in various areas of modern life. Heidegger, however, defines technology as a determining ground of knowledge, as the paradigm of knowing that has become dominant in Western cultures.

As the modality of knowing proper to Western thought, technicity marks the beginning of modernity and defines knowledge in terms of rendering things and nature open to measuring and calculation. This technological modality of revealing underpins the matrix of thought as rational calculation, and in this capacity, sets up *(gestellt)* nature in terms of calculable objectivity (*US,* 17). As the *Gestell,* that is, as various modes of setting up and making available, technology makes possible modern science, in the specific sense that it "presents" nature as in "essence" calculable and measurable, that is, as prestructured and available for scientific discovery and appropriation. It is technology in this "fundamental" meaning that shapes the modern world in the image of a grand resource and defines social and political relations in terms of calculation and management of resources. The role technology plays in the formation of experience is to inaugurate, and, in the same gesture, to foreclose, the differential emergence of the world in terms of the opposition between resources, both "natural" and manufactured, and the human mastery of the world secured through technological means. Modern experience becomes technologized not as a result of the omnipresence of technologically produced objects or the forms of calculation and regimentation of everyday life but by virtue of the technic schematization of experience which marks the beginning of modernity. In the modern world, technicity is both what occasions experience and what determines its form and boundaries.

Technicity is understood as the mode of disclosing and perceiving things which unfolds the techno-scientific picture of modern reality: "The revealing that rules in modern technology is a challenging [*Herausfordern*], which puts to nature the unreasonable demand that it supply energy which can be extracted and stored as such" (*BW,* 320). Heidegger describes the forms of technic disclosure with a cluster of terms that emphasize the forceful, penetrative, and unlocking strategies assumed in relation to nature and world from the position of the power inherent in techno-scientific thought: setting upon *(Stellen),* ordering *(Bestellen),* challenging-forth *(Herausfordern),* standing-reserve *(Bestand).*[11] The umbrella term for the modes of technic revealing, *das Gestell* (the enframing), expresses, in a concentrated fashion, the meaning of technology conceived as constitutive of the very element or domain of experience and thought: calculation, definition, orderability.[12]

Heidegger's reflection on technology allows us to make a distinction between techno-scientific progress and industrialism, on the one hand, and *Technik,* which describes the patterning of experience, the unfolding of the world in what might be called a "technic" manner, on the other. The technic designates here the underlying existential structure of modern experience and its forms of representation: It reflects the "modern" proclivity for encountering the world in the manner of a calculus, or a tabulation of differences, which reveals being in its contemporary manifestations to be increasingly, and inherently, orderable and presentable as information. Presenting the world as a schema of calculations convertible into the order of information, the technic predetermines being and thought, and, thus, channels and regulates the practices through which the world is experienced and represented. What appears to worry Heidegger is that technological production increasingly obscures the "other" meaning of technology as revealing, and becomes indistinguishable from the reality which it is supposed to describe: "[T]he frenziedness of technology may entrench itself everywhere to such an extent that someday, throughout everything technological, the essence of technology may unfold essentially in the propriative event of truth" (*BW,* 340). At this point the technological would no longer correspond to a historically determined constitution of being but would become interchangeable with the fiction of a "true" essence—it would lay claim to being *the* truth of being.

I would argue that the problem of technology points beyond the total scope of the techno-scientific image toward what makes such a global perspective possible: the idea of basing the very nature of relating (humans/world; thought/nature, and so on) on the model of a forceful ordering and uniformity. Technicity describes above all the principle of relationality itself, the matrix of relating whose principle is based on the possibility of measurement and calculation. This technologically conceived relationality, which constitutes the underlying paradigm of techno-scientific thought and the practices of modern life, affects in advance—prescribes, as it were—the articulations of difference, determining the scope of their socio-political and ethical implications. This type of relationality—the product of the historical development of the metaphysical tradition into scientific thought—regulates the entire spectrum of modern experience, dictating, in effect, the manner in which the world occurs: its technic modality of revealing.[13]

By contrast with technicity and its modes of representation, I read Heidegger's poietic revealing or *poiēsis*,[14] in terms of difference as alterity whose play remains elusive for thought and comprehension. Difference read as the index of alterity retains the unboundedness of its event *(Ereignis)*, where the fold of historicity renders the event already different from itself or from any grasp or comprehension its articulation affords. This distinction between difference conceived in terms of comprehension or calculation and difference as the index of alterity reflects the tensions that mark modern experience and provides another venue for the discussion of the historicity of the event described in chapter 1.

Conceiving of technicity in terms of relationality, that is, as predetermining the very shape of relations in the modern world, puts us in a position to unpack Heidegger's notion of *poiēsis* or poetic revealing and to develop its implications for understanding the work of art. Just as Heidegger's notion of technology refers to a force constitutive of how human beings relate to what is, *poiēsis* is also thought on the same level: The poetic event of experience critiques the idea of a private aesthetic, the notion that art pertains to an aestheticized region of being, separate from "real life" problems and concerns. *Poiēsis* here refers to the historial force—the historicity of happening—which unfolds experience as "inessential" and disjoined. It also exposes the limits of technicity, showing how it effaces the historial aspects of experience, saturates it with meaning and renders it commensurate with calculative thought. If technology becomes synonymous with the formation of experience in the contemporary world, the revelation of the "poetic" character of the historicity of experience, the historial *poiēsis* of the world's coming into being, concerns directly the work performed by art, the work whose postaesthetic scope falls outside of the realm of the aesthetic categorizations of art. In Heidegger's words, "in our sheer aesthetic-mindedness *(lauter Ästhetik)* about art we no longer guard and preserve *(bewahren)* the essential unfolding of art" *(BW,* 340–41); that is, we no longer recognize art's relation to experience and, instead, try to resolve all questions about art's work within the binary scenario of the "aesthetics" of isolation versus the "politics" of integration.

Heidegger's term *bewahren* ties the preservation of the work of art, of its figuration of historicity, to the possibility of opening, through a confrontation with the "essence" of technology, a poietic organization of experience. To reappraise the technic production of modern experience, to inflect the calculative relationality that (in)forms its practices, is to rethink the formation of thought and experience figured in the work of art. This formation Heidegger designates with the term "poetic": It bears the name of poetry *(Dichtung)* or of poetic revealing. Though both *technē* and *poiēsis* are modes of revealing, of bringing-forth *(BW,* 319), poetic unconcealment, in contrast to the setting and framing *(stellen)* characteristic of technic revealing, proceeds as letting-be. Since it is grammar that describes the matrix of relations obtaining within a language, I refer to *technē* and *poiēsis*—two interlinked variants of relatedness—as the technic and poietic grammars of experience, respectively. The interplay and contestation of those two patterns of relating makes up the interstices of experience, the grammar of everyday practices. Both modes constitute the play of *alethēia;* they negotiate the ambiguous scission of the true and the untrue, but the upper hand in disposing the relations which obtain within this play belongs to the technic disclosure, to the enframing or the *Gestell.* Figuring a possible rupture of the uniform framework of the *Gestell, poiēsis* indicates a narrow opening marked by historicity, a sort of a grammatical lapsus, in which it may be possible to renegotiate our understanding of the work of art through the link between art's poetic *Gestalt* and the poietic unfolding of experience.

In order to avoid an all too easy misunderstanding that this rethinking of technology amounts to a form of aestheticization, I introduce a distinction between the poetic and the poietic, between the poetic figure at work in art and the poietic historicity of experience. Although this difference is only implicit in Heidegger's thought, the way he recasts *poiēsis* and calibrates it with art's historico-philosophical role in the critique of modernity suggests that *poiēsis* constitutes the structuring moment of experience—the texture of the differential manifestation of the world. Drawing a link between *physis* and *poiēsis,* Heidegger indicates that *poiēsis* delineates the workings of the event of manifestation: "*Physis* . . . the arising of something from out of itself, is a bringing-forth, *poiēsis. Physis* is indeed *poiēsis* in the highest sense" *(BW,* 317). Beyond craft, and artistic or poetic creation, *poiēsis* refers to the historial character of the event, to the opening of the world, irreducible to subjective or private experiences. It is in this specific sense that I write about the *poietic* event of experience and keep it differentiated from the poetic configuration of the work of art, which "The Origin of the Work of Art" describes as *Dichtung*—poetry or the poetic domain of art: "*All art,* as the letting happen of the advent of the truth of beings, is as such, *in essence, poetry*" (*BW,* 197). The bifurcation of the notion of poetry into *Poesie,* the genre of poetic writing, and *Dichtung,* the poetic element of art, opens the door to rethinking art through its relation to *poiēsis* in the broad sense, that is, with regard to the poietic structure of experience. The poietic as I have defined it here is not limited to or reserved for art and poetry but delineates instead the structuration of experience. The poietic and the poetic remain distinct, even though their linguistic and etymological proximity suggests reference to the same structure of experience. While not all poetry and art is poietic, the discourse at work in "poetic" art—its "poetics"—registers in its very structure what I have termed the "poietics" of experience. In this context, "poetic art" becomes the site where the historial *poiēsis* of experience marks itself against the dominant technicist formations of the everyday.

This kind of *poiēsis* does not just constitute a new aesthetic but revises the notion of relation and produces a new relationality alternative to the figures of relation which ground calculative thought. I develop this poietic relatedness in reference to Heidegger's notion of nearness *(Nähe),* which in his late works describes the complicated and shifting weave of relations within the propriative event *(Ereignis).*[15] *Nähe* specifies a type of relationality which, in order to mark and yet preserve the alterity of the other within the relation, conceives the relating bind in terms of a proximity that "unbinds" or lets be. Unlike difference, which remains calculable and representable within the binary optics of identity and difference, proximity binds by releasing. Relationality figured as nearness—which, as I show in the next chapter, is also crucial to Irigaray's critique of sexual difference—marks an attempt to think the very optics within which difference first becomes possible and representable as difference.

Since measurable, graspable difference is the key parameter of representational and calculative thought, the relationality implied in the notion of nearness figures an alternative to the technological relatedness, a poietic unfolding alternative to the technic mode of revealing. In other words, nearness conceived as the very element of relation, the middle *(Mitte),* so to speak, where relating becomes possible in the first place, refers to the poietic weave of relations which structures experience as event. This poietic relationality becomes thinkable only as an inflection or a torsion within the differential matrix of manifestation. What nearness figures is the very distinction between difference as *poiēsis* and difference appropriated technologically, that is, difference conceived as the pivot of calculative thought. It marks the distinction within *Ereignis* between propriation as dispropriation or depropriation *(Ent-eignis)* and the eventual appropriation into the representational schema. This distinction keeps in play the critical effects of the remainder which does not enter into the matrix of calculation and which excuses itself from the differential (re)presentation of the event. This remainder indicates the historicity of experience, a certain untimeliness which dislocates the event and which is marked in the irreducibility of the signification of proximity to the representation of difference. I read Heidegger's nearness as a poietically conceived relatedness, as a way of rethinking technology and critiquing calculative thought, which would keep experience in view of the irreducibility of its event. The problematic of nearness and difference indicates how the technic and the poietic constitute two sides of manifestation, whose identity and separation remain constantly at play.

The poietic reinvention of relationality involves rethinking the role that the other and alterity play in thought and the ways in which otherness affects the formation of experience and everyday practice. To the extent that this relationality crystallizes relations in a nondeterminate, nonsaturated way by letting the other remain other, it operates a different kind of temporality, one distinct from the binary temporality of presence and absence. Its time is historial and not simply historical, that is, it marks the temporal torsion which has always already opened the present, as noncoincident with itself, to the future. This poietic relationality does not concern itself with bringing into presence, and thus with representing, but with articulating experience as already dislocated, fissured: an *Erfahrung*, which, as I show in chapter 1, constitutes itself by reinscribing its own historicity. By contrast, technicity forms beings into relations of power, maintaining differences only as an index of power, and thus effectively canceling them within the overall calculus of resources. Taken as historial *and* poietic, experience opens its social and aesthetic constructs to the inessentiality of the event, which remains incommensurate with experience constituted in terms of power, representation, and resource. Poietic relationality, both a mark of alterity and a remainder of the historicity of the event, defines an attempt to conceive of relation on the pattern of proximity and inflection of difference, where the differential matrix of thought, rather than being rigid or schematic in its calculation of differences, becomes pliant, adaptable to the indeterminateness of alterity.[16]

The Avant-Garde *Poiēsis*

This reading of *poiēsis* constitutes the frame for my understanding of the terms "poetry" and "poetics" in reading avant-garde poetry: Beyond their conventional reference to the genre of poetic writing or the aesthetic code regulating it, they designate, in a specific and limited way, the "poetic" operations through which art registers and figures the poietics of experience. As I demonstrated in chapter 1, this poietics functions as a critique of the dominant ideologies of experience and their grounding in the metaphysics of subjectivity. The link between this poietics of the event and the poetic in art defines the postaesthetic or the avant-garde working of art. As my discussion of Duchamp's ready-mades shows, this postaesthetics is at work in the historical avant-gardes but it also operates in contemporary poetry, manifesting itself in the poetic redefinitions of the relation between language, everydayness, and technology. This postaesthetic poietics of experience defines the function of the avant-garde in my argument: The avant-gardes are historical, they belong to the epoch of technological thought and the critique of modernity, but the avant-garde *work* of art is irreducible to any of the historical avant-garde "isms." It describes the continuing critical rethinking of the poietic and the technological figurations of experience. If on the basis of the works of Heidegger and Benjamin we regard language as a translative event, then avant-garde poetics replays the torsion of the poietic into the poetic, the configuration of the event of manifestation into the work performed by art. What is avant-garde about avant-garde art is its engagement with this specific language fold, which transcribes the poietic into the poetic *Gestalt,* or into the instant, as Tzara calls it. The distinction between the poietic and the poetic, complementing the difference between *technē* and *poiēsis,* clarifies how the poietic event escapes the boundaries of aestheticization and questions the technological formation of experience. At issue is not an arbitrary choice of art as a safeguard against the domination of technology but the matter of opening within the technological forms of experience an alternative figuration of *Erfahrung.*

Calling the alternative to technology *poiēsis,* Heidegger is not at all sure whether this distinction can still be meaningful, whether the poietic can mark a difference from the technological or whether, instead, it explains itself fully within the fold of technology. The avant-garde, in particular Dadaism, seems to be, by contrast, a celebration of precisely that very possibility of art as a different, postaesthetic *poiēsis.* The tenor of avant-garde art, the frenetic pace of its linguistic and artistic innovations, stands in marked contrast to Heidegger's cautious meditative approach. While Heidegger investigates the historical conditions in modernity under which such a transformation into a postaesthetic art could be possible, the avant-garde advertises its works as the very stage where such transformation takes place. It is obvious that Heidegger would have had little patience for the irony with which Dada questions and refashions the links between art and the everyday, for the playful mundaneness of Duchamp's ready-mades or the clowning meanders of Tzara's manifestoes. And yet, underneath the cautious, almost skeptical look with which Heidegger regards contemporary art and the bravado with which Dada dismisses the past and ridicules the present in its works, a common thread of concern with the event of experience connects these two, so different, approaches. In his insistence that "Dada does not mean anything,"[17] Tzara does not simply scandalize the literary public and upset their expectations of meaningfulness and coherence. He also indicates that the level on which Dadaism wants to engage being reaches beyond the play of signification into the event structure of experience which Dada attempts to release from the conventions of everyday being.

This kind of *poiēsis* becomes visible in Tzara's various Dada manifestoes, which consistently, through their mazes of jokes, irony, and contradictions, draw the sign of equation between Dada and being: "***DADA DADA DADA;***—the roar of contorted pains, the interweaving of contraries and of all contradictions, freaks and irrelevancies: LIFE."[18] The Dadaist attack on bourgeois society, family, and state institutions, its anti-establishment and anti-aesthetic stance, appears to be a result of attempts to renegotiate the relation between art and being:

> We must accelerate this quantity of life that spends itself so readily here, there, and everywhere. Art is not the most precious manifestation of life. Art does not have the celestial, general value that people are pleased to accord it. Life is far more interesting. Dada boasts of knowing the exact proportion that is to be given to art; it introduces it with subtle, perfidious means into the acts of everyday fantasy. And vice versa. In art, Dada brings everything back to an initial, but relative, simplicity. (*SM*, 110)

Art "going Dada" constitutes more than an aesthetic or artistic phenomenon because it concerns "LIFE," that is, it sets out to reconceive relations between artwork and world, literature and experience. Art (re)claims a portion or a layer of experience, a *poietic* dimension of historicity, which cannot be filled "with words or conventions," and which opens the possibility of re-figuring art's relation to the technological organization of experience. What remains to be investigated is "the exact proportion" to be given to art so that its relation to experience can be renegotiated within the matrix of the everyday and yet outside or beyond the framing opposition between the separation/integration of art into social practice.

To release the Dada in being, Tzara demands specifically a break from the futurist fascination with technology, a distancing from Marinetti's attempt to replace literary sensibility with machinelike "feelings": "We declare that the motor car is a feeling that has cosseted us quite enough in the dilatori-ness of its abstractions, as have transatlantic liners, noises and ideas. And while we put on a show of being facile, we are actually searching for the central essence of things, and are pleased if we can hide it . . ." (*SM*, 1). For Dada, which is "definitely against the future" (*SM*, 1), what matters is not the future that will one day become present but the instant, the event of experience in its futural temporality. It is the self-concealing rupture of the event that Dadaism attempts to both reveal and conceal in the irony and contradictions of its language. This "show of being facile" which Tzara puts on in his poems and manifestos seeks precisely this hiding "central essence of things"—the instant or the event. To transpose experience into its di-mension of the event, Tzara constantly undermines logic and the principle of noncontradiction, creating a convoluted series of self-canceling asser-tions which lead his language beyond the discursive confines it inhabits. As he humorously puts it, "Even if logic were confirmed by the senses it would still be an organic disease" (*SM*, 9). Rather than the key to truth and meaning, logic appears a sort of a degeneration of experience, which covers over with its machinery of rules and axioms the Dada event of being. Logic "infects" not simply language but experience itself, imperceptibly altering its fabric so that it appears intrinsically calculable and graspable—technic. What we can recognize within Dada's "non-sense" and its ironic crusade against logic, is precisely the tension between the technic and the poietic unfolding of being. This is why Tzara wants to lead art to a state where "Beauty and Truth in art don't exist" (*SM*, 110), that is, to a state where art, to the extent to which it escapes the techno-aesthetic categories which obscure its work, begins to matter for experience precisely because art's significance cannot be accommodated within the related schema of truth-based cognition, aesthetic judgment, and social usefulness.

What emerges from Tzara's pronouncements is a postaesthetic notion of art, whose main impetus is less to propose a new aesthetic or even an anti-aesthetic than to attempt to altogether leave aesthetics to itself. Perhaps it is time to abandon aesthetics, the way Heidegger wanted to leave metaphysics to itself in his late essay "Time and Being." Since a simple overcoming of aesthetics is impossible (hence "postaesthetic" sounds a somewhat false note), we should probably talk about letting aesthetics cease to be so important and allowing art to reinvent a different set of exchanges with the world. Such a reinvention or reimaging puts into question the idea of returning to an orderly picture of art integrated into social practice, because this paradigm, which conceptualizes art in terms of its either outside or inside status with respect to the social sphere, effectively performs art's incorporation into the technical ordering of experience. To the extent that notions of social practice as either a space structured technologically or its opposite, a pretechnological realm immune from the reification of experience, are indebted to the metaphysico-technological schema of being and increasingly speak this language, the wager implicit in Picabia's remark about the technological destiny of modern art rings false. Picabia frames the issues in a way that predetermines the outcome of the discussion, making art spin between the opposites of the autonomy of aestheticist art and the avant-garde dream of integration of art into social practice. By contrast, Duchamp's ready-mades and Tzara's manifestoes suggest that the avant-garde critiques this entire opposition and tries to rethink art's relation to experience beyond the aesthetic dilemmas of separation and integration.

Picabia's remark appears to resolve the tensions at play in Duchamp's ready-mades, locating art, without any remainder, within the fold of technology, and, implicitly, extending the machinist domain over the entirety of experience. The seemingly innocent and merely aesthetic query about the provenance of art, and the issue of its residue or remainder over the technological, touches upon the problem of the structure of experience in modernity. Its importance becomes immediately visible when we realize that the tenuous possibility of a remainder above the technological configurations of experience—of art as the moment of the contestation of technicity and the inauguration of an otherwise—becomes the placeholder for alterity. As Tzara notes, "[a]rt is a series of perpetual differences. . . . The strength to transmute this succession of ever-changing notions into *the instant*—that is the work of art" (*SM,* 76). The precarious architectonics of the work of art consists in holding together, both *in* an instant and *as* an instant, a constellation of differences, a series of shifting images and notions, which open up a distance marking the historicity of experience. In effect, the constellation, not unlike Benjamin's dialectical image, configures itself as a difference which holds the instant open toward what it no longer is (the past) and what it is not yet (the future). Through this peculiar opening up of the event-ness of experience — the reproduced instant of displacement — art constitutes itself as its own remainder, as always above and beyond what it comes to be in the instant of its work. To be exact, the work "proper" or idiomatic to art consists in constituting the instant, that particular "instantaneous" *Gestalt,* as Heidegger would say, as the moment of its own undoing and reproduction, that is, as a "series of perpetual differences."

The understanding of experience as event has a direct bearing on the problematic of the everyday, with which so much of avant-garde art concerns itself. In Tzara's manifestoes, art transmutes the ever-shifting differences into an instant, thus remarking the self-concealing historicity of the everyday. As such, the instant points to the fold within the everyday: between the routines, knowledges, and perceptions characteristic of the ordinary, underpinned and regulated by the "disease" of logic, and the instant in which the everyday shows its ironic Dada face. As in Dadaism, much of the energy of contemporary art and modern thought is directed at rethinking the everyday: from ordinary language, everyday practices, and banal topics, to mundane events and prosaic situations. Both phenomenology and ordinary language philosophy have made it the backbone of their philosophical practice to consider dimensions of the everyday, from Husserl's *Lebenswelt,* Heidegger's everydayness, or Merleau-Ponty's "prose of the world," to Wittgenstein's language games and Cavell's quests of the ordinary, to name just a few. Twentieth-century art (from Duchamp's readymades to Newman's "abstract" paintings with their banal titles, "Here," "Now," and so on) to literature (from Gertrude Stein's writings to Beckett's prose and Białoszewski's miniature poems and narratives) engage the modern world by bringing art to the level of the ordinary and the mundane. What remains crucial to contemporary debates, however, is how one interprets the everyday: whether the ordinary signifies a realm of immediacy, givenness, and direct communication, or whether it itself becomes a matter of contestation and critique. Apart from differences in interpreting everydayness, at issue here is the understanding of experience, of how its "poietics" revise the familiar and "stable" significations of the everyday.

Heidegger's conception of technicity *(Technik)* articulates a certain "universal" coding of the everyday which underwrites the plurality of representational strategies and social practices. These heterogeneous forms of the lived differential do not escape, in Heidegger's view, the fold of calculative thought, which reflects the technological determination of being intrinsic to modernity. For Heidegger, as much as for Duchamp, the lived differential of the everyday has become determined by the enframing "essence" of technology, and its practices have been synchronized with and become increasingly indistinguishable from the technological patterning of experience. When Heidegger refers to the ordinary as "reliable," he indicates the degree to which everydayness is indebted to technology and its models of grasping the world in terms of reliability and availability, the extent to which the ordinary works on the principle of the technological representation of being as "reliable." Duchamp's urinal or bicycle wheel, though certainly operative in a very different tonality, likewise stand the ordinary on its head, disconnecting everyday tools from their functional context and, thus, bringing into the open the invisible regulative force with which technicity forms modern being. Tzara's conception of art as the instant involves a similar turn within the everyday, a "regeneration" from the ordinary logic of being, invisibly constructing and orchestrating the purported immediacy of experience. In other words, the concept of the ordinary as immediate, as a place of common knowledge or a sphere of prelinguistic experience, sheltered from the influence of technology and mass culture, has to be called into question. The ordinary is already mediated, it is enframed technologically and functions as a font of availability, as resource or *Bestand*.[19]

The distinction between the ordinary and the poietics of everyday experience, which I locate in the *work* performed by art, reveals a dehiscence, a rift, within the very formation of the ordinary. The event estranges and defamiliarizes the habitual, as in Brecht's aesthetic or in Russian formalism, but it also emphasizes the simultaneously constitutive and de-constituting role of historicity, and underscores its "de-essentializing" impact upon experience. In other words, the event marks the irreducibility of the *everyday* to the *"ready-made" significations of the ordinary.* Williams's early poetry or the work of Objectivists comes to mind here. But perhaps the most interesting examples of unmaking the significations of the ordinary come in Stein's *Tender Buttons* and Białoszewski's poems. While *Tender Buttons* playfully dissolves labels and names into linguistic patchwork, Białoszewski's poetry continuously resignifies the everyday and the trivial in a gesture that parodies both high poetic language and the sense that the everyday is just routine and ordinary. In such works, the indication of a fracture within the everyday—of the ambiguous interface of the technic and the poietic—is clearly different from the familiar modernist gesture of escaping the dreary daily existence, a nostalgic poetic retreat from the vulgar and crass everydayness into its mystical and mysterious verso, an attitude which Henri Lefebvre in his *Critique of Everyday Life* identifies with Surrealism.[20] The avant-garde resignification of the everyday questions the idea of a mystical or esoteric verso of everydayness as much as it interrogates the technicity which underpins and regulates the modern ordinary. Distinct from the idea of the ordinary as immediate, as a sphere of familiarity and direct communication, the poietics of experience questions the way in which the technic relatedness pervades the domain of ordinary life and language. Since the poietic signification of the everyday is always mediated, paired with the technological, it effectively undercuts the common figures of the ordinary: self-presence, immediacy, common sense, and common knowledge. The poietic model of relatedness, based on alterity and proximity rather than on the idea of graspable and assimilable difference, renders problematic the "ordinary" relationality and its comforting sense of familiarity and transparency. The displacement from the "ordinary" to the "poietics of everydayness" takes the form of a critical incision, which, securing "an openness of beings," attempts to bring into language the "ungraspable" historicity of everyday experience.

In this perspective, the poetic event as the *work* proper to art becomes tantamount to a restaging or a reproduction of the linguistic torsion, that is, to the translation which transcribes the poietic into the technic, in an attempt to prevent the erasure of their play and the establishment of a univocally technic domain of experience. At stake in the reproducibility characteristic of the work of art is the possibility of modalizing the everyday into different significations, of keeping in the "instant" of art the play between the technic and the poietic inherent in the unfolding of the world. Near the end of "The Question Concerning Technology," Heidegger tries to reproblematize the meaning of *technē* in order to render it polyvalent, open to semantic possibilities which would exceed the meaning of technology as enframing: "There was a time when it was not technology alone that bore the name *technē*. Once the revealing that brings forth truth into the splendor of radiant appearance was also called *technē*. . . . The *poiēsis* of the fine arts was also called *technē*" (*BW,* 339). The possibility of a post-aesthetic reading of the work of art hinges upon the signification of *technē,* that is, upon our ability to read *technē* as both identical to and yet as more than, or other than, technicity. It depends upon the possibility of keeping alterity in play within the semiosis of *technē,* upon opening technicity to the historicity marked in the poietic unfolding.

This way of approaching the problem of technicity and modern experience modifies the optics for our discussions of the avant-garde. The avant-garde preoccupation with technology is not simply a sign of their fascination with and acceptance *tout court* of the technological age. As is clearly the case in Khlebnikov's work, the avant-garde also pushes technicity to its very limit, discovering in the process the proximity between the technic and the poietic. Khlebnikov's "beyonsense" *(zaum)* takes both linguistic invention and mathematical calculation into an uncharted language territory, where technicity reverses itself into a new form of poetic language which registers the poietic event of experience. In Khlebnikov or in Dadaism, the signification of the work performed by art is tied to the question of whether the modern experience as *technē* understands and exhausts itself within the "essence" of technology or whether an other poietics of experience is at work in it. This issue remains important beyond the confines of the debates about the avant-gardes, because what hinges upon the distinction between the poietic and the technic is precisely the question of the aestheticization of the political. A folding of *poiēsis* into technicity—the disappearance of the difference between them—specifies a juncture between aesthetics and politics which produces the possibility of remythologizing the state and its politics. The equivalence between *poiēsis* and technicity has two interrelated effects: On the one hand, it makes the everyday into a humdrum, repetitive routine, from which one seeks relief in the various forms of entertainment; on the other, it can render the ordinary auratic, to paraphrase Benjamin, and lead to aesthetic practices which mythologize the everyday. Reducing the event to its "ready-made" significations, such equivalence collapses the historicity of happening into the uniform space of representation and neutralizes the disjoining which marks the structure of experience. The way in which the avant-garde artworks reopen within the everyday this fold between the technic and the poietic bespeaks a larger political significance for the avant-garde, which complicates the political commitments and endorsements explicitly adopted by the various movements.

3. Sexuate Experience

Irigaray and the Poetics of Sexual Difference

The interrelated questions of gender *in* and *of* modernity have become the arena for critical reappraisals and contestations of what constitutes modernity itself—its cultural, political, philosophical, and literary manifestations. Within this optics the problem of the figuration, positioning, erasure, or strategic appropriation of the feminine (for example, a certain reading of the largely male avant-garde in terms of writing the feminine) redoubles itself to reflect back upon modernity and open the issue of *its* gender, that is, of the role of gender in the very construction and self-perception of modernity. In what way is the problematic of gender and sexual difference already inscribed in the production of modernity and how does it affect its various manifestations? To what extent can the reading of this inscription alter the operative concepts of experience, thought, and language? In *The Gender of Modernity*, Rita Felski argues for the necessity of a more nuanced and complicated reading of modernity, beyond its readily available identifications with masculine rationalization and production, on the one hand, and the antithetical association of the modern with the irrational and the libidinal, "exemplified in the figure of the voracious female consumer," on the other (30–31). At the same time, such a reading of the gender of modernity, Felski suggests, has to revise the predominant oppositional association of the figures of the masculine and the feminine with high art and popular or mass culture, respectively. If this way of redescribing modernity increasingly refines the picture of gender and its modern(ist) figurations, it still leaves unquestioned the foundational concepts of modernity's cultural and intellectual project: experience, consciousness, technicity, temporality. To the extent that in the twentieth century modernity becomes indisassociable from its own critique, the matter of gender constitutes precisely one of the critical points where modernity, putting its own legacy into question, opens the door to a reinvention of gender(s) in relation to experience and where the rethinking of sexual difference becomes the conduit for conceptualizing the transition into "postmodernity." The crisis of modernity—the judgment that modernity renders upon itself—marks the point at which the questioning of the metaphysical provenance of the modern calls for rethinking everyday experience in the context of sexual difference, with the proviso that such a critique also puts into question the concepts of consciousness, representation, and time that underlie modernity.

To rethink the role of the avant-garde and its poietics of experience in the critique of modernity, it becomes important, then, to examine the links between the feminist critique of experience and the poetic work of language. For this reason, I look at the writings of Luce Irigaray, who explicitly ties her rigorously and provocatively articulated critique of modernity to the task of formulating a new *poetics:* a new language of thinking, which would set the stage for the reappraisal of the role of sexual difference and gender in the very structuring of experience. Critical responses to Irigaray seldom focus on the complexity of poetic thinking in her work as they try, in what remains an important and necessary move, to articulate the critical claims and political accomplishments of her project. Interest in Irigaray's style has centered largely on her textual strategy of mimesis, which produces a defamiliarization of and provides the protocols for a different reading of the feminine.[1] Among most recent contributions to Irigaray criticism, Elizabeth Weed shifts the discussion of style from the defamiliarizing and disruptive effects of Irigarayan mimesis toward a "discursive positivity" of sexual difference.[2] Irigaray's idiosyncratic language produces a "positive" mapping of sexual relations, which moves beyond Lacan's analysis of the nonexistence of sexual relations and evokes "a different symbolic organization." [3] Against the privilege which much of the current U.S. feminist criticism gives to the thematizable and the intelligible as the necessary conditions for change or effective intervention, Weed offers Irigaray's "style" as the arena where the very conditions of intelligibility—including those of Irigaray's own texts— are brought into question and refigured.[4]

The fact that the poetic in Irigaray is rarely seen as central to her philosophical and political critique seems to be a symptom of a broader distrust of aesthetics in current debates. Feminist criticism seems to be weary of the by now well-known, even worn out, aesthetics of *écriture féminine,* and regards it with suspicion as a form of displacing political concerns into the realm of aesthetic experimentation. In the case of Irigaray, however, the poetic cannot be confined to aesthetic categories or textual strategies, but has to be reconceived as a sexuate mode of being and experience. More than a defamiliarizing strategy of interpretation, Irigarayan mimicry needs also to be read in terms of a critique of modernity and its reigning categories of being and technology. It is only in recent critical assessments that Irigaray's work has been considered more explicitly against the background of the philosophical critiques of modernity, in particular, the thought of Heidegger, Levinas, and Derrida. Chanter's benchmark *Ethics of Eros* presents Irigaray's writings through a series of dialogues with key philosophical figures in the Continental tradition—from Hegel and Nietzsche to Levinas and Derrida—as a chain of exchanges which influence and complicate Irigaray's critique of the patriarchal discourse of modernity.[5] Likewise, a recent volume of essays on Irigaray's thought, *Engaging with Irigaray,* emphasizes for the first time the critical role of Irigaray's encounter with Heidegger's work for the formulation of her ideas about the ethics of sexual difference.[6] Both studies are immensely helpful in showing to what extent Irigaray's revision of the patriarchal logic of modernity borrows, radicalizes, and critiques the postmodern or poststructuralist idioms in which such reappraisals have been articulated.

Like Foucault, Irigaray continues Nietzsche's and Heidegger's questioning of aesthetics in the context of rethinking being, inflecting it through the problematic of sexuate experience. To reassess the importance of Irigaray's deployment of the poetic, the decisive role it plays, first, in her questioning of technology and the logic of commodification, and, second, in her remapping of sexual difference vis-à-vis the historicity of experience, I read Irigaray in the context of Heidegger's redefinition of *poiēsis,* reconsidering her poetics of sexual difference[7] through the prism of *das Ereignis,* or the propriative event.[8] The event tends, on the one hand, to become obfuscated in the techno-calculative schema of being, even to be denied actuality and assigned to the irreal, and, on the other, to question the familiar modalities of signification and elicit a reinvention of language in the form of what Heidegger calls "poetic thinking." Reassessing the importance of Irigaray's deployment of aesthetics, my approach stresses specifically the doubly *critical* role of her poetics to the very constitution and aims of her project: First, *poetic* thinking is significant, even pivotal, to Irigaray's articulation of an ethics of sexual difference, and, second, this poetics becomes the bearer or "performer" of the most radical insights of her critique.

Irigaray's reinvention of the parameters of modern experience by means of a critical reading of the erasures of sexual difference in Western thought can, and, I argue, should be read in terms of a poetics, in part at least because it explicitly sets out to revise the very (patriarchal) syntax of thought. I emphasize precisely these nodal points where Irigaray's work presents itself as a poetics, and I often proceed beyond Irigaray's sketchy remarks on this new poetics in order to underscore the critical intersections between the poietic unfolding of experience and the project of rethinking sexual difference. Situating Irigaray in the context of Heidegger's remarks on art and technology, I examine her work in terms of another venue for discerning the complexity of art's critical involvement in figuring modern experience. Irigaray's remarks on the erasures of sexual difference in the context of technology and commodification provide the perspective in which I look at how avant-garde poetics functions as a critique of the commodification of art.

Keenly aware of the historical conditions of gender in/of modernity, Irigaray's work moves within the broad philosophico-cultural perspective of metaphysical thought to diagnose the crisis of modernity as a critical juncture that opens both the possibility of rethinking "feminine experience" and of revising the understanding of experience *through* what might be envisioned as the fluid and flexible *poietics* of sexual difference. For Irigaray, the auto-critique of modernity, while itself not sufficiently radical for her purposes, opens the space for a further creative rewriting within the optics of sexual difference, of the metaphysical categories like being, experience, subjectivity, otherness, space, and time. Putting in question the manner in which philosophical, psychoanalytic, and cultural constructions of femininity effectively serve the purpose of effacing sexual difference, Irigaray's project reinvents the feminine and sexual difference as catalysts for rewriting experience. In a typically Irigarayan double gesture of mimicry—of simultaneously replaying and dislodging the inherently patriarchal logic of Western philosophical discourse—Irigaray both models her project upon and displaces Heidegger's questioning of Being:

> Sexual difference is one of the major philosophical issues, if not the issue, of our age. According to Heidegger, each age has one issue to think through, and one only. Sexual difference is probably the issue in our time which could be our "salvation" if we thought it through. (*ESD,* 5)

This forceful articulation of the problem suggests that thought has come, historically and discursively, to a point where it faces both the opportunity and the necessity of reinventing itself specifically through the problematic of sexual difference. If modernity is to rethink itself, to indeed open the possibility of a *post*modernity, it needs not only to remap femininity but also to reinvent *discourse* through sexual difference.

Recent Irigaray criticism has shown how the early dismissive readings of Irigaray as an essentialist thinker[9] misread her project either as reclaiming an autonomous or essential femininity or as locating the feminine outside the masculine logic of modernity. Contrary to these mischaracterizations, Irigaray's critique suggests that the contestations of modernity and its patriarchal logic do not go *far enough* to enable both a reinvention of language through the problematic of sexual difference and a rethinking of the pivotal role of sexual difference in the constitution of experience: a rethinking that could inscribe sexual difference into the very matrix of experiencing. For Irigaray, the patriarchal figurations of sexual difference—where the feminine is erased, rendered esoteric, or identified with the prelinguistic immediacy of nature—effectively efface sexual difference from language and, at the same time, from the discursive formation of experience. In other words, what is absent are the discursive practices that would allow experience to articulate itself in a sexed or sexuate manner—to constitute, think, or "experience" itself within sexual difference conceived otherwise than through the optics of the patriarchal logic of sense. Such a (dis)figuration of sexual difference leaves its imprint upon experience in its everyday and mundane dimensions, which makes it necessary for the project of rethinking femininity to extend beyond reclaiming everydayness or reinscribing it onto the cultural map of modernity. Instead, Irigaray's project contests the ordinary and opens up the possibility of a different approach to sexual difference and experience, one that Irigaray imagines in terms of an ethics of sexual difference. This reappraisal of the feminine—tantamount, in Irigaray's view, to the possibility of finally inaugurating sexual difference: its experience, language, and thought—is meant to refigure experience through the exchanges of proximity, where the feminine, historically and discursively the erased or the appropriated other, would reformulate the very optics in which otherness becomes capable of signifying. I show how Irigaray's work, in addition to describing and theorizing female experience, offers resources for inventing such a new legibility of experience, with sexual difference as its fluid, poietic, matrix.

The Matter of Proximity

One can read Irigaray's work as both a transposition of the problems and limitations of the differential economy of signification—signaled already, among others, by Heidegger's work on difference and Levinas's writings on alterity—into the problematic of sexual difference and as a further critique of the specular logic of difference from the perspective of the erasure of the sexuate character of experience produced by such a logic. Heidegger's questioning of difference eventually effects a move away from the priority of the ontico-ontological difference toward the question of *Ereignis,* language, and nearness. A similar shift of emphasis is operative in the thought of Levinas, who progressively abandons the correlation between difference and otherness in favor of the notions of nonindifference and proximity, which imprint ethical signification upon difference. In the context of Heidegger's and Levinas's work on language and difference, it becomes clear that the revision of otherness from its negative signification of absence or lack to the positive meaning of multiple differences may not be enough. In fact, Irigaray's own work appears to continuously question the idea that the play of the differential economy of meaning will ever ensure the distinctness of the sexes and reflect a sexuate poietics of experience. Since difference is always implicated in a possible return to sameness and in the cognitive effacement of the other, it becomes necessary to look for an alternative economy of thought. As in Heidegger's work, difference for Irigaray becomes inflected by proximity, the between or the interval. But since for Irigaray the proximity is sexuate, this inflection acquires not only ethical but also political signification: Irigaray regards it as inaugurating the possibility of reappraising the intellectual and cultural effects of the sexual "indifference" of metaphysics.

Irigaray provisionally describes this new economy of thought through the images of double syntax and two lips:

> What a feminine syntax might be is not simple nor easy to state, because in that "syntax" there would no longer be either subject or object, "oneness" would no longer be privileged, there would no longer be proper meanings, proper names, "proper" attributes. . . . Instead, that "syntax" would involve nearness, proximity, but in such an extreme form that it would preclude any distinction of identities, any establishment of ownership, thus any form of appropriation.[10]

Like the double syntax, the two lips indicate an interplay that refuses the terms of difference and identity. The lips, both sexual organs and the organs of language are neither two distinct and different lips nor one, unified, "same," structure. Instead, what defines their specificity is their nearness or proximity, which indicates an economy of exchange apart from difference, identity, and sameness: "From that ceaseless to-ing and fro-ing that upsets any opposition between here and there, from that endless embrace, from that 'in the self' and at the same time and same place in the other, and neither the one nor the other, neither the same nor its other, how is an idea to be had?"[11] This reserve prevents the two lips and the double syntax of language from merging into one, as it makes it impossible for (the idea of) the one to emerge and disallows the en-gendering of "one and the same." The excess and residue cannot be read in terms of difference, for the proximity is so radical that it does not let difference and distinct identities trace themselves. Its sense, its direction *(un sens)* is not cognitive but instead ethical, and as such it refuses to fold back into the specular optics of difference.

Both invoking and inflecting the issue of respect for otherness in Heidegger and Levinas, Irigaray conceives the ethical dimension of the relation to the other as an aspect of sexual difference. Challenging the Levinasian supersession of sexuality and eros by ethics, and its requisite substitution of "the son for the feminine,"[12] Irigaray puts in question the possibility of difference *without* or *outside* of sexual difference, and, hence, the possibility of ethics outside of an ethics of sexual difference. "Questions to Emmanuel Levinas" begins with the paramount query: "Is there otherness outside of sexual difference?" (*IR,* 178). This rhetorical question sets the stage for a re-sexualization of Levinas's notion of proximity, which signifies ethically but in a carnal manner:

> For Levinas, the distance is always maintained with the other in the experience of love. . . . This autistic, egological, solitary love does not correspond to the shared outpouring, to the loss of boundaries which takes place for both lovers when they cross the boundary of the skin into the mucous membranes of the body, leaving the circle which encloses my solitude to meet in a shared space, a shared breath, abandoning the relatively dry and precise outlines of each body's solid exterior to enter a fluid universe where the perception of being two persons [*de la dualité*] becomes indistinct, and above all, acceding to another energy, neither that of the one nor that of the other, but an energy pro-

duced together and as a result of the irreducible difference of sex. (*IR*, 180)

Irigarayan proximity is not one of absolute height and difference (as in Levinas's *Totality and Infinity*) or of the figure of the other under my skin—the irrecusable vocative "me" before any positioning of "myself" as the subject in *Otherwise Than Being or Beyond Essence*.[13] Instead, proximity is a sexual energy, a dynamic of "the irreducible difference of sex," which itself falls outside of and, therefore, cannot be read according to the logic of difference. Irigaray's opening query to Levinas resituates the question of difference within this new space of inscription figured as the ethical and carnal proximity of sexual difference. In other words, there seems to be no difference "outside" proximity: the possibility of thinking and maintaining difference becomes connected here to the unstable inflection of difference by the "energy" of proximity. The porousness of boundaries signified by proximity—"a fluid universe" of no precise outlines of the body and the energy of the encounter—serves as the "guarantee" of maintaining difference in play.

As Irigaray demonstrates already in *The Speculum*, the specular dialectic of representation, the effacing logic of specularization at work in texts ranging from Plato through Hegel to Freud has implicitly structured experience along the lines of sexual differentiation, only to erase this difference in the elevated claim to universality, to the generalized, always "the same," form of experience. In a section of "Plato's *Hystera*," aptly titled "The Misprision of Difference," Irigaray illustrates the attempt to control the specular optics in the following way:

> Being not simply a-sexuate or trans-sexuate. This is not to say that it explicitly re-marks one sex, or the other. Rather it maintains the partition without allowing itself to be cleaved by the difference at work there. For Being's domination requires that whatever has been defined—*within the domain of sameness*—as "more" (true, right, clear, reasonable, intelligible, paternal, masculine . . .) should progressively win out over *its* "other," its "different"—its differing—and, when it comes right down to it, over its negative, its "less" (fantastic, harmful, obscure, "mad," sensible, maternal, feminine . . .). Finally the fiction reigns of a simple, indivisible, ideal origin.[14]

The misprision of difference appears here to be an inherent feature of the differential economy, making difference a sublatable, effaceable effect of the multiple reincarnations of the same. Differential economy produces difference in order to annul it and deploy the very erasure in the service of its logic of unification. This logic of sameness, produced at the price of the double gesture of a simultaneous sexuation and desexuation of experience, forecloses the space of its own inscription and renders it off-limits to sexual difference. How effective this proscription has become is visible in the false equation of the problematic of sexual difference with reclaiming an autonomous, natural, or prelinguistic form of femininity, that is, with positing an essentialist conception of the feminine. Assigning femininity to the material, the bodily, or the natural, only to reinscribe and efface it within the universal sameness of the spiritual—the self-reflective and totalizing logic of the true—the economy of specularization renders experience specular and speculative, pliant and heterogeneous only to the extent that it enables, or in fact ensures, the "eternal return of the same."

To expose and counteract the misprision of difference at the very heart of the specular economy of differentiation, Irigaray deploys the trope of proximity, which allows her to position sexual difference as an originary moment of differentiation and yet to read it precisely as an inflection of the differential economy, located, as it were, "before" or "on the other side" of difference. Proximity, which has to be read as neither one nor two, destabilizes the logic of identity and difference, allowing experience, the body, or the feminine, to constitute itself only in proximity to and through a constant exchange with its other: thought (or language), the spirit, the masculine. As the figure of relationality that occurs otherwise than through difference, proximity interrupts and inflects the differential logic from its dialectical trajectory of completion. Proximity keeps difference in play in spite of and against the dialectical pull of sublation precisely because it remains, as it were, illegible to difference, refractory to its logic of separation and identity. It acquires the status of a passage, a between, never reducible either to the polarity of two distinct moments or to the suture of unification. Signified in Irigaray's work by the figures of lips that are "strangers to dichotomy," by mucosity, angels, and the sensible transcendental, proximity figures sexual difference as a "near-differential" modality of relating. Because of its mode of occurrence and its materialization as "neither one nor two," proximity is neither predifferential nor nondifferential *sensu stricto*. Inflecting and curving the symmetrical exchanges of difference, proximity positions itself, unimaginably as it were, "athwart" difference, deregulating the economy of differentiation.

Irigaray's rethinking of proximity emphasizes the double valency of the term in her work: On the one hand, proximity refigures the difference be-tween the sexes outside of the binary optics of difference as a nearness—as "neither one nor two"—which cannot be properly signified within the spectrum of differential relations; on the other, proximity understood as a resignification of the relation between the sexes beyond the reach of the speculum and the dialectic of mirrors produces a broader critique of dif-ference, an inflection in the differential economies of signification and re-lation. I read this constant overlaying of the two roles of proximity as an event of double materialization, in which *matter* is taken as both materiality and signification. This doubling allows us to rethink the split between the sensible and the intelligible as escaping and remarking the binary economy of speculative logic. The traditional division into matter and signification evidences gendering in accordance with the phallogocentric economy of thought, in which matter becomes "signified" as feminine and inferior, and the spiritual becomes coded as masculine. This sexualization of the divi-sion between matter and signification is deployed, however, only to be, Iri-garay shows, immediately effaced and speculatively reinscribed in the uni-versal, de-sexualized economy of thought. In order to expose this double gesture and to rethink the sexual morphology of experience in a way that cannot be effaced through the binary mechanics of difference and iden-tity, Irigaray proposes to see experience in terms of an event that "mat-ters" or "mat(t)erializes" as the unsettling and changing proximity between materiality and signification. The double valency of matter—what I call here the event of mat(t)erialization—reflects Irigaray's revision of experi-ence through the prism of proximity, where matter is "neither one nor two," that is, where materiality can neither be separated from signification nor collapsed into its discursive construction. Reading the event of experience in terms reminiscent of the feminine morphology of the two lips resignifies matter outside of the patriarchal discourse of modernity and links it to prox-imity, Irigaray's figure for the fluid and changing relation between the sexes. The dislocating and disruptive effects that the proximity of matter and sig-nification produces in the binary logic of separation operative in speculative thought become the places of the "originary" inscription of sexual differ-ence—inscriptions that resist the effacement mandated by "asexual" and universal economy of thought.

Irigaray's insistence on maintaining the material inscription of sexual difference against the dialectical logic that "dissolves" matter in its "spiri-tual" significations, thus superseding or denying it, an insistence which consistently deregulates and questions the specular legibility of experience, does not signify an essential (essentialist?) determination of experience by the body. As Judith Butler remarks, "the body signified as prior to signification is an effect of signification" and the presumed mimetic or representational status of language is, in fact, "productive, constitutive, one might even argue, *performative*" with respect to the body.[15] The body neither stands for an unmarked, prelinguistic plentitude nor becomes reducible to a set of signifiers. As Butler illustrates it in "Bodies That Matter," "matter" (related to both *mater* and *matrix,* and thus to the question of origination and reproduction) suggests an indissoluble link between materiality and signification, a constant tension that both differentiates the two senses of matter—the two ways that it "matters"—and effectively undercuts the possibility of a decisive scission between them (145). The occluded and opaque event of mat(t)erialization owes its ambiguity as much to the impenetrability of matter as to the tenuous boundary between materializing and mattering. Read by Irigaray in terms of proximity, this event envelops the double signification of matter, and resignifies—literally, de-polarizes—one of the most pervasive effects of this signification: the division between nature and culture.

To think of sexual difference it is not enough to conceive experience and thought as embodied, and the body, in turn, as already constituted discursively. This optics needs to be reversed in order to recast experience *as* the originary fission into the material and the immaterial, into the sensible and the intelligible. What I am proposing is that experience takes place as "mattering" in the double sense of the word. Two positions are put in question here: the idea that experience is originarily bodily, natural, and immediate, and, thus, somehow prelinguistic or precultural; and the approach in which the body is always discursively constituted and mapped in toto. Rather, experience first unfolds and transpires as the rift into the material and the immaterial, the body and the mind. Using Butler's terminology, we could say that experience in its always singular event performs the difference between the material and the immaterial. In other words, the rift between matter and spirit does not ground experience, but, *au contraire,* is always already an effect of the event, a sign that experience has taken place and articulated itself into the very dichotomy of materialization and signification. In this context, the proximity of the lips—both the figure of female sex and the "agent" of the refiguration of sexual difference itself, the inflection and the "half-open" threshold of difference as such[16]—begins to rewrite difference and experience through the double: material and signified morphology of the feminine.

Irigaray's mimicry shows how the event of experience, when read along the traditional lines of the feminization of matter and the spiritualization of the masculine as the universal signifier for all people, separates rigidly the feminine and the masculine: It incarnates them across the divide between the sensible and the intelligible, only to reclaim and cancel this difference within a higher claim of (spiritual) universality. Irigaray positions sexual difference as the erased (non)foundation of this logic of specularization, and, therefore, as the unacknowledged element of experience the occlusion of which has been necessary for the construction of the specular matrix of difference. To the extent that the effacement of sexual difference—that is, its characteristic institution in a manner that always already neutralizes the rift of this difference—ensures the efficacy of specularization, Irigaray's reinscription of sexual difference undermines the economies of experience produced and legitimized within the patriarchal discourse: economies based on the devaluation of matter, on the unified, "sexless" morphology of experience, on the neutral subject of thought. Irigaray refashions this conventional patriarchal matrix, deploying the difference between the sexes on both sides of the divide, doubling the matter and multiplying the significations, as it were, in a gesture that dislodges the feminine and the masculine from their fixed significations. Depolarized, both the feminine and the masculine become reassigned and redoubled across the matter/spirit, sensibility/intelligibility divide, as they both become the "matter" of those differences. The feminine is no longer just the province of the material, the bodily, the natural, or the maternal. Instead, it figures *across* the conceptual and discursive oppositions, spelling out a proximity between them that confounds the fixed economy of difference and distribution along polarized lines of sexual difference. The traditional tropes and polarities of discourse are both used to figure sexual difference and, at the same time, become themselves disfigured by it. Only through this double play of figuring and disfigurement can sexual difference be resignified, rematerialized and remattered, into a practice of proximity that cannot coincide with or be reabsorbed by the logic of polarity.

Remapping the crossings of matter—between the body and the mind, between the material and the intelligible—with the feminine and the masculine, Irigaray reinscribes sexual difference into the practice of thought, making the proximity of the multiple exchanges characteristic of her figuration of sexual difference the very space of inscription for experience. Experience as the event of the difference between the material and the intelligible is the matter of difference itself, that is, it signifies and materializes difference, *through* sexual difference. It "experiences" itself within the inflected optics of this proximity. This characteristic reinscription of difference within the optics of proximity makes it possible for Irigaray's thought to work parallel movements of projecting backward into the history, and unraveling the economy, of patriarchal discourse, on the one hand, and writing (toward) the future of experience, where the morphology of experience becomes articulated within the proximity of sexual difference, on the other. This double movement—the gesture of mimicry—forms the "avantgarde" moment of Irigaray's work: a new space of inscription, sexed or sexually differentiated through the inflections of proximity, a space where Irigaray's writing projects itself almost literally *avant la lettre* of the patriarchal discourse.

Technology and Sexual Difference

Irigaray's reformulation of sexual difference as an event of proximity has interesting, though rarely discussed, implications for the problematic of technology's influence on modern experience. Reading Irigaray's notion of poetics against the background of Heidegger's remarks about technology and *poiēsis,* I place Irigaray's poetics within the larger discussion of experience and technology and flesh out more concretely the critical implications of this poetics, often only intimated in Irigaray's few direct remarks pertaining to it. I situate Irigaray's poetics in terms of a double reading of the Heideggerian diagnosis of being within the twin fold of technology and art for two reasons: On the one hand, Heidegger's approach to these problems provides Irigaray with a nonmetaphysical space of inscription, within which the figurations of femininity and sexual difference can be divested of their logocentric determinations; on the other, the double axis of reformulation of experience *(Erfahrung),* technology and poetry, is rethought *through* sexual difference—not only to advance a feminist critique of the critique of metaphysics but also to bring forward the sexuate dimension of experience latent, as Irigaray suggests, in Heidegger's reflection.[17]

Heidegger defines technology beyond the notions of instrumental reason and calculability, as a modality of revealing, a representational-calculative comportment toward reality, constitutive of modernity: "The essence of modern technology starts man upon the way of that revealing through which the actual everywhere, more or less distinctly, becomes standing-reserve" (*BW,* 329). For Heidegger, technology, as either production processes of industrialism or the rational, scientific, and commercialist worldview, results from the already "technological" unfolding of the world as a standing-reserve of resources *(Bestand)*. The unfolding of the world into a standing-reserve determines the regulatory parameters of representation as techno-scientific ones, rendering the representational scene into what Heidegger refers to as the "enframing" [*Gestell*]: a manner of "unconcealment in accordance with which nature presents itself as a calculable complex of the effects of forces [that] can indeed permit correct determinations" (*BW,* 331). The problem that Heidegger identifies with the enframing is that it covers over, renders unreal or nonexisting, the modalities of being—specifically unconcealment as *poiēsis*—that do not conform to the "technological" standards of representation, that is, modalities whose occurrence cannot be represented in terms of ordering, availability, correct calculation: "Where this ordering holds sway, it drives out every other possibility of revealing. Above all, enframing conceals that revealing which, in the sense of *poiēsis,* lets what presences come forth into appearance" (*BW,* 332).

Irigaray's approach to technology seems more conventional than Heidegger's, as it primarily underscores the increasing mechanization of everyday life and the de-sexualizing effects of the gender neutral machine. Therefore, I rethink here Irigaray's take on technology and, inflecting it through Heidegger's critique of the *Gestell,* extend her remarks to the level of the structuring of experience as event. As Irigaray notes in "The Female Gender" from *Sexes and Genealogies,* "We are in the process of passing into another environment, which, for many people, replaces the natural one. For many of us today the technological milieu necessarily becomes the normal, everyday environment."[18] The historical environmental change reshapes the conditions and the milieu of experience, but it also leaves its stamp upon the structure of experience, instituting the regime of the everyday based upon the repetitive operation of the machine. Experience in the modern world is increasingly structured as a repetitive machinelike rhythm, a rhythm that dominates and orders the inappropriable temporal and sexual contours of experience. To the extent that Irigaray associates sexual difference with alterity that ruptures its own presentation and remains foreign to its own presence, the technological modality of revealing, based on the neuter, mechanical rhythm of repetition, effaces both the sexual dimension of nature and its becoming: "A machine has no sex. Nature, on the other hand, always has a sex. Obviously there are times when a machine mimics sex. And, moreover, machinery is more akin to one sex than the other, particularly in its status as tool" (*SG,* 107), and "The machine is to be trusted only if it repeats. When it ceases to be able to repeat, it is flawed, broken. Nature, on the other hand, does not repeat. It is in continuous be-coming" (*SG,* 108). Keeping sexual difference as the "matter" of experience turns, therefore, into the question of renegotiating the relation between technology and "nature," refashioned in the context of Irigaray's writings on the elements. The trilogy on the elements (*Elemental Passions, Marine Lover,* and *The Forgetting of Air*) reinscribes the materiality of the elemen-tal—air, water, fire—into philosophical discourse, deliberately confusing the boundary between the sensible and the intelligible and reclaiming the material from its abjected, "feminine" status. Such a reconstruction and revaluation of the elemental as the repressed force of fluidity and disrup-tion—a poetic insinuation of nonpresence into the specular logic of same-ness—allows Irigaray to dismantle "the solid mechanics" of the phallogo-centric logic and put into question its determination of the technological domain of experience.

I read the concept of nature which Irigaray invokes as a counter to tech-nology along the lines of Heidegger's rethinking of *physis,* which places the emphasis upon the occurring of being and its temporal destructuration of presence. The way Irigaray weaves this idea into the conceptual web of her work indicates that "nature" does not denote a pristine, pretechnological presence, the immediacy or transparency of sensible experience, but serves the purpose of renegotiating experience between the technological everyday and the elemental, poietic space occluded within modern culture. Irigaray's strategic mimicry of the patriarchal figuration of nature—its association with the feminine, the immediate, the fully present—dispropriates these figures in order to open a space of inscription for a new, nonmetaphysical conceptualization of nature as a possible entry into the poetics of sexual dif-ference. I would suggest here that the most productive reading of Irigaray's reinscription of the "natural" leads us to rethink Heidegger's "translation" of *physis* into *Ereignis* as the moment that opens modernity not only to the possibilities of self-critique but to an even more radical reinscription of sexual difference and materiality. This reinscription takes the form of ex-perience based on the feminine morphology of proximity—rather than on sublatable and specularizable difference—in which discursive articulations of experience would preserve sexual markers.

Although Irigaray often focuses her remarks about technology on the issue of the neutralization or dematerialization of gender in the mechanisms of production, the overall scope of her rethinking of Heidegger suggests that technology, as in Heidegger's thought, can be taken to coincide with the metaphysical underpinnings of experience. The question of technology is more than the conflict between nature and the machine, as it involves examining the effects that the technological structuring of experience has upon sexual difference. Far from being an external addition to "natural" experience, technology constitutes the very matrix of experience: Its demands produce experience as a gender-neutral pattern, where sexual differentiation disappears in the face of the repetitiveness of production: "The human spirit already seems subjugated to the imperatives of technology to the point of believing it possible to deny the difference of the sexes" (*SG*, 107). What troubles Irigaray most are the effects of the technological imperatives of uniformization and efficiency of production upon the sexual dimension of experience, which functions as a reflection, in fact, an embodiment, of the patriarchal ideal of the neutral subject/locus of being. As experience assumes the repetitive structure of mechanical reproduction, sexual difference becomes erased from it, since the permeable, shifting elemental significations of proximity fall outside the horizon of technologically reproducible difference. Sexual difference ceases to matter—in its double sense—within the general dialectics of the technological neutralization of experience.

Technology reconfirms and solidifies the effacement of sexual difference as the basis of the metaphysical systems of thinking. The technological modality of the unfolding of the world as a standing-reserve, constitutive of the experience of high modernity, becomes historically and conceptually possible because of the ostensible erasure of sexual markers from speculative thought. Reinscribing sexual difference requires, therefore, a new poetics of thinking, which, in a manner parallel to Heidegger's project, becomes capable of responding to the poietic event of experience foreclosed in the technological scenario. In the previous chapter, I developed Heidegger's diagnosis of modern experience in terms of the contestation of the everyday and the technological through a poietics of experience. This specific resignification of the poietic—where experience is seen as always dislocated, its occurrence disjointed and remarked by historicity—will serve as the venue for my exploration of Irigaray's poetics of sexual difference. For Heidegger, the occlusion of the poietic modality of being—its representation as irrational or unreal—surrenders the inscriptional space of being almost thoroughly to the powers of the technic mode of revealing. Such a (re)presentation and (re)production of experience makes possible the articulation of the everyday as a sphere devoid of, even antithetical to, the poietic modality of experience. What Heidegger categorizes as the technic eventuation of being institutes an effective separation between the everyday and the poietic, a division which, disconnecting the poietic, and with it poetry and art, from the ordinary, throws art into an impossible double bind: The technological either renders the poetic *a priori* ineffectual, by definition alienated from reality, or permits us to read poetic contestations of the everyday only as forms of aestheticization, as venues for an artistic escape from *praxis* and the "real" concerns of day-to-day living.

For Irigaray, the rethinking of technology in relation to sexual difference similarly requires a new ethical poetics of sexual difference which would be able to reimagine the relations between the sexes in a nonphallocratic manner: "Sexual difference would represent the advent of new fertile regions as yet unwitnessed, at all events in the west. By fertility I am not referring simply to the flesh or reproduction. No doubt for couples it would concern the question of children and procreation, but it would also involve the production of a new age of thought, art, poetry, and language; the creation of a new *poetics*" (*IR*, 165). What is never underscored in critical responses to Irigaray is that her "manifesto" for a new poetics of thinking and writing comes on the heels of her underappreciated critique of Heidegger's questioning of being in *L'oubli de l'air*. Discovering another layer of forgetfulness unmarked in Heidegger's *oeuvre*—the erasure of the "maternal" air, of the feminine and of sexual difference—Irigaray's book on Heidegger suggests that the rethinking of sexual difference is inextricably intertwined with the reappraisal of the poetic and the technological. The contextualization of *An Ethics of Sexual Difference* within Irigaray's entire opus indicates that it is indeed the thought of being, of the poetic unconcealment and the technological determination of being, that opens the space for thinking sexual difference in terms of proximities "that are strangers to dichotomy" (*IR*, 175).[19]

Similarly to Heidegger's rethinking of *poiēsis*, such a reinvention involves refiguring experience, against the techno-scientific determination of existence. Irigaray proposes this poetics of sexual difference as a contestation of both the culturally dominant logic of experience produced through the metaphysical ideal of sameness and the power relations instituted as the result of the double gesture of sexualizing and desexualizing experience. To the extent that sameness becomes associated with a techno-philosophical logic of thought capable of producing and sublating difference, Irigaray calls on the notion of a poetics to disrupt the operations of this logic and even to reinvent them so that the excluded or covered "feminine" significations—materiality, fluidity, proximity, "neither one nor two"—reemerge within discourse and remark sexual difference within the asexual space of experience. In the closing section of *L'oubli de l'air*, in a move reminiscent of Heidegger's remark from "The Way to Language" about the necessity for change in language as a prelude to the disclosure of the poietic dimension of experience,[20] Irigaray invokes the need for refashioning language in a way that would abandon the traditional schema of signification. She writes about the need to "abandon all calculation. All language [*langue*] and all meaning already produced. In risk" (*IR,* 218). This quotation is important for at least two reasons. On the one hand, it makes clear that Irigaray's critique of language responds to the idea of language as a disembodied social code, a system of signs in play on the model of Saussure's *langue.* In other words, Irigaray leaves ample room for refashioning language into a poetics of sexual difference, where the culturally available and historically produced meaning could be put in question and "exchanged" for a different map of "sexed" experience and culture. On the other hand, the quotation links the possibility of such a remapping of discourse to the abandonment of the calculative practices of technological culture. Such a double contextualization of the problem of the poetics of sexual difference makes Irigaray's ethics hinge upon a simultaneous contestation of both technological paradigms of experience and their reflection in the discursive practices operative in modernity.

The last section of *L'oubli de l'air* contains in its seven pages a web of allusions and critical remarks, from Heidegger's idea of the poet and Lacan's notion of the imaginary to technology and commodification, which Irigaray uses to weave a poetics of sexual difference. Characteristically for Irigaray's earlier work, *L'oubli de l'air* accomplishes most of its work through a concatenation of questions, poetic images, and critical points, rather than through a tightly woven discursive presentation. That is to say that Irigaray writes her text *as* a poetics—a feminine *and* feminist poetics—openly critical and disruptive of the argumentative and expository modes, codified by the patriarchal tradition of philosophical and critical thought. Any negotiation of Irigaray's work into a set of arguments incurs the necessary risk of forgetting and even effacing the very poetics that underpins and animates her project—the poetics that questions the possibility and the stakes of maintaining the translatability of the poetic into the argumentative. This is an obvious point but, nonetheless, one all too often neglected in critical encounters with Irigaray. For it is equally untenable to act as though Irigaray's ethics of sexual difference were not, first and foremost, a poetics, as it is to maintain that, because her work is "poetic," it forecloses its own critical potential, which even in some feminist projects seems to be arrogated almost exclusively—and in a patriarchal discursive gesture *par excellence*—

to the clear, transparent, and "logical," *prose* of argumentative discourse. There is no room here to rehearse the problems inherent in the division into theory and practice or the stylistic ramifications of this difference reflected in the all too easy identification of "politically engaged" writing with a certain style of presentation, which privileges "prosaic" transparency of language, logical coherence, and explicit invocation of the domain of politics, often to the exclusion of the attempts at revising the inscriptional space *for* politics that, like Irigaray's work, call for a new poetics. It has to be born in mind, however, that Irigaray's project of sexuating experience *is* a poetics; on the one hand, it reinscribes an "elemental," poietic experiential domain, which is either effaced, like the feminine, in the "prosaic" logic of technological modernity or safely contained within an aestheticized, irrational, space of inaction; on the other hand, it also reworks the specular logic of difference into the nonsignifiable proximity of the other and resignifies sexual difference into a new, nondichotomous morphology of experience.

It is more than fitting that *L'oubli de l'air,* which invokes Heidegger both to situate Irigaray's project within the broader critique of modernity and to resituate that very moment with respect to its blindness to, or at least inexplicitness about, sexual difference, would end with a meditation on the poet and poetic language. Characteristically for Irigaray, this section mimics the viewpoint of the male poet, of the "he who risks" evocative of Heidegger's poet of the poets: Hölderlin, in order to carry out simultaneous critique and redefinition of the poetic thinking proposed by Heidegger. Exposing the co-dependence between speculative logic and the argumentative and propositional language, Irigaray writes in a style that deliberately indulges in accumulating questions and syntactically fragmented or inverted structures in order to alter the morphology of representational space. Disrupting the propositional either/or logic of patriarchal thought through its fluid discursive proximities of "neither one nor two," this Irigarayan morphology of writing attempts to "resex" the poietic event of experience. It is already within this refigured morphology of discourse that Irigaray invokes and resignifies the Levinasian sense of radical alterity: "Immediate perception in an openness barred by no consciousness. Native bonds, foreign to any reflection. Being together before any face to face encounter in which evaluation is inaugurated. . . . No geometry, no accounts here. What opens up does not stop in any direction. No waymarkers in this total risk" (*IR,* 214–15). Irigaray suggests that the risk taken in the encounter with radical alterity allows for no road signs, no markers for the paths to choose; the exposure required becomes more radical than the listening to the saying of being, which, in Heidegger's text, is always interspersed with *Wegmarken,* with waymarkers. No decisive mapping, no alignment, no geometrical figuration is possible within the morphology of experience that refuses the binary schema of speculative thought.

Part of Irigaray's strategy consists in leaving Heidegger, Hölderlin, and Levinas unnamed: unidentified yet intimated through a nexus of terms and images evocative of their work. In this way, Heidegger, together with the unnamed figure of the male poet/philosopher, becomes both the point of view enacted and inflected by Irigaray and the other addressed by her text. This performative inversion adopted by Irigaray—a mimicry that doubles and exchanges roles—constitutes one of the most important aspects of her project. It marks the invention of a discursive practice which works through the nondichotomous exchanges, the in-betweens of roles and positions, rather than by establishing its own position, argument, or point of view. Irigaray's texts deliberately prevent, or at least render highly problematic, a "complete" identification of their argument, preferring instead to illustrate their points by enacting the textual and conceptual plays. This fluid textuality not so much "argues for" as literally "writes" a new space of inscription for sexual difference. This inscriptional space opens itself precisely in the passages and reversals characteristic of Irigaray's mimicry, in the proximities between Heidegger's poet and Irigaray's poetics, between being and the alterity of the other, between the masculine and the feminine resignified outside of the paradigm of negation and absence. The manner of writing which Irigaray adopts or, rather, invents, is crucial here. It goes beyond the matter of a style or mode of writing and shows that the mat(t)erialization of experience into the material and the intelligible itself has a "style," a poetic energy, which is not preserved in the argumentative-critical discourse. The poetics which Irigaray attempts to write exceeds the idea of an extraneous form or a device added to the critical "content" of her presentation, because it resignifies the event of experience as fluid, ruptured by alterity, and imaginable only as the in-betweens and proximities rather than as representational solids and discursive claims. If the "solid" spaces of representation become markers of the patriarchal logic that installs the masculine as the universal subject of experience, then the intervals and proximities of Irigaray's discourse reintroduce the feminine, and with it, sexual difference, onto the scene of representation.

One of the most important and remarkable features of Irigaray's work is her ability to reinvent philosophical and critical terms in ways that underscore precisely the proximity between the argumentative and the literary, that, in fact, render the very space of this interaction poetic. Irigaray's writing both makes an argument and presents a poetics in the same gesture, or, to put it differently, it makes its argument poetically. Although the strategies of allusion and playful indetermination constitute a vital moment of Irigaray's work, her poetics points beyond a "merely" poetic use of language. Irigaray's poetics replays her point that the bifurcation of discourse into the poetic and the philosophical (and subsequently into the technological, informational discourse of modern culture) and the parallel attempt to control language, already at work in Platonic dialogues, effaces the poietic dimension of being. It covers over the fluid morphology of experience which still reflects the "positive" significations of the feminine, quite different from its "negative" representations within the specular logic of sameness. This is why Irigaray prefers to enact her points by rupturing discursive practices and rendering fluid the boundaries between conceptual signification and poetic reimagining:

> It is lived, lavished without safeguards. Before the subject-object distribution — that effect of the means useful to an imperialist will on the part of man. The establishment of a market where nothing is delivered without being introduced into a system of exchanges that blurs or erases tangible reality in a speculative spirituality. No one encountering or apprehending anything without coming before the court of a general calculation, whose reign is all the more imperative in that numbers do not appear there. So it is with love. (*IR,* 215)

This paragraph is typical of Irigaray's poetics, mixing together cornerstones of philosophical thought (the subject-object distribution), economic (un)realities, and the imperceptible workings of techno-scientific conceptuality, with the issues of the materiality of experience, relations to alterity without safeguards, and love.

Already such a concatenation of various regimes of discourse and conceptualities regarded as incommensurate or foreign to each other deregulates discursive regimentation and suggests an inscriptional space of experience in advance of, *avant la lettre,* the already produced language and signification: "[W]e abandon all calculation. All language and meaning already produced. In risk" (*IR,* 218). What Irigaray sets against the calculative practices of "a speculative spirituality" and against the general regime of calculation that "condemns" experience to a certain techno-logic is the figure of love as the carnal incalculable *par excellence* — love that has no desire to either calculate itself or to calibrate its relations to alterity.

Risking and challenging the standards of meaningfulness and representationality, the poetic work of language intrinsic to an ethics of sexual difference resignifies the relations between the sexes on the model of an incalculable, reciprocally inflected exchanges which exceed the "meaning already produced" and the standards of visibility regulating the desire to will, to know, or to represent:

> From which there escapes the very content of desire. Unpredictable, uncoerceable. Free of domination—in itself or in the other. . . . A call in a will that wills nothing, but abandons all resistance. Responds without knowledge or intention which give account of obedience to anything. . . . Still innocent of appropriate(d) techniques. (*IR,* 215)

Composed mostly of sentence fragments, this paragraph undercuts the propositional logic of statements, the syntactical and rhetorical formulas that enable the "calculation" of meaning and the assignation of stable, firm, and "knowable" discursive positions. With empty subject positions, even the assertive modality of writing is turned inside out by Irigaray's work, rendered "unassertive" and "incalculable." The opening of syntactic structures through fragmentation and incompletion, coupled with the prevalence of questions sequenced into entire sections of her texts, marks Irigaray's nonpropositional, unassertive modality of writing.

The nonassertive language of this poetics is mobilized by Irigaray specifically against the calculating logic of desire, which she regards as the primary structuring force in the philosophical project of the West and, in particular, its modern incarnation: techno-scientific culture. Refashioning and sexing Levinas's notion of desire as uncontainable excess, Irigaray adjusts the optics of desire from lack and negation to the overflowing of proximity: "Objective and subjective lose their limits. Each one and all 'things' resting in one another, spilling into one another, without limits" (*IR,* 217). Desire no longer signifies an absence to be filled, recuperated, or "calculated," but an openness to the proximity of the other within an elemental, differentiated, and sexed dimension of experience. The risk at issue in the last section of *L'oubli de l'air* involves specifically opening thought beyond the "negative" economy of desire, and thus beyond the monological, "specular" desire at work in economy and technology. With the volatile figure of "neither one nor two" lips marking the proximity of the feminine and the masculine, where they find themselves dependent upon yet excessive with respect to their reciprocal determinations, Irigaray breaks the hold of negation and its speculative reversals over the articulation of experience. The prominence she assigns to sexual difference in the formation of experience disarticulates the uniformity characteristic of the technological morphology of experience, where the notion of being as resource provides the standard which renders the inappropriable events of experience representable in terms of productionist logic. Irigaray's poetics links the project of rethinking desire and sexual difference in terms of proximity to a wide-ranging critique of cultural practices: from language, thought, and art to economy, politics, and technology. Her frequent critical remarks about productionist logic suggest the importance of thinking about experience in a nonproductionist manner in an attempt to disconnect it from the dominance of the techno-economic logic, which forms experience in the image of production.

Risking the Specular Economy of Production: Women, Commodities, and Art

For Irigaray, both the economic operations of exchange and the technological paradigm of experience as production constitute the most pervasive and wide-reaching modes of the deployment of "speculative spirituality." Both have their roots in the philosophical paradigm of the distribution of being along the subject—object axis. Through her critique of the specularization of experience, Irigaray attempts to inaugurate a nonspecular poietics of experience, which approaches the bifurcation of "matter" as "prior to" the institution of the speculum and the dialectic of mirrors, that is, as the poietic "element" of experience which becomes covered over and dissembled within the subjectivist economy of being: "Before the subject-object distribution—that effect of the means useful to an imperialist will on the part of man" (*IR*, 215). Redistributing experience outside the patriarchal optics of the subject-object division, this poietics questions the very logic of distribution and the effects of domination it produces in the realms of thought, economy, and technology. With the interrogation of the phallogocentric logic of the philosophico-critical tradition undertaken in Irigaray's early readings of Freud, Hegel, and Plato comes also the examination of the spiritualizing logic of economic thought. Irigaray claims that economy presents and calculates the material conditions of production in a way that inevitably dematerializes experience. *L'oubli de l'air* considers economy in terms of "[t]he establishment of a market where nothing is delivered without being introduced into a system of exchanges that blurs or erases tangible reality in a speculative spirituality" (*IR*, 215). Economy works as an extension of the technological thought, of the speculative logic of philosophy, dematerializing experience for the sake of obtaining a general calculus, a generalized market where "being" can be calculated for the purposes of exchange and profit. Irigaray tries to rethink here not only the ties between the economic market and the technological calculus of being but the overall economy of experience—the very idea of experience as a certain *economy,* which renders experience specularizable at the expense of its unrepresentable dimensions, the feminine and sexual difference in particular. When economy opens the possibility of exchange and figures costs and profits, it does so by suppressing a cost that cannot be calculated or exchanged, a cost that ungrounds the very idea of calculation. To have an economy of experience, Irigaray argues, is to already have exchanged tangible experience and the mat(t)erializations of sexual difference for the profit of "knowing," for the infinitely marketable "speculative spirituality."

In Irigaray's view, it is the commodification of women that, historically, guarantees the stability of the social order, of the passage from nature to culture. It does so precisely through the gesture of the demat(t)erialization of experience, that is, through the erasure of experience as the fractured "matter," as the nonbinary proximity of the sensible and the intelligible: "*In order to become equivalent, a commodity changes bodies.* A super-natural, metaphysical origin is substituted for its material origin. Thus its body becomes a transparent body, *pure phenomenality of value*" (*TS,* 179). The double logic at work here renders women objects of exchange and prepares the ground for the eventual sublation of sexual difference within the specular economy of experience. The passage to culture, equivalent to the institution of the homosocial economy of experience, allows male subjects to maintain the commerce of women without having to take into the account the double gesture of sexualization and desexualization of experience, that is, without thinking experience as itself a matter of "exchanges" within the proximity of sexual difference: "A sociocultural endogamy would thus forbid commerce *with* women. Men make commerce *of* them, but they do not enter into any exchanges *with* them" (*TS,* 172). What makes exchanges as such possible is the subject-object distribution of experience, a parceling of being that guarantees the essential sameness of the subjects of transactions. This distribution conceives of the other as an object exchangeable for other objects according to a calculus that always holds open the possibility of totally specularizing experience. The exchanges between the sexes figured as proximity would not only disrupt the homosocial commerce underscoring the uniformity of being but also resignify experience as itself outside economy and calculation: "Without worries, for without calculation. Foreign to exchanges and business. Outside the market" (*IR*, 217). The model of experience I see at work in "Sexual Difference" would open a *poietic* reserve of experience, "free" from the logic of commodification and its "meta-physics." It would allow us to see experience as an event whose doubling "materiality" remains irreducible to commodities and speculative values.

If a commodity is an entity whose exchange value supplements its materiality in a way that introduces the metaphysical dichotomies into the commodity itself, then the specular distance inscribed in commodities leads in the end to the supersession of their materiality and to the satisfaction of the specular nature of desire: "The commodity, like the sign, suffers from metaphysical dichotomies. Its value, its truth, lies in the social element. But this social element is added on to its nature, to its matter, and the social subordinates it as a lesser value, indeed as nonvalue" (*TS*, 179). The exchange value of commodities, which is the representation of the needs and desires of the (male) subjects, codes experience with the male logic of desire. It makes it impossible to think of desire otherwise than as lack and negation, and excludes the figuring of experience as the proximity of the other (and her desires). In other words, commodification is a reflection of the monological dynamic of desire, of a paradoxical desexualization of experience. What Irigaray presents in the form of the poetics of sexual difference is an alternative reading of experience as an incalculable crossing of desires, which makes impossible the distribution of this proximity along the subject-object axis, and, therefore, preempts, as it were, the "production" of the relation to an other in terms of a commodified object.

To the extent that art can be thought on the model of a poietics that complicates and contests what we might call the techno-economic profile of being, Irigaray's notion of poetics also opens a new context for thinking of the relation of art, materiality, and sexual difference. If, as Irigaray claims in "Women on the Market," "*[t]he economy of exchange—of desire—is man's business*" (TS, 177), then the importance of art which "reproduces" experience as the event of double mat(t)erialization, and thus remarks sexual difference, lies in reworking the economics of desire that underpins symbolization. Thus, art can be seen as a "work" that unworks the techno-economic logic, remapping in the process the operations of desire. It is precisely for this reason that the work performed in/by art needs to be seen in terms of the disruption of the logic of commodification and its effects on art. In this context, I explore how the links between the logic of commodification, on the one hand, and the traffic in women and the erasure of sexual difference, on the other, allow us to rethink the work of art vis-à-vis commodification and sexual difference.

Transplanting into her work Heidegger's unstable opposition between *technē* and *poiēsis,* Irigaray reorganizes the stakes of this opposition through sexual difference and, in particular, through the ethical and political "risks" involved in respecting this difference. The final section of *L'oubli de l'air* certainly draws out and emphasizes the ethical undertones of Heidegger's notion of poetry, refocusing, however, the matter of poetic saying through the lens of sexual difference. In contrast to Heidegger, Irigaray's poet is much more explicitly willing to risk the poetic saying for the other, for the other whose alterity is not only gendered and sexed but signified specifically through these differences: "The only guide there being the call to the other. Whose breath subtly impregnates the air, like a vibration perceived by those lost in love" (*IR,* 217). What is risked for the sake of the sexed other is not only the poetics but also the technological "infrastructure" of experience, its reliance on calculation, the market, economic computation, and exchange. Far from being limited to language, Irigaray's poetics tries to break and revise "the foundation of the economic, social, and cultural order that has been ours for centuries" (*TS,* 170). This seemingly exorbitant claim originates from Irigaray's analysis of production, of the influence that the productionist logic animated by male desire has on the representation of experience: "[A]ll the systems of exchange that organize patriarchal societies and all the modalities of productive work that are recognized, valued, and rewarded in these societies are men's business. . . . The work force is thus always assumed to be masculine, and 'products' are objects to be used, objects of transaction of men alone" (*TS,* 171). Irigaray suggests that experience is produced in ways that "mediate" it socially through the symbolic order reflective of the male desire and consonant with the homosocial determination of culture. In short, through social mediation, the very paradigm of experience becomes coded in masculine terms, and the venues for understanding and articulating experience come to be determined through the subordination and devaluation of the "feminized" matter in relation to the "standards" of specularization. The poetics suggested in "Sexual Difference" would open the possibility of a sexuate ethics of experience by questioning how the relations between production, commodification, and calculation come to constitute the mapping of being in terms of the labor of male desire.

To the extent that the commodification of women becomes the model and the condition for economic exchanges, it also implies the paradigm for analyzing the commodification of art—in terms both of privileging the exchange value over the work performed by art and of evacuating the importance of the materiality of the artwork. In this context, reinscribing sexual difference and undercutting the exchanges based upon commodification opens the possibility of approaching art not through the binary understanding of matter and form but through the notion of double mat(t)erialization, where materiality and signification are understood in terms of their nondichotomous proximity within the event of experience. The link that Irigaray establishes between commodification and femininity can, in turn, be inverted in order to bring sexual difference to bear upon the poetics of modern art. The approach to art which can be developed from Irigaray's writings is a result of two factors: the critique of commodification and of the model of experience based on the specularity of male desire, on the one hand, and the rethinking of the opposition between the sensible and the intelligible through the poetics of the elements, on the other.

What Irigaray identifies as a necessary link in the logic of commodification is the abstraction from the materiality of experience, the distanciation from matter, the body, and the feminine: "when women are exchanged, woman's body must be treated as an *abstraction*" (*TS*, 175). To paraphrase Marx, the production of a commodity involves a suppression of coarse materiality, a gesture which replicates, Irigaray adds, the devaluation of matter/*mater*/woman throughout discursive, philosophical, technological, and economic practices. The commodification of art replicates this gesture of devaluation and erasure of the materiality of the work of art, of what Heidegger describes as the thingly *(dinghaft)* character of artworks. What is required to take art as a commodity and to invest it with exchange value is an abstraction from the work performed by art and from its inscription in the materiality of the artwork. As I suggested in the first chapter, the increase in the means of mechanical reproduction characteristic of art's function in modernity leads to the widespread commodification of art. However, mechanical reproduction also draws our attention to reproducibility as the modality of art's being. To the extent that reproducibility can be identified as the modality, the "element," in which art "works," the plasticity with which art reproduces its work disrupts the logic that enforces commodification and places art within the arena of exchange and calculation. Mechanical reproduction secures the possibility and provides the means for a rapid commodification of artworks, but it also, paradoxically, counters this tendency by highlighting the ways in which the historicizing modality through which the work of art "reproduces" itself disrupts and complicates the investment of desire in commodities.

If the logic of commodification proceeds generally by abstraction from the material existence of objects, from their function and their use value, in order to codify the labor of desire as the new exchange value superimposed over the object, then what becomes subordinated and effaced in the case of art is the very work performed by artworks. When art becomes a commodity, what is devalued is the indisassociability of the work performed by art from its sensible existence, that is, from the manner in which the work as which art reproduces itself is "mattered," conditioned and inextricably intertwined with its material. Commodification of art involves, therefore, the abstraction from the way in which the restaging of the historial work of art literally figures *through* the materiality of art. The commodification of artworks results in the occlusion of the material, experiential, and cultural conditions of the production and reproduction (reception) of art, conditions which, as I argued in the first chapter, all come into play and are configured in the specific historial work of art's *Gestalt*. The emphasis on the historicity of experience in the work of art becomes occluded and "exchanged" for the objectification of the monological operations of desire, which, transforming an artwork into an object, disregards and covers over what art is as a work.

The notions of use or exchange value do not appear in Heidegger's analysis of the poetic workings of art in "The Origin of the Work of Art," but it can be shown nonetheless that the essay constructs an implicit argument against the "appropriation" of art involved in the imposition of these values upon it. If Irigaray sees the use value as the moment of retention of the sensible substrate of the object against the pressure of abstraction into the exchange value, Heidegger's discussion of the differences between work, thing, and equipment leaves little doubt that even the notion of use value is already a form of the supersession of the materiality of things. Usefulness and reliability associated with equipment, in fact, constitute the equipmental modality of being by occluding the materiality of the thing transformed into equipment: "[t]he 'mere' [thing], after all, means the removal of the character of usefulness and of being made. The mere thing is a sort of equipment, albeit equipment denuded of its equipmental being. Thingbeing consists in what is then left over" (*BW*, 156). The process of making or producing equipment changes the constitution of the thing by inscribing it into the dialectic of form and matter. What is already implicit in the matter-form structure, however, is the eventual subsumption of the material into the immaterial, of the sensible into the formal. This is why Heidegger quite emphatically discards the matter-form structure as the optics for the discussion of the thingly aspect of things, that is, their "materiality": "Matter and form are in no case original determinations of the thingness of the mere thing" (*BW*, 154). In other words, the use value imparted to a thing when it is made over into equipment is already part and parcel of the conceptual operation that leads to the eventual devaluation of usefulness and its supersession by the exchange value. Usefulness functions already as an element of the economics of desire which desubstantializes entities and reinvests them with the objectified forms of its own labor.

This is why "The Origin of the Work of Art" will seek to place the work of art outside of the parameters set down by the "equipmental" economy of being. Early in the essay, Heidegger questions the generalized nature of equipment which serves as the paradigm for the representation of being in the technological age: "Because equipment takes an intermediate place between mere thing and work, the suggestion is that nonequipmental beings — things and works and ultimately everything that is — are to be comprehended with the help of the being of equipment (the matter-form structure)" (*BW*, 155). "The Origin of the Work of Art" links the poietic character of art to the possibility of thinking materiality outside the moment of its "forming," that is, as materiality that escapes the logic of "dematerialization" and the negative valuation implied in the matter-form distinction. Although the work performed by art cannot be understood in terms of the thingly character, it makes possible a reformulation of the question of materiality. "To be sure, the work's work-character cannot be defined in terms of its thingly character, but as against that the question about the thing's thingly character can be brought into the right course by way of a knowledge of the work's work-character" (*BW*, 194). What Heidegger suggests is that the rethinking of the work of art outside of the parameters of aesthetics makes possible a new appreciation of what perhaps can no longer be simply conceived as the "materiality" of being. The reinvention of the work of art characteristic of modernity becomes thus associated with the problematic of "rematerializing" matter, of reinstituting experience within the double fold of mat(t)erialization.

Insisting on the reinvention of the work of art outside of the matter-form structure, Heidegger's thought deliberately counters the effects of commodification; it provides the possibility of a very different "logic" of art's work, which exposes the conceptual underpinnings of commodification and presents "materiality" in a way that renders it resistant to the logic of commodification. Thinking in terms of both the use value and the exchange value is predicated upon a certain conception of matter, which tries to nullify the work performed by art and the manner in which this work "re-presents" things. Heidegger's claim that the work performed by art has to be conceived as poetic (as *Dichtung*) can be read as opening the door to rethinking being on a model alternative to the economics based upon the matter-form duality and regulated by a techno-logic. Such poietics of experience remarks materiality in a way that derails the operations of the meta-physical conceptuality already *en route* to dematerialization. It is probably most productive to see Heidegger's effort to overcome metaphysics in this specific context: as an attempt to inaugurate a thinking that would not be subordinate to the dematerializing logic of meta-physics, that is, to the logic the preempts the dual event of mat(t)erialization and represents it as an opposition only to specularize the relation in a reunifying gesture. To critique metaphysics is to think about experience outside this closure.

For Irigaray, the rethinking of the commodification of women entails a critique of this very same "meta" gesture Heidegger identifies, but from the point of view of the ethics and politics of sexual difference. Irigaray sees the logic of commodification as reproducing the metaphysical gesture that envelops and cancels materiality within the spirituality implied in the "meta" of the metaphysical thought. Referring to the patriarchal character of the social order in Western cultures, Irigaray claims that "[t]his type of social system can be interpreted as *the practical realization of the metaphysical. As the practical destiny* of the metaphysical, it would also represent its *most fully realized form*" (*TS,* 189). She diagnoses an inseparable link between metaphysics and the social order it produces, a bond that makes her see this social system as the "fulfillment" of metaphysical conceptuality. The critique of the specularization and effacement of sexual difference in metaphysics is, then, directly connected to the questioning of the inherently meta-physical gestures of the social, economic, and political orders. If we extend Irigaray's analysis to illustrate the link between the commodification of women and the commodification of art, we can set the stage for explaining how the poietic and performative force of art refigures mat(t)eriality and sexual difference.

Implicit in Heidegger's thought on art is the indispensability of the critique of commodification for the rethinking of the links between art and experience. Irigaray's work allows us to underscore the fact that such a rethinking must account for the double erasure of sexual difference: from the logic of commodification and from the poetics of the work of art. Thinking of the work of art outside of the economy of exchange takes us also beyond the technological modalities of representation, into the new, and Irigaray would say "risky," poietics of proximity. Irigaray's own work prepares such an approach through the familiar double gesture of the critique of commodification and the inauguration of the poietics of sexual difference. Where I connect Heidegger's thought on art and Irigaray's poetics of sexual difference is through the "different" trace of mat(t)eriality implicit already in Heidegger's work, through its double fold prior to the inscription of the metaphysical chains of oppositions. For the remembrance of such mat(t)erializations and their historicity can be said to be the very "work" performed by art, the work, which, in Irigaray's reading, entails a reworking of the ways in which sexual difference in-forms experience.

Art "works" through a poietic dynamic rather than within the economy of exchange that characterizes the operations of the social order. What "resists" the commodification of art in this approach is precisely the emphasis on the fact that the work performed by art "materializes" outside of the subject-object dichotomy, apart from the aesthetic appreciation of art. If the commodification of women becomes disrupted by the inseparability of materiality and signification figured as the proximity of the lips, the "materiality" of art does not, in turn, allow the work to be reduced to an art object and thus rendered appropriable as a value that can be exchanged apart, as it were, from the artwork and its material *Gestalt*. Because of how the double materiality inscribes historicity, the work performed by art remains excessive and disruptive with regard to the economy of exchange. Perhaps such a poietics should be thought in reference to what Irigaray terms the "economy of abundance" (*TS*, 197) as an alternative to the meta-physics of exchange. Irigaray's poetics of sexual difference indicates the possibility of the transformation of the social order, in which various relations, relationality itself, would be socialized nonmetaphysically: "Not by reproducing, by copying, the 'phallocratic' models that have the force of law today, but by socializing in a different way the relation to nature, matter, the body, language, and desire" (*TS*, 191). This poietics—"Foreign to exchanges and business. Outside the market"—is a rigorous critique of commodification as the modern incarnation of the metaphysical logic; it draws attention to how the operations and exchanges certified by such a logic turn art into an object in the patriarchal economy of desire and cover over the critical effects of art's work, the possibilities it opens for resignifying experience through sexual difference.

For Irigaray's poet, the task becomes double: both a critique of technology and an inflection of the poetic saying through sexual difference. This double poetic task illustrates Irigaray's move from *Dasein,* through Levinas's ethical other, gendered male in a replication of the homosocial bond, to a poetics of sexual difference which inflects both the Heideggerian and the Levinasian positions in order to resignify the relation to the other according to gender differences. Realigning the relationship between poetics and technology through the optics of sexual difference, Irigaray specifies a new venue for thinking experience: a venue where Heidegger's rethinking of technology and Levinas's radical alterity are redeployed beyond their intended scope and linked in ways that enable an alternative mapping of experience in view of sexual difference which has become resignified through the double valency of "matter." Irigaray's investment in writing *within* this poietics frames the philosophical, ethical, and political issues addressed by her work in terms of a certain poetics of thought and writing. It suggests that the project of rethinking modernity through the problematics of sex and gender involves placing the entire nexus of issues like experience, body, technology, and economy, with their ethical and political stakes, within the scope of the gendered poetics of discourse.

Part Two : **The Avant-Garde Moment in a Transatlantic Frame**

Poetics, Sexuality, and Revolution

4. Gertrude Stein's Poetics of the Event

Avant-Garde, the Ordinary,
and Sexual Difference

Gertrude Stein's writings are most often discussed in two contexts: as part of the "experimental" tendencies of the avant-garde or with regard to the question of feminist/lesbian writing and politics. Estimations vary widely in either case: from the acceptance of Stein as a precursor of contemporary "language writing," to Stimpson's reservations about Stein's importance to feminist/lesbian criticism, or Meese's counterclaim that Stein foregrounds lesbianism in her writing. Value judgments aside, these responses indicate that Stein's work poses the problem of the relation between the two "avant-gardes": on the one hand, the modernist textual practices and formal innovations and, on the other, the "avant-garde" of feminist writing, with its critique of cultural formations, sexuality, and politics. These two avant-garde moments in Stein's work illustrate the convergences between avant-garde textual practices and a reconceptualization of experience outside of the parameters of patriarchal discourse. Raising the question of Stein's avant-garde aesthetics in the context of feminist critiques of patriarchy and representations of sexual difference requires, nonetheless, two disclaimers. On the one hand, considerations of modernist aesthetics are now all too readily dismissed as a return to formalism or, worse, to the aestheticization of reality. On the opposite side, coupling aesthetics with feminist critique evokes easy generalizations about sexual/textual politics, the idea of an equivalence between aesthetic subversion and political critique posited in the wake of *écriture féminine*. At least since Toril Moi's in-cisive critique of the feminist reception of Woolf in *Sexual/Textual Politics,* the connection between textual and sexual radicalism, as well as its politi-cal import, has become almost a cliché in many feminist debates, easily acknowledged but not always carefully scrutinized.

Returning to the question of Stein's poetics, I want to complicate and re-vise the assumptions underlying both these arguments. I argue that Stein's avant-garde practice is never a matter of a formalist aesthetics, for it is en-gaged in remapping the very structure of experience, against the predomi-nant representational and linguistic practices, that is, against what Stein calls "patriarchal poetry." Moi's claim that an anti-humanist reading of the aesthetic categories invented by the patriarchal tradition would disclose "the political nature of Woolf's aesthetics,"[1] also opens the door for a nec-essary rereading of Stein, whose textually far more radical work poses a daunting challenge to aesthetics. Employing similar parameters to those of Moi, DeKoven's study interprets Stein's subversive "experimentalism" as a critique of patriarchal language and the systems of representation contin-gent upon it.[2] My reading reinterprets this connection between sexuality and textuality in terms of Stein's poetics of the event, that is, her refigura-tion of the everyday as a fluid nexus of events whose historicity calls into question the ideal of the stability and transparency of representational and grammatical structures. Such a recoding of experience requires a rethinking of language in order to expose and undermine a deep-seated bind between representational thought and patriarchal grammar. I suggest that it is within this juncture between experience as event and experimental language that we can see how the issue of sexual difference and lesbianism in-forms Stein's work, and does so in a literal sense: it "forms" and shapes the textuality of her works, for instance, "Patriarchal Poetry" or "Lifting Belly." To gauge the transformative effects of Stein's writing, one has to map the connections between her reappraisal of the ordinary, the notion of experience as event, and the question of feminine identity and sexual difference. These three interrelated issues define the parameters of Stein's avant-garde practice— they have to be considered jointly in order to recognize the place of Stein's poetics within the avant-garde revision of the work of art.

The two avant-gardes mentioned above interlace in Stein's text to pro-duce certainly one of the most provocative articulations of experimental poetics offered by twentieth-century literature. In order to begin to under-stand Stein's challenge to literature and aesthetics, it is necessary to describe how the textuality of her works reflects the relation of art to experience in its *everyday* temporal, bodily, and sexed dimensions. It is through the confluence of these issues that Stein's work, sorely neglected by most theoretical discussions of the avant-garde and modern aesthetics, becomes crucial to assessing the role of modern art and its relation to experience in the context of the critique of modernity. In chapter 3, I underscored the importance of the *poietics* of sexual difference in Irigaray's critique of technocratic patriarchy and its discursive regimes. At the crucial junctures of her project, Irigaray links the possibility of rethinking sexuality and developing a new culture of sexual difference to a reinvention of language, to a creation of a new poetics of thought: "If we don't invent a language, if we don't find our body's language, it will have too few gestures to accompany our story." [3] Irigaray's poetics is a matter of transforming the morphology of discourse: from the one dictated by the patriarchal representations of sexual difference to one reflective of a new, "ethical," morphology of experience respectful of alterity and sexual difference. This poetics rethinks experience through a nonpatriarchal economy of desire and sexual difference. As Irigaray remarks, it becomes necessary to reimagine the imaginary in order to "write" the diversity of feminine pleasure: "the geography of her pleasure is far more diversified, more multiple in its differences, more complex, more subtle, than is commonly imagined—in an imaginary rather too narrowly focused on sameness" (*TS*, 28).

It would be an oversimplification to claim that Stein's work constructs a similar sexuate poietics of experience, even though the issues of sexual difference and lesbian desire are central to the textuality of her key works: from *Tender Buttons* through "Lifting Belly" and "Patriarchal Poetry" to *Ida*. It would be equally inadequate, however, to disregard the fact that Stein, even when she does not explicitly treat sexuality or lesbianism, often writes it out as the question of language and literary code. Like other issues prominent in her work—experience, everydayness, naming—Stein's understanding of sexuality is never simply declared or given but always communicated through the forms of textuality she invents. As Karin Cope suggests, Stein's lesbianism is played out mainly in her subversions of linguistic and literary codes: "For 'the truth' of Gertrude Stein's lesbianism is certainly not disguised in any other way than in language, so if the manifestations of her sexuality look *like* language, this should not be surprising." [4] Similarly to Irigaray's poetics of sexual difference, it is Stein's characteristic reinventions of textuality that "perform" the most radical insights of her work. These insights are rarely rendered thematic or communicated as content, but are often produced by Stein's practices of rearticulating experience through the reinvention of language: they are, strictly speaking, the effects of her way of writing. Since her works become commentaries on the nature of textuality, the writing becomes inseparable from thinking experience as an event, whose everydayness is marked by the historicity and incompleteness of its happening. Stein's texts do not so much comment on the historicity that makes experience "inessential"—that is, *without* an essence or the possibility of ever becoming fully "present"—as they render the event structure of experience into the structure of the text.

In Stein's work, the thought of experience as an event links the question of the representation of the ordinary with detaching experience from the patriarchal framework of thought, as is the case, for example, in "Patriarchal Poetry." Stein's writings connect the inessentiality of experience with the fluid coding of sexual difference, with undercutting the rigid separation between femininity and masculinity installed by patriarchal modes of representation. In "Lifting Belly," such a writing out of sexual difference constitutes the texture of the work, the undecidable exchange between voice(s) that is/are, to invoke Irigaray, "neither one nor two." As I will show later, the notorious question of identity, "twinning," and recognition in Stein's work is bound with the problem of sexual difference and experience. Stein's complicated relation to the feminism of her days notwithstanding,[5] there is an undeniable link between her "radical poetics" and her interest in shaking up "patriarchal poetry" and rethinking sexuality; in her case, sexual politics coincides with the texture of writing.

Linking the questions of event, historicity, everydayness, and sexual difference, I see Stein's writing as a preeminent locus for interrogating the conception of avant-garde poetics proposed in the first part of my book. Since Stein's texts, through their various forms of textuality and language, reinvent experience as an event, they foreground the fashion in which avant-garde writing reworks the relation between aesthetics and experience. Her attempt to write without names forms one of the ways in which Stein tries to sidestep the structuring influence of metaphysical/patriarchal forms of representation, which operates already on the level of the linguistic constitution of relations. In order to show how these issues become interlaced in Stein's practice, I divide this chapter into three sections. The first one examines Stein's figuration of experience as event in the context of Lyotard's definition of the avant-garde in terms of the question "Is it happening?" and Heidegger's notion of *Ereignis*. The second part investigates the relation between the inessentiality of event and the radical refashioning of the ordinary performed by Stein's *Tender Buttons* and "Stanzas in Meditation." The

final section outlines the connection between textuality and sexual difference and develops the Steinian morphology of the text, which questions the
idea of (re)constructing experience in terms of narrative coherence and representational clarity, preferring instead to figure being as an event of unrepresentable proximity and destabilizing exchanges. Writing "Lifting Belly"
as a text that forms itself in terms of the body interacting and touching the
other, a formation enacted through the touching and mixing of voices and
words, Stein makes the body into an event, an occurrence "embodying"
the historicity of experience. Event, everydayness, and sexuality all become
critical elements of Steinian poetics, which I take to be a form of imagining
a nonpatriarchal morphology of experience. Crucial to this project is the
fact that Stein rewrites the relations constitutive of experience on the elemental linguistic level: relations between words and syntactical rules. Her
writing is a continuous redoing of the elemental relations structuring experience through, often literally, rewiring language circuits. The degree of
unfamiliarity generated by these operations is symptomatic of the radical
shift Stein's texts offer in the way we think of the "work" performed by art.
This shift marks the avant-garde moment of her writing.

The Event of the Avant-Garde

In his two essays on Barnett Newman's painting, "The Sublime and the
Avant-Garde" and "Newman: The Instant,"[6] Jean-François Lyotard defines
the avant-garde as the attempt to disclose the event-character of the work of
art, as the effort to move beyond the limit of expression and, interrupting
the conventions of representation, to inscribe in art the instance of happening. For Lyotard, the avant-garde coincides with the gesture of presenting
the unpresentable moment of art, that is, the elusive opening from which
the work of art emerges: "The avant-gardist attempt inscribes the occurrence of a sensory now as what cannot be presented and which remains to
be presented in the decline of great representational painting" (LR, 208).
The attentiveness to the performativity of the instant of the unfolding of
a world—to its becoming present—requires a departure from the system
of representation which has dominated both artistic sensibility and forms
of expression. Unlike previous art and literature, Lyotard claims, avant-
garde works no longer purport to represent the world or manifest its truth,
whether real or ideal, but instead examine the occurrence of the world's unfolding, the temporality of its constitution. The focus on the event and its
temporality displaces our thinking about art and literature in terms of struc-

ture and representation, accentuating instead the instability and heterogeneity at play in the unfolding of language. In a sense, then, the avant-garde work of art locates itself "before" representation, signification, meaning, and truth, and preoccupies itself with the very "element" in which representing and signifying become possible. I will argue that focusing on this element, its elusive "now," which has remained unreflected upon within artistic practice and aesthetic speculation, entails a radical questioning of the very idea of aesthetics, and a displacement of the forms of aesthetic categorization and institutionalization of art and literature. This is true insofar as aesthetics and its institutional practice require the erasure of the heterogeneous and singular character of the event in order to ensure the stability of the representational order and guarantee the transparency of meaning.

The avant-garde's subversive, even transformative, potential vis-à-vis aesthetic tradition comes specifically from its preoccupation with the event-character of experience and the impact that such a change of perspective has upon thought and understanding. When juxtaposed with the aesthetic ideals of the presentation of truth (content) or of the mastery over artistic vision (form), the avant-garde's preoccupation with the event may appear to be "weak," interested only in the apparent simplicity of the event's elementary "there is." Yet it is this simplicity of the event, as manifested in the minimalist poetics of Stein, Beckett, Białoszewski, or Coolidge, and a correspondingly sharpened awareness of the erasure of singularity even at the elemental—lexical, grammatical, syntactic—levels of the articulation of meaning, that puts in question the very practice of presenting artistic truth or producing comprehensive representations of reality. Paradoxically, the "poverty" associated with the indefiniteness and temporal unboundedness of an event provides the avant-garde with the room and the freedom to displace not only artistic ideologies and conventions but also the very aesthetic and cultural framework which has produced them. Though this issue lies beyond the scope of my discussion here, for Lyotard the performativity and radical singularity of an event is certainly not limited to aesthetics. In the context of Lyotard's writings on ethics, politics, and justice, the event is always implicated in the problematic of the absence of ultimate normativity and the necessity of judging without pregiven criteria.[7]

Within the avant-garde, the challenge to artistic norms implies also the undercutting of the linguistic, social, and cultural formations that have served as their origin and authorizing foundation. The avant-garde's contestation of aesthetic art and its forms of institutionalization consists, therefore, in producing postaesthetic art, in developing ways of thinking capable of replaying and reproducing the subversive unboundedness of the event with respect to the dominant discourses of knowledge, rationality, and aesthetic sensibility. Hence the project that Lyotard identifies in "The Sublime and the Avant-Garde" as "the avant-garde search for the artwork event" (*LR*, 209) is an act of thinking that directs the unboundedness of the event against the power of intelligence that would turn it into a thing or an object that can be represented, grasped, and understood:

> Letting-go of all grasping intelligence and of its power, disarming it, recognizing that this occurrence of painting was not necessary and is scarcely foreseeable, a privation in the face of *Is it happening?* guarding the occurrence "before" any defence, any illustration, and any commentary, guarding before being on one's guard, before "looking" *(regarder)* under the aegis of *now,* this is the rigour of the avant-garde. (*LR,* 199)

The rigor with which the avant-garde attends to the event is directed in particular against the objectifying tendency in thought — its "grasping intelligence" — and the way this predilection has shaped artistic practice: thematic interests, aesthetic precepts, and institutional forms. This is why this rigor realizes itself above all in the avant-garde exploration of language, regarded — whether we are talking about the language of painting, music, architecture, or literature — as both the vehicle of and the means of subverting the aesthetic inheritance. Since such a consideration of the event means attending to the unfolding of experience and signification, its poetics has to consider specifically how the play of language and meaning solidifies into structures that make representation and comprehension possible.

What is at stake, then, in the avant-garde's characteristic letting-go of the grasping intelligence in favor of foregrounding the open-endedness of the event is a mode of thinking that attends precisely to the nonsubstantive character of experience and its resistance to conceptual mastery. Moving language toward the practice of such thinking of letting-be is the main preoccupation of the later works of Heidegger, where his thought focuses on the proximity between the poetic and the philosophical or on what he himself refers to as "the neighborhood of poetry and thinking."[8] In Heidegger's late texts, this proximity between poetry and thinking serves the purpose of highlighting the event *(das Ereignis)* as the most significant problem that confronts contemporary thought. For in Heidegger the question of the event describes not only the philosophical crisis of metaphysics but, and above all, the historical predicament of technological culture, a culture in which the ways of objectifying and schematizing being cover over its event-character: "the work of modern technology reveals the actual as standing-reserve *(Bestand)*."[9] As "The Question Concerning Technology" argues, such a schematization of being where all beings, including humans, are perceived as resources to be calculated and utilized, as "standing-reserve," deprives experience of its heterogeneity and hence of the power to put in question and displace the forms of objectification that culture imposes upon it. Calling the calculative schema of being regulating modern society "technological," Heidegger shows how our dominant form of thinking—measurement and computation—obscures, almost obliterates, the nonsubstantive character of experience. To Heidegger[10] this always singular event of being has a poietic character, one of disclosing, letting-be, and opening, as opposed to the instrumentalization and objectification that are characteristic of the metaphysical/technological model of thought.[11] One way to think of experience as an event against the culturally dominant forms of perception and calculative or systematic reasoning is to bring into language, often by dislocating and estranging it, the poietics of experience. This is why in Heidegger's work from 1950s and 1960s modern art, and poetry in particular, offer resources for a critique of both the "technological" mentality pervading modern society and art and aesthetics, to the extent that, like technology, they represent reality according to the principles of the metaphysics of the subject.[12] Together with his work on poetry, Heidegger's idiosyncratic employment of language and philosophical terminology is motivated by the desire to disrupt these calculative and objectifying patterns of rationality and to accentuate the nonsubstantive moment of thinking—its poietic space in which thought lets its object be "before" it proceeds to grasp and represent it.

In Heidegger's view, poetic thinking is a response to the historical circumstances confronting modern society: the development of mass culture and its progressive rationalization, together with the effects these processes have had upon being. This aspect of Heidegger's thought is similar to Benjamin's or Adorno's work on modernity and its continued instrumentalization of experience. Faced with the cultural effects of modernity and its primary agent—calculative and systematic rationality—both Benjamin and Adorno turn to art for ways of disrupting the monological models of thought and experience operative in modern society.[13] The historically motivated thought of the event proposed by Heidegger requires that we begin thinking "between" poetry and philosophy, between the poietic and the technic schema of experience.

Gertrude Stein is hardly ever mentioned in the context of the critiques of modernity and the so-called aesthetic turn of philosophy, even though her work, more than that of Mallarmé, Kafka, Joyce, or even Beckett, is centrally engaged with the event, in particular with its bearing upon literary writing in relation to propositional (philosophical) discourse and ordinary language.[14] Lyotard is the only thinker who, against the backdrop of the avant-garde, underscores Stein's importance for confronting the limits of metaphysical thinking and language and for letting go of the power inherent in all grasping intelligence. In addition to devoting one of his notes in *The Differend* to Stein, Lyotard singles out her work in "The Sublime and the Avant-Garde" as exemplary for the avant-gardist preoccupation with the event: "In the determination of literary art this requirement with respect to the *Is it happening?* found one of its most rigorous realizations in Gertrude Stein's *How to Write*" (*LR*, 199). Even though Lyotard does not pursue this point about Stein, his remarks about the rigor with which avant-garde art and writing treat the event—the rigor that, by contrast with the philosophical-scientific exactness which relies on conceptual clarity and absence of contradictions, reflects the precision with which one attends to the unfolding of words and language—suggests the manner in which we can begin to articulate the importance of Stein's writing to avant-garde practices. What needs clarification above all is the extent to which Stein's idiom—its characteristic disfiguration of grammar and syntax and subversion of the rules of literary writing—is a response to the event character of experience and its erasure from linguistic practices.

I am interested in how Stein's unbounding of language, of the English word order and the play of signification contingent upon it, together with a deliberate elision of nouns and nominal forms, leads her away from representational language to a "thinking" of the event, as, for example, the section "A Vocabulary for Thinking" from *How to Write* suggests.[15] Stein directs this thinking of the event, of "intense existence" as she puts it, against the patriarchal culture around her, challenging its standards through her alternative literary practice. This Steinian "rewriting" of the English language—her practice of "naming without names"—becomes significant for the critique of calculative rationality and its influence on everyday life. Above all, I want to explore how the inscription of ordinary language in Stein's work serves the purpose of subverting culturally and linguistically coded patterns of experience and thinking.

No matter how variable in style, Stein's texts, from the repetitions and incessant variations of the early prose to the increasingly indeterminate semantic field of her later poetic writings, are characterized by the rigor and exactitude with which they attend to the event of writing, language, and meaning. Most important for our consideration, the playful rigor of Stein's work is a direct result of her approach to the literary text as the event of writing—of the unfolding of the world and its meaning through the "grammars" of writing. *How to Write* is emblematic of this Steinian project, because there she explicitly articulates the insights into the writing process elaborated in her other works—from *Tender Buttons* to "Patriarchal Poetry" and "Stanzas in Meditation"—into a poetics of the event. The basic premise of this poetics is that the rules and conventions of grammar—as a reflection of cultural practices and their dominant modes of representation—constrain the language field in a manner that, by nominalizing the event into an object of perception and identifying it with its represented content, results in the erasure of what Stein refers to as "intense existence." To counteract this power of nominalization, Stein claims in the first chapter of *How to Write*, "Saving the Sentence," that sentences, as the basic units of writing, have to be seen as the open-ended events of meaning: "A sentence has wishes as an event" (*HTW,* 18), and, later on in "Sentences": "This is a sentence if it is an event" (*HTW,* 144). Indeed, the whole of *How to Write* is constructed in a way that specifically foregrounds the text as an event of writing/reading. Divided into sections that read like the table of contents of a grammar book—sentences, paragraphs, grammar, narrative, and vocabulary—*How to Write* is composed mostly of fragments of sentences, cut and intersected phrases, that explicitly subvert grammatical and syntactical rules. Many chapters read as if they were composed of fragments of several sentences, intersected and run together into discursive blocks that vacillate between being sentences and paragraphs. Writing her singular "narrative of undermine" (*HTW,* 243), Stein successively undercuts, even explodes, syntactical, grammatical, narrative, and discursive rules and conventions, in an apparent gesture of liberating the event of literary writing from linguistic and discursive ("narrative") constraints.[16]

The result is texts that both unfold and spend themselves in the event of writing/reading, texts that are eminently performative.[17] Stein's way of writing deliberately makes it impossible for the reader to retain the text, to form an image or a memory on the basis of which one could claim to know, remember, or understand these works. Most of the time, there is no plot, no narrative development, no set of ideas or even an aesthetics or poetics strictly speaking, by means of which one could hold onto a Stein text. In fact, as *How to Write* playfully indicates by undoing linear progression and parodying argumentative reasoning, Stein refuses narrative and discursive emplotment as constricting the event of writing: "A reason for having re-fused a narrative for having refused a narrative for reason for reasons for re-fusing for reasons refusing narratives for reasons refusing narrative refusing for reason refusing reason for refusing narrative for reason refusing narrative a reason for refusing for refusing narratives narratives for a reason" (*HTW*, 268). Instead, the reader's relation to the text exhausts itself almost without reserve in the moment of reading—in the *event* of the text. Reading Stein's writing, especially in the case of texts like "Stanzas in Meditation" or "Patri-archal Poetry," one has the distinct impression that those texts are designed for the reader to slide in and out of them, without being able to remember what transpires in them or to reconstruct the text in one's memory.[18] Stein's literary idiom—its parody of sequentiality and linearity, its subgrammatical and subsyntactical "rules" of composition, its disavowal of nouns and thus of a conceptual apparatus—purposefully prevents the possibility of such a reconstruction, forcing us to read the moment in which the text transpires rather than to interpret or understand it.

This writing strategy allows Stein to focus many of her long poetic texts, and the reader's attention, away from the conventional nodes of writ-ing—content, plot, imagery, characters, and so on—and directly upon the process through which a text emerges and produces meaning. "Stanzas in Meditation," a form of language meditation upon the unfolding of the poetic text, places most emphasis upon the difference (and its erasure) be-tween the constituted text and the "space" within which the text is written, between the stanzas themselves and the event of writing:

> For they can claim nothing
> Nor are they willing to change which they have
> Oh yes I organise this. But not a victory
> They will spend or spell space
> For which they have no share
> As so to succeed following.
> This is what there is to say.[19]

In this one of the numerous moments of explicit self-commentary, "Stan-zas in Meditation" acknowledges that "what there is to say" is precisely the proto-linguistic space which words only spell and spend. In other words, this "semiotic" space, to borrow Kristeva's term, is accessible only as traced in words: It both marks (says) and spends itself in tracing upon words, grammar, and meaning.[20] Even though Stein remarks ironically that she (the I) organizes the text, what there is to say spells itself through the language play itself; it is not a matter of the victory of the subject or a unity of meaning but, conversely, of their rupture and displacement. The title of Stein's text suggests the necessity and the difficulty of keeping in play the distinction between text as object, with more or less determinable meaning/content, and the event of writing, with its unboundedness and repeated ruptures of constituted meaning. In "Stanzas in Meditation," the play, erasure, and reemergence of this tenuous distinction make up the poetic text itself; with the text understood here as the tension between the disappearance of writing as the event and the constitution of poetry as an aesthetic object.

In the "Gertrude Stein Notice" from *The Differend*, Lyotard emphasizes this tension in Stein's texts, and, because of its irreducibility to narrative frameworks or discursive commentary, correlates it with the Heideggerian notions of the event, happening, and Being: "In Stein's text, a phrase is one time, an event, it happens. The anxiety that this will not start up again, that Being will come to a halt, distends the paragraphs."[21] In an attempt to inscribe Stein in his Burkean-Heideggerian paradigm of the modern sublime, Lyotard seeks the motivation behind Stein's literary idiom in the feeling of anxiety and apprehension about Being, about the possibility of its coming to an end: not-being or death. However, I would argue that Stein's preoccupation with the event follows a somewhat different trajectory, in which the anxiety about the event's possible cessation gives way to the pleasure of its occurrence: "In the midst of writing there is merriment" (*YGS*, 54); or, in "Stanzas in Meditation": "They could have a pleasure as they change / . . . / They will stop it as they like / . . . / Liking it as they will / . . . / Nearly often after there is pleasure / In liking it now" (*YGS*, 317) and "Should it be mine as pause it is mine / That should be satisfying" (*YGS*, 347). Apart from explicit references to pleasure and liking, Stein's writing generates a sense of enjoyment specifically through its patterns of repetition and its continuous undermining and putting in play of grammatical and logical rules. In Stein's texts, anxiety arises in the face of the impossibility of imposing the strictures of understanding and interpretation upon them. When allowed to unfold in their own idiosyncratic way, Stein's works can be more readily described, as many critics have remarked, through playfulness, irony, pleasure, perhaps even *jouissance*, reminiscent of *écriture féminine*.[22] For even though Stein subverts literary and linguistic conventions in order nearly to bring to words the unwritten or blank space from which language unfolds, her texts derive ironic, often perverse "pleasure" from the linguistic play and freedom they induce.[23]

Bringing the poetic forward, onto the page, has to do in Stein with undoing conventional grammar and writing new, *poietic,* "grammars." Stein styles herself, especially through her "distaste" for and avoidance of nouns, as a grammarian in search of a grammar and a vocabulary for a thinking that would see the world in its "intense existence" as an event, rather than as a static collection of things or entities: "I am a grammarian," she explains in *How to Write* (105); section titles from *How to Write,* "Arthur A Grammar" and "A Grammarian," and the title of the essay "Poetry and Grammar" bear testimony to Stein's interest in playing with and undoing the grammatical by means of the poetic. In Stein's work, the poetic becomes synonymous with the intratextual space, so often evoked in "Stanzas in Meditation," which, by withdrawing itself, both lets the text constitute itself and continuously holds open the possibility of its own reemergence and rupture of grammatical and discursive structures: "Or only once or not with not as only not once / Could they come where they were / . . . / Letting once make it spell which they do" (*YGS,* 348). Related indirectly to Heidegger's thought of the event, Stein's "language in meditation" explores the space of writing in which the text emerges. The sense of an always already delayed grasp of the "immediacy" of the text, of the difficulty that thought has attending to and "spelling" its own presence ("Could they come where they were") is produced in Stein's work through the tension between the structures of literary language and their continually erased poietic intratext.

In "Stanzas in Meditation" and "Patriarchal Poetry," Stein attempts to bring this interplay directly to the surface of language: "For before let it before to be before spell to be before to be before to have to be to be for before to be tell to be . . ." (*YGS,* 106). After the first paragraph of "Patriarchal Poetry" announces Stein's desire to unfasten and "carry away" the structures of patriarchal language, poetry, and culture, the second paragraph, quoted above, begins to mark a space "before" words, before language has to spell and to be (as signification or representation), and thus to spell "to be." Trying to retain the performative character of this linguistic occurrence, Stein avoids nouns and undoes grammatical strictures to give her language more of a dynamic and an ever-shifting, protean, quality. The tireless repetition and variation of the same phrases—for, before, let it, to be—combined with the absence of punctuation marks, creates the impression of language in a melted state, free to combine and coalesce in ways unexpected, unacceptable, or even repressed by discursive practices. In order to spell what transpires "before to be before to have to be"—before language congeals into its historically and culturally authorized forms—Stein's texts engage, as it were, in their own form of cryptography, in the continuous process of transposing the space before words into the written text. As a form of intra-lingual or intratextual transposition, such writing aims to bring to words the erased, unknown "language," often sought by feminist critiques of aes-thetics—what DuPlessis provocatively calls the "Etruscan language." [24]

"Patriarchal Poetry" makes clear that it is in this poietic state or space that language possesses its most disruptive potential, one that Stein's texts induce in order to subvert, put into question, and play with not only literary or textual practices but also with the culture and society that have instituted them. *How to Write* suggests that Stein's reimagining of literary language has as its specific purpose the development of a new mode of thinking that would overhaul traditional ways of conceiving the world in terms of rep-resentation and signification. In "Poetry and Grammar," Stein proposes to subvert literary practice, especially its predilection for nouns and their defi-nitional function, by means of writing as it were apart from substantives and thus gaining access to the "intense existence" of things and the world: "I had to feel anything and everything that for me was existing so intensely that I could put it down in writing as a thing in itself without at all nec-essarily using its name." [25] "Intense existence" refers to things regarded in terms of the event—as the ever-shifting matrix of relations reconstituted into the singularity of its occurrence—rather than as objects endowed with an essence and definable by means of nouns or substantives. The intensity Stein has in mind describes the idiomatic character of each happening, the particularity of its configuration and circumstances, which are lost in the generality of linguistic naming. Existing intensely, that is, as always singular events, things evade grammatical and semantic categories, and Stein's writ-ing proposes to revise and adjust literary language accordingly. "Poetry and Grammar" offers then another way of formulating what in *How to Write* takes the shape of the poetics of the event characteristic of the avant-garde's challenge to aesthetics and focused on the unfolding of the world into lan-guage rather than on description, definition, and propositional statements. This difficult and elusive poetics has the task of finding what the last section of *How to Write* describes as "a vocabulary for thinking." This "vocabu-lary" extends beyond lexical items and offers, in fact, a matrix for thinking the event that would be different from thinking in substantive forms: in concepts, ideas, propositions, or, in short, in "nouns."

Reimagining thinking away from concepts and definitions, away from its practices of nominalization/objectification, and toward its poetic form, makes Stein's work central both to the avant-garde's revision of aesthetics and to the critique of modernity and its cultural manifestations. The relevance of Stein's writing is less in terms of specific representations, images, or cultural practices and more with respect to the very elements—linguistic, conceptual, iconic—that make up the order of representation. In *Tender Buttons,* Stein's implicit critique of the exclusion of domesticity and ordinary language from high modernist art takes the form of undoing definitional and descriptive patterns in reference to everyday objects, utensils, meals, and living spaces.[26] In "Patriarchal Poetry," it is not the images of femininity (with the exception of the sonnet) that Stein takes apart but instead the discourse of patriarchal culture: objectification, definition, possession through cognition, erasure of difference, linear progression, propositional forms of language. Stein often identifies these features with the "poetry of nouns"—the objectifying discourse characteristic of modern rationality—which, operating exclusively in terms of the name, the proper, property, identity, and substance, obliterates experience as event. Stein appears to descend in her texts to this elemental level of engagement with language in order to put her critique into play at the roots of language, as it were, where it can most disconcert and call into question language practices that other radical discourses still have to follow, even if their "content" may explicitly disavow and criticize them. This elemental linguistic energy that Stein's texts produce, her playfulness and irony, serve purposes that reach across literary practice, into its cultural and social significance and into the critical potential inherent in the social functions of art.

In "Patriarchal Poetry," the declared literary, cultural, and, by extension, philosophical aim is the resistance to patriarchal culture and its dominant "poetry":

> How do you do it.
> Patriarchal Poetry might be withstood.
> Patriarchal Poetry at peace.
> Patriarchal Poetry a piece.
> Patriarchal Poetry in peace.
> Patriarchal Poetry in pieces.
> Patriarchal Poetry as peace to return to Patriarchal Poetry at peace.
> Patriarchal Poetry or peace to return to Patriarchal Poetry or pieces
>   of Patriarchal Poetry.
> Very pretty very prettily very prettily very pretty very prettily.
>
> (*YGS,* 133)

Ironically playing "piece(s)" against "peace," Stein indicates the desire and the possibility of withstanding Patriarchal Poetry and leaving it "in pieces" rather than "in peace." Although Stein's poem makes clear that we have to "return" to Patriarchal Poetry, since there is no easy exit from patriarchal forms of culture and writing, the trajectory of this return and the shape in which Patriarchal Poetry will find itself depends above all upon what kind of writing one performs and upon the use to which one puts language.[27]

Works like "Patriarchal Poetry" suggest that Stein's literary practice moves toward uncovering the link between elemental linguistic configurations and their potential to both identify and explode the "patriarchal grammar" of the world: its matrix of the relations of difference, dependence, and power. As Stein indicates in *How to Write*, grammar holds the key to the order of discourse and representation that the tradition seeks to repeat and perpetuate. The repetitiveness of grammar, its insistence on following rules, reflects for Stein the cultural order that links stability with the figure of the father and with patriarchal power—the order of sameness, repetition, and predictability that erases difference. Sections of "Patriarchal Poetry" parody the connections between the orderliness of reason, military discipline, and the logical ordering of experience: "Patriarchal Poetry reasonably. / Patriarchal Poetry which is what they did. / One Patriarchal Poetry. / Two Patriarchal Poetry. / Three Patriarchal Poetry. / One two three. / One two three. / One Patriarchal Poetry. / Two Patriarchal Poetry. / Three Patriarchal Poetry" (*YGS*, 126). This sentiment is reinforced in the last line of the text: "Patriarchal poetry and twice patriarchal poetry" (*YGS*, 146). Stein's linking of this repetitiveness and predictability of grammar with the central role of nouns in language suggests that the everyday itself is "patriarchal"—structured and regulated by the hierarchical rules of representation that assure the dominance of the "more valuable" substantive forms of objectified knowledge.

At the same time, though, "Grammar is in our power" (*HTW*, 73)—it is open to revision, transformation, and rewriting, the operations that Stein's texts continuously perform on their language and inherited conventions. Identifying the phallocratic complicity of traditional grammar with the grammar of culture—"Grammar is contained in father . . ." (*HTW*, 99)—Stein counters the hegemony of this "patriarchal poetry" by bringing to our attention the disruptive and transformative power of language, especially of its poietic space. In this gesture, she points out the pertinence of the avant-garde revisions of aesthetics, even in their extreme, exploratory articulations, to the critical and transformative forces within culture.

Her writing allows us to identify the intersections of the "elementary" work that avant-garde artists undertake on the discourses of art (for example, Malevich in painting, Khlebnikov, Beckett, or Białoszewski in literature) with the issues of power, domination, and cultural monopoly. One could argue that it is texts like "Patriarchal Poetry" that show that literature is never, even at the apparent extreme of experimentation, purely formal or "for its own sake" and demonstrate how such elemental and seemingly confined texts in fact recode cultural constructions through their very mode of writing.

"Do Not Call It by the Name by Which It Is Known": Rewriting the Everyday

Redefining literary practice, Stein's project of dismantling and then refocusing language and writing through the prism of "naming without nouns" transforms our understanding of the ordinary. From *The Making of Americans* to "Stanzas in Meditation," Stein explores and alters literary perceptions of the everyday, often, as is the case in *Tender Buttons,* focusing on its most mundane and feminized aspect—domesticity. As Stein herself explains, the strategy of stripping poetry of nouns results from the need to approach things in their everyday being, their ordinary, even mundane, particularity, rather than knowing and appropriating them objectively, scientifically, or philosophically. If for Heidegger the elusive occurrence of the event creates apprehension about the philosophical idiom and its calculative, systematizing tendencies, Stein's idea of capturing in words the "intense existence" of things intertwines avant-garde literary practice with the exploration of ordinary language and its cultural conditions and functions. For Stein "intense existence" does not signify some elevated, poetized state—the aura of the extraordinary emanating from the art work—but, conversely, the quotidian, even the commonplace: "anything and everything." However, rendering everydayness in terms of the event requires the same kind of redefinition of the everyday and of ordinary language to which Stein's work submits literary language. This revision gains urgency in view of the fact that quotidian experience and its articulations in ordinary language are as much determined by the calculative rationality of the technological and patriarchal culture as are the categorizations of experience in specialized discourses, whether scientific, philosophical, or literary. For Stein, undoing the conventions of ordinary language is intertwined with the critique of the patriarchal grammar of the everyday and becomes a requisite for recognizing and reinscribing in language the event structure of (everyday) experience.

Reading Stein's revision of the everyday against Heidegger's work on poetic thinking and naming allows us to articulate better both the philosophical and the poetic contexts for Stein's project of writing without nouns. This connection between the redefining of the poetic and the ordinary in both Stein and Heidegger has been often missed or at least de-emphasized. It is rarely remembered that Heidegger's turn to poetry constitutes an alternative attempt to rethink everydayness, one that follows upon the realization that the philosophical categories that Heidegger applied early on in his analysis of the everyday are themselves the result of the same process of instrumentalization that has structured everyday reality. For Heidegger, poetic language, being the least instrumentalized genre of discourse, is capable, therefore, of revising both the understanding of language and the practices of representation.

Heidegger counterposes the paradigm of experience at work in poetry *(Dichtung)*—thinking as letting the world unfold and be in its difference and otherness—to the technicization of experience in modern society and to its reflection in ordinary language and the calculative thought of social sciences. The poietic, by which he refers not simply to literary language but, more broadly, to the unboundedness of experience approached as the event, is Heidegger's way of loosening the grip of technological rationality on both the organization and representation of being. What Heidegger calls "poetic thinking" involves, therefore, rethinking everyday experience and recognizing the performative singularity of the event—its poietic occurrence as opposed to its instrumental articulations within the regimen of calculative rationality. Because "metaphysical" thought, whether philosophical, scientific, or literary, is itself built upon the erasure of the "constant concealment" (*BW*, 179) at play in the everyday, it is incapable of rethinking the ordinary outside of the parameters it has already internalized in its own structure of reasoning. To the extent that this rationality has determined both specialized and everyday forms of discourse, the regulative notions of both philosophical and ordinary thought—truth, representation, signification—cannot register the "dissembling" in the ordinary. They overlook or erase its event-character, the fact that it constantly ruptures and overflows the forms of representation given to it—its "nouns."

In order to think the everyday as concealment and event, it is necessary to disassemble its dominant representations in both formalized discourses and ordinary speech as familiar, immediate, and common. This refiguration of the everyday is contingent upon the poietic, upon the ways in which poetic language exposes and undermines the restrictive conventionality of both specialized genres of discourse and ordinary speech. As Heidegger indicates in "The Way to Language," ordinary or natural language is as much implicated in the metaphysical constructions of reality as the idiom of philosophy; the use of "natural" or "ordinary" language provides only a false sense of liberation from the strictures of calculative reasoning while coming nowhere near recognizing the concealment characteristic of the everyday:

> For the "natural language" that perforce must be invoked here is posited from the outset as a language that, while not yet formalized, has already been ordained to formalization. . . . What is "natural" in language, whose existence the will to formalization finds itself compelled as it were to concede for the time being, is not experienced with a view to the originary nature of language. (*BW,* 421)

Erased and nonexistent within the instrumental conception of language as a means of representation and communication, this poietic moment of language is capable of inscribing the event character of the everyday. This poietic moment both precedes and ruptures the formalizations of specialized idioms and the apparent "informality" and "naturalness" of ordinary language.

Similarly, Stein's poetic writings employ ordinary language and everyday situations, though often in a parodic way which Heidegger would probably find difficult to recognize and accept as poetry,[28] in order to undermine the literary representations of experience and to expose the "false" naturalness of the ordinary. The best example of this is *Tender Buttons,* where Stein literally undoes "the poetry of nouns" and, parodying and deforming the definitional mode of calculative thought, makes the quotidian signify "intensely" in her journallike entries:

A Little Bit of a Tumbler

> A shining indication of yellow consists in there having been more of the same color than could have been expected when all four were bought. This was the hope which made the six and seven have no use for any more places and this necessarily spread into nothing. Spread into nothing.[29]

Set up as a catalogue of domesticity, a series of definitions of ordinary objects, foods, and rooms, *Tender Buttons* immediately proceeds to dismantle the categories and images according to which the everyday has been coded and constructed.[30] It is a text in which Stein attempts to "tenderize" nouns, precisely in order to break away from the complacency of ordinary language with the logic of representation and its "patriarchal grammar."

She defines the procedure for such writing as "looking at anything until something that was not the name of that thing but was in a way that actual thing would come to be written" (*LA*, 237). The entries turn out to be a subversion of the very schema of definition, as they dispense with the grammar of predication and erase the boundaries between subjects and objects. As sentence fragments, repetitions, and gerunds take the place of ordinary syntactic patterns, the focus of the text is transferred from the description of objects in terms of their characteristics to a nexus of active, verbal relations in which things are sustained and exist. Instead of naming things and turning them into substantives, Stein unfolds fields of verbal energy in which things "exist intensely." As she explains in "Poetry and Grammar," "As I say a noun is a name of a thing, and therefore slowly if you feel what is inside that thing you do not call it by the name by which it is known. . . . And therefore and I say it again more and more one does not use nouns" (*LA*, 210). The conspicuous limitation of the use of nouns in Stein's later texts and the prevalence of pronouns and modifiers with their indeterminate significations[31] make the emphasis fall on the verbal and the adverbial constructions, and thus on the event itself, on the happening or the occurrence rather than on its subject or agent: "Once not. / Once and not. / Let it be remembered that at once and once. / Let it be remembered / It is not remembered" (*YGS*, 105).

Reinforced by the use of commonplace events and stories and the largely quotidian vocabulary, this characteristic Steinian gesture redefines poetic language and returns it to the everyday precisely by dismantling both the language and the categories operative in the discourse of the ordinary. In *Tender Buttons,* the definiteness and stability associated with things and nouns, normally ensuring the clarity and efficiency of everyday communication, give way to a chain of verbal associations which, as in the entry entitled "A Box," undo the transparency of both ordinary objects and their expression in language: "Out of kindness comes redness and out of rudeness comes rapid same question, out of an eye comes research, out of selection comes painful cattle. So then the order is that a white way of being round is something suggesting a pin and is it disappointing, it is not, it is so rudimentary to be analyzed and see a fine substance strangely, it is so earnest to have a green point not to red but to point again" (*TB*, 11).

The ordinary appears to be as much a construct as the specialized discourses from which it claims immunity; it is in fact a corollary of meta-physical thought, determined by the same system of categories, values, and images. The ordinary is never immediate, simple, or pure, because ordinary language already locks us into the noun, only on the obverse side of it, as it were, from philosophical-scientific discourse. In other words, it is not enough to return to ordinary language, to abandon the idiom of the poetic tradition and reclaim the habits of everyday communication. Instead it is necessary to disassemble both literary practice and the structures of ordinary language and to show their respective conventionalities. Ostensibly returning to the discourse of the everyday, and repossessing its most ordinary and least "poetic" part—domesticity—*Tender Buttons* performs a defamiliarization or demystification of the ordinary and its language, in an attempt to circumvent the oppositional logic that underlies the distinction between the everyday and the extraordinary, between ordinary language and specialized idioms.

To the extent that Stein's critique of the noun has to do with singularity and finitude, as opposed to the "infinite" envelope of generality, her idiom is often seen as underscoring the immediacy of the particular: "For Stein the immediacy of language is not the immediacy of self-presence but the immediacy of difference as measure."[32] At the same time, this "immediacy of difference" is, paradoxically, notable for its indeterminacy and abstractness. Mixing immediacy and concreteness with abstractness and indeterminacy, Stein manages to interweave and foreground both the singularizing and the generalizing tendencies of language, rendering immediate the "general" scope of the singularizing effects of difference. Making this tension the source of textual production, Stein inscribes into the very working of her texts this par excellence philosophical problem. Her output then makes its own characteristic contribution to the problematic of the everyday and the common: Stein's everyday questions the ideas of common knowledge and transparency of communication, and subverts them in the name of the fluid and heterogeneous character of experience and language.

One of the links between Stein's work and feminist thought is precisely this critique of common knowledge or knowledge of the commonplace, which are said to somehow return us to a sense of a "substantive," even if only local, community.[33] Stein's articulation of the everyday explodes the notion of common knowledge by turning her poetics of domesticity into the arena for the problems of gender, femininity, and lesbianism. In her texts the ordinary is precisely the locale where conflict, difference, otherness, and oppression mark themselves. In other words, the local is the locus of difference: of sexual, gender, and language difference. "Patriarchal Poetry" associates the local with gender difference, with the feminine subverting the masculine (patriarchal) hegemony of sameness through the parody of its "mean" practices of erasing differences and imposing the unity of meaning: "Patriarchal Poetry is the same. / . . . / Patriarchal Poetry connected with mean" (YGS, 139). "Lifting Belly," through the contrast between homosexual relationship and married life ("Kiss my lips. She did. / Kiss my lips again she did" and "Lifting belly is so kind. / Darling wifie is so good. / Little husband would" [YGS, 19 and 49]), emphasizes the differences in sexuality, the pleasures and dangers of lesbianism diverging from the dominant heterosexual culture: "Lifting belly is good. / Rest. / Arrest. / Do you please m. / I do more than that" (YGS, 9–10).

To maintain difference and heterogeneity on the "local" level, in *Tender Buttons,* "Stanzas in Meditation," and "Patriarchal Poetry," the ordinary and the domestic become a place for initiating a different language: the poetic language "without names" as opposed to the language of communication. It is as if Stein were trying to say that common knowledge is itself a patriarchal myth, one that erases the particularity of differences, especially gender difference, not on the universal level but on the local one. Through her idiomatic strategies of writing, her innovations and transformations of language, Stein uses the ordinary and the domestic to undermine the myth of their familiarity and commonness. For in Stein's texts it is in the commonplace that difference, incomprehensibility, and indeterminacy arise. In these works, the ordinary vocabulary and everyday expressions lose their aura of familiarity, as they become the very agent of critique and exposure to the unfamiliar and the other. To the extent that Stein's is indeed the poetics of intense existence, the strangeness and unfamiliarity of her language both encode otherness and difference and keep the text open to them.[34]

Without ever succumbing to the allure of the rhetoric of existentiality, Stein's work fits well in the context of the modern preoccupation with the ordinary as a means of critiquing and displacing the traditional structures and concerns of thought: Wittgenstein's ordinary language games, Heidegger's everydayness, Białoszewski's poetry of the mundane, Cavell's ordinary. Stein's difference, though — the fact that the everyday in her work can be seen as both a poetic project and a feminist critique of culture — puts her writing in a unique position to expose the cultural ramifications of the revision of the ordinary and to avoid the temptation to aestheticize it. It is indeed vis-à-vis the issue of the ordinary and the common — the problematic that seems to be gaining momentum as a response to the thought of difference and multiplicity—that Stein's poetics can be of particular significance for current debates. If the "crisis" in philosophy—from Kierkegaard's existential concerns, Nietzsche's "aesthetic" critique, to Heidegger's thought of everydayness, Derrida's exploration of the interplay between the singular and the general, and Irigaray's ethics of sexual difference—has been precipitated by the issue of the everyday (existence) and the importation of the singular into the generalizing and universalizing idiom of thought, then Stein's work, her attempts to write the singularity of "intense existence," can be seen as a revision of the optics through which we approach the issue of singularity and commonality. Because of both her employment of ordinary vocabulary and her express attention to language and meaning as event, Stein's texts appear to be uniquely predisposed to explore the shifting linguistic and textual boundaries between the singular and the general. Her extraordinary sensitivity to the workings of the differential matrix of language and her ability to free language from conceptual, grammatical, and semantic constraints, coupled with her predilection for irony and playfulness, give Stein the most room for distending language so that it can attend to the critical demands that the event of experience places upon thought. More than any other avant-garde writer, Stein shows that such a change in optics is contingent upon linking the refiguration of the everyday with an avant-garde poetics, with a simultaneous undoing of literary idioms and ordinary language.

"A Measure of It All": Sexual Difference and the Pleasure of the Text

The sense of the inessentiality of experience which lies behind the fluidity and indeterminateness of Stein's language underscores the historicity of the everyday. Despite appearances of routine and ordinariness, everyday objects and occurrences in Stein's texts remain open fields, without essences or names, indicating only the radius of their happening. These two factors—the event structure of experience and the historicity of the everyday—determine the shape of Stein's writings and, in effect, define the relationship between art and experience. If Stein is "avant-garde," in the sense my study gives to this word, it is because her writings work out an alternative linguistic matrix to reflect the "nameless" ways in which historicity opens up the constructedness of experience. The notorious fluidity of Stein's language—fluidity that extends beyond the differential play of signification and the nonessential status of meaning to radical syntactic refigurations—

is a mark of "intense relatedness" which characterizes experience for Stein. To reflect the intensity with which such relatedness de-essentializes things and incidents and emphatically renders them into events or happenings, Stein deforms the representational structures and aesthetic conventions by opening up the English syntax to various alternative and "ungrammatical" configurations. As Judy Grahn puts it, Stein calls into question "our very basic patterns of relationship, at the level of linguistic relationship."[35]

The third element which informs Stein's rethinking of experience as a web of intense relations is sexual difference, and, in particular, the issue of feminine/lesbian identity. I mean "inform" here in a literal sense: sexual difference *forms* Stein's texts, constitutes their design and texture. "Lifting Belly" and "Patriarchal Poetry" show how femininity, no longer represented in accordance with patriarchal models of discourse but refigured through lesbian relations, offers an alternative way of constructing the very idea of relationship. Placed outside the binary opposition between masculinity and femininity, femininity in Stein becomes the basis for an economy of relations that undercuts the binary logic of identity. The characteristic blending of voices in "Lifting Belly" undoes the notion of the unity and discreteness of the self, and produces a text whose basic modality of relation reflects the intersecting and blurring of boundaries: a textual logic which departs from the norms of representation and becomes reminiscent of Irigaray's poetics of proximity.

Irigaray articulates her notion of proximity as an alternative mode of describing the relation of the self to the other, which eludes the dialectical scenario of identity formation. Irigaray's objective is to reimagine the relation between self and other(s) in nonbinary terms, according to a feminine paradigm which, unlike the patriarchal logic of identity, would actually preserve differences between the sexes instead of foreclosing or suppressing them in a homosocial economy of experience. Since the oppositional logic of identity and difference serves to enforce the homogeneity and sameness of both experience and language, only a radical reimagining of experience through an economy of proximity could break the hold that patriarchal discourse has on how we understand relation. Proximity, therefore, comes to signify the ruptures effected within the logic of identity by a femininity which does not obey the rules of sameness and difference: "*She is neither one nor two.* Rigorously speaking, she cannot be identified either as one person, or as two. She resists all adequate definition. Further, she has no 'proper' name" (*TS,* 26). Refusing the properness of a name or a noun and the adequacy of definition prescribed by representational logic, Irigarayan "she" undoes the clarity and comfort of oppositional and binary thinking: "As for woman, she touches herself in and of herself without any need for mediation, and before there is any way to distinguish activity from passivity. . . . Thus, within herself, she is already two—but not divisible into one(s)—that caress each other" (*TS*, 24). "She" folds the conceptual paradigms, which, obliterating sexual difference, enable the production of a discursive regime that, through the subtlety of dialectics and specular logic, infuses sameness into the heterogeneous event of experience: "The same attractions and separations. The same difficulties, the same impossibility of making connections. The same . . . Same . . . Always the same" (*TS*, 205).

What makes possible the avoidance of mediation, and hence of the inevitable dialectical assimilation, is the logic of proximity, which enables a discourse which works without the familiar parameters of "either one or two." The nonassimilational logic of "neither one nor two" suggests a different mapping of relations, one no longer based on forging links between definable and discrete elements. In "When Our Lips Speak Together," the figure of two lips speaking simultaneously and touching each other in an exchange which suspends both identity and difference signifies a space of relating which cannot be described within the representational regime of language. It is a modality of relating where neither identity nor difference matter, to the extent that one can never assert either one or the other: the very terms "one" and "other" cease to "mean" and be distinct. Instead, relating transpires as an event of proximity, according to a modality of exchange where economies of discrimination and definition have not yet taken hold: "Nearness so pronounced that it makes all discriminations of identity, and thus all forms of property, impossible. Woman derives pleasure from what is *so near that she cannot have it, nor have herself.* She herself enters into a ceaseless exchange of herself with the other without any possibility of identifying either. This puts into question all prevailing economies . . ." (*TS*, 31). Nearness produces the pleasure of alterity, of "touching" (upon) the other without assimilating it, that is, it instigates the pleasure of the impossibility of identity—of never completing or possessing oneself (or the other)—because of the other's touch. Irigaray makes clear that proximity involves a rigorous yet fluid exchange, a "nearness so pronounced" that it renders discrimination, in its many senses, impossible. It is a rigorous exchange where one can neither possess oneself nor distinguish between oneself and the other. Yet proximity means also that one cannot assimilate or cancel the other, merge the one and the other into the same: It denies possibility of representing human beings in terms of a plurality of discrete yet exchangeable, hence, the same, entities. In other words, the impossibility of discrimination remains distinct from the possibility (or necessity) of indiscriminateness or sameness. The rigor Irigaray describes refers precisely to a modality of relating which, without resorting to the terms of identity and difference, produces a relation of proximity.

The notion of proximity offers a feminist revision of the patriarchal/metaphysical logic of relating. The nonassimilative and nondialectical economy of relating epitomized in the figure of the two lips suggests, first and foremost, the possibility of a new syntax, a new "grammar" of thinking. Traces of the erasure of sexual difference and the exclusion of femininity internal to the patriarchal economy of the same disturb the pretense of achieving a total representation of experience and open the possibility of transforming the masculine discourse from within. Indeed, Irigaray is quite explicit about the need to provide an alternative to the patriarchal grammar of discourse and representation, to construct, in other words, a new language: "If we don't invent a language, if we don't find our body's language, it will have too few gestures to accompany our story" (*TS,* 214). Articulated in the argumentative layer of Irigaray's texts, this demand is also reflected in the styles and modalities of her writing, so evident for example, in "When Our Lips Speak Together" or *L'oubli de l'air.* My argument here is that a similar bind between a nonbinary and nonassimilative model of relation and avant-garde poetic practice exists in the work of Stein. This link would make Stein an often unacknowledged precursor to feminist revisions of the patriarchal order of representation. More important, this insight helps us construct the context in which it becomes possible to flesh out in more detail the links between sexual difference, lesbianism, and the radical textuality of Stein's works.

Since Stein's relation to feminism and its cultural and political objectives was complicated, if not conflicted, the debate about her place in the spectrum of feminist writing or about her importance for feminist critique is likely to continue for a long time. What should be emphasized in these polemics is the connection between sexuality and textuality in her work: the way in which her rethinking of relation on the basis of the proximity characteristic of lesbian sexuality feeds into how she constructs the matrix of relations that constitute "intense existence," that is, her no longer "straight" English or patriarchal grammar of the everyday. Objections to such an approach, articulated, for instance, at the end of Stimpson's "The Somagrams of Gertrude Stein," have to be taken with a grain of salt: "[Stein's] literary language was neither 'female,' nor an unmediated return to signifiers freely wheeling in maternal space. It was instead an American English, with some French twists and a deep structure as genderless as an atom of platinum. It could bend to patriarchal pressures, or lash against them." [36] The problematic supposition of a deep structure aside, the claim to its genderless status casts Stein's work as a recovery of a neutral core of language which can be refashioned and deployed according to one's intentions. Yet there is nothing more striking about Stein's writing then her attempt to play with and deform the "deep structures" of American English, to unwork and de-order the principles of word order and syntactical relations.

The bind between metaphysical and patriarchal practices of representation and discursive structures is so deeply embedded in language that it requires Stein to perform a kind of a playful rewiring of grammar: a double move of unmasking the historically gendered linguistic practices that makes them repetitions of the same, and of recoding sexual differences in ways that imprint themselves within language through a new grammar of writing. Stein's works are clearly about finding, or inventing, language resources capable of undermining the metaphysical horizon of intelligibility and questioning the accepted protocols of meaning. There is no a priori need to regard either the structures called into question or the means employed in the process of their dismantling in terms of a determinate and unchangeable essence: that is, as, in truth, either gendered or neutral. Yet, given the history of Western culture, Stein's challenge to aesthetics and grammar does become an anti-patriarchal gesture and the language strategies she employs, at least in "Lifting Belly" and "Patriarchal Poetry," can be described in terms of what Irigaray calls "feminine syntax." As "Patriarchal Poetry" or the following excerpt from *Everybody's Autobiography* indicate, Stein seems well-aware of the patriarchal framework against which she has to work in order to literally bring into words the new economy of relating constitutive of intense existence: "The periods of the world's history that have always been the most dismal ones are the ones where fathers were looming and filling up everything . . . perhaps the twenty-first century . . . will be a nice time when everybody forgets to be a father or to have one." [37] Both "Lifting Belly" and "Patriarchal Poetry" make clear that she also employs the subversive effects of a nonpatriarchal reading of sexual difference and lesbian sexuality to unground the representational economy of experience.

Among Stein's texts, "Lifting Belly" provides perhaps the most poignant illustration of how the feminine paradigm of nonassimilative relation becomes worked into the very texture of writing. As Chessman observes,

"Stein attempts both to call into her writing the female body and love between women more directly than in *Tender Buttons,* and to avoid reproducing the structures of representation in which the female has been constrained" (*PID,* 101). Chessman suggests that, as an alternative to the monological patriarchal structure of discourse, Stein adopts the model of dialogic exchange. However, the idea of a dialogue implies an intersubjective relation, an exchange between two discrete subjects willing to elaborate a common or shared space of interaction and intimacy. I would argue that, in "Lifting Belly," Stein goes *beyond* dialogical conversation, both conceptually and textually. The fabric of "Lifting Belly" is not so much woven dialogically as it is constituted through a "pronounced" proximity of voice(s) that remain "neither one nor two," and cannot therefore be described as either one voice or two distinctive voices in a dialogue. As Stein refuses to give the sexual/textual intimacy underlying "Lifting Belly" stable or clear representations, she also makes the voice or voices involved in the collaborative production of the text rupture the very texture of identity and dialogue. As the text indicates, "lifting belly" becomes quickly "mixing belly": "Mixing belly is so strange. / Lifting belly is so satisfying" (*YGS,* 13). The "confusion" of identity constitutes the basic text-generating device in "Lifting Belly," suggesting not simply epistemological uncertainty or representational crisis but a different modality of relating. The voice(s) remain indistinguishable because language in Stein arises out of the space of proximity free of the either/or logic, where relating takes place without the discrimination of identity and property. The whole point of "Lifting Belly" seems to be the construction of a textuality within such an economy of exchange that would operate without a foundation in a determinate identity or a representable difference, and, hence, without the requirement of nouns, naming, and definition. The text arises out of the "touching" of one voice against the other (itself?) and experience in it opens up through such "intimacies" and exchanges, which remain unsystematizable and overflow the parameters of the logic of identity.

Taking our cue from *Ida,* we can describe "Lifting Belly" in terms of a characteristically "twinned" textuality. The echoes of this strategy of writing can be found in other Stein texts, notably *Many Many Women* and *Ida.* In *Many Many Women,* after a series of repeated statements designed to confirm the existence of certain and discrete identities: "Each one is that one the one that one is," Stein suddenly reverses her position and demonstrates that "one" is never without the "other": "That one being that one was one needing something, was one needing something to have been that one. That one being that one was one needing something to be that one. *That one was not that one*" (emphasis mine).[38] Logically speaking, the last sentence is a contradiction. It comes as a sharp counter to the long, repetitive sequences in which Stein parodies the patriarchal penchant for the reiteration of the same. The text first plays along, albeit ironically, with the obsessive need to confirm and reconfirm the possibility of "that one," of a self-contained and secure identity, only to defy (patriarchal) logic and indicate the possibility of a nonassimilative relation where "that one is not that one." Stein suggests that difference is neither assimilable nor representable, and, as such, cannot constitute the foundation for determinate identity. On the contrary, difference continuously "twins" identity, splits it up, making it neither one nor two. This alternative paradigm of relation is indicated already in the text's title, as *Many Many Women* exposes the impossibility of the patriarchal ideal of a totalized representation of "the woman." The notion of "twinned" identity, ceaselessly recoded through the proximity of the other, frames also Stein's late novel *Ida:* "There was a baby born named Ida. Its mother held it with her hands to keep Ida from being born but when the time came Ida came. And as Ida came, with her came her twin, so there she was Ida-Ida."[39] Opening the novel, the scene of Ida's birth presents a paradigm of the origin of identity. Ida's identity does not come from a secure foundation of self-recognition, which would guarantee the presence of a stable and contained self. Instead, her identity is always already twinned—it comes into being through the proximity of its "twin," neither simply one nor two. The hyphenated and doubled name indicates the inflection of the self's mirroring and replication in the other. This rupture of the protocol of self-recognition marks the extreme nearness involved in the relation of Ida-Ida. As I already indicated, this type of proximity underscores also the peculiarities of the textuality of "Lifting Belly," whose rhythm is predicated upon the ambivalent exchange between neither one nor two voices.

Unlike *Tender Buttons* or "Stanzas in Meditation," "Lifting Belly" comprises mostly full and regular sentences, clauses, or phrases. The use of relatively conventional, for Stein, syntax enhances specifically the sequencing and the interplay between the lines composing the text. Most of the poem is written in a way that allocates each separate and usually short line to one sentence or phrase, presumably spoken by one voice. Because most lines are quite short, the text creates the image of a continuous shuttling between points (voices) that remain indistinct and ungraspable. This construction underscores the fact that what matters in the poem is how the lines enter into exchanges with one another: The text focuses itself on the interlinking of the voices, constantly raising the question of whether it is "spoken" by one voice in conversation with itself or by two or more voices: "Lifting belly. / What was it I said. / I can add that. / It's not an excuse. / I do not like bites. / How lift it. / Not so high. / What a question. / I do not understand about ducks. / Do not you. / I don't mean to close. / No of course not. / Dear me. Lifting belly. / Dear me. Lifting belly" (*YGS*, 7). The way this typical passage is constructed leaves various interpretations open. At first, it seems that we have here one voice conversing with itself, reflecting an interiority of consciousness which associates freely and asks itself questions — in a word, a characteristic modernist literary practice. It could be the case, however, that the text comprises several discrete voices, each thinking along different lines. Finally, the passage can be read, especially toward its end, as an exchange between two voices. It is worth noting that the repetition which closes this quote is a rare instance in "Lifting Belly," as though suggesting that Stein deliberately avoids the effects of mirroring and specular dialectics which often lead to totalization.

For the most part, "Lifting Belly" appears to be a mixture of sometimes anxious and tense, sometimes very ordinary, but also joyous and pleasurable, exchanges between two voices. In the first part of the text, the interplay between the voices focuses on the tension between describing and praising "lifting belly" and a clear resistance to even talking about it: "Lifting belly is so satisfying. / Do not speak to me. / Of it. / Lifting belly is so sweet" (*YGS*, 13). The tabooed and unrepresentable subject of lesbian relations is thus openly introduced by Stein as the site of conflict and the contestation of the social and discursive spaces of representation. In the subsequent sections of "Lifting Belly," as the proximity between voices and the intimacy of exchanges intensifies, this conflict gives way to sexual and textual pleasure, to the relishing of lifting belly: "Lifting belly for me. / I can not forget the name. / Lifting belly for me. / Lifting belly again. / Can you be proud of me. / I am. / Then we say it. / In miracles" (*YGS*, 46).

One of the "miracles" of "Lifting Belly" is that the voices register without "exposing" the speakers, that is, the speakers remain unseen or unknown, never firmly distinguished or graspable in the rapid concatenation of lines. What this strategy questions is the priority allotted to visibility, or, to put it more precisely, the reliance of experience on vision, or on knowledge and understanding gained through seeing. This is by now a very familiar gesture of questioning the metaphysical and patriarchal privileging of seeing over other senses, an interrogation of the familiar trope equating visibility with knowledge, possession, and power. In Stein, this gesture of subverting the priority of seeing is produced through various forms of undercutting literary and grammatical conventions; in other words, rather than forming a thematic concern, it structures her textual practice. The fact that her texts are staged as "events" that exhaust themselves in the moment of reading underscores precisely the impossibility of knowing or "possessing" them through interpretation. All these strategies can be factored into how Stein's writings unwork the aesthetics of seeing, based on various forms of perception reflected in the structure of representation and textual practices. One could say, therefore, that Stein's works are not scopic, but use other senses as models for their textuality. Certainly they undercut the prevalent scopic economy and its ways of signifying experience and sexual difference.

In *This Sex Which Is Not One*, Irigaray associates the undermining of visibility and scopic economies with feminine pleasure: "Woman takes pleasure more from touching than from looking, and her entry into a dominant scopic economy signifies, again, her consignment to passivity: she is to be the beautiful object of contemplation" (*TS*, 26). And later: "Her sexuality, always at least double, goes even further: it is *plural*. . . . Is this the way texts write themselves/are written now?" (*TS*, 28). Feminine sexuality and pleasure exceed the order of visibility: Within the scopic economy they can only signify through absence and, as Freud illustrates it, mean nothing. In order to give voice to this pleasure, a new mode of writing, a new type of textuality is necessary. It seems hardly a coincidence that "Lifting Belly" is about pleasure, about feminine and lesbian pleasure articulated through touch and hearing rather than through seeing: "Lifting belly is a miracle. / I am with her. / Lifting belly to me. / Very nicely done. / Poetry is very nicely done. / Can you say pleasure. / I can easily say please me. / You do. / Lifting belly is precious" (*YGS*, 42). Stein explicitly links the pleasure of sexual intimacy ("lifting belly") with textuality: "Poetry is very nicely done." The parallel between sexuality and textuality suggests that Stein's text is based on touching, its "sensible" texture is formed of senses other than seeing.

This is perhaps why both sound and grammatical junctures between words and phrases play such a crucial role in Stein's writing. Phonetic plays and the manner in which words link with and "touch" each other are clearly instances of pleasure: playful, ironic, and "belly well" at the same time. Since they so obviously undermine the "patriarchal poetry" of conventional grammar and ordered expression, these instances express textual pleasure, which in the case of "Lifting Belly" is quite explicitly recoded as feminine pleasure. A challenge to "seeing," Stein's language is one of listening and "tactile" effects, which produce a different grammar, as suggested in *How to Write,* excessive and uncontainable within patriarchal grammar. This excess marks a reconceptualization of the textuality of experience: a move away from a scopic economy toward a tactile one. As Chessman puts it, "A continuum emerges between a bodily intimacy and the 'composing' of this work . . . the literal touching of belly to belly enters into the writing" (*PID,* 104).

In "Lifting Belly," the female body—neither one nor two—and the lesbian intimacy of touching bellies, give shape to the rhythm of writing, the rhythm which operates on the principle of plurality: a plurality of the body and pleasures that, as Irigaray puts it, are "already two—but not divisible into one(s)." "Lifting Belly" continuously undercuts the idea of distinguishable voices which could be ordered into a comprehensible conversation and follows the rhythm of proximities produced by the text. It links Stein's familiar textual practices from *Tender Buttons* or "Stanzas in Meditation," where objects and occurrences lose the shape of entities and become webs of shifting relations, with the figuration of the female body. The link between the proximities of the body and the nearness to the other(s) characteristic of the event structure of experience suggests that the female body and feminine pleasure become the figures of Stein's avant-garde poetics, and the signs of perhaps the most radical "feminist" exposition of a deeply embedded correspondence between patriarchal representations of sexual difference and the conventions of grammar and writing. At the same time, this pronounced cross between textuality and sexuality draws attention to the possibility in Stein of articulating the body in terms of an event, radically marked by the historicity of its happening.

Thinking of the body as event, I want to call into question both the idea that the body is a mute, passive substratum of experience and the notion that it is entirely a historical product of social and discursive construction. Instead, I see the body in Stein as shaped by the event structure of experience, influenced and effected by the "touching" of the other(s). The body in "Lifting Belly" emerges and reshapes itself constantly through interaction with the other, through events of pleasure, conflict, anxiety, celebration. In Stein's work, the event can be approached as signifying nonessentialism in thinking the relation between the sexes. It writes the body beyond the opposition between biological essentialism and social construction, suggesting a much more fluid and highly historicized bodily morphology. One moment in "Lifting Belly" indeed seems to be an ironic comment about the desire for essence: "Lifting belly waits splendidly. / For essence. / For essence too" (*YGS,* 51). The question implicit in "For essence" gets a sarcastic answer, which grants, somewhat reluctantly, a place to the desire for essences but clearly denies it priority. In the context of Stein's preoccupation with "intense existence," this curt exchange acquires considerable importance as a typically playful revision of the thought of essence into the thinking of the event. The touching and mixing bellies, sentences, and phrases of "Lifting Belly" make the body the space of the inscription of experience as event, a text which "embodies" the historicity of happening. Apart from the historical character of the various cultural constructions of the body, we can also talk about the historicity of the body in terms of the body itself being an event which transpires according to an economy of proximity: as neither one nor two. Already double—both past and future—but never divisible into one(s), the body in Stein is marked by the futurity of its exchanges with exteriority, by the proximity to the other(s) marked in the relations that shape it without ever allowing it to grasp itself as "one." This active sense of the body as event shaping itself through proximity to the other(s) is emphasized by the quick turns and rejoinders characteristic of "Lifting Belly." The different modality of relating constitutive of the body is also marked by the suspension of conventional syntax which makes it difficult to grammatically order and parse long sequences of "Patriarchal Poetry": "Let her be let her be let her be to be to be shy let her be to be let her be to be let her try" (YGS, 120). If we accept this "pleasurable" mapping of the body as the source of the textual morphology of "Lifting Belly" or "Patriarchal Poetry," then we have to agree with Meese that Stein is indeed insistent about her lesbianism, though most often in subtle and textually complex ways. For Stein, textual figurations of sexuality require radical displacement in the conventions of language, which, in their ordinary and everyday expressions, duplicate the links between patriarchal representations of sexual difference and the clarity and orderliness of grammar.

The textuality of "Lifting Belly" is a counter to what Stein calls "patriarchal poetry," because it presents a dynamic of the relation between self and other outside the dialectics of recognition and assimilation. It constructs a "nonpatriarchal poetry," a poetics which subverts the patriarchal economy of meaning and identity based on the paradigm of visibility as knowledge, and substitutes for it the model of relations based on the morphology of proximity. "Between women" could be taken, then, as a model for nonpatriarchal relations of difference and exchange, for an alternative mapping of sexuality. In her writings, Irigaray introduces proximity as the figure for female sexuality and pleasure and, later, extends this notion to open the possibility of a nonpatriarchal representation of sexual difference marked by futurity and transformation. Her phrase "neither one nor two" becomes a critique of the identity paradigm, a questioning of differentiation and dialectical assimilation between consciousness and self-consciousness, the self and its other. The impossibility of ever being "one" and the "same" illustrated by the two lips indicates a different paradigm of relations between women: woman to (her)self, lover-lover, mother-daughter, sister-sister. What matters for Irigaray is that, as the figure for proximity, the lips allow us to think femininity and relations among women through a discursive practice that avoids the specular assimilations characteristic of metaphysical discourse. Beginning with the refiguration of autoerotics and homoerotics outside the homosocial logic, Irigaray extends the "non-economy" of proximity to delineate the structure of sexual difference in a fashion that would avoid collapsing it into the language of the same. This remodeled sexual difference proposes an ethics of sexual difference which cuts across homo- and heterosexuality, circumventing binary oppositions and maintaining differences through proximity "so pronounced" that difference remains, even *without* discriminations of identity and property.

Even if there is no such progression in Stein's writings, the textual morphology of "Lifting Belly" with its encoded lesbian sexuality does link up with Stein's revision of language and sexual difference in "Patriarchal Poetry." Chronologically, "Patriarchal Poetry" follows "Lifting Belly," extending the idea of tactile textuality to reconfigure female sexuality and, with it, sexual difference. As much is at least suggested in "Lifting Belly," when Stein asserts that "Lifting belly is so a measure of it all" (*YGS,* 12). Stein's trope for the proximity of the other, lifting belly is also her figure for the measure of experience, articulated in "Lifting Belly" through the event of multiple and fluid exchanges. As the measure of experience, "lifting belly" is closely linked with historicity and the refiguration of everydayness. Both "Lifting Belly" and "Patriarchal Poetry" are about everyday experiences: weather, current events, eating habits, emotional and sexual intimacy, and so on. Yet this very "comforting" everyday milieu is also "subversive," because it questions patriarchal versions of experience and identity, and, in the case of "Lifting Belly," models the everyday experience on lesbian sexuality. Fashioning the body and the intimacy of sexual relations in terms of event, Stein combines her refiguration of the ordinary with the rethinking of experience and sexuality. The end of "Lifting Belly" signals this intersection, linking the moment of sexual release with writing and the joy of happening: "Lifting belly enormously and with song. / . . . / In the midst of writing. / In the midst of writing there is merriment" (*YGS,* 54).

The intersections between the three factors—experience as event, revision of the ordinary, and sexuality—illustrate the complexity of Stein's poetics of the event. It is a poetics informed by a desire to inscribe in language an attentiveness to the excessive "inessentiality" of happening, and to recode writing in ways that allow for the "unsuspected" pleasures of circumventing linguistic and literary conventions and expectations. From the perspective of this poetics, even literary approaches to language appear "ordinary," ripe for a subversive play that attempts to tease out an alternative matrix of thinking, that is, of thinking (like) "lifting belly": "I do think lifting belly" (*YGS*, 51). I have illustrated some of the linguistic and textual parameters and effects of Stein's practice of "thinking lifting belly," identifying in them parallels between the revision of writing and experience. Fleshing out the importance of this revision for the critique of modernity depends on a broader negotiation of the avant-garde in the context of Heidegger's and Irigaray's radical rethinking of experience. Without such negotiations, Stein can be all too easily declared a writer of a disembodied textual space, with no obvious or immediate link to "external" reality or experience; and this apparent disconnection only intensifies with Stein's best, though also more difficult and experimental, texts. My contention is exactly the opposite: It is precisely in texts such as "Patriarchal Poetry" or "Stanzas in Meditation" that Stein's recoding of the structure of experience through "subgrammatical" linguistic operations is most convincing and successful.

5. History and Revolution

Khlebnikov's Futurist Revision
of Modern Rationality in *Zangezi*

The work of Velimir Khlebnikov (1885–1922), still known outside Russia primarily in the Slavist circles,[1] remains one of the most interesting examples of the characteristic avant-garde confluence between poetic/literary invention and fascination with science and technology. Much less known than Mayakovsky, Khlebnikov moved in the same avant-garde circles and was often regarded as the most important poet to come out of the futurist movement in Russia. This opinion finds its justification in the versatility and inventiveness of Khlebnikov's writings as well as in their extraordinary range of interests: from ornithology, geology, and mathematics to history and mythology. What makes Khlebnikov particularly important for my study of the affinities between avant-garde and technology is the fact that no other modernist poet is more seriously or explicitly engaged with a poetic project that relies so heavily on correlating poetic language and the scientific, mathematical idiom. This parallel is often echoed in Khlebnikov's call for a "science of word creation": "If it turned out that there were laws governing the simple bodies of the alphabet, identical for a whole family of languages, then a new universal language could be constructed for the entire family of peoples who spoke them—an express train bearing the mirroring words 'New York-Moscow.'"[2] The poetic possibilities of language, the new spaces they open for rethinking experience, depend upon understanding the inherent rationality of scientific conceptuality and its formative influence upon the very conditions of representation and legibility of modern experience. The intensity of Khlebnikov's mathematical and biological studies, his continued interest in explaining history through mathematical equations and numbers, is perhaps best reflected in Zangezi's monologue in Plane Six of *Zangezi: A Supersaga in Twenty Planes:* "Numbers, eternal numbers, sound in the beyond; / I hear their distant conversation. Number / Calls to number; number calls me home."[3]

In his obituary after Khlebnikov's death, Mayakovsky wrote that Khlebnikov was almost impossible to read, not a "poet for consumers" but a poet for producers, for other writers.[4] As Cooke suggests in his important English language study, *Velimir Khlebnikov,* this less than congenial appraisal from another futurist set the tone for an early reception of Khlebnikov, known at the time mostly for his neologistic poem "Incantation by Laughter" and for his invention of beyonsense *(zaumniy)* language and verse. With the publication of his *Collected Works* between 1928 and 1933, many misconceptions about Khlebnikov's work were dispelled, but it is only more recently, especially in the 1970s and 1980s, that his writings have begun to receive steady critical attention. Cooke's book-length study and the continuing publication by Harvard University Press of the translation of Khlebnikov's *Collected Works,* which has made accessible a large and growing body of Khlebnikov's work, mark a critical change in the English-language reception of Khlebnikov.

Khlebnikov was a leading figure of Russian futurism, arguably its most important poet, and a poetic and intellectual inspiration for the most radical strand of Russian literary modernism known as cubo-futurism. The cubo-futurists were a group of writers and artists which, in addition to Khlebnikov, included at various times the three Burliuk brothers (David, Nikolay, and Vladimir), Kruchonykh, Mayakovsky, Livshits, and Kamensky. The group first became known as Hylea, the Greek name of the part of Russia where the Burliuk family lived. Among its most important programmatic collections and publications were *Trap for Judges* (1910), "A Slap in the Face of Public Taste" (1912), and two short manifestoes, "The Word as Such" and "The Letter as Such," both co-authored by Khlebnikov and Kruchonykh, who used the opportunity to call for a new art of writing in which a poem could be based entirely on one word.[5] Khlebnikov's poetry, especially his emphasis on the word as such, was a response to the aesthetic of Russian symbolism and its preoccupation with what transcended the word. What started as contributions to early futurist publications, became a steady stream of poems, stories, plays, theoretical writings, mathematical calculations, and so-called supertales, which all culminated in Khlebnikov's late masterpiece, *Zangezi,* printed in 1922, shortly before his death. This often ironic text, constructed in twenty language planes, presents Khlebnikov's theories of language, time, and history through his alter ego Zangezi. Because of *Zangezi'*s importance in Khlebnikov's *oeuvre,* its almost paradigmatic status in relation to the characteristic futurist exploration of the possibilities of language and signification, I make this text the linchpin of my analysis.

Dissatisfied with the label "futurism," in part at least because of its association with Italian futurism, Khlebnikov coined his own alternative, a Russian neologism *budetlyanstvo* (from the word *budet,* it will be), a kind of a domain of "what will be." This region of *budet* specifies a future time which Khlebnikov imagines in his many "prophetic" texts about radio, future language, architecture, and so on, but it also refers, I suggest, to a certain futurity inscribed in the structure of experience, to a nonsynchrony which marks language's relation to meaning and presence. It is through the word creation and the exploration of the possibilities for "beyonsense" meaning in Russian that Khlebnikov's writings open this space of futurity within the present. These efforts to open, and preserve as "beyonsense," this futurity of experience must be read together with Khlebnikov's preoccupation with science and mathematical calculations, and yet also as a challenge to the technical organization of being in modernity.

Khlebnikov's extravagant and idiosyncratic claims about mathematical laws of historical development, repeatedly voiced in his essays and theoretical writings, lead critics like Jean-Claude Lanne to read his work in terms of an ultrarationalist language: a poetic/literary language which, using scientific knowledge, becomes more rational than science itself. Together with a mathematical conception of time and history, such a language discovers the essence of rationality itself.[6] It is indeed possible to interpret Khlebnikov's notorious quest for a numerical conception of history and for a poetic language capable of rendering it in new words and syntax as fully explainable within the scientistic, techno-rational paradigm of modern experience. Khlebnikov's inquiry would be, then, largely in agreement with Picabia's statement about the technological soul of modern art, which projects art as a reflection and development of the technological "essence" of being. However, when the emphasis is placed solely on rendering history in mathematical formulas and the companion procedure of compressing language into a system of "most significant" syllables and letters of high semantic and cultural density, it is all too easy to forget Khlebnikov's interrogation of the very limits of scientific rationality. These limits are tested and transgressed by a poetic language that specifically refigures the historicity of experience as event beyond the rational. As the Russian term *заум* suggests, this is an event beyond the parameters of sense and established meaning. Focusing on one of Khlebnikov's last texts, *Zangezi,* I will argue that this other, and sometimes self-ironic, strand, works against the overtly scientific and frequently pedagogical posture Khlebnikov assumes. As the ultimate prophet-scientist of nearly mythical proportions, Khlebnikov's poet finds himself in conflict with the uncontrollable, singular contours of experience, which he tries to master through poetic formulas, paradoxically approximating in their scientific exactness the power of magical incantation. It is this contestation over the poetic space between these two directions in his writings that makes Khlebnikov's work so important to the question of poetry's role in understanding experience in modernity.

Perhaps the most poignant indication of this tendency to transgress rationality and invert it against itself is Khlebnikov's description of the temporality of experience as an event by reference to an "impossible" number $\sqrt{-1}$, a number which indicates a temporal structure beyond the binary opposition of presence and absence and points to a (non-)time that falls outside the scope of representation. This peculiar "nonorigin" dislocates experience, rendering it noncontemporaneous with itself. Because of this noncoincidence, experience finds itself always "out-of-joint" with the very space of representation. This form of experience, which both *is* and *is not* representable, or becomes representable only as the impossibility of its own presentation, provides the fold or the scaffolding (*основа*) for thought—the space of visibility where representation, even rationality itself, as a Russian critic, Duganov, suggests, become possible.[7] Against the idea of rationality and the speculative matrix of experience, the number $\sqrt{-1}$ functions as the preeminent figure of the beyonsense language (*заум, zaum*) at work in Khlebnikov's writings. I read it as the sign of a poetic rethinking of experience that reaches beyond (*за/za*) reason (*ум/um*) toward a poietic, "beyonsense" configuration of experience. In order to open language to the possibility of experience that unfolds as "beyonsense," without at the same time collapsing beyonsense into the irrational, I link the exploration of the poietic (beyonsense) dimension of language with the historicity of event and its political implications. In this context, I propose a different reading of Khlebnikov's engagement with mathematics: as the sign of employing the resources of science, and its paradigms of (re)presenting experience and being, within a poetic enterprise that opens an alternative event temporality of experience. Seeking parallels between scientific imagination and poetic writing, Khlebnikov's language inscribes what Heidegger calls the technic modality of revealing—in which experience transpires as the ordering of the world into a standing-reserve at the willful disposal of the technological subject—into another "meaning" of experience, whose sense becomes legible only at/as the limit of signification.

It is this tension between the idea of technology as the overall framework of Khlebnikov's work—a feature generally characteristic of futurist art—and an alternative interpretation which sees techno-scientific rationality as complicated and questioned by Khlebnikov's poetry, that I would like to explore here, placing a particular emphasis on the link between Khlebnikov's understanding of language and historicity. I want to develop the links between *zaum* and the conception of the event which takes shape inseparably from language: that is, as both articulated, "presented," into words and dislocated beyond the constancy of presence by this articulation. This approach underscores the importance of the event for Khlebnikov's conception of history and revolution, and allows us to think the historical relevance of the poietic, or *zaumniy,* moment of experience. I understand historicity here in terms of a fold of history, or as the "space-time" of historical occurrences. It instantiates a dislocating movement of historialization, through which being becomes history, and, as being, remains incompatible with the order of representation. Historicity both makes it possible to read being as history and does not allow history to be conflated with the field of experience. In the context of Khlebnikov's writings, the task of poetry is to think historicity "beyonsense," that is, as located at the limits of representation and the rational-calculative organization of being. Always on the edge of history, historicity both inaugurates the event and withdraws, as it were, to the reverse side of what becomes present and meaningful. I read Khlebnikov's conception of *zaum* as a form of the aesthetic critique of modernity, in which his linguistic innovations amplify the effects of historicity within syntax and semantics. They reinscribe the "translation" of experience into language by making historicity into the verso of sense, into a beyonsense fold of signification.

It is in the context of beyonsense that one should read Khlebnikov's "futurian" visions and consider how in his poetic experiment the very possibility of thinking future as revolution hinges upon historicity. One of the effects of Khlebnikov's decomposition of words into multiply signifying, often semantically overdetermined, syllables and letters is the inscription of noncoincidence and openness into the structure of experience. This inscription is also reflected in how he subsequently recombines these linguistic elements into a different pattern of legibility. As a result, experience loses "substance" and becomes detached from the constancy of the present, extracted from the uniform continuum of time. The way Khlebnikov conditions legibility in linguistic noncoincidence and difference both complicates the modernist gesture that renders interpretation problematic and locates in historicity the moment of the inscription of the future within the present. Khlebnikov's work allows us to clarify the relation between the historicity of the event and the possibility of transformation or revolution, that is, between an absence or a nonpresence around which the present is always configured and the opening to the new. His writing both projects itself into the future, proposing a new or utopian vision of what is to come, and investigates the very conditions of futurity opening itself within the disjunctive structure of experience.

I argue that Khlebnikov's conception of futurianity *(budetlyanstvo)* relies specifically upon understanding experience as opening to a future which is marked within the present as the noncoincidence of the event. This poietic opened-endedness of the event unfolds the space of prolepsis, where thinking the future becomes possible in the first place. As Kristeva remarks, Russian futurism "paid strong attention to the explosion of the October Revolution. It heard and understood the Revolution only because its present was dependent on a future."[8] The futurist poetic language works in the modality of a "future anterior," which projects an alternative historical space that cannot be reduced to the linear progression of punctual presents. As such, it contests the linguistic, social, and political articulations to which history is submitted. The very possibility of transformation and of a different future lies within this opening marked by the historicity of the present.

"Each Moment Producing Words": *Zaum* and Historicity

The issue of the relation of beyonsense to signification becomes central to understanding Khlebnikov's poetics for two reasons: first, because it is tied to his conception of being and its linguistic modality of occurrence, and, second, because it illustrates the role of beyonsense language in his conception of history and revolution. Language and the discursive inscription of the event become the terrain for negotiating the temporal structure and the historical meaning of experience. The continuously resignified boundary between beyonsense and "ordinary" forms of language constitutes a reflection of the event temporality of being. Let us illustrate this conjunction in a preliminary manner by reference to two quotations characteristic of Khlebnikov's approach to language. The first one comes from *Zangezi,* a "supersaga" or "beyonstory," which crosses and rewrites the genre boundaries between drama, poetry, and theoretical treatise on language and history. The quotation is taken from a prophetic, but also parodic, speech Zangezi delivers at the end of Plane Eight:

> Have you heard all I've said, heard my speech that frees you from the fetters of words? Speech is an edifice built out of blocks of space.
>
> Particles of speech. Parts of movement. Words do not exist; there are only movements in space and their parts—points and areas.
>
> You have broken free from your ancestral chains. The hammer of my voice has shattered them; your frenzied struggle against those chains has ended. (*KT,* 205, translation modified)

In this speech, revolution and revolutionary rhetoric signify liberation from the bonds of language, from the traditional linguistic usage. Written in 1922, *Zangezi* cannot but be read against the background of historical and revolutionary turmoil, perhaps as an ironic commentary on revolutionary change, which, in addition to transforming political, social, and economic orders, must alter relations on the level of discourse and revise the parameters of representation. Zangezi's speech underscores the link between altering the workings of language and changing the "building blocks" of experience. It seeks to transform precisely the manner in which the world opens (into language).

Treated by other characters in the "superstory" both as a prophet and a visionary, and as a joke or a blabbering idiot, Zangezi resembles more Zarathustra or Eastern sages than a political revolutionary in the modern European sense. Still, the rhetoric he employs is unmistakably revolutionary: breaking the ancestral chains, the shattering hammer (a reference to the Soviet emblem of the revolutionary hammer symbolizing the working class), frenzied struggle. Tapping directly into the political and cultural rhetoric of postrevolutionary Russia, *Zangezi* sets up its own "revolutionary struggle" in terms of a fundamental change in the understanding of the relation between language and reality. It is a change that involves recognizing how the event temporality of experience is interwoven with language. Zangezi's speech associates the freedom from the fetters of language with the idea that words cannot be understood as autonomous, as part of a language system existing separately from the happening of being. Instead, they are interlinked, one wants to say, interfaced, with "movements in space and their parts": in fact, language seems to be built of the same material as the space-time of experience and history.

Zangezi's "revolution" has to do with the notion of language as built out of the "blocks of space" and "particles of movement," as constructed from the pieces and traces of the space-time of history or from the particles of experience. This particular expansion of the idea of language focuses on the passage between language and its beyonsense fold. Interrogating the notion of language as a social and representational code superimposed upon historical reality, beyonsense ties the poetic (re)invention of language to the happening of being, to the particles, movements, and planes of experience. The Russian word that Khlebnikov uses for speech — *rech* — signifies speech, discourse, talk, or language, but also thing and matter, in a manner similar to the German *Sache*. Language for Zangezi becomes the matter of thinking, which needs to be reconsidered, "revolutionized," vis-à-vis experience. Similarly to Heidegger's approach, it is the matter of language in a double sense: First, it produces and sustains language, and, second, it constitutes the matter *for* language, that is, what is to be thought and signified. The reworking of this "fundamental" difference between materiality and intelligibility — of the distinction which structures the parameters of visibility, understanding, and meaningfulness — constitutes the object of Zangezi's pronouncements.

The second quotation comes from "Our Fundamentals" *("Nasha osnova")*, one of Khlebnikov's most interesting essays on language and word creation. The title word *osnova* could be rendered into English as "basis" or "fundament," but this translation loses the root meaning of weaving and interlacing at play in Russian. A more appropriate rendition in this context would be "envelope," or even "fold," since *osnova* suggests intertwining, a pattern of weaving that forms the fold for experience and history. *Osnova* also implies spinning a tale, a "beyonstory" *(zapovest)* that describes the "laws" of experience. Read this way, the title suggests the interlacing of experience and language, which informs Khlebnikov's poetic work and his speculation about history:

Word creation — the enemy of the bookish petrification of language. It relies on the fact that in villages, by rivers and forests, language creates itself to this very day, every moment producing words that either die or gain the right to immortality. Word creation transfers this right to the world of literary creativity. A new word must not only be named, it must be directed toward the named thing. Word creation does not break the laws of language. (*CW I*, 382, translation modified)

At first, it seems that Khlebnikov describes here simply the appearance and codification of new words, a phenomenon common in the history of any language, and a regular feature of language change. Poetic word creation appears as a justified form of an intense invention of new words, an amplification of a "natural" linguistic process.

However, Khlebnikov's description is more nuanced, as it links the intrinsic creativity of language directly to the event of being. The Russian text emphasizes the fact that language is an activity: It is not created or invented, but, rather, it *creates itself (tvoritsa)*. The statement indicates a nonsubjective view of language, where word creation falls outside the domain of the creativity of the poetic subject and belongs to the event of language. Khlebnikov's remark also ties the constant reinvention of words with the event structure of experience. For it is language itself that functions as the "subject" of the phrase "every moment producing words." Every moment "speaks," that is, occurs as a form of language, producing words that, perhaps no longer identifiable simply with linguistic signs, make up a configuration singular to that particular happening. The singular historicity of the moment is obviously lost or veiled in the "petrification of language," in the customary forms and rules of language usage, whether everyday or literary. Word creation becomes here more than the poetic procedure of introducing new words into the lexicon, as it describes the mobilization of the plasticity of language against the ossification of its articulated forms and structures. Since language structures the event of experience, constituting the modality in which "every moment" happens, each instant of being becomes tantamount to producing language anew, to a continuous resignification of the linguistic matrix. This conception of the linguistic character of experience sees the world—"villages, rivers, forests"—or, in other words, "nature" *(priroda)*, as a form of language, as appearance or manifestation that is linguistic. Khlebnikov's remarks imply that the plasticity of being is itself word-creative, that every minute reinvents itself in words. The *osnova* or the envelope within which experience becomes readable in historical terms traces this interweaving of language and being. We could say that the "fundament" of being has the form of this peculiar, shifting interlace, thanks to which experience occurs as always already translocated or "translated" into words.

These two quotations set up the parameters of my discussion of the relation between experience and language in Khlebnikov's work, which extends the notion of experience beyond empiricist or rationalist terms. As I have suggested in the previous chapters, modern experience does not fit into essentialist conceptions and must be rethought apart from the idea of the constancy of the present. In the context of Khlebnikov's writings, I read experience in terms of the distinction between word creation and the petrification of language. Furthermore, the undermining of the familiar practices of signification through word creation becomes the venue for the critique of representation of the everyday. The word *osnova* ties historicity with the dislocation which language undergoes from the fluid manifestations of the world as a saying ("every moment producing words") to intelligible expressions and "normal" syntactic structures. Historicity becomes marked as the excess or residue of the event over what becomes present or disclosed as its result. "Every moment producing words" overflows the bounds of the play of signification and the totality of possible meanings, differentiating itself from the meaning of the event "petrified" in words.

"Our Fundamentals" describes this dissymetrical relation between happening and presence in terms of two distinct senses of the word: "A word divides itself into the pure word and the daily existing word. We may even imagine a word that contains both the starlight intelligence of nighttime and the sunlight intelligence of day. This is because whatever single ordinary meaning a word may possess will hide all its other meanings" (*CW I*, 377, translation modified). A lot depends here on what Khlebnikov understands by the "pure" part of the word, on whether this "purity" is indicative of a supra-rational, universal language or, conversely, can be interpreted in terms of the inappropriable historicity of the event, excessive and dissymetrical in relation to the order of representation. Khlebnikov himself remarks that our approach to language is not scientific enough and that we have to learn to treat language the way science interprets nature: "It is evident that language is as wise as nature, and only now with the growth of science are we discovering how to read it" (*CW I*, 378–79). Such a scientific explanation of language could produce a classification of fundamental sound elements that would be as universally valid as chemical elements: "The plentitude of language must be analyzed in terms of fundamental units of 'alphabetic verities,' and then for these sound elements we may be able to construct something resembling Mendeleev's law or Moseley's law — the latest achievements of the science of chemistry" (*CW I*, 376). It would be easy to conclude that Khlebnikov's text is motivated by a certain naive, "poetic" scientism, which sees in science the equivalent of a procedural model for artistic creation and regards poets as the engineers of language. The enthusiasm with which Khlebnikov outlines his "scientific" decomposition of language into alphabetic verities in order to prepare the ground for the invention of a new language is obviously symptomatic of the avant-garde fascination with science as the modern model for representing and understanding reality. It also evokes, as several critics have remarked, Leibniz's and Pascal's idea of language as a system of algebraic signs (*VK,* 73).

Large parts of Khlebnikov's theoretical writings, in particular his reflections upon the mathematical theory of history, indeed rely upon the scientific ideal of investigation and describe the task of poetry in terms of the science of language or word creation.[9] His writing practice, however, inevitably reshapes this alliance between science and art, enlisting the scientistic model in the service of his poetic reformulation of language. This kind of ambiguity in relation to science is evident also in the text of "Our Fundamentals," where Khlebnikov's "scientistic" belief in the possibility of inventing a rationally understandable "supra-language" is undermined by the plasticity of the event that "produces words every moment." I would argue that the remarks about word creation, in which Khlebnikov defines each moment in terms of its ability to (re)produce itself as words—as an excess over the "ordinary" and "petrified" meaning—strongly suggests the reading of the split between "pure" and "everyday" word in terms of the event temporality of experience. The "overflow" of the event over the order of presence singularizes "every moment" and opens it to future reproduction and rereading in ways that cannot be tabulated and, thus, undermine the idea of a scientific calculation of the play of signification. It indicates that experience takes place as the petrification of its happening into the order of representation. At the same time, however, it also underscores the possibility of a poetic language that could maintain the disjunction between "creation" and "petrification" by distinguishing between the two senses of the word.

Because of this ambiguity reflected in the futurist approach to word creation, critical controversies have always surrounded the idea of *zaum:* Is it linguistic nonsense rather than beyonsense, a failed attempt at inventing the "absolute" word and a scientific-poetic approach to language, or is it indeed a genuine poetic proposition of a creative rethinking of language and experience? The discussion is further complicated by the fact that various Russian futurists differed in their understanding and interpretation of the function of beyonsense language. The word *zaum* was coined by Kruchonykh[10] and, even though "[t]o both men *zaum,* beyonsense, was an extension of poetic language that rejected the mediation of common sense and deemphasized denotative meaning,"[11] their approaches are quite distinct. While Kruchonykh creates beyonsense through "intuitively invented neologisms, grammatical confusions, sound puns, and nonsequiturs," Khlebnikov's attitude is that of a "scientist of word creation": "more analytical construction of neologisms, building new words carefully from meaningful linguistic elements" (*CW I*, 20). Khlebnikov's explanations of beyonsense always proceed on two levels: On the one hand, they involve scientific descriptions, diagrams, and mathematical formulas, and, on the other, they incorporate illustrations from nature, quite distinct from the aesthetics prevalent among the city-oriented futurists. In "Our Fundamentals," Khlebnikov refers to word creation in terms of semantic configurations: "[T]hese free combinations, which represent the voice at play outside of words, are called beyonsense. Beyonsense language means language situated beyond the boundaries of ordinary reason, just as we say 'beyond the river' or 'beyond the sea'" (*CW I*, 383).

Zaum is a combination of the preposition *za* (beyond, past, behind)and the noun *um*, whose range of meanings comprises reason, understanding, knowledge, and thought. Later in the essay, Khlebnikov characteristically phrases his definition of beyonsense in terms of a number of propositions underlying his poetic experiments with word creation:

Beyonsense language is based on two premises:

1. The initial consonant of a simple word governs all the rest—it commands the remaining letters.
2. Words that begin with an identical consonant share some identical meaning; it is as if they were drawn from various directions to a single point in the mind. (*CW I*, 384)

Khlebnikov's linguistic search for "alphabetic verities" consists in finding semantic correlations between various words that begin with the same sound element in Russian (and sometimes other Slavic languages) and distilling the meaning of each initial element. For instance, comparing several Russian words beginning with the sound ч (*ch*): *chasha* (cup), *choboty* (a kind of boot), *chulok* (stocking), *chuviak* (slipper), *cherep* (skull), and so on, Khlebnikov concludes that "all these words coalesce at the point of the following image: whether we speak of a stocking *(chulok)* or a cup *(chasha)*, in both instances the volume of one body (foot or water) fills up the emptiness of another body which serves as its surface" (*CW I*, 384).

This descriptive determination of the semantics of sound elements becomes the basis for constructing an alphabet of "linguistic verities"—or underlying linguistic elements—a tabulation of basic sememes at the root of languages. Such fundamental elements would have the same universal intelligibility and application as mathematical numbers: "The second language of poetry. Number-nouns [*chisloimena*]" (*CW I,* 318). This numerification of language elements constitutes the prolegomena to a future supra-rational language: "[b]eyonsense language is thus the universal language of the future, although it is still in an embryonic state. It alone will be able to unite all people. Rational languages have separated them" (*CW I,* 385). It is worth noting that the compatibility of the beyonsense language with the universal intelligibility of numbers has an explicit social and revolutionary agenda in Khlebnikov's work. The proleptic vision of a pre-Babelian language common to all humankind becomes an "internationalist" poetic/linguistic plane, which would make possible a radical renegotiation of cultural, social, and linguistic differences through word creation.

This utopian vision of a universal language running through Khlebnikov's work is, however, complicated by his poetic practice, in particular by his correlation of word creation with the event, which belies the possibility of ever "completing" the beyonsense alphabet. If we take Khlebnikov's remarks about the mathematical laws of history and the construction of a supra-rational language intelligible to speakers of various languages as the primary defining characteristic of his work, and thus treat his writings as a parallel to the Leibnizian dream of a universal algebraic language, then Khlebnikov's project becomes equivalent to a poetic alchemy, a quest for the "poet's gold" in the form of an absolute alphabet. Doomed to failure from the start, Khlebnikov's poetry would fit comfortably within the interpretation of the avant-garde, and, particularly, futurism, as a utopian venture, naively optimistic about the possibility of influencing the future and of constructing art in the image of a "hyperrational," techno-scientific calculus of being. Yet, as much as Khlebnikov's works are pervaded by this idea, they also read experience in terms of an event whose historical occurrence demands continuous word creation without producing an absolute semantic key to reality.

The aspect of *zaum* I want to explore here illustrates Khlebnikov's attempt "to recognize the corners of events in the instantaneous foam of words."[12] The "instantaneous foam of words" is the effect of how "every moment producing words" registers in language, generating deliberate violations of linguistic and semantic norms. These semantic and phonetic experiments are figures of historicity, of the excess of the event over the order of its representation. In Kristeva's words, "by thus suspending the present moment, by straddling rhythmic, meaningless, anterior memory with meaning intended for later or forever, poetic language structures itself as the very nucleus of a monumental historicity" (*DL,* 32). The instantaneous multiplicity of semantic planes produced, for example, by "Incantation with Laughter" or "Incantation with Names" exceeds conventional representational and perceptual structures and opens language to "the corners of events" inaccessible to normative linguistic usage. In the words of Zangezi, such poems free one "from the fetters of words." If those fetters refer to "the stable intentional, appellative and denotative relationships with long-established referents,"[13] then, releasing the semantic energy by disassembling words and putting in motion the particles of language, Khlebnikov hopes to produce within the poetic text the dynamic of the event.

This poietic relationship between language and experience is often rendered in the image of the world as a book. In a long monologue that makes up Plane Nineteen, Zangezi describes nature as a form of writing, a book:

> See the patterns of waves of sand
> And the curly hair of the sea —
> The beach, the branches, the debris.
> Pinetree branches move a hand
> And a book is written on the sand —
> The book of the pine, the shore, the sea.
>
> (*KT,* 227)

A similar conflation of writing with the "course of nature" informs the imagery of "The Only Book," in which the book signifies the always already linguistic status of reality, the fact that the world manifests itself as a form of saying: "to speed the coming / Of the only book / Whose pages are large seas / Trembling like wings of a blue butterfly."[14] Khlebnikov's repeated presentation of the world and natural phenomena as an inscription, a text to be "read" into words, is consistent with his notion of the "divided word" and with the idea that beyonsense language reaches beyond conventional perception and expression to register in word creation the unpresentable "corners of events." Even though the world appears as a form of writing, it still requires inscription in words: It finds itself in need of translation. Chastising readers for carelessness — "Please pay more attention"[15] — and calling for a more attentive approach to language, Khlebnikov boasts of the authorship of such a translation, of the book of the (world) book. This seems to be a reference to the project of beyonsense language, which attempts to "translate" the multifarious happening of the "book of the world" through word creation. While not new, Khlebnikov's images of nature as forms or spaces of inscription are less an attempt to spiritualize the natural world than an exemplification of his understanding of experience, according to which the event takes the shape of an already accomplished "translation" into discourse. One could see beyonsense language in terms of maintaining through its deregulated semantics the force of this "translation" against the imperative of representation, against the reduction of the event to discursive structures.

This Khlebnikovian view of the event is textually tied to the figure of Zangezi and to frequent references to water images. In "The Only Book," the allusion to a butterfly and the list of great rivers that follows refers the poem to Zangezi, who describes himself as a butterfly (*KT,* 198) and whose name may well be a conflation of two river names, both cited in "The Only Book": Zambezi and Ganges. Both the text and the character of Zangezi are often linked to water images: rivers, seas, oceans, foam, beaches, and to the idea of sand writing. In the context of this water imagery, the facility with which Zangezi produces his monologues and addresses his listeners makes for an apt comparison of his pronouncements with what Khlebnikov describes as the "instantaneous foam of words." Zangezi's language experiments—which will be analyzed in more detail below—instantiate Khlebnikov's idea of producing the sense of multiple instantaneity, irreducible to the temporal dimension of the present.

Such a link between historicity and poetic language forms the pivot of Heidegger's reflection on poetry. In "The Way to Language," Heidegger's understanding of experience in terms of the propriative event *(das Ereignis)* depends upon the idea that manifestation is a form of "soundless" saying: "The saying is by no means the supplementary linguistic expression of what shines forth; rather, all shining and fading depend on the saying that shows." [16] Being and occurrence, presence and absence ("shining and fading"), constitute forms of saying through showing, a sort of manifestational saying, where events and beings have an intrinsically linguistic status. Language here exceeds social codes and discursive practices, since it describes the event of experience simultaneously reaching and breaching articulation, an event whose historicity is marked specifically by what remains unsaid, "untranslated" into words. As Heidegger remarks: "The event of propriation *(Ereignis)* is telling *(sagend),*" it occurs in the manner of a saying *(BW,* 420), or, in other words, the event is "the saying's way-making movement toward language" *(BW,* 418). The movement of the saying toward words constitutes the historial unfolding of experience: the rift or the distance which remains unsaid in words: "[t]he saying will not allow itself to be captured in any assertion" *(BW,* 424). The propositional and appropriative modalities of language fail to register the poetic saying, which, as Heidegger suggests, requires a different relation to language, a relation that puts into question the representational paradigm: "In order to think back to the essence of language, in order to reiterate what is its own, we need a transformation of language, a transformation we can neither compel nor concoct. The transformation does not result from the fabrication of neologisms and novel phrases. The transformation touches on our relation to language" *(BW,* 424–25).

Albeit implicitly, Heidegger appears here to be extremely cautious, even skeptical, about the avant-garde treatment of language, in particular about the avant-garde penchant for word creation, about the kind of inventions that proliferate in Khlebnikov's work. Khlebnikov himself seems to be more than optimistic about the success and future importance of his beyonsense project. In spite of this difference, I see in Khlebnikov's work an attempt to force, or, at least, to quicken, the transformation in our relation to language through the emphasis on the beyonsense aspect, the "hither side," of signification and experience. There is no doubt that beyonsense aims at changing the attitude toward language, at transforming it through a different, "beyonsense," interweaving of language and experience. The Khlebnikovian "instantaneous foam of words" traces the movement of the manifestational saying/writing—of the world as a book—into "ordinary" words. The distance Khlebnikov's word creation opens between ordinary signification and the semantic fluidity of the beyonsense enacts the movement of the saying ("pages of large seas") into language.

Suggesting that manifestation has a linguistic form, Heidegger sees the world both as opening itself to thought and as being shaped by its relation to thinking, that is, as ready for "translation" into words. Conceiving of language as the riftlike field of an event, Heidegger avoids absolutizing the saying, and, in fact, historicizes its occurrence. As part of the way-making of language, the saying has a history, and takes place in specific historical circumstances. As I suggest in chapter 1, it also marks the opening of history, because the translation of the saying into words opens up the distance which makes history thinkable. Paradoxically, historicity both inaugurates and eludes the space-time of history. This simultaneous proximity and distance, which structures experience, is reflected in Heidegger's distinction between words *(die Worte)* and terms *(die Wörter):* "Words are not terms *[Die Worte sind keine Wörter]*, and thus are not like buckets and kegs from which we scoop a content that is there. Words are wellsprings that are found and dug up in the telling, wellsprings that must be found and dug up again and again, that easily cave in, but that at times also well up when least expected." [17] The transformation in language Heidegger mentions in "The Way to Language" has to do precisely with the difference between words and terms, that is, with a poetic opening of language as a set of terms with a "stale" semantic content (*WTC,* 130) to the saying that "wells up" in words, exceeding and "historicizing" the signification of terms. While terms describe the functioning of language as a social code, words circumscribe the manifestational saying, that is, they bring into play the distance, the way-making of the saying into "terms." Words in Heidegger's sense are inscribed in what is said without being reduced to "terms" or linguistic signs: "As hearers, we abide in the sphere of what is spoken, where the voice of what is said rings without sound. From this sphere [*Spielraum*], whose essential nature we have barely caught sight of, much less thought about, the words, without coming to the fore, disclose themselves as speaking in what is spoken [*öffen sich die im Gesprochenen sprechenden und eigens gar nicht hervortretenden Worte*]" (*WCT,* 130, modified). Both marked in linguistic signs and irreducible to them, words register, precisely at the point of their shattering, the historicity of experience.

I draw a parallel between Heidegger's distinction between words and terms and the relation between Khlebnikov's beyonsense language and normative linguistic expression. What characterizes Khlebnikov's poetic practice is a continuous reopening of words ("terms"?) to what they tell or inscribe beyond their codified meaning. Word creation extends terms or language signs into their beyonsense sphere, as it reaches an underlying stratum of language which corresponds to Heidegger's words that "speak through" the signs of language. This poetic reorientation of language allows Khlebnikov to link word creation to the space-time of history and to read the telescoping or compressing of the "beyonsense" potential of language into linguistic codes as equivalent to the occlusion of historicity within the presence-bound representational space.

Zangezi's Vision of History

Zangezi represents an unusual literary form, which, although ostensibly a theatrical drama designed for performance, crosses generic boundaries in a way parallel to how beyonsense reformulates the confines of signification. In fact, one of the supra-generic names that Khlebnikov gives to his text, *zapovest'* or "beyonstory," suggests this correlation between the structural aspects of the text and beyonsense language. This constant movement across boundaries and between planes describes a sort of a "geometry of language," which unfolds various planes of the existence of words: "The supersaga resembles a statue made from blocks of different kinds of stone of varying colors—white for the body, blue for the cloak and garments, black for the eyes" (*KT*, 191). The hybrid textuality of *Zangezi*—a series of discrete "narrative" and language planes—reflects a typical modernist gesture of undoing the unity of the literary text and presents language as a complex and layered structure existing on several planes. This particular hybrid geometry of language constitutes a crucial part of Khlebnikov's conception of the relation between reality and language. Both *Zangezi,* the text, and Zangezi, the mouthpiece for Khlebnikov's theories, show how beyonsense language provides the hybrid space beyond the conventions of representation and understanding necessary, in Khlebnikov's view, for rethinking the interface of language and reality.

Before we proceed with explaining the specifics of how *Zangezi* presents language and history, it is important to underscore the ambiguous status of the character Zangezi in this text. Modeled after Nietzsche's prophetic figure of Zarathustra, Zangezi is presented by Khlebnikov as both a prophet of the future—a visionary capable of seeing history through mathematical laws and the calculations of the "tables of destiny"—and ironized as a foolish character who has lost touch with reality. The image of Zangezi changes from plane to plane, oscillating between the veneration of the crowd of followers and the jeering of disappointed listeners. Plane Five begins with the crowd calling out to Zangezi: "Speak to us! We hear you. Our souls are a floor beneath your feet. Brave comer! We believe in you, we await you" (*KT*, 197). In Plane Seven, however, Zangezi appears in quite a different light: "But he hasn't got the true poetic fire. It's all just raw material, his sermon. Just a lot of unworked stuff. A lot of green wood. Go dry out, thinker" (*KT*, 202). The fact that Zangezi is treated alternately either with veneration or with disrespect, even with condescension, indicates that, even when taken as a self-portrait or a speaker for Khlebnikov's theories, Zangezi has to be seen with a dose of irony. The text of *Zangezi* is indeed at least as ironic and comic as it is serious. It contains numerous jokes, linguistic puns, and robust folk expressions, and the epilogue, which turns out to be a joke about Zangezi's apparent suicide, puts an additional twist on this intentional ambiguity. Bursting onto the stage to deny the newspaper story about his suicide, Zangezi exclaims that it was only a silly, nonsensical *(neumniy)* trick. Yet the joke is much more important and "serious" than it appears. It underscores a thin but crucial line between *zaumniy* (beyonsense) and *neumniy*, where *zaum*, taken too literally as a drive toward a final calculation, an ultimate poetic-scientific formula, turns from the flexibility of beyonsense to an absence of *um* (reason), a bungled attempt implied in the prefix *ne*. Too strictly overdetermined and ordered, sense empties and dehistoricizes itself; it becomes "silly" by virtue of its overreaching formulation. As serious as Khlebnikov appears to be about his calculations of the future, *Zangezi* inscribes an ironic distance to the mathematical laws of history. It is an important gesture, in line with Khlebnikov's questioning of linguistic, literary, and scientific authority, a displacement which it seems only fitting for him to perform with respect to the textual "embodiment" of his own theories. This move assures that Zangezi's ideas about language and history are always situated in an ironic frame in which their "value" oscillates between prophetic genius and "forest fool" (*KT,* 195).

The hybrid textuality of *Zangezi,* the various planes of its "action," presents several attempts to explain historical reality—the historical and physical forces at play in the world—in relation to the event of language. Zangezi's prophetic speech about freeing humanity from the fetters of words redefines language in terms of the building blocks of space-time: "Speech is an edifice built out of blocks of space" (*KT,* 205). Language exceeds the idea of a system of signs: It is thought in terms of spatial and temporal movements, of the interacting forces and unfolding spaces:

> Particles of speech. Parts of movement. Words—they do not exist; only movements in space and their parts—points and areas . . .
>
> Planes, the lines defining an area, the impact of points, the godlike circle, the angle of incidence, the fascicle of rays proceeding from a point or penetrating it—these are the secret building blocks of language. Scrape the surface of language, and you will behold space and the skin that encloses it. (*KT,* 205, translation modified)

The geometries of text and language become here parallel to the geometrical representation of space, as they are constructed out of the spatio-temporal occurrences and relations. Zangezi's emphatic statement that words do not exist as signs or entities but only as movements in space, reflects Khlebnikov's revision of the understanding of the word: It is movements, occurrences, spatial relations, points, planes, and angles—a kind of a "geometry of happening"—that constitute the hidden building blocks of language. Scraping the surface of language, that is, dislocating language signs into their beyonsense play, reveals that language extends beyond the play of signification, that the space-time of experience itself has a linguistic composition.

Particles of experience—parts of movements and space—are also particles of language. In other words, language extends beyond the idea of a system of signs or a social code, and refers to the invisible spatial and temporal relations and forces. It forms the very matrix of happening, the event structure of experience. In "The Language as Such and the Language of Man," Benjamin explains that things and beings have their own language, which means that their "being," though nameless, is linguistic: "language has its own word, and this word applies also to that conception which is enacted by the nameless in names. It is the translation of the language of things into that of man." [18] In "On the Mimetic Faculty," he describes this translation in terms of a "nonsenuous similarity" which exists between the linguistic being of things and their names (*R,* 335). The translation Benjamin has in mind becomes possible because objects and phenomena take place in a linguistic manner, and, one might say, have part of their existence or reality in the language matter. The idea of beyonsense language seems to go even further, as it reinterprets the "nameless in names" in terms of historicity: What in experience escapes representation, what cannot be presented in terms of things or entities, is precisely the happening of being, its event. This happening constitutes the "matter" of language, the linguistic material beyond the play of signification, or, in other words, beyonsense. Defining letters and sounds in Plane Eight, Khlebnikov reads movement and occurrence as linguistic particles: for example, "*L* is the cessation of fall, or motion generally by a plane lateral to a falling point. / *R* is a point that penetrates a transverse area" (*KT,* 204). Khlebnikov's "geometry of being" draws a linguistic map of forces in which history itself, taken as event or occurrence and not as idea or content, has the status of a language. As in Benjamin's model, Khlebnikov's distinction between beyonsense and "regular" language describes the moment of translation from the language of things to the language of names. Khlebnikov, however, does not leave the language of things nameless: he regards poetry as the labor of extending language beyond names in order to retrieve the beyonsense language of things and occurrences.

I refer here to Benjamin's notion of translation and Heidegger's idea of language in order to contextualize Khlebnikov's conception of *zaum* and show how his practice of rendering explicit the linguistic character of the "particles of experience" by means of beyonsense upsets the very idea of representation and mimesis. When Zangezi remarks that words do not exist as entities or signs but find themselves in motion, much as forces or occurrences do, he discounts the idea that experience, the "secret building blocks of language," remains prior to or independent from language. Representation depends upon the distinction and separation of the represented from the medium or the moment of representation. It relies upon the possibility of a mimetic reflection which doubles the mirrored object, both instituting and suspending the difference between the thing and its representational double. By contrast, Khlebnikov regards experience as inextricably interfaced with language: The form experience takes is negotiated linguistically, with words playing a constitutive role in this event. The event never transpires outside or before language but, instead, happens *into* words. Beyonsense functions as the edge upon which the world opens itself as a linguistic configuration of the particles of experience, the edge continuously blunted by discursive practices and linguistic conventions. This noncontemporaneity, or, we might say conversely, a paradoxical contemporaneity that lacks self-coincidence and presence, marks the "translation" constitutive of experience. The phenomenality of being is structured as this translative event, nonsynchronous with the representational optics.

In Heidegger's view, the fold of representation, the *es gibt* or "there is" which opens the space-time of experience and representation, functions already as language beyond words and signification. It forms the saying which, "signifying" through words, remains itself in the register of silence, as the unsaid of signification. For Khlebnikov, this sense of happening, and its historicity elusive to representational schema, constitute the beyonsense *(zaum)* matter of language, the building blocks of speech and writing. Where Khlebnikov differs from Heidegger is in the means necessary to achieve a transformation in our relation to language which would make it possible to see the "linguistic matter" of history. While Heidegger distrusts neologism and word creation for their own sake, Khlebnikov intensifies word creating capabilities of language beyond any known scope.

Word creation in Khlebnikov extends beyond playfulness and innovation and posits as its goal the uncovering of the building blocks of language. To see the relation between "particles of speech" and "parts of movement," Khlebnikov broadens the scope of language, moving beyond the zone of sense into *zaum,* into a sphere in which the space-time of history becomes visible underneath the "codified" skin of language. It is in the field of beyonsense—a sphere beyond normative understanding of language and yet a space, as Khlebnikov's poetry suggests, more densely linguistic than language—that the particles of experience become visible as particles of language.

The planes immediately preceding and following Plane Eight, which contains Zangezi's speech about language, present various takes on beyonsense language, in which individual letters and sounds—the particles of language—become elements of being, parts of movements and spaces. The alphabet of letters Zangezi constructs becomes the alphabet of various forces of happening, and, thus, an alphabet, one might say, of what the Greeks understood under the name of *physis*—not simply nature, but, as Heidegger explains, the emergence of what is. Plane Seven of *Zangezi* develops this notion of poetic language by describing the expansive semantic range of individual letters/sounds *R, K, L,* and *G* in terms of the elementary forces of history. For example, the letter *L* and the sound "el" become associated with a string of words which begin with or contain the letter/sound *L,* and which, according to Khlebnikov's version of *zaum,* are semantically connected: sun (*solnyshko,* translated as "light"), laziness *(lenia),* love *(lyubov),* grace (*laska,* translated as "languor"), and people (*lyudi,* translated as "multitude"). Khlebnikov amplifies this semantic undercurrent in order to characterize historical forces and to describe the features of historical time: "The weather changes—*L* days are upon us! / *L,* the sweet light of laziness, of love and languor! / In 'living multitudes' you lull us twice" (*KT,* 199). This fragment is characteristic of the semantic and phonetic density Khlebnikov generates in Russian: using and amplifying the resources of ordinary Russian, Khlebnikov rewires, as it were, the semantic and phonetic relations and opens new linguistic circuitry that pushes language beyond sense and signification to register "the corners of events" illegible within the order of representation.[19]

Plane Eight presents what Khlebnikov calls the "star-language," or a language which, moving beyond compilations of words with the same phonetic and semantic components, defines letters/sounds in terms of "particles of experience":

The *VE* of branches [*vetok*] on [*vdol*] the pinetree trunk
The *VE* of stars [*zvezd*], the night-world turning overhead.
A *CHE* of girls—golden [*chervonnaya*] shirts. . . .

(*KT*, 203)

The entire plane is based on those largely untranslatable linguistic relations
which establish connections between various elements of reality: the secret
building blocks of language that Zangezi mentions in his speech at the end
of Plane Eight.

Plane Nine, titled "The Plane of Thought," involves elaborate extensions and redefinitions of thought and reason *(um),* a series of linguistic
inflections of "reason" which describe the opening of rationality to a range
of beyonsense *(zaum)* possibilities (*KT*, 205–9). Khlebnikov provides his
own notes to explain the various meanings of "reason" *(um)* which reaches
beyond its own linguistic and representational constraints, and becomes
a liberated reason, as the first composite on the long list—"free-sense" or
"out-sense" *(vyum)*—suggests. These possibilities are immediately put to
work in Plane Ten, which constitutes perhaps the most impossible "level"
of language in *Zangezi* to translate. The plane is almost entirely based on
the inflectional and neologistic plays around the word *mogut':* can, may,
might, be able to, and other words associated with it through the letter
M. Khlebnikov deploys here several new "beyonsense" relations, combining sememes from two or more different words to create neologisms like
mogatyr: a cross between "might" and "ability" and the Russian word *boga-
tyr,* which signifies a noble and powerful man; or *mog,* a combination of the
verb "can" and the noun *bog,* god. He also invents entirely new words, like
mogoon, a "can-er," or *mogach',* a "can-ist." Khlebnikov's extensions and inflections of standard Russian are particularly difficult to render into English
because they rely largely on complex inflectional paradigms. Let me illustrate the principle of Khlebnikov's inventions on the basis of one strand of
word creation: "*Moglets! Ya mogu! Mogey, ya mogeyu!*" [20] Beginning the line
with a neologism *moglets,* an "enable-er," Khlebnikov then uses the standard expression "I can, I am capable of," and immediately creates another
noun from the verb "*mogu*"—*mogey,* say, a "mighter" (from the verb *might*).
Then he proceeds with a sort of a second degree of invention, creating a
first person singular verb form *ya mogeyu:* "I mighterize," on the basis of the
previously invented noun "*mogey.*" Subsequently, the plane spirals through
a series of second, third, and fourth degrees of word creation, all revolv-
ing around the verb *mogu* and various related words beginning with *M*. As

the basis for the development of the entire plane, Khlebnikov expands and modifies the system of inflectional and derivational morphemes, deploying standard morphemic structures well beyond their prescribed context of application. A parallel example in English might be to apply the derivational morpheme "ness" to verbs which normally use other morphemes to form nouns: kingness, capableness, leverness, and so on. In Plane Ten, the letter *M* together with the verbs and nouns invented from the verb *mogu* create an entire matrix of the semantic vectors of "can" or "be able to," a field of the forces of change and transformation already at work in *priroda* or *physis*.

On the level of plot, the verbal innovations of Plane Ten, gravitating around the notion of power, perform an overthrow of divine authority, as the letter *M* invades the land of *B,* and god *(bog)* becomes replaced by the human "enabler" *(mog)*. Zangezi fulfills his role of prophet and helps people assert their own authority over language, as the vanquished gods flee and humanity assumes the position of a god. The mythological allusions so critical to many of Khlebnikov's works culminate here in the ascension of humankind to a godly, mythical status.[21] Zarathustra- and Prometheus-like, Zangezi is both a scientist and a magician, who represents the point at which science reaches such power that it assumes the status akin to magic: It begins to play the role of an all-powerful tool for explaining and manipulating reality. The Plane validates the poet's claim to being the "King of Time," who, combining poetic inventiveness and scientific exactness, places himself at the center of the universe from which the world and history appear transparent and calculable according to the laws of destiny.

Yet the Plane may be also read against itself, in terms of that paradoxical moment in modernity, perhaps the turning point for the Enlightenment, when science, impressing intelligibility and unity upon reality and empowering human beings to assume control over it, begins to recognize itself, as Adorno and Horkheimer suggest, as myth: "The principle of immanence, the explanation of every event as repetition, that the Enlightenment upholds against mythic imagination, is the principle of myth itself."[22] The staging of the fall of divine power becomes also the moment of mythologizing science and technology, so characteristic of futurist aesthetics. Is, then, Khlebnikov's *zaum* the moment when science achieves such a point of cohesion that it reverts to myth and the scientific formula speaks with the all-embracing force of poetic/magical incantations?[23] While such a reading is certainly plausible, especially in the context of Khlebnikov's earlier works, we have to remember that Plane Ten does not end *Zangezi* but comes merely midway through the text, and the supersaga closes with Zangezi's joke about the thin line separating *zaum* and *neum*. I would suggest that, as in Adorno's reflection on modernity, this narrow line marks the reversal of rationality into the irrational, which happens at the historical point when rationality achieves global calculative abilities.

This point of generalization and all-inclusiveness, reflected in the alphabetic and historical verities sought by Zangezi, is contextualized and questioned by Khlebnikov's irony and by the continuing "expansion" of word creation, which opens an "elsewhere" to the established calculations and formulas. In Plane Thirteen, the accepted rules of word formation become deliberately "overgeneralized" to create a sense of language in flight, a language which moves in the direction of an elsewhere or otherwhere *(inesa):* "These nestlings of nowhere, a lattering flutter / Of wings in flight to some otherwhere, / Of ledglings in flight, seeking their selfland!" (*KT*, 212–23, translation modified). Khlebnikov's intention is to draw attention to and keep open the possibilities of inflection and derivation as a form of opening toward the "otherwhere." What Khlebnikov achieves here is a radical revision of the order of representation: from legibility structured along the norms of syntax and the rules governing the play of signification to a different legibility, where language displays a broader scope, or a beyonsense reach. These possibilities become foreclosed by the "limited" scope of the language code, where they get subordinated to the communicational function of language.

My argument is that beyonsense is more than a "poetic" play with linguistic standards: It is the disclosure of a language field which underlies the "limited" code employed in various discursive practices. Heidegger hints at a similar field of saying "beyond" words in "The Way to Language": "Various modes of saying and the said permeate the rift-design, modes in which what is present or absent says something about itself, affirms or denies itself—shows itself or withdraws. What pervades the rift-design in the essence of language is a richly configured saying, from various provenances" (*BW*, 409). Khlebnikov's poetry tries to maintain the distinctness of the beyonsense field of language against the prescribed, "constrictive," articulation into discourse. A good illustration of this difference is the graphic opposition between the inappropriable "radiation" of meaning and signification based upon the linearity of language in Khlebnikov's diagram of the particle "*so*" in "Here is the way the syllable *so* is a field" (*CW I*, 272). If historicity becomes effaced at the very moment when experience becomes represented as history, then the reconfiguration or the rezoning of sense into beyonsense is meant to counter this reduction.

On the Beyonsense of Art: Nature, Technology, and the Possibility of Revolution

Khlebnikov's complex relation to technology has to be considered in relation to his concept of beyonsense language and its link to *priroda* (nature). His writings on technology form an integral part of his poetics, and their futurist message depends upon his understanding of time and experience, reflected also in his linguistic conceptions. Rezoning language into beyonsense, Khlebnikov places most emphasis on the very occurrence of being over and against its (re)presentable content or sense. Situated in the foreground, the event temporality of experience shapes the optics of Khlebnikov's poetics so that the technological representation of being finds itself supplemented and inflected by art. My argument is that the capacity for refiguration intrinsic to beyonsense language is linked to the idea of change and transformation: It is Khlebnikov's response to the historical changes and revolutions he witnessed. The link between the linguistic potential unlocked in beyonsense poetics and the constitution of experience becomes the very locus of transformation. The disjunction between beyonsense and the order of representation, replayed in the distinction between art and technology, becomes the site of Khlebnikov's thoughts on revolution, which forms the undercurrent of his futurist visions.

On the one hand, beyonsense language incorporates the scientific modes of representation in order to test the limits of their production of sense and to explore the very boundaries of the legibility they institute. On the other, *zaum* is a critique of how aesthetics reduces art to aesthetic experience and effaces historicity. The reason we tend to forget historicity is the eclipse of *poiēsis* in art and in history. Remapping experience, Khlebnikov extends the representational paradigm into beyonsense in order to recover the poietic in art and to bring it to bear upon our understanding of history and historicity.[24] Opened into beyonsense, the poietic space becomes pliable, adjustable to the shifting, inappropriable lines of the event, to what Khlebnikov calls *priroda,* or nature.

Khlebnikov's interest in nature, reflected in his studies and ornithological writings, complicates his apparently straightforward futurist commitment to a technological vision of the future evident in his writings between 1916 and 1920. His futurist pronouncements about technology and his interest in quasi-scientific laws of history appear in a different light through the prism of *priroda*. Since *priroda* describes the force of unfolding, the *poiēsis* of the world, the techno-scientific character of the modern changes which fascinated the futurists become, for Khlebnikov, the sign of the intensification of the "nature" of happening itself. Technology does not so much qualitatively alter the character of happening as it changes the optics of history. Khlebnikov's interest in the laws of history finds both its motivation *and* its condition of possibility in this emphasis upon time, captured well in "The Trumpet of the Martians," a futurist proclamation co-signed by Khlebnikov in 1916: "The human brain until now has been hopping around on three legs (the three axes of location)! We intend to re-furrow the human brain and to give this puppy dog a fourth leg—namely, the axis of TIME" (*CW I*, 321).

Although *priroda* literally means nature, it functions in Khlebnikov more like the force of occurrence, which underscores the historicity of experi-ence. As Duganov remarks, it refers to the active emergence which questions and rewrites the "artificial" boundary between nature and culture.[25] Khleb-nikov's fascination with technology and the machine clearly implies that his idea of *priroda* calls into question the notion of a pretechnological or precultural natural world. Comparing Khlebnikov's *priroda* with Heideg-ger's critique of the concept of nature, I want to underscore how Khlebni-kov's poetry highlights experience as event. Heidegger critiques the idea of nature because it presents the world as an aggregate of objects, as a collec-tion of already existing and determined things. Such an understanding of nature as *natura* covers over the temporality of being and obscures the fact that beings emerge and become rather than "are" simply present—the idea still recognizable, in Heidegger's view, in the Greek notion of *physis*: "Tree and grass, eagle and bull, snake and cricket first enter into their distinctive shapes and thus come to appear as what they are. The Greeks early called this emerging and rising in itself and in all things *physis*" (*BW,* 168).

Khlebnikov's references to nature—from his ornithological and botani-cal writings to his nature imagery—form part of his preoccupation with *priroda* and, therefore, become closely linked to his interest in time and historicity. *Priroda* represents a force not opposed to technology but play-ing an active role, even regulating, the technologically determined forms of becoming. In "The Trumpet of the Martians," the favorite image of the locomotive speedily moving away from the past certainly signifies fascina-tion with speed and technology, but it also demonstrates how the break from the past hinges upon thinking time, or, as the text puts it, "kidnap-ing" it: "What better answer is there to the danger of being born a man than to *carry off time?*" (*CW I,* 322). This hijacking of time suggests that technology fails to supersede "nature," finds itself reinscribed into it, and signifies the intensification of the "natural" happening which defines *physis*. The intensified awareness of temporality, of being as continuous occurrence, is reflected in the rhetoric of the triumphant privileging of time over space. "The Trumpet of the Martians" refers to the people of the past as "the vulgar inhabitants of space," while the new "government" of artists and scientists it proposes to establish is defined specifically in relation to time: "to form an independent government of *time* (no longer dependent on space)" (*CW I*, 323). Khlebnikov's challenge to the pervasive "spatiality" of thought is tied to his nonessentialist notion of experience, manifest in the reproduced discursive disjunction between sense and beyonsense.

The idea of technology as part of and subject to the same laws as *priroda* may account for Khlebnikov's ambivalent place within Russian futurism and for his problematic relationship to the Italian futurists, Marinetti in particular. Although Khlebnikov participated in many futurist ventures in Russia—including the early "A Slap in the Face of Public Taste" (1912) and *The Word as Such,* coauthored with Kruchonykh—his relationship to cubofuturism[26] is as uneasy as the relation between Russian futurists and their Italian counterparts. The differences in Khlebnikov's notion of "nature," his less than enthusiastic attitude toward urban life and environment, and his need to anchor his brand of futurism in Russian culture and history, may explain his unusually hostile reaction to Marinetti during his first visit to Russia in 1914, an outburst very uncharacteristic for the rather shy Khlebnikov, in which he joined the vociferous attack on Italian futurism initiated by Mayakovsky. If polemic and provocation were Mayakovsky's "normal" mode of interaction and artistic existence, they are so unusual for Khlebnikov that his attack on Marinetti warrants a closer look, especially because it provides clues about the critical junctures of Khlebnikov's own work.[27]

On one level, Khlebnikov's dismissal of Marinetti as a precursor of Russian futurism reflects an attempt to claim priority and uniqueness for the Russian version of futurism, an idea colored by nationalist overtones and linked to the postulate of a different genealogy which would ally Russian art with Asian heritage against the Western European claim to cultural superiority: "Today some natives and the Italian colony on the Neva's banks, out of private considerations, prostrate themselves before Marinetti, thus betraying Russian art's first steps on the road to freedom and honor, and placing the noble neck of Asia under the yoke of Europe."[28] On the other hand, Khlebnikov's polemic highlights the specificity of his own brand of futurianism *(budetlyanstvo),* as he preferred to call it. In contradistinction from the Italian futurists and Mayakovsky, who almost unconditionally reject the past and call for the destruction of cultural heritage in the name of starting anew from scratch, Khlebnikov tends to reappraise the past, both historical events and cultural heritage, in an effort to produce mathematical laws of history which would both allow for the prediction of the future and facilitate the understanding of the turbulent historical context of his own work.

Though in 1914 Khlebnikov renounced Marinetti, distancing himself from the homage that some Russian futurists paid to him, in his later futurist pronouncement published in cooperation with the Society of 317,[29] Khlebnikov appears to stand firmly on the side of futurist ideas. In his less known, but perhaps most articulate, futurist manifesto, "The Trumpet of the Martians," Khlebnikov announces the formation of "the Martian Council" and includes Marinetti as its honorary member: "The following are invited to become honorary nonvoting members of the Martian Council: H.G. Wells and Marinetti" (*CW I,* 323). The inclusion of Marinetti's name seems less surprising in the context of a text which teems with typical futurist images and slogans, such as radical break from the past, denigration of the older generations, building a new future, exultation of technology, frequent evocations of speed, glorification of youth, the future and the power of change: "We believe in ourselves, we reject with indignation the vicious whispers of people from the past who still delude themselves that they can bite at out heels. Are we not gods?" (*CW I,* 321); or "How can we free the speeding locomotive of the younger generation from the insolent freight train of the older generation, hitched on without our permission?" (*CW I,* 324).

In "The Trumpet of the Martians" and other futurist visions like "The Radio of the Future" and "Ourselves and Our Buildings," which describes "the-yet-to-be city of the Futurians" (*CW I,* 350), Khlebnikov appears to be perfectly aligned with the futurist dream of a superbly technological and radically redesigned future. "In the Radio of the Future," technology becomes identified as the agent which, altering and reforming consciousness, defines the future shape of thought: "The Radio of the Future—the central tree of our consciousness—will inaugurate new ways to cope with our endless undertakings and will unite all mankind" (*CW I,* 392). Technology becomes the central nervous system of the future, because it structures the forms of experience and shapes the consciousness of this experience. Technological interconnectedness and dissemination of information, coupled with the scientific forms of knowledge, become the locus of supraindividual consciousness, the functional matrix of experience and thought.

Technology signifies the fulfillment of the Enlightenment idea of the unity and universality of humankind: "Thus will Radio forge continuous links in the universal soul and mold mankind into a single entity" (*CW I*, 396). If technology becomes the epitome of future experience as well as of the experience *of* the future, then this idea finds its perfect culmination in the concept of a universally understandable hieroglyphic language which Khlebnikov proposes in "Artists of the World! (a written language for Planet Earth: a common system of hieroglyphs for the people of our planet)." This language unites the "work of the artist" with the "work of the thinker" in an effort "to create a common written language shared by all the peoples of this third satellite of the Sun" (*CW I*, 364). The naive utopian enthusiasm of this venture aside, Khlebnikov relates here the technological project with the idea of a universal script that would supersede the differences between languages and cultures and retrieve the lost, pre-Babelian unity of experience. In this scenario, the artist complements, perhaps even fulfills, the technological "destiny" of being. The conclusion from those texts would have to be that Khlebnikov inscribes his artistic project within the technological understanding of being, where experience and thought take their form from the technic paradigm of reality. Art becomes a manifestation of the fact that reality is "technologically nerved," that technicity determines the very mode of being of what is.

Yet we know already that Khlebnikov's poetic practice and his beyonsense experiments, so heavily dependent upon the idiomatic features of Russian and the flexibility of inflectional systems characteristic of Slavic languages, belie this interpretation. The reading which allies Khlebnikov with the technological paradigm of experience—and the Picabian idea of the technological soul of modern art—becomes inflected through the ironic prism of *Zangezi*. The notion of the common system of hieroglyphs becomes complicated, if not undercut, through the multiple linguistic planes and the event temporality of experience. In *Zangezi*, words, letters, and sounds become readable in terms of temporal and spatial movements, as vectors and indices of forces and events. If we can talk in this context about words or particles of nature *(priroda)* in Khlebnikov, those words are not universal hieroglyphs but singular manifestations of the moment, "every minute producing words," as "Our Fundamentals" suggests.[30] It seems that the often exuberant linguistic creation of *zaum* tries to keep pace with the constant alterations and reconfigurations of the particles of experience. The expansion of language into the field of beyonsense responds to and registers the inappropriable contours of experience, or "corners of events," as Khlebnikov calls them. Reaching beyond the prescribed limits of signification, beyonsense emphasizes the distinction between the idea of history as a historical *datum* and history as continuously disarticulated by its historicity.

The difference between reading *zaum* as a universal hieroglyphic script and *zaum* as an expansion of language which marks the beyonsense status of historicity problematizes the position of technology within Khlebnikov's thought. On the one hand, technology spells out the "essence" of modernity and promises to define the nervous system of future experience. On the other hand, technology becomes reinscribed into "nature" and contextualized vis-à-vis the beyonsense moment of experience. Marking the historicity of the event, beyonsense remains incalculable to the mathematical laws designed by Khlebnikov to establish numerically computable relations between significant events in world history. These laws may well draw the links between more or less arbitrarily privileged moments in time, but they fail to register the "momentary" surplus of beyonsense that characterizes the *poiēsis* of experience. However overambitious and idiosyncratic Khlebnikov's idea of calculating historical distance, his notion of beyonsense extends beyond it: While the tables of destiny calculate the equations according to which the main events of history take place, they also hint at the fact that all calculations and mathematical tables of being become possible within the fold of historicity, represented by Khlebnikov through the impossible number $\sqrt{-1}$. The way in which the beyonsense experiments of Khlebnikov's poetry continuously complicate his thought about technology and history can be summed up by reference to Heidegger's insistence on the poetic structure of being: "[I]f . . . thinking knowingly avoids the vicinity of poesy [*Dichtung*], it readily appears as the super-science that would be more scientific than all the sciences put together" (*WCT*, 135). The ironic plays of *Zangezi* portray the dangers of such a thinking that becomes "more rational" than science itself.

This ambiguous attitude toward science and technology is also indicative of the double status of revolution in Khlebnikov. The idea of revolution as a violent and sudden change in the social and political order is certainly reflected in Khlebnikov's futurist predilections, especially in a series of manifestoes which he wrote or coauthored for various futurist groups. It is also reinforced by his laws of history, since the calculations in the "Tables of Destiny" are structured around "revolutionary" events in Russian and world history. In fact, Khlebnikov's obsession with understanding history in mathematical terms derives apparently from Russia's loss to Japan in 1905 and the revolution which followed this defeat within the same year. On the other hand, as I suggested earlier, a different conception of revolution is at work in *Zangezi,* one which links transformation to historicity and beyonsense language. Such a revolution refers to a radical change in the representational order itself, to the revision of the structure of experience through the beyonsense "subfield" of language. Both those conceptions continuously feed into each other in Khlebnikov's writings, in particular in *Zangezi,* where the augmentation of language into beyonsene is linked to Zangezi's reflections on the forces of history.

As is the case with many other Russian futurist writers and artists, Khlebnikov's work becomes at some point inextricably linked to the historical events in Russia: the First World War, the two revolutions of 1917, and the Russian Civil War. Never as politically active or ideologically committed as Mayakovsky, Khlebnikov clearly sympathized with the social and political changes happening in Russia through the revolutions of 1917 and the Civil War, which may explain why his most openly futurist and "revolutionary" proclamations were written between 1916 and his death in 1922. Finding himself almost constantly on the move during the time of the World War I, the revolutions, and the Civil War, Khlebnikov identifies movement as the constitutive feature of modern life and comes up with a daring architectural idea for mobile house units in his "Ourselves and Our Buildings." In need of finding lodging everywhere he goes, Khlebnikov proposes a vision of "the yet-to-be city of the Futurians," where a mobile apartment could be transported between cities and reattached to stationary frames in any location: "[A] container of molded glass, a mobile dwelling module supplied with a door, with attachment couplings, mounted on wheels. . . . It is set on a train . . . or on a steamship, and inside, without ever leaving it, its inhabitant would travel to his destination. . . . Once it had been decided that the primary building unit would no longer be an incidental material like brick, but rather these modular units inhabited by individuals, they began the construction of framework-buildings whose open spaces were filled in by the inhabitants themselves with their moveable glass cubicles" (*CW I,* 350).

While Khlebnikov's visions of the future definitely gather their energy from the transformations that took place around him, he distances himself from the rhetoric of war at work in Italian futurism. Side by side with his futurist visions, Khlebnikov writes a remarkable series of anti-war poems, collected under the title "War in a Mousetrap." As Markov suggests, "[t]his work could become the bible of modern war protesters, and Khlebnikov their prophet, if only they knew about it: it combines his avant-garde technique, the anti-war theme, and an orientation toward youth" (*RF*, 299). The title of the cycle suggests the entrapment of war, which locks all sides into a conflict in which everyone loses. One of the most poignant expressions of Khlebnikov's anti-war and anti-violence sentiment can be found in his poem "Refusal":

> I would rather
> Watch stars
> Than sign a death warrant.
> I would rather
> Hear flowers murmur
> ("It's him!")
> When I'm out in the garden
> Than see a gun
> Shoot down a man
> Who wants to shoot me down.
>
> (*KT*, 34)

This dramatic disavowal of violence distances Khlebnikov from the futurist glamorization of war or violent transformation and indicates that revolution has to find another venue in his work: the beyonsense potential of language. Khlebnikov's itinerant or nomadic lifestyle during the Civil War in Russia becomes itself an icon of de-localized experience—experience deprived of a site, ground, or essence—which keeps (dis)articulating itself through its historicity. The mobile modules of Khlebnikov's futurian cities signify both the transformation of the conventional modes of habitation and the displacement intrinsic to experience—the absence of a permanent temporal site that "structures" the event.

Doubting the effectiveness of military revolution and social upheaval, Khlebnikov links the possibility of change to the futurity inscribed in the event, which ruptures the present and holds it open to the future. In Kristeva's words, "[t]he poem's time frame is some 'future anterior' that will never take place, never come about as such, but only as an upheaval of present place and meaning" (*DL*, 32). The idea of the particles of experience forming the "secret building blocks of language" becomes, for Zangezi, the moment that revolutionizes language and revises our understanding of history: "We breathe like a wind upon you, / We whistle, our breath moves, / We blow blizzards of nations, / We cause waves, we bring ripples and waves"

(*KT,* 228). Though this gesture could be read as an attempt to construct a secret historical code which would explain through a numerical scenario the occurrences of important historical events, disasters, and revolutions, I argue that the link between the beyonsense field of language and historicity points to a nonessentialist, language-based conception of experience. The recovery of *poiēsis* in art and language brings into the foreground historicity, which remains occluded in different analyses of history. The effects of such a transformation in experience can be found throughout Khlebnikov's poetry, from his very short and experimental poems like "Incantation with Names" to more traditional and longer poems like "Russia and Me." "Russia and Me" is particularly significant in this context because of the explicit parallel Khlebnikov draws between "transformative" poetics and the revolutionary events in Russia: "Russia has granted freedom to thousands and thousands. / It was really a terrific thing to do, / People will never forget it. / But what I did was take off my shirt / And all those shiny skyscrapers the strands of my hair, / Every pore / In the city of my body / Broke out their banners and flags" (*KT,* 35).

The poem develops parallels between the image of Khlebnikov's body (and the body of his work) and the embodied, material experience of existence. The gesture of taking off the shirt becomes equivalent to the fall of Bastille: "The Bastille of my shirt has fallen!" (*KT,* 36), and the liberation of the body from the conventions of dress signifies freeing experience from the conventions and norms of language. The poem becomes a figure for the expansion of language into its realm of beyonsense, an expansion parallel to the revision of experience, which replaces its foundationalist notion with the idea of a disjointed, noncontemporaneous event. Khlebnikov certainly does not propose to substitute the poetic liberation of language for the freedom gained through political changes. Yet, the analogy he establishes between granting political freedoms and the freedom of beyonsense language underscores the importance of how we understand experience for thinking any possibility of transformation. This analogy shows that Khlebnikov, disappointed by the carnage of the Russian revolution and the suffering and poverty precipitated by the Civil War (which he describes in the simple and direct poems of the 1920s), rethinks freedom in terms of a transformation in the very modality of happening, in the relationality that subtends experience. There is an ironic undertone in "Russia and Me," which suggests that grand political gestures of granting freedom to humanity would perhaps not be necessary if experience were rethought in terms of historicity and its "liberating" effects, if freedom, extended beyond the idea of an individual's rights, were grounded *poietically:* "It was really a terrific thing to do, / People will never forget it. / But what I did was take off my shirt."[31]

The distance and dislocation opened up by historicity makes any closure of the present impossible and, thus, keeps open the possibility of a different future. One of the effects of historicity, as Derrida puts it, is that the present is always still to come, that its closure remains always deferred, projected toward what is to come—the future. Calling in *Spectres of Marx* for a new way of thinking or a new experience of the event, Derrida associates the event-ness of the event with "[t]he disjointure in the very presence of the present, this sort of non-contemporaneity of present time with itself" (*SM,* 25). The unexpected, the new, or the possibility of transformation finds its space of possibility in the disjunction of the event, in what Derrida calls the "event-ness" *(événementialité)* of experience (*SM,* 28). Since futurity is inscribed in the very structure of the event, it destabilizes experience and renders it intrinsically open to rereading. Such an open-ended or unbounded conception of event is at work in Khlebnikov's "beyonsense" understanding of history. It is exemplified by the ways in which *zaum* ruptures grammar and semantics, opening the conventions and norms of language, together even with the beyonsense inventions themselves, to poetic "re-invention."[32] Though obviously not directly translatable into changes in the social or political realm, the transformation of language and the different way of thinking experience contingent upon it become for Khlebnikov the venues for thinking the future. To the extent that it keeps in play the "beyonsense" of the representational space of history, poetry makes it possible to think experience through historicity, and to reimagine the present in terms of its unstable opening to the future—both to possible future histories and to future rereadings of the present as a historical moment.

Describing a poietics of historicity, *zaum* links art to the possibility of reinventing the present. This is the sense in which Khlebnikov's poetry is *futurian:* it reimagines the present as the realm of what "will be," as the sphere of what beyonsense language allows to come into being.[33] Khlebnikov charges poetry with the linguistic energy that inflects the representational order to allow for the "revolutionary" moment of experience to preserve itself against the discursive petrification of meaning. If Derrida writes about the need for a new, postmetaphysical thinking of the event, then we can see Khlebnikov's beyonsense poetry as an attempt at a postaesthetic concept of art: art that rebels against its reduction to the aesthetic paradigm, against the erasure of the productive and liberating effects of historicity. The importance of such art lies in its ability to figure experience without totalizing or splintering it into isolated points within the order of representation. Distinct from the idea of an art of the future, of art that "simply" remains ahead of its time, such avant-garde art figures the futurity of experience. Questioning the aesthetic paradigm, it works as *poiēsis* and brings its transformative effects to bear upon our understanding of history. It is perhaps in this sense that Khlebnikov's futurian art remains transformative, open to the future within and beyond its own historical context.

Part Three : **From the Avant-Garde to Language Poets**

To się nie da przepisać

z faktyczności

na wyrażalność

(This can't be rewritten

from facticity

to expressibility)

—Białoszewski, *Oho*

6. How to Write the Everyday
in Eastern Europe

Miron Białoszewski's "Minor" Poetry

Among many modern poets and fiction writers who make everyday experience and ordinary language central to their writing—from Williams, Stein, or Ponge to Musil, Joyce, and Beckett—Miron Białoszewski, a Polish poet and prose writer, still largely unknown in the United States,[1] may hold the distinction of producing a uniquely iconoclastic body of work, which remakes literature into a continuous rewriting of the everyday.[2] Part of the distinctive character of Białoszewski's work comes from the often "unpoetic" themes of his poems, concerned predominantly with details of ordinary life: with such banalities as problems with the plumbing or the elevator in his apartment building, changes introduced into his life by the acquisition of new dentures, or the specifics of his hospitalization and kidney operation comprised in a series of poems entitled "Encounters with the Knife." What contributes to the "shock value" of these topics, unpoetic even by modern standards, is Białoszewski's systematic displacement, or, to use Deleuze and Guattari's idiom, deterritorialization, of poetry and literary writing: a reciprocal demythologization of literature and everyday life. Treating the everyday as an event which constantly defamiliarizes and remakes itself, Białoszewski incorporates the colloquial and nonstandard registers of language into a literary practice whose critical and ironic force comes specifically from its "intensely" minor status: in relation to cultural centers, literary traditions, or political orientations, but also with respect

225

to the "myths" which writing inescapably engenders. As Białoszewski remarks in an interview: "My diarylike pieces-poems are indeed diarylike. That is, writing and life go together. And at times, they are the same. . . . Working on life as it happens. Demythologizing. Demetaphorizing. . . . In order to do literature, one should never go to literature. One has to do it from something more alive and other, precisely from life. From life and experience [*Z życia i przeżycia*]." [3] In order to question literary conventions and the social functions of literature, Białoszewski invents a "minor" language within the "high" literary language, a poetic language which unworks poetry. One could say that he deliberately produces an "inferior" idiom or a sub-language that undoes the mythology of writing and the cultural and literary idealizations it generates, a Białoszewski vernacular, relentlessly ironizing the pretensions of writing. This poetic idiom reflects the fact that, as Barańczak observes, "Białoszewski always chooses the world of popular culture against elite culture. . . ." [4]

For Białoszewski, writing becomes a matter of inventing a language of a continuous interface, contestation, and parody between literary discourse and idioms of ordinary speech, a language which would be capable of registering everyday experience without transforming it into an aesthetic construct. My reading draws some parallels between Białoszewski's poetics and Heidegger's critique of the everyday in order to rethink the relation between poetic thinking and everydayness, both beyond the scope Heidegger gives to it and in a tenor quite different from the one characteristic of his work. I read Białoszewski's work as a unique venue for reworking this connection between the poetic and the everyday: a link which animates much of Heidegger's project and yet remains undeveloped in his texts on poetry.[5] Białoszewski underscores the proximity between the poetic and the everyday by juxtaposing the intensity and surprise of everyday experience—which his work produces through stylistic and linguistic innovations—with the accepted routine of the ordinary. Interested in the temporality of the everyday, in the poietic space of the mundane, he pushes language to its semantic and stylistic extremes where distorted, reinvented words and fragmented syntax map the overlooked dimensions of the commonplace. As in the previous chapters, I make the distinction between poetics as a literary category and *poiēsis* as a modality of unfolding, as a poietic event. In Białoszewski's case, such *poiēsis* explicitly undercuts nostalgic sentimentalization or aestheticization of the ordinary: It strips everydayness of any mythologizing inclinations, expressly de-sentimentalizes poetry, and evacuates any pathos that might accrue precisely as a result of the poetic (re)writing of the everyday.[6] These deterritorializing literary, cultural, and political effects of Białoszewski's exploration of the historicity of the everyday mark the avant-garde moment of his writing—the place of an intense refiguration of experience.

Miron Białoszewski (1922–83) occupies an interesting and, in many ways, unique position in Polish literature. Much less known abroad than contemporary "main stream" poets like Miłosz, Różewicz, Herbert, or Zagajewski, whose aesthetics have clearly met the literary world's expectations about poetry from Eastern Europe, Białoszewski is both an outsider to that tradition and one of its most severe critics. Like other poets of his generation, for example, the better known Różewicz, Białoszewski's poetry is distinctively "anti-poetic," devoid of metaphors and other poetic devices, employing ordinary language and everyday imagery.[7] Although his first texts did not seem to fit the profile of his generation, whose members were intensely preoccupied with the devastating experience of World War II, the publication of Białoszewski's memoir from the Warsaw Uprising *(Pamiętnik z powstania warszawskiego)* in 1970 made clear the extent to which his approach to poetry and experience had been influenced by the war. Similarly to Zbigniew Herbert, Białoszewski published his first volume, *Obroty rzeczy,* in 1956, after the end of Stalinism in Poland, and was hailed as belonging to the "new wave" of Polish poetry which burst upon the literary scene after the years of the state-mandated dominance of socialist realism. With the publication of his subsequent volumes— *Rachunek zachciankowy (Calculus of Whims,* 1959) *Mylne wzruszenia (False Thrills,* 1961), *Było i było (Was and Was,* 1961)—it became clear, however, that Białoszewski's poetics eschewed classification and developed an individual, "plebeian" and iconoclastic approach to writing quite distinct from the main trends of Polish poetry which, in the face of the repressive regime, emphasized Poland's place within the cultural tradition of Western Europe. Rather than seeking aesthetic, ethical, or political legitimation within this tradition, Białoszewski opted for an unprecedented project of a radical remaking of literature in terms of diverse "genres" of everyday experience, and, in the process, invented a different "literary" language, which, reshaped through everyday speech and colloquial idioms, was instrumental in unworking both the representational constraints and the cultural imaginary in relation to everydayness. In the course of his career, Białoszewski wrote numerous volumes of poetry, a book of plays, and several volumes of prose, which became his main preoccupation after the publication of *A Memoir of the Warsaw Uprising.*

As it evolved over the years, his writing began to increasingly blur the boundaries between literary genres: His texts became fragmentary, focused within the moment, usually "dramatic" in tone, and the differences between poetry, prose, or drama became more a matter of typographical arrangement then content or diction. Białoszewski's last writings tend to be organized by major events in his personal life: *Zawał* (*Heart Attack*) describes his heart attack and hospital stay; *Konstancin* chronicles his convalescence in a sanatorium in Konstancin near Warsaw; *AAAmeryka* describes his trip to the United States. To underscore the connection of his writings with the everyday, Białoszewski groups his poetic texts into cycles, inventing unconventional "generic" names for them, which reflect the multiplicity of the "genres" he discovers in the everyday. Often funny and even ridiculous titles such as "Cites," "Leaks," "Frivols," "Noises," "Paste-Ups," "Chains,"or "Dartings" refer to diverse aspects of everydayness and have their origin in colloquial speech.[8] This unconventional approach to literary writing met during Białoszewski's life with both enthusiastic welcome and severe criticism, especially from those cultural quarters interested in preserving the high and noble style of the national literary tradition. It is only recently, however, that Białoszewski's work has become regarded as a truly major force within contemporary Polish poetry. As the 1993 volume of essays from the conference of the Institute for the Literary Studies of the Polish Academy of Sciences dedicated to Białoszewski's work suggests, literary critics have started talking about a Białoszewski "tradition," an alternative trend within Polish postwar poetry inspired by Białoszewski, which contests and ironizes the notion of the "Eastern European" writer as a moral legislator.[9] The continuing publication of the collected edition of his works by Państwowy Instytut Wydawniczy seems to be the confirmation of the growing importance of Białoszewski's work for contemporary Polish literature.

Two major factors which played a determining role in the development of Białoszewski's poetics should be mentioned here. In the 1960s, Białoszewski was regarded as part of the so-called language poetry *(poezja lingwistyczna)*[10] trend, associated with the writings of Karpowicz, Wirpsza, Barańczak, and Krynicki, whose linguistic innovations changed the landscape of Polish poetry and predated the better known American language poets. Although not a misnomer, this label fails to do justice to the complexity of Białoszewski's work, in particular because it occludes the fact that in his case linguistic deformations and inventions result from a "poetics of the mundane," from a transformative engagement with the genres of everydayness. Another important factor in situating Białoszewski's writings is his experience of the 1944 Warsaw Uprising: As he himself observed about his *Memoir of the Warsaw Uprising*, his poetic experiments were partly a result of the effort to register in language the dislocating effects of the experience of war, in particular of the days of the Warsaw Uprising against the German occupational forces in 1944. Chronicling Białoszewski's relocations and wanderings through the basements of destroyed buildings in Warsaw's Old Town, where the civilian population "lived" during the uprising, *A Memoir* registers in its language and writing style the proliferation of "alternative" routines of daily life literally displaced into the underground. For Białoszewski, the reality of the uprising and almost complete destruction of the city did not simply abolish "ordinary life." In addition to uprooting the routine of everydayness, the uprising produced a new kind of "ordinariness" of daily bombardment and deprivation, which drew attention to the inconspicuous and often overlooked details, things and affairs, taken for granted in "normal" circumstances. While life during the uprising rendered simple amenities like habitation, food, and hygiene "extraordinary," it also produced its own substitute practices and habits. Białoszewski's subsequent preoccupation with the arcana of everydayness, with exposing the routines of ordinary experiences and their unsuspected, surprising, and often comical underside, can be traced to this war experience of a forcibly dislocated, "upside-down" everydayness.[11] This kind of persistent dislodging of the everyday in order to apprehend its other, poietic dimension becomes the trademark of Białoszewski's work.

Białoszewski's writings obviously do not fit the standard Deleuze and Guattari definition of minor literature as "that which a minority constructs within a major language."[12] To begin with, Białoszewski already operates within a comparatively "minor" language on the cultural map of Europe, and his circumstances are less complexly and multiply dislocated than are those of Kafka's work, which Deleuze and Guattari use as their main example. Yet, it is possible to read Białoszewski's situation differently: In a way, Białoszewski's poetic and cultural deterritorializations could be seen as forceful in a different manner than those of Kafka; for if Kafka's were precipitated, even to a certain extent "arranged," by historical and cultural circumstances, Białoszewski had a language and a tradition, even if a "minor" one, within which to recuperate his experiences but, instead, expressly chose to challenge it. We should also not underestimate the fact that by focusing his challenge on poetry, Białoszewski *is* in fact working within a major and highly prestigious cultural "language." Realizing the already marginal or minor status of Polish literature, he opts for a second degree marginalization — a displacement from even the "minor" safety of the margin — in order to question both the familiar topography of the Polish literary tradition and to rechart the territory of poetry. Like a minor literature, Białoszewski's writings develop the "tensors" and "intensives"[13] which intensify the internal tensions of language and push Polish literary language to its limits. They deploy colloquialisms, childlike distortions, nonstandard expressions, and neologisms to create a map of surprising semantic and grammatical intensities which reflect the intenseness of the historical and linguistic paste-up of being, unsuspected in ordinary occurrences.

Białoszewski's texts work on the principle of a double movement between the poetic and the everyday: On the one hand, poetry is deglamorized, brought into everyday experience and focused on the apparent banality of commonplace things and events, and, on the other hand, constant experimentation with ordinary language and colloquial or nonstandard expressions undercuts the illusory immediacy and familiarity of everydayness. His writings consistently deterritorialize poetic language through everyday idioms, colloquialisms, and nonstandard, even ungrammatical, expressions. Yet, these imported language registers do not constitute a new terrain for poetry: a comfortable space of transparent, ordinary language, underlined with nostalgia for the supposed obviousness and immediacy of the everyday. Instead, they themselves are immediately defamiliarized by poetic experimentation: word inventions, grammatical and inflectional innovations. As though this were not enough, Białoszewski's writing puts itself in question through yet another inversion: Many of the poetic techniques are often employed in a deliberately clumsy and exaggerated, distortive fashion, generating what Białoszewski refers to as little poetic "monstrosities." In effect, these innovations avoid aestheticizing the nonpoetic registers of the everyday or recuperating them for poetic practice. These operations produce a distinctively two-pronged textuality, which keeps reinventing both the poetic and the everyday in order to open writing to the "surprising" poietic dimension of everydayness — to what Białoszewski calls *dziwienie*, or "wondering." To counteract language's tendency to self-mythologization, Białoszewski gives to such *dziwienie* the form of deliberately "minor" poems, or, in the case of his later prose writings, "little narratives," as critics call them.[14]

Dziwienie, or the Everyday as a Situational Paste-Up

Białoszewski's poetry does more than construct a "minor aesthetics": an alternative poetic practice, a counterpoetics, which would concentrate upon the domains of experience which, too commonplace or mundane, either remain excluded from aesthetics or can serve as poetic material only through deliberate beautification. Its aim is to rethink poetry as a venue for understanding experience through its everyday *poiēsis.* Białoszewski's poietics describes a dimension of everydayness which opens up when both poetic language and the ordinary are stripped of their customary connotations, when they are brought, through poetic experimentation, into the state of wonder *(dziwienie).* Wonder—a state of thinking and, primarily, a state of poetic language—constitutes the paradoxically deterritorialized "territory" of Białoszewski's work, a terrain without set perimeter or parameters, where even the most insignificant elements, like dust, walls, or stairs, can unexpectedly become the fleeting and contingent "fundamentals" of the everyday.

I read this rethought idea of wonder as a critique of high aesthetic experience, which for Białoszewski aestheticizes the everyday and forecloses its meaning in terms of poetic affect. What is characteristic of Białoszewski's "wonder" is the complexity and heterogeneity of the everyday event, of the paste-up character of the ordinary: "what is at stake . . . is the whole situational paste-up. That which happens. . . . The comings, the associations, dialogical situations, some stories. . . . Without this there is only literature, aphorism, the absence of the human."[15] The idea of a situational "paste-up" *(zlep)* defines writing in terms of the shifting and metamorphosing character of happening, of the hybridity of a situational paste-up, which is kept in play by the parallel paste-up of literary and ordinary idioms. As a space of demetaphorizing and demythologization, wonder becomes important for underscoring this paste-up character of the event and for ironizing the way in which literature and aestheticization evacuate the everyday. As Białoszewski indicates in the cited interview, his texts work expressly against "distilling" the meaning of what happens, against reducing the hybridity of *zlepy* to the necessarily aphoristic space of representation. Keeping in play the event of experience and its dislocating effects within the practices of representation and literary conventions, wonder opens up the spaces of inscription for the elusive historicity of being. If art, as Heidegger suggests, is to produce a turn within the technological modality of revealing away from articulating being in terms of the universal calculability of resources, then it has to refigure being specifically in its everyday dimension. And it has to do so without lapsing into the familiar debacle of aestheticization, without resorting to the nostalgic mythology of immediacy and fullness. Białoszewski's work certainly meets these criteria, as it demythologizes both poetry and everydayness through reciprocal questioning and ironization. It is along the lines of this reciprocal demythologization that I want to explore the relation between Białoszewski's writing and Heidegger's notion of poetic thinking, in order to demonstrate the poietic character of experience as event.

It is relatively easy to write separately about the importance of everydayness for Heidegger's early "phenomenological" work and the role of poetic thinking in his late writings but more difficult to discern how Heidegger's remarks about poetry and the critique of aesthetics bear upon the everyday. Heidegger's project of the critique of metaphysics begins in *Being and Time* with an attempt to redirect thinking along the lines of everyday being, *das alltägliche Sein*,[16] and this interest, although muted to some degree by his later investment in Hölderlin's poetry and its hymnic rhetoric, nevertheless underpins the entirety of Heidegger's thought. In order to recognize how the problem of the ordinary inscribes itself in Heidegger's definition of poetic thinking, let us read a rarely discussed part of "Letter on Humanism," where Heidegger, reflecting on a story about Heraclitus, expressly brings together thinking and everydayness. Heidegger comments there on Aristotle's story in *De parte animalium* (I, 5, 645a 17) about the disappointment that unknown guests experience upon visiting the most famous of the pre-Socratics, Heraclitus, and finding him in the middle of a most banal activity—a story which, as it turns out, engages the problem of the "essence" of thinking:

> The story is told of something Heraclitus said to some strangers who wanted to come visit him. Having arrived, they saw him warming himself at a stove. Surprised, they stood there in consternation—above all because he encouraged them, the astounded ones, and called for them to come in, with the words, "For here too the gods are present."[17]

Depicting a commonplace, daily occurrence, the story underscores the paramount importance of the ordinary: the house, the stove, the act of warming, with the words εἶναι γὰρ καὶ ἐνταῦθα θεύς, "For here too the gods are present."

The Heraclitus story suggests that what matters for thinking, what in fact constitutes its very matter, is a certain attentiveness to the everyday. Heidegger's commentary, though preoccupied primarily with setting up his notion of thinking as proto-ethical, with explaining the word ἦθος as an abode, a place of dwelling (W, 350), indicates in passing the importance of the everyday in the enterprise of thinking, as it underscores the banality of the situation in which the visitors encounter the thinker:

> The group of foreign visitors . . . believe they should meet the thinker in circumstances which, contrary to the ordinary [übliche] round of human life, everywhere bear the traces of the exceptional and rare and so of the exciting [die Züge der Ausnahme und des Seltenen und darum Aufregenden tragen]. . . . The foreigners who wish to visit the thinker expect to catch sight of him perchance at that very moment when, sunk in profound meditation, he is thinking. . . . Instead of this the sightseers find Heraclitus by a stove. That is surely a common and insignificant place [Das ist ein recht alltäglicher und unscheinbarer Ort]. . . . At this disappointing spectacle even the curious lose their desire to come any closer. What are they supposed to do here? Such an everyday and unexciting occurrence [alltägliche und reizlose Vorkommnis] — somebody who is chilled warming himself at a stove — anyone can find any time at home. (BW, 257)[18]

All the words that guide Heidegger's reflection on the passage about Heraclitus and the nature of thinking refer to the opposition between the normal and the extraordinary. The disappointment that the visitors show at the sight of Heraclitus expresses itself in the rhetoric of the absence of anything "exceptional," "rare," or "exciting." The site and the event, which Heraclitus proclaims worthy of the presence of the gods, or, to be more exact, whose being is godlike or holy, are perceived as "ordinary," "common," "insignificant," "everyday," and "unexciting."

The focus of Heidegger's brief remarks falls specifically on the "alltägliche und reizlose Vorkommnis"—the everyday and unexciting occurrence, which, at least for the visitors, appears to have nothing to do with thinking. Implicitly, for them thinking constitutes a special event, an extraordinary occurrence, which, though based on the everyday and common experience, is at the same time divorced from it, separated by a distance which allows for reflection, understanding, and knowledge. For the visitors, the extraordinary character of thinking should, not surprisingly, be reflected in the posture in which they expect to see Heraclitus—"sunk into meditation." Heidegger clearly distances himself from this view, as the phrases used in this passage reveal his ironic, even parodic, attitude toward such a representation of the thinker and thinking, a representation distinctively reminiscent of Rodin's famous sculpture.

What remains only implicit in Heidegger's commentary is the question of how wonder *(thaumazein)* in the pre-Socratic sense of the word, underlies the properly philosophical notion of thought as the enterprise of obtaining knowledge. At the start of his remarks about the rise and nature of thought in *Metaphysics,* Aristotle locates the origin of philosophical questioning in wonder: διὰ γὰρ τὸ θαυμάζειν οἱ ἄνθρωποι καὶ νῦν καὶ τὸ πρῶτον ἤρξαντο φιλοσοφεῖν *(Metaphysics* A, 2, 982b 12–13) — "For it is owing to their wonder that men both now begin and at first began to philosophize. . . ."[19] The Aristotelian wonder defines the roots of philosophy in terms of a desire to know, which springs from the astonishment at the world.[20] Wonder comes to be treated as the origin of philosophy, an origin which, however, remains excluded from philosophy proper. Acknowledging the originary importance of θαυμάζειν, Aristotle makes clear that thought and philosophy arise out of this wonder and change it into knowledge — ἐπιστήμη (983a 25). The Aristotelian wonder triggers philosophical thought (φιλοσοφεῖν) but itself cannot claim the same status, for philosophy as such is an attempt to give systematic and lucid answers to the phenomena that cause the human mind to wonder. For one wonders only when one does not know the cause of things, and philosophy by providing answers allows us to achieve a "better state" of knowledge: "[b]ut we must end in the contrary and, according to the proverb, the better state, as is the case in these instances when men learn the cause" *(M,* 1555). As the beginning of *Metaphysics* makes clear, Aristotle's concern lies with seeking ἐπιστήμη and, thus, with transforming the human mind from the state of wonder to "the better state" of knowledge. The distinction between the originary wonder and philosophy defined as a search for knowledge implies that θαυμάζειν is prephilosophical and as such belongs with philosophical inquiry only indirectly, as a way of anchoring and explaining the initial philosophical impulse. Heraclitus's statement, however, complicates the distinction between wonder and philosophy and indicates that θαυμάζειν is already a kind of thinking, a thinking that precisely remains unexplored by philosophy as it takes shape with Aristotle's definition of knowledge. The visitors' surprise results from their inability to comprehend that warming at a stove is a "matter of thinking," that it is worthy of the concern of a thinker. The stove and the mundane necessity of keeping warm become the place holders for what constitutes the "proper" site of thinking — everyday experience. Conceived this way, wonder is not deficient but excessive in relation to *epistēmē:* It describes a poietic modality of thinking irreducible and untranslatable into the order of representation and knowledge. In relation to wonder, the parameters of *epistēmē* represent a restricted scope of thinking: They obscure the "ordinary" site of thought, and, reducing the poietics of everydayness to the parameters of signification, render it "foreign," even unreal, to the enterprise of accumulating knowledge.[21] This link between wonder and *poiēsis* opens a postaesthetic venue for thinking art, in which the poietic dimension of experience puts into question both the customary figurations of the everyday and the aesthetic "reduction" of poetry.

In the context of this double displacement, it becomes easier to recognize the ramifications and motivations of Białoszewski's work. If Heidegger uses the Heraclitus story to question the idea that knowledge is the "better state" of thinking, Białoszewski's writing can be read in terms of undermining aesthetic construction as a better or finished state of representation. As much as Heidegger's work reformulates the very notion of what it means to think and to know, Białoszewski's poetry interrogates the sites where language and representation, achieving the aesthetic quality of expression, fail to register the historicity of the event. Białoszewski's early poem about the loss of his stove, " 'Oh! Oh! Should They Take Away Even My Stove . . .' My Inexhaustible Ode to Joy," is one of his most explicit instances of reconceptualizing thinking and language through everyday experience.

> I have a stove
> like a triumphal arch!
>
> They're taking away my stove
> like a triumphal arch!!
>
> Give me back my stove
> like a triumphal arch!!!
>
> They took it away.
> All that's left
>   is a grey
>   gaping
>   hole
>   a gray gaping hole.
>
> And that's enough for me:
> grey gaping hole

> grey-gaping-hole
> grey-gap-ing-hole
> greygapinghole.
> (*RT*, 12, translation modified) [22]

The poem is punctuated by the repetition of the phrase "like a triumphal arch" *("podobny do bramy triumfalnej")* and "grey gaping hole" *("szara naga jama"),* which insistently draws attention to the two focal points of the text. The first one emphasizes the importance of what seems to be an ordinary, old heating stove, while the second encapsulates the role that language plays in mapping experience, literally filling with words the hole exposed by the removal of the stove. Although the text describes an apparently painful experience of losing an important object, emphasized through the repetitions and the increasing number of exclamation marks after each of the first three stanzas, it is surprisingly subtitled "My Inexhaustible Ode to Joy."

The loss of an object which constitutes a basic necessity of life and a vital part of the poet's experience of having a home (note here the stress that the title places upon the word *nawet,* "even"), disrupts the sense of dwelling. The poem hinges upon the fact that this disruption becomes, paradoxically, a source of linguistic proliferation, which fills the gaping, or "naked" *(naga)* hole with words—a process which moves from the repetition of the phrase "gray gaping hole" through its syllabization, and culminates in the erasure of the boundaries between words and the invention of a foreign sounding sound string "greygapinghole." [23] Unexpectedly, the disruption of the everyday routine becomes a positive experience, which generates a sense of an inexhaustible joy of language and turns the poem into a celebration of the linguistic form of dwelling. Filling the hole exposed by the removed stove with words suggests that dwelling has a linguistic constitution, that it takes its shape from how the event of experience comes into words. The sudden absence of the stove accentuates the "rising" of language and it draws the poet's attention to the fact that being has a language of its own—an inexhaustible rising of words even in the absence of objects and things. The text underscores this point by using the word *"jama"* (translated as "hole"), which plays on the idea of the link between language and dwelling. On the one hand, *jama* refers to a den or a burrow, and thus suggests a subterranean dwelling place, and, on the other, it also signifies the oral cavity and alludes to the process of the articulation of sounds. The poem suggests that the nature of habitation is primarily linguistic, less determined by the constellation of the objects that make up our surroundings than constituted as a map of unstable significations, a web of multiple and shifting referrals, into which the world opens. This is why Białoszewski can say emphatically that the "grey gaping hole" becomes an inexhaustible source of joy, worthy of a continuous writing of an ode.[24] Stripping his place of everything but emptiness, Białoszewski is happy to discover that he is left with language, with "naked" words. This "joyous" recognition of how language arranges and builds one's dwelling—the hole inexhaustibly pouring out words— functions parodically as the origin, the continuous "spring" of poetry.

The "naked" words deflate the celebratory rhetoric of "the triumphal arch" while the poem's references to mundane things and technologically produced objects—the missing stove, walls, and the hole—ironize nostalgia for the immediacy of ordinary experience. These underlying strands of irony make it possible for Białoszewski to link poetry with the everyday without mythologizing the connection and to keep a playful distance in his own project of "defamiliarizing" the ordinary. The joy of the mundane is always mediated by language, and the site of wonder is an ordinary, even ugly hole in the wall, whose "nakedness" brings into focus the linguistic configuration of experience. Białoszewski's "ode" marks the recognition of the inexhaustible, "infinite," singularity of even such an apparently simple event as the appearance of a hole exposed by the removal of an old stove. This event remains without essence, without the assurance of the ontological constancy or semantic transparency associated with presence. As the ending extends language beyond its accepted rules, it suggests the noncoincidence of the event with its representation. It points to dislocation and displacement as the very mode of occurrence proper to the event, a disjoining figured in the poem by the removal of the stove and the opening of a gap or a "hole" in the structure of experience. The exuberant repetition of the words "grey naked hole" underscores the deferral of signification which marks the event's historicity: an event which has no essence, and which empties or "holes" itself with each attempt at representation. This repetition outlines the poietic dimension of experience, which, manifest as the open-ended field of the event, finds its reflection in the poetic plasticity of language.

In an early poem "Of My Hermitage with Calling" *("O mojej pustelni nawoływaniem"),* this plasticity takes a form of *dziwienie,* of wonder or amazement:

> Wall, I am not worthy
> that you should fill me with constant wonder,

and you too, fork . . .
and you, dusts . . .

(RT, 10)[25]

In a faintly ironic, quasi-religious idiom, the poet confesses his unworthiness to accept the "grace" of the most ordinary objects and things, which fill him with wonder. The objects are deliberately the most mundane ones—fork, wall, dust—the objects of everyday surroundings, signifiers of domesticity, and overlooked trivialities, which, though always present as part of everydayness, hardly ever draw our attention. These are the details and corners of everydayness which certainly have very seldom been graced with poetic or philosophical regard:

> Yes
> my hermitage has its temptations:
> solitude
> memories of the world
> and that I consider myself a poet.
> I wonder
> I wonder me
> and comment on the lives of the surrounding.
> *(RT,* 10, translation modified)[26]

I modify slightly the existing translation of the poem in *The Revolution of Things* to underscore the fact that wonder coincides with linguistic innovations and displacement. The lines "I wonder / I wonder me" *("Dziwię się / dziwię siebie")* transform, in violation of grammatical rules, the reflexive verb *dziwić się,* which takes indirect objects in the dative case (in English the verb "wonder" is nonreflexive but functions as a transitive verb with the use of prepositions "about" or "at"), into a nonreflexive transitive verb, which can take direct objects in the accusative. To approximate this effect in English, it would be necessary to use the verb "wonder" in a transitive form, with a direct object but without the intervening preposition. The invented phrase, *"dziwię siebie"* ("I wonder me"), a deliberate transgression against grammatical propriety, functions as the emblem of Białoszewski's reconceptualization of poetic language. The derivation of *dziwić* as a nonreflexive transitive verb, abolishing the prepositional distance between the subject of wonder and its object, shows how wonder exceeds the subject-centered paradigm of being. This linguistic "perversion" produces a redefinition of wonder: Wonder no longer signifies a state of curiosity or ignorance, a question that expects an answer in the form of understanding or knowledge, but an openness to the event through which the world unfolds into language. Wonder changes its role from being a preliminary stage to the institution of a rational subject in search of knowledge to functioning as the opening up of a space in which a thing can be "something" in the first place.

Białoszewski's language disclaims both the representational function and the authority of a commentary, illustration, or exemplary status with respect to the experience of the ordinary. The displacements, distortions, and ironic playfulness specifically serve the purpose of ridiculing the mimetic pretensions of language. A decisive shift in the conception of poetry, such an attitude denounces the mistakes, the "sins" of past poetic writing:

> Put paper flowers in teapots,
> pull the ropes of clotheslines
> and the bells of boots,
> for the carnival of poetry,
> for a solemn unceasing amazement [*dziwienie;* wonder].
>
> (*RT,* 11) [27]

Eschewing conventional poetic themes and imagery, "Of My Hermitage with Calling" links the idea of poetic carnival with the minutiae of the ordinary: boots, clotheslines, and paper flowers. Defining what constitutes the poetic, the poem opts for accouterments of the everyday, banal, and "cheap" (paper flowers) reality. The invocations of the mundane disclaim the "offenses" of poetic writing, making the carnival of poetry contingent precisely on the recognition of the ordinariness. The Polish word *odpust* (translated as "carnival") is an equivalent of the Latin *absolutio,* and ties the celebration with the Church designated days of absolution, a play which another passage makes clear:

> Switch off the light:
> Here's a storehouse of contemplation,
> you are all covered with heart,
> give me absolution [*rozgrzesz mnie!*]!
>
> (*RT,* 11/*UZ I,* 72)

Asking the objects of his everyday surroundings for forgiveness, Białoszewski implies that poetry finds itself in need of atonement for the "aesthetic" excesses and extravagances of its portrayal of experience. It is the ironic wonder at the "mundane," manifest in the twists and distortions of language, that secures the absolution for poetry's mythologization of experience.

The linguistic pun in the title of another poem, *"Zmysłów pierwoustroje"* (*UZ I*, 130) demonstrates precisely the "originary" character of this poetic wonder. The neologism *"pierwoustroje"* ("firstelements") plays on the Polish equivalent of "microorganisms" *(drobnoustroje)* by replacing the first segment, *drobno-*, which indicates the minimal size, with a derivative of the adjective *pierwszy*—first, initial, originary. The coined word suggests that the linguistic lacunae in Białoszewski's poetry are of originary and principal importance for his understanding of poetic language. These blanks constitute the "firstelements" of language, which arrange, structure, set up, and program writing (all those "activities" are implicit in *ustroje*, which carries the connotation of arranging and organizing—not yet a sign of actual arrangement or order, but an index of the structural play which enables ordering). The full title of the poem can then be rendered as "The Firstelements of Senses," where "senses" itself carries an additional load of playful ambiguity. The word *zmysły* refers to the senses as the mechanism of perception but it also plays in this specific context on *myśl* (thought) and *zmyślanie* ("making up" or "imagining"). The text leaves no doubt that the "firstelements" are themselves linguistic, a kind of first *zmysły* (constructs of thought), even if they signify only as blanks or lacunae. Consequently, these "firstelements of senses" cannot be quite categorized under the rubric of either the sensible or the intelligible, as their ontologico-linguistic status puts this opposition into question. They point, instead, to what might be called the "element of sense," the space that opens up the very distinction between materiality and intelligibility, without, however, becoming signifiable through this opposition. Wonder marks the poietic dimension of experience, which inaugurates binary conceptual configurations—matter-sense, subject-object—only to exceed their parameters. The perceptual senses are always already linguistically coded—they perceive or "sense" inseparably from language senses, like the sweetness of the beet root felt already in word from the cycle "Romance with the Particular": "sugar! sweet / already in the beet-root of the word /. . . / our gluttonous well / trimmed / with the taste buds of language" (*UZ I*, 158–59). Since sensations are felt through words, experienced as inseparable from their meaning, wonder describes experience not simply as embodied but, rather, as opening an inscriptional space where flesh can be experienced as a socio-linguistic body, signified through its functions.

The figures through which Białoszewski describes everyday experience all refer to habitation, to forms of dwelling and habitual, customary occurrences—from the "hermitage" of his apartment to the series of poems describing the minutiae of life in a high-rise apartment building. His poetry functions as a poetic building of an open-ended and historical map of significations, within which writing opens up access to the *ēthos* of everydayness.[28] This *ēthos* takes the form of poetic thinking, built of the "first elements of sense," in which things emerge as what they are. Białoszewski's term *dziwienie* refigures the Heraclitean wonder into this specific venue of poetic thinking, which emphasizes the paste-up character of the event. This poetic dimension of thinking requires a reinvention of the everyday as an "inexhaustible" happening, whose continuously erupting singularity can never be brought fully into presence: It remains foreign to knowledge and aesthetic representation. Białoszewski's poetry parodies the divorce of thinking from the everyday, its abstraction—for the sake of knowledge—from the mundane, though perhaps never really ordinary, minutiae of experience. It uses the disruptive effects of this parody to question the reductions of the everyday to the "event-less" and ordinary scope it is given within the order of representation.

The "Avant-Garde" Peripheries of Culture

On the face of it, Białoszewski's favorite strategy of writing, *dziwienie,* poses a challenge to at least some of the tenets of avant-garde aesthetics: It espouses a plebeian rather than an elitist viewpoint; it deploys countless forms of low culture and folklore; it uses substandard and peripheral forms of language; and it is highly individualistic, anti-ideological and anti-communal.[29] These points of contention do not mean, however, that Białoszewski simply takes an anti-avant-garde stance. Rather, his work is a constant demystification of the myth of the avant-garde and its emblematic features: super-experimental aesthetics, group ideology, elitist attitude, utopian social vision. As usual with Białoszewski, his irony cuts both ways: His work parodies the avant-garde's tendency to self-mythologization *and* the cultural stereotypes and misreadings of avant-garde art. This dismantling of avant-garde myths constitutes, as Burkot shows, a necessary "destructive" part of Białoszewski's radicalization of avant-garde poetics, in particular of the problematic of everydayness. Rejecting what he finds obstructive to the rethinking of experience as event, Białoszewski develops the idea of the avant-garde as a "poetics of the mundane," where the questioning of the most commonplace forms of experience motivates linguistic experimentation.

Białoszewski's individualism and extreme privacy, his withdrawal from official forms of literary life and cultural exchange into the minutiae of everyday life, constitutes a challenge to the public function of art. This contestation is particularly significant in the context of the expectations of moral and political leadership which Polish culture has placed on artists and intellectuals. As Jarosław Anders remarks in his review of the new translation of Gombrowicz's *Trans-Atlantyk,* "Eastern European writers, as we have been told for years, are moral legislators of their people. They are supposed to stand like immovable rocks in the turbulent sea of the region's history." [30] Against this dominant image of literary life in Eastern Europe, reinforced by Western perceptions of the political struggle during the Cold War years, Białoszewski appears to be almost an anti-writer, a kind of anti-intellectual, who openly displays a lack of interest in playing the ready-made role of a literary and moral authority. His stance suggests that modern literature can remain important only if it deflates its own stature, ironizes its cultural significance, and takes leave of its conventions. This kind of "individualism" is a calculated political and anti-ideological posture, which mocks the artist as a moral legislator or a creator of beauty and sees art's work in terms of discerning the critical forces implicit in the event texture of the everyday. As Burkot argues, Białoszewski's emphasized privateness is not a sign of narcissism but a way of problematizing the distinction between the private and the public (*MB*, 20). His writings could indeed be analyzed from the perspective of how they continuously reappraise the linguistic work through which the always singular, "private" experience gets articulated and enters the public domain of meaning. The idiosyncrasies of his language illustrate the constant renegotiation of this process, an attempt to articulate in the general social code the singular shape of experience as event. The emphasis upon the particulars of personal life, daily routine and conversations, suggests a challenge to "naive" autobiography, taking the form of writing that details the varying shape of things and events (*MB*, 26). Such writing breaks up the confines of the lyrical subject with its self-transparent interiority and becomes, as Bauer suggests, a form of "being-in-the-world," a turn to the outside, to the nonsubjective space of experience, which results in "a deconstruction, an unmasking and demystification of the accumulated, as well as of the ways of experiencing exteriority."[31] The hybrid texture of Białoszewski's language, its always tenuous position between articulation and disarticulation, inscribes historicity into the very matrix of experience. Exteriority marked in a certain untimeliness or nonpresence of historicity inlays experience and shapes it by extraverting language into a modality of "being-in-the-world."

I read Białoszewski's departure from the avant-garde mythology as a gesture of making prominent the "real" problematic of the avant-garde: its engagement with the aesthetic and political implications of the idea of experience as event. The difficulty of sustaining this focus without rendering the everyday marvelous or exotic manifests itself in the strain that avant-garde poetics places upon language, which now carries the burden of *both* questioning the ordinariness of the everyday and counteracting the effect of aestheticization. Białoszewski's work is, then, avant-garde in the sense that Lyotard ascribes to this word, that is, according to a conception in which the insistent question "Is it happening?" functions as the defining moment of avant-garde art. Lyotard's emphasis on the event has both aesthetic and political implications, as it calls for a "letting-go" of grasping and controlling modalities of cognition and comportment to the world. It is only in the moment of such a releasement/questioning that experience shows itself in an inessential manner, as an event. This Lyotardian avant-garde question "Is it happening?" is amplified and intensified through Białoszewski's practice of making language "dwell" within the event. *Dziwienie* (wonder) expands or decompresses the moment of happening, registering in linguistic innovations and inconventionalities the ways in which the production of experience, its *poiēsis,* marks itself in consciousness and language. The expansion and hybridization of language performed by Białoszewski offsets the reduction or compression of the everyday into the significations of the ordinary, into the representable spaces of normalcy regulated by the increasing commodification of experience and time. In " 'Oh! Oh! Should They Take Away Even My Stove . . .' " the variations on the phrase "grey gaping hole" enact such an intensification of the event: Repeating the phrase, they extend it into syllables and then collapse it into a sound string, which underscores the surprising effects of the exposed hole and the sudden realization that it is language, more than any material object, that "preserves" experience as always untimely, as nonsynchronizable with presence and representation.

A good example of such an intensification of an ordinary event is "A Ballad of Going Down to a Store" from Białoszewski's first collection of poetry:

First I went into the street
down the stairs,
would you believe it,
down stairs.

Then acquaintances of strangers
and I passed one another by.
What a pity
you did not see
how people walk,
what a pity.

I entered a complete store
There were glass lamps burning,
I saw someone—who sat down
And what did I hear? . . . what did I hear?
The rustle of bags and human talk.

And indeed,
indeed
I returned.

(RT, 13, translation modified) [32]

Part of a series entitled "Grotesques," the poem invokes both the conventions of a Romantic ballad, which in its typical formula incorporates the mysterious, the threatening, and the marvelous, and the aesthetic of the grotesque, with its characteristic distance and distortion. These two explicit citations of literary conventions allow Białoszewski to construct a "grotesque" optics in which the commonplace undergoes multiple dislocations to reveal an unsuspected complexity.[33] A routine trip to the store discloses an unexpected sensual and existential intricacy; it becomes what it, in fact, always is, a singular event. Yet what is "wonder-ful" about this event is precisely its singular ordinariness: walking, seeing, hearing, that is, an experience of what Białoszewski calls the "firstelements of sense." Devoid of nostalgia for immediacy or familiarity, which would aestheticize the unappealing aspects of the ordinary, the poem reclaims the intricacy of the "normal" firstelements of experience from the dullness of unquestioned normalcy. The ending indicates that this descent to the store is precisely a return to the everyday, which returns experience to its *poiēsis*.[34]

Białoszewski's typographical arrangement of the poem enacts the temporal extension of the event, thus allowing the firstelements of sense to register their inexhaustibleness within the space of the poem. This inexhaustibleness comes from the fact that the event is never synchronous with its articulation, as its historicity dislocates the routine of the senses in its double, sensible and intelligible, play. Seeing, hearing, and walking return to their place within the *poiēsis* of the event and produce a cascading reaction in language against the norms of signification and representation. Reclaiming the firstelements is a linguistic, avant-garde venture, which entails dislocating language so that the "firstelements" of experience can emerge. The event unfolds its multiple surfaces, extending, as in "A Ballad . . . ," through the elements of its senses: audible, visual, tactile, semantic, syntactic.

In some cases, this practice of focusing on the inexhaustible texture of the event has also political effects. The most persuasive example is obviously *A Memoir of the Warsaw Uprising,* which deliberately parodies the myths of national martyrdom and heroic patriotism. At the same time, *A Memoir* can be read as a statement of political defiance in the face of a regime for which the very mention of the Warsaw Uprising of 1944—militarily directed against the German occupational force but politically aimed at the incoming Soviet troops and the Soviet imposed communist government—was a political embarrassment. Ironizing both sides, *A Memoir* unmasks the folly of invoking the myth of national sacrifice during the Second World War against another myth: the necessity of introducing the communist rule in the face of historical circumstances. This parody of the politics of myth goes even a step further and discloses its underlying seriousness through repeated references to the uprising in the Warsaw Ghetto and its final destruction in March 1943. *A Memoir* depicts the isolation of Warsaw during the Warsaw Uprising of 1944 as a repetition, a reminder about the seclusion and abandonment of the Jews of the Warsaw Ghetto during their uprising over a year earlier: "And afterwards—it was the famous, beautiful, late Easter eve of 1943. The Aryans—we were still called that—in the churches—dressed up for the holiday—and over there—this hell—this well-known, only without hope. . . . And now we were the ones isolated, unadmired. At least with the hope for the front" (*MWU,* 80–81, translation modified).[35] The reminder about the Ghetto uprising both draws a parallel between the situation of the helpless civilian population of Warsaw and the exterminated population of the Ghetto and indicates a pivotal difference between them: the difference between hopelessness and the possibility of hope. It also shows how the very quality of myth and its cultural functions can allow the myth of Polish heroism often to "forget" this other uprising, of which the Warsaw Uprising was, in a sense, a repetition.

As Wacław Lewandowski suggests, Białoszewski opposes the "heroic" tradition in Polish literature in order to foreground the "civilian" experience and to place this experience in the context of the Holocaust.[36] The stark deflation of heroism which constitutes the framework of *A Memoir* illustrates how the mythologization of suffering, instead of opening up to the suffering of others, can serve to consolidate the narcissism of cultural and national identities.

This is probably why Białoszewski avoids an appeal to universal humanity, to the "politics" of a unifying sameness of human nature, and opts for describing the minutiae of the ordinary sensations. His interest in the mundane details of experience takes the form of three principal textual strategies: irony, linguistic playfulness or "monstering," as he calls it, and an aesthetics of the periphery. Such a form of linguistic open-endedness, coded into elaborately and playfully perverse and parodic language constructs derived from but no longer classifiable as ordinary language, becomes identified, especially in later works, with a peculiar kind of irony directed both at the literary and cultural tradition and at Białoszewski's own productions. This idiosyncratic irony is so significant that Białoszewski invents a name for it: *m'ironia* (m'irony). This word appears as the title for a series of poems which outline Białoszewski's *ars poetica* in a discussion which parodies the labor of writing, the notion of poetic inspiration, and the desire for truth. *M'ironia* is a clever play on the poet's first name, Miron, and its linguistic proximity to the Polish word for "irony": *ironia*. Prefixing an *M* to "irony," Białoszewski coins a self-ironic term which describes his strategy of continuous parodic displacement, an irony turned against Miron and his writing or "mironizing." This irony has a specifically Białoszewskean tone — warm and playful, occasionally harsh, but still full of affection for the mundane details of being. More than a poetic device, "m'irony" functions as a form of textuality which, playing with words and idiomatic expressions and parodying ideas through mixing discursive modes — for example, the discourse of philosophy with colloquialisms — transforms the predictability of ordinary language into *dziwienie*.[37] As a constitutive feature of the textuality of Białoszewski's work, "m'irony" ironizes both the discourses from which he wants to distance himself and his own texts, in order to prevent them from assuming a position of authority, of the air of self-importance generated by their critical impetus.

The double twist of this ironic mode of writing comes explicitly to the fore in "About My Rising," which, exposing the absence of inspiration in the poet's work, ridicules the naive and affected assumptions about poetry:

"I've fallen / from my inspirations / . . . / when they cut me open / there will be a scandal" (*RT,* 31). The Polish text works even more effectively because of its substandard, "unpoetic" phrasing: for example, a careless use of *"z"* instead of *"ze"* in *"z swoich natchnień"* (*"from* my inspirations"), as well as the colloquially sounding *"oklapłem,"* translated as "I've fallen," but which, in fact, plays on the colloquial verb designating deflation and alludes to the loss of poetic power. The poem parodies the idea of poetic inspiration as a special state of consciousness or capability of the imagination. This (m)ironic strategy marks an effort to remain open and candid, emphasizing the need to expose every pretense and affectation to which language succumbs, and to which, Białoszewski seems to suggest, his own texts are also prone. Such ironic treatment involves not only the thematic, ideological, or figural aspects of poetry, but also its linguistic and discursive practices. In other words, in its most important gesture, it affects the syntactic and lexical levels of language as well as style and discursive mode: ungrammatical constructions, colloquialisms, fusion of different modes (written/spoken, educated/uneducated), and inflectional forms considered "inferior" to the standard ones. Białoszewski undercuts the segmentation of language into various spheres of discourse—literary/nonliterary, colloquial/educated—and explores the effect that this compartmentalization has had upon literary, in particular poetic, language. A very short poem entitled *"mironczarnia"* is one of such grammatical and stylistic hybrids:

> *męczy się człowiek Miron męczy*
> *znów jest zeń słów niepotraf*
> *niepewny cozrobień*
> *yeń (UZ I,* 246)

> a human being agonizes [suffers, struggles] Miron agonizes
> again he is a word-incompeter
> unsure whattodoer
> oer

The title of the poem resists direct translation, as it plays again on Białoszewski's first name, Miron, combining it with an incomplete word, *czarnia,* which suggests agony and suffering *(męczarnia)*—that is Miron's suffering or m'ironic suffering. The text chronicles the labor and the pain of writing, its uncertainties, difficulties, and hesitations. Its ingenuity lies in the manner in which it fuses the thematic and the formal, as the idea of agony over words is literally enacted by the text's often deliberately awkward or overdone verbal acrobatics: "unsure whattodoer" *("niepewny cozrobień")* regis-ters the hesitation in its transformation from a verbal phrase into a noun, echoed in the next line by the separated and modified ending, *"yeń"* ("oer"), which begins to reverberate with another possible connotation—*leń*—a lazy, idle person (here an ironic reminder that perhaps the poet, despite his claims to agony over each word, does not work enough). The difficulties of the writing process are even more trenchantly illustrated by the phrase *"słów niepotraf,"* which, in the form of a mocking self-accusation, points to the poet's deficient ability with words.

This poem also illustrates the second form that Białoszewski's undoing of the reduction of everydayness to the significations of the ordinary takes, namely, a calculated, self-parodic deployment of the avant-garde tech-niques of word creation. These techniques are often deliberately misapplied, or used "carelessly," in order to produce what Białoszewski calls *"wypadki z gramatyki"*—a phrase which plays on the etymological meaning of "falling out" implicit in *wypadek* (accident) and means both "accidents (or inci-dents) of grammar" and "falling out of grammar." Cutting, disabling, or distorting words, Białoszewski attempts to exit or leave the word, as he indicates in another poem entitled "I cannot write" *("Nie umiem pisać")*: *"którędy wyjść ze słowa?"* "which way to exit the word?" (*UZ I,* 111). His cal-culated "errors" implement a careful dissection of language in an attempt to cut into the word and turn it inside out in order to put into play its poten-tial, even if erroneous or mistaken, meaning.[38] Białoszewski's avant-garde poetics takes on the form of an exploration of the inability to exit words, of an inconceivable, preposterous demand that makes this impossibility the very condition of the possibility of poetic writing. For an exit from the word can be made only by means of language: through dissecting words, distort-ing existing words or creating new ones. Language affords no ultimate exit, but this is clearly not the way out that Białoszewski seeks. His intention is to exit the literary and cultural conventions and to enter a poietic dimen-sion of language, whether within, outside, or on the inverse of words. If the event horizon of experience loses its historicity upon entering the codified space of language and becomes a (hi)story, then these exits from the word are opened up in order to increase the plasticity of language to a degree that would allow it to keep the signification of the event flexible, irreducible to what it means to be "ordinary."

Białoszewski explains this procedure in a short and playful poem *"Tłu-maczenie się z twórczośsci"* ("Explaining one's creations"), which illustrates his reasons for writing semi-colloquially, for creating odd and humorous but quite trenchant little linguistic "monstrosities": ". . . *łapię za słowa/ po tocznie/ po tworzę"* (*UZ I*, 167). The first line is an idiomatic expression which refers to an overliteral interpretation of one's words, both grasping *at* but also *for* words; the next two lines play with two words, "colloquially" *(potocznie)* from which the text separates the first syllable *po,* corresponding to the initial syllable of the word from next line (it reads as one word though its opening syllable is written separately). It is on this word that the entire poem pivots, since the double meaning of the word codes into itself the governing play of the text. The word *po tworzę,* is a pun on two words: *tworzyć,* "to create," and *potwór,* a monster. On one level, the pun "colloquializes" the verb "create" into *potworzyć* (to create casually, in an off-handed manner); on the other, it invents a verb form from the noun *potwór,* something on the order of "to monster" or "to invent monstrosities." It can be paraphrased into English in two ways: as "I will create [write] monsters [that is, linguistic monsters or monstrosities]" and, at the same time, as "I will create [write] casually," nonchalantly and unceremoniously. This easy-going manner of writing is echoed, structurally and semantically, by the word from the previous line—*po tocznie* ("colloquially"). In a direct response to his critics, Białoszewski formulates his artistic credo in a way that evacuates any solemnity and pathos from writing.

The third idiom in which Białoszewski's poetics of wonder works is that of peripheral linguistic and cultural regions. As Barańczak's excellent study of Białoszewski's poetic language, *Język poetycki Mirona Białoszewskiego,* points out,[39] this project of parodying generic literary distinctions, poetic devices—metaphors, rhymes, rhythm, versificational and stanzaic canons —and the distinction between literature and nonliterature, underlies the entirety of Białoszewski's work. Białoszewski consistently "compromises" and parodies established poetic strategies and forms as well as the basic rules of the educated language by "contaminating" them with the likes of children's mistakes, colloquial expressions, and new words and idioms generated with the help of the above practices. Disrupting literary and grammatical conventions, Białoszewski's texts ironize high culture in order to elevate the trite and the commonplace, the artifacts of mechanical reproduction, folk art or craft. The parody, however, does not end there, as the same texts also play ironically with the manifestations of "low" and provincial culture.[40]

This contestation of high culture through minor and peripheral aesthetics finds a characteristic expression in one of Białoszewski's best and most popular ballads, *"Karuzela z madonnami"* ("A Merry-go-round with

Madonnas"). Cast in the circular rhythm of a merry-go-round in motion, the poem stages a confrontation between popular entertainment and high art. The motion of the merry-go-round, inscribed into an extremely intricate and skillfully constructed rhythmic and rhyming pattern in the text, "sings" a "Magnificat" of the ordinary: "—white horses /—carriage /—black horses /—carriage /—brown horses /—carriage /—Magnificat!" [41] The dashes punctuate the intervals between horses and carriages into a musical rhythm which the poem equates with a magnificat. The title madonnas are invested with significance through comparison to the madonnas of Leonardo and Raphael. Sitting in each carriage, they have about them the air of Leonardo *("A one w Leonardach min")* while the motion of the merry-go-round becomes the "turns of Raphael" (of Raphael's brush?): *"W obrotach Rafaela"* (*UZ I*, 38). However, the text immediately reminds us that those "splendid" madonnas exist on the peripheries of towns and are nothing more than an embodiment of Sunday pastime and amusement (*"W przedmieściach i niedzielach"* [38]; "in the peripheries and Sundays"). In a linguistically and aesthetically acrobatic move, the text describes them as the "periphe / rafa / elite / madonnas / of sub / urbs" (*"peryfe / rafa / elickie / madonny / przed / mieścia"* [*UZ I*, 38]). The entire texts works around this ironically coined adjective: peripherafaelite. Running together "peripheral" and "preraphaelite," Białoszewski comes up with a parodic word emblematic of the tensions between high and low culture that underpin his poetics.

With this one "stroke" Białoszewski parodies here both the Raphaelite idea of beauty and the pre-Raphaelite aesthetics, as he finds his own everyday and trite "beauty" in the machineries of amusement parks, somewhere on the peripheries of towns or in suburbs. Overcharged with meaning, the word "peripherafaelite" collapses together high aesthetic ideals and the superficiality and insignificance of the peripheral. In fact, this neologism is so overinvested with multiple and often contradictory connotations that it practically self-destructs, and its dissolution is graphically indicated by the segmentation of the word ("periphe—rapha—elite"), which, punctuating the rhythm of writing, mimics the slowing motion of the merry-go-round. The poem intensifies the opposition between high and low culture only to dissolve it, to ease the tension with the double stoppage of the motion and of the text. Fusing two words, "peripheraphaelite" enacts the meltdown of the oppositional logic and articulates Białoszewski's challenge to the binary value system. It suggests the need for opening up a zone between the "high" and the "low," the poetic space of experience and language unencumbered with the conventional paradigms and aesthetic judgments.

Willfully situating itself on the fringes of literature and official cultural life, Białoszewski's writings continuously enact this meltdown of boundaries and parody the logic of the center and the margin. Since the margin is always a margin "with respect to" a center or a core, in a dialectical relationship with what marginalizes it, Białoszewski prefers periphery, with its connotations of supposed banality, absence of stylishness, even triteness.[42]

The two most salient examples of this contestation of the high/low divide are *A Memoir,* and a short poem *"Stepy amerykańskie"* ("American Steppes"), a parody of both the rhetoric and the themes of Polish Romanticism. "American Steppes" is an ironic reworking of one of the most famous poems of Polish Romanticism, the sonnet *"Stepy akermańskie"* ("The Steppes of Akerman") by Adam Mickiewicz, a national icon and paragon of high culture. Mickiewicz wrote the series of "Crimean Sonnets"—which includes *"Stepy akermańskie,"* cited or, in fact, reinvented, by Białoszewski—as a symbolic representation not only of his personal longing after his country but also of Poles' desire for lost independence. The sonnets are regarded as among the very best literary texts ever written in Polish. Białoszewski, by contrast, situates his "sonnet" as an outcome of his trip to America and a total failure at taking a prophetlike posture characteristic of Mickiewicz:

> Kicia Kocia
> Wpłynęłam na mokrego przestwór hm hm anu
> dalej nic . . . nic . . .
> zawał talentu
> aaaaa
> (drze włosy i rękopis)[43]

> Kitty Kattie
> I sailed onto the wet expanse of the hm hm ean
> then nothing . . . nothing . . .
> a total collapse of talent
> aaaa
> (she tears her hair and manuscript)

In a deliberate contrast to the lyrical "I" of Mickiewicz's poem—a male poet, a Romantic prophet *(wieszcz)* in exile longing for his country (fatherland)—the "speaker" of Białoszewski's text is female. "Her" unusual and silly nickname jars with the poetic vocation, especially the way it is defined by the Romantic tradition, and ironizes the masculine stance widely adopted by Romantic poets. It is important, however, to note that *"Kicia*

Kocia" functions as the poet's *alter ego,* extending the parody to his own texts and making the gender play even more immediately relevant for their lyrical subject(s). Subverting, almost literally turning Mickiewicz's text into a stutter, *"Stepy amerykańskie"* parodies the inflated notion of poetic inspiration, pointing out the difficulties, exertions, and labor involved in writing. The poet is not at all inspired, the writing, in a reversal of Mickiewicz's metaphor, does not "sail." On the contrary, the whole experience is presented as frustrating and depressing, though it is obviously "lightened" and eased by the text's explicit exaggeration and irony. The ironic treatment of the idealized picture of an inspired prophet becomes here the vehicle for Białoszewski's critique of cultural and literary traditions. Since Białoszewski openly admired Mickiewicz's poetry, this attack is clearly aimed at the cultural mythology which mystifies literary figures and constructs idealized canons.

Białoszewski's contestation of the political mythologies of Polish culture receives its most poignant expression in *A Memoir of the Warsaw Uprising* and a series of texts called "cabarets," written in the politically and socially turbulent years of the rise of Solidarity and the imposition of martial law. *A Memoir* consistently breaks the historical and literary stereotypes about the 1944 uprising; it demonumentalizes the struggle and evacuates any lingering pathos by focusing exclusively on the ugly and mundane aspects of the everyday fate of civilian population. Although Białoszewski opts here for the form of the memoir to make problematic the fictionality of literature, at the same time, he foregrounds the imperfection and incompleteness of memory on which he has to rely in writing this text in 1967, twenty-three years after the uprising took place. He therefore supplements his account with information from newspapers, documentary footage, his father's recollections, and so on. According to Białoszewski, the twenty-three years that elapsed between the uprising and the moment he was ready to write his *Memoir* were necessary to prepare language for it, to find a way of writing that would not succumb to conventionalized representations of war and the apocalyptic rhetoric associated with them.

What is most striking about *A Memoir* is the apparent discrepancy between its theme—the most disastrous event in the history of Warsaw, the destruction of the city and its inhabitants—and the style of presentation, with its ordinary, spokenlike language and the focus on the cycles of escalating disintegration of daily routines and attempts to construct new ones. Choosing the form of linguistic chatter or prattle *(gadanie)* in order to follow scrupulously, almost day by day, the forced relocations and increasing suffering of the civilians caught in the fighting, *A Memoir* avoids both the glorification of the heroic struggle doomed to defeat and the rhetoric of catastrophism characteristic of Polish war poetry. It also deflates the stereotypes and myths that accumulated around the uprising as one of the "primal" scenes of modern Polish identity by presenting it, as Lewandowski argues, as a replica, already imperfect and hence never "primal," of the uprising in the Warsaw Ghetto: "The consciousness that this is a replica and — as a replica — less 'perfect,' less intense. Therefore the narrator of *A Memoir* does not hide that, although the [Warsaw] uprising was the most important experience, it was not what shaped his perception and understanding."[44] Avoiding the familiar gesture of intensifying the images of terror and apocalyptic rhetoric, Białoszewski presents the war and the gradual destruction of Warsaw by showing, as one critic put it, the destruction of all ordinary points of support that organize everyday life: from cooking and eating to sleeping and defecating.[45] The chatter prose of *A Memoir,* colloquial and often onomatopoeic, is composed mostly of fragments, one word sentences and sentence equivalents, which effectively heightens the sense of increasing disorder and destruction. It emphasizes the chaotic darting and sprinting around *(latanie)* which both paste the text together and unwork it on the syntactic and semantic levels. The dominant image of a frenzied darting around *(latanie)* is also an ironic commentary on the image of the aesthetic, Icarus-like flight *(lot)* and the patriotic surge *(wzlot).* As usual, Białoszewski achieves this effect by mixing high tone with the colloquial: *latać* means to fly or to soar, but, colloquially, it refers to a disorganized and frenetic running around. As Maria Janion remarks, *latanie* in *A Memoir* ironizes lofty and aestheticized representations of the struggle for independence within the post-Romantic tradition of Polish literature. It renders problematic the literary monumentalization of the Polish form.[46]

As a quasi-organizational principle, *latanie* in Białoszewski's *Memoir* accounts for the fragmentary and disjointed description of haphazard, often seemingly insignificant events and the absence of military struggle, political debates, or heroic deeds. The colloquialism of *latanie* also reinforces the semi-official, semi-literary, and unsystematic aspects of the language of *A Memoir.* It sets the tone for the unheroic portrayal of the inversion of the securities of everydayness into a multiplying threat of death: In Białoszewski's script, satisfying the basic necessities of everyday life — cooking, washing, or urinating — entails exposure to bombs and machine gun fire and the possibility of sudden death. The characteristic deflation of *lot* (flight, soaring) into mundane and chaotic *latanie* describes well the way in which Białoszewski, even when dealing with a "central" event in Polish cultural memory, locates his writing on the peripheries, on the margins of what gets represented and passes into the national iconography and memory. Such "peripheral" writing makes *A Memoir* one of the most poignant critiques of the cultural practices of selecting and centralizing the material that becomes the "substance" of history. It recalls Benjamin's warnings about appropriating ordinary danger and suffering into a uniform vision of history.[47]

Similarly ironic is Białoszewski's treatment of the events of early 1980s, which takes the form of a cabaret. It is possible to argue that at this particular point in Polish history, it was the numerous cabarets that served as the critique of the social and political manifestations of the regime (for example, "Sixty minutes per hour," *"Pod Egidą,"* or "The Olga Lipińska Cabaret"). Nonetheless, even the cabarets themselves tended to hit a high patriotic note whenever it came to voicing opposition to the regime. Białoszewski's cabaretlike texts, interspersed with both patriotic and parodic songs, constitute an ironic commentary on the political, social, and cultural events from that period. When the title heroine of the cabaret, Kicia Kocia, receives the Nobel prize for literature, we are reminded of Miłosz's award, and both the attacks of jealousy and the prophetlike welcome he received upon his arrival in Poland. Another of the cabaret texts, bearing as its title the date May 3, refers to the events of May 3, 1982, approximately six months after the introduction of martial law, when Warsaw was paralyzed by a mini-uprising, a day of clashes with the riot police. In this short sketch, Kitty Kattie's walk with her dog is interrupted as she runs back into her apartment screaming that she has been attacked by Bolesław Chrobry (Bolesław the Brave).[48] Bolesław Chrobry, a famous Polish king who solidified the Polish state in the twelfth century, and his troops, turn out to be the riot police in their full armor, with helmets and transparent plastic shields. In another immediate reversal, the king-commander of the police reveals her true identity as Kitty Kattie's friend who has come to protect her. With one caricature of Bolesław the Brave, Białoszewski pokes fun at Polish historical mythology and the way that the regime and its opponents use its armor for their political purposes. This elaborate and humorous masquerade runs the full gamut of allusions which play on the desires of both sides of the political conflict to appropriate the national(istic) imagery and heritage.

Białoszewski's most self-conscious comment about his literary and cultural iconoclasm is the title of an early poem, *"a teraz ja — pisarz pism nie św"* (*UZ I*, 268) — "and now me — the writer of non-holy scriptures," a work that again invokes and breaks down the oppositions between the everyday and the extraordinary, the sacred and the profane, and so on. The poem leaves no doubt that Białoszewski's writings attempt to avoid any pretensions to a special cultural status enjoyed by poetic discourse and opposed to the pragmatic efficiency of ordinary language. Rather than validate its discourse, the poem both emphasizes its "imperfections" and "weaknesses" *("złe strony")* and ironizes the literary standards that produce such aesthetic judgments. The phrase *"złe strony"*—which suggests both bad and wrong sides, parts, or aspects—can be read as an ironic acknowledgment of how Białoszewski's poetry fails to conform to aesthetic standards. One of the most interesting moments of the poem, the phrase *"kupa ładu"* ("a pile [or heap] of order), announces and subverts, in a catachretic turn, any desire for order, completeness, or clarity. The meaning of this figure/disfigurement is further complicated and undermined by the polysemy of *"kupa,"* which also signifies poop or shit. This semantic play indicates an order turned inside out, a disorder produced by too much order, which one of the meanings of *kupa,* pile, implies—a dissolution of the opposition between order and chaos. The poem's ending parodies aspirations to conclusiveness and closure, as the final phrase *"ciąg dalszy nastąpi"*—"to be continued"—suggests that Białoszewski's "scriptures" are not only not sacred, untouchable, and unalterable, but in fact need constant rewriting and appending. The unmistakable echo of serialization in this last line suggests that Białoszewski's cycles function as serialized observations, as reproductions of the same situational paste-ups for the purpose of underscoring the inexhaustibleness and noncoincidence marked in the structure of the event. As a writer of "unholy" scriptures which parody national literary and cultural myths, Białoszewski opts for the peripheries of aesthetics, for a poetics of the peripheral, as the site of his writing. His focus on the irreducibility of the event suspends the logic of the opposites in order to let language dwell within the historicity of the event. Concentrating his texts on the moment of in-betweenness— between logical opposites, between high and low culture, between writing and poietics—Białoszewski produces the effect of an openness of language and perception to that quality of happening, or to the burst of experience as Nancy calls it, that does not register within the order of representation. This quality of nonsynchronicity means that *poiēsis* marks the "critical" peripheries of representation, whether at issue is the linguistic order, literary and cultural significations, or political mythology.

I explore Białoszewski's poetry of the peripheries also as a contrast to that problematic moment in Heidegger's work when his reclaiming of the everyday as the site of thinking tends to lose its critical edge and disappear into a certain solemnity of poetic annunciation. In Białoszewski, the objective of "reinventing" the everyday becomes sharpened through a critical look at a certain pathos that sometimes underlies Heidegger's, or for that matter Cavell's, philosophical project of reclaiming and redefining the ordinary.[49] Attempting to reclaim the ordinary as the "proper" site of thought, Heidegger appears to undercut his project when he resorts to a hymnic, celebratory rhetoric in which the poetic is apparently to be found. Because of their explicit irony and humor as well as their continuous contrast between the special and the ordinary, Białoszewski's texts successfully resist any sense of pathos. Białoszewski prefers to weave his texts around things of everyday use and of apparently no special value or importance. Although Białoszewski too writes about the holy, invoking the structures and vocabulary of religious rituals, songs, and invocations, his holy is no longer that of gods, but of everyday objects and events. His "gods" are utensils, floors, dentures, routine activities, small and ugly towns—in all cases, the examples of what one would more readily call the unholy or the profane. By placing Białoszewski and Heidegger together, I hope to expand and make concrete what is already at work in Heidegger's notion of *poiēsis*, even though it is often dissimulated by the tenor of his writings. It seems to me that, although Heidegger wants to engage the everyday in his work on poetry, he continues to slip back into a certain solemnity of the poetic,[50] precipitated by his readings of Hölderlin, Rilke, or Trakl: poets who are quite unconventional, and yet fit well into the tradition of solemn, hymnic poetry. One of the functions of my reading of Białoszewski is, therefore, a simultaneous rhetorical deflation and a sharpening of the critical implications of Heidegger's redefinition of *poiēsis*.

Keeping a Watch in an "Ant-Rise": Technology and Everyday Life

Białoszewski's late poems, focusing on the changes precipitated by his move to a new apartment in a high-rise building on the other side of the Vistula river, reflect the increasingly technological "location" of modern everydayness. These texts from 1975 to 1979 underscore the extent to which everydayness becomes structured by the elements of life which evolved as a result of the technologically conditioned mass society. Treating various aspects of city life in Warsaw, where technology and mass produced objects become the "element" of daily experience, these poems chronicle the minutiae of life in a high-rise apartment building, or an "ant-rise" *(mrówkowiec)*, as Białoszewski ironically, though aptly, calls it, with all the technological accouterments and problems it involves: from elevators and staircases, to corridors, sidewalks, renovation of building facades, pipes, electrical wiring, and light bulbs. For example, a long poem *"Korytarzowiec"* ("A Corridorer" or "A Corridor-poem") dramatizes the events and features of a corridor as the important place, a sort of crossroads, in the life of the apartment building dwellers (*MśT,* 156–58). A cycle of late poems bears a parodic title "Renewvating the Anthill" *("Trynkowanie mrówkowca"),* and describes how the renovation of the facade of Białoszewski's building changes the circumstances of everyday living, upsetting the routine, introducing the element of the unknown and the new: "**I am running away** / **going down** / in the elevator into the world. / I strain my head up / and the renewvators look out / from up high / from the bridges. . . ."[51] Producing both a threat and a temptation of the new, the invasion of technology into the privacy of the poet's life is figured through the literal heights of the scaffoldings that encircle the building whose facade is being given a new paint job. The "ant-hill" *(mrówkowiec),* Białoszewski's favorite ironic image for the congested living conditions in the high rise apartment buildings that populate most of Warsaw's landscape, is doubly ironic: because of the external conditions that regulate and replicate the entire flow of life in the building into a familiar routine (identical stairs, corridors, apartments, balconies, sidewalks, and so on) and because, in spite of the standardized, highly organized conditions, as though in an ant-hill, life constantly produces surprises, disrupts the routine, and disorganizes itself.[52] How important these technologically produced circumstances of everyday life become for Białoszewski's writings is evident even from the titles of many poems from the collection *Odczepić się (To Let Go,* or "to detach oneself"), which chronicles the poet's move to the new apartment and the process of "detachment" from his old place of dwelling: "Looking Through the Window," "Warsaw from the Ninth Stairs," "A High-Rise, Me in It," "In My High Apartment," "On this 9th Floor I Sit, I Stand," "This Apartment Can Be Inspired" (*UZ VII,* 30–73). The tone for the entire collection is set by the two liner: "**Elevation** / happened" (*UZ VII,* 31), which alludes to the move to the poet's new apartment on the ninth floor, later echoed again in "My Own Place": "the city chopped itself off. // I elevatored. / Onto the ninth."[53] In place of a "ballad" of walking to a store, we have a text about being mechanically "lifted up" to the poet's ninth floor apartment. The space between walking and being "elevatored" thematizes the difference between event as *poiēsis* and event as circumscribed within the technologically "built" or determined space of experience.

As though to watch over this difference, Białoszewski appoints himself the watchman of the life of his "ant-hill": He is a chronicler of the new, mundane reality of city life, as he constantly reminds his fellow residents to pay attention to the inconspicuous. The late poems become even starker and shorter than the already brief early poems. The simplicity of structures and words seems to become emblematic of the increasingly compressible space of experience, which allows for the repetition of situations and events as unmarked and unremarkable spaces: corridors, elevator shafts, stairwells, and so on. The growing presence of whiteness on the page remains, however, ambiguous in its significations. On the one hand, it reflects the uniform space of high-rise housing, where only infrequently something breaks the routine and marks itself in a few words on the page. On the other hand, the whiteness also contains increased possibilities for inscription, for a possible turn within apparently "empty" events of everyday life, foreshortened to the calculable spaces of work, entertainment, daily chores. In "I, the watchman, broadcast from the ant-hill," Białoszewski calls to others not to get lost and lose sight of the everyday by becoming inoculated by its routine appearance: "Do not get lost // Be. // Pass, let's pass each other, / but let's not pass each other by. // Let us pass. // We! / You! Who run around / and are pushed around." [54] The poem is structured around the play on the word "to pass" *(mijać)* and its double sense of passing by and passing away. We have to pass away, but this passing should not become equivalent to passing each other by without paying attention to one another and to what happens around. The closing line alludes to the congested conditions of city life, where one gets jostled by the passers-by, but it may also function as a political allusion, calling on fellow "ant-hill" dwellers to resist being pushed around by the political and social conditions of their life. It is Białoszewski's unique talent to compress into a poem of only eight very short lines both a portrait of modern city experience and a mini poetic and political "manifesto."

In these late poems, everydayness and technology are fused together, and the opposition between technology and nature no longer seems to obtain or be important for Białoszewski's work. It is quite significant that while almost all of his later poems contain technological elements or mass produced objects, there are essentially no poems about nature. In a cycle entitled *Siekierki* (the name of a Warsaw suburb), the fragmentary evocations of the natural landscape are set against the background of a huge heating plant in Siekierki which supplies Warsaw with energy. The first poem in the cycle begins with the sentence: "A Portrait with Siekierki in the Background." The landscape appears dominated by the plant: "**Siekierki** / a big place, separate / unknown / millions of little leaves /as in the Middle Ages"; or "**Siekierki** / a cloud, bushes / here lurks This one / and this one walks / attacks / with force / revelation" (*UZ VII*, 213). The landscape of Białoszewski's poetry is inevitably an industrial landscape, a cityscape, where "nature" remains vestigial, no longer playing a significant role in the scheme of things. Its elements enter into the picture but only as complements or part of the larger landscape that is dictated by the conditions and demands of mass society. Białoszewski writes his poetry quite openly as a city dweller, for whom there is no other known or imaginable sphere of experience and for whom the question of the judgment as to whether the circumstances in which he finds itself are "good" or "bad" seems irrelevant. For Białoszewski, technology is neither fascinating nor threatening. It is just an integral part of the space of experience, often it seems to be its constitutive component: Technology is just "there," inseparable from daily reality. The question as to whether technology is aesthetic or anti-aesthetic, whether modern art, as Picabia claimed and Heidegger worried, is technological in its essence, or whether it provides an alternative to technology, is absent in this form.

Białoszewski casts the question about technology in a different way: Since the distinction between technology and nature no longer really obtains and is not significant for his poetics, at issue really is the thinking of what might be called a technological everydayness. Is the everyday, and the technology which has become inextricably interlaced with it, as transparent, immediate, and familiar as it seems? I do not mean here the fact that on a daily basis the workings of technological contraptions around us are transparent to us, even if one fails to understand why and how technological inventions work, but, rather, that daily practice is based on the sense of the transparency of technology, a certain obliviousness to the technological within one's environment. For Białoszewski, even those most "familiar" and ordinary among mass products that occupy most of our daily spaces and whose functions pose no secrets, become the objects of wonder *(dziwienie),* and their ordinary recurrence is refracted through the "untimeliness" and the surprise of the event. Białoszewski often depicts the dull objects of everyday use with epithets reserved for exceptional things and high art: in *"Sztuki piękne mojego pokoju"* ("The beaux arts of my room") a closet becomes "a Semiramis, a pyramid, an Aïda," and "an opera in three doors": *"Szafo szafo Semiramido / piramido / Aido / opero w trzech drzwiach!"* (*UZ I,*

65). *"Szare eminencje zachwytu"* ("Grey Eminences of Rapture") describes a colander as shining "in a monstrance of brightness" (Białoszewski, *RT* 8) (". . . *tak świecisz w monstrancji jasności"* [*UZ I,* 57]). What fascinates the poet is how the utterly functional mass-produced objects of modern life do not completely disappear into their usefulness, how their existence does not become transparent or wholly explainable through their use as tools or objects of fantasy and desire. A certain "untimeliness" of their existence, their excess over presence and representation, renders them noncoincident with their "essence" as tools or commodities.

The idea that technology is integral to everyday experience, that ordinary life is no longer "natural" but technological in its daily business, seems to be an unquestioned assumption of Białoszewski's work. But if the practices of everyday life are pervaded and structured by technological thought, then Białoszewski plays with technology the way he plays with the everyday. The question of the opposition between (high) art and technology, between aesthetics and technologically produced mass entertainment, gives way to the possibility of disclosing the poietic dimension of the technologically determined everydayness, that is, to the possibility of a turn, a subversion within the technological texture of experience. There is no "critique" of technology, no gesture of escapism, for, clearly, none is possible or desired. It would be a mistake to look at Białoszewski's work in terms of existential anxiety brought about by the progressive mechanization of contemporary life, just as his interest in the deceptively simple, mundane aspects of everydayness evidences no nostalgia for the supposedly "natural" immediacy of experience, extinct in the multiple technological mediations modern life involves on a daily basis. Instead, Białoszewski is interested in following the details of experience so closely and carefully that a different map of everydayness would break through the script—where no routine is ever possible, for no "simple" moment ever repeats itself: "I try to give expression in my poems to new categories of experience and concepts, and this is often misunderstood. In my opinion, the expression of unnamed feelings—that is the aim of poetry." [55]

On the one hand, these new categories refer to ordinary spaces and moments of experience Białoszewski introduces into poetic writing: corridors, elevators, walls, dusts, microexperiences, and events of apparently minuscule significance. Rejecting or modifying generic classifications, he invents his own names for those new categories of experience, assembling his poetic "microseconds" into cycles which resist inscription into aesthetic categories.[56] On the other hand, these new categories refer to the displacements which the *poiēsis* of the event introduces into the uniform space of the everyday. The new "generic" headings Białoszewski continuously constructs for his cycles—"Cites," "Frivols," "Asleeps," "Lyings," and so on—attempt to name the different structure of the everyday which his writing injects into the representational space. The degree to which they depart from literary categories reflects the distance opening between technology and *poiēsis*, between the ordinary and the everyday. Białoszewski questions the cognitive, linguistic, and cultural habits that form the grid of everydayness and finds the linguistic and conceptual energy for this questioning in the apparent inconspicuousness with which the everyday happens. The inconspicuous, however, has to be brought to the fore through the avant-garde manipulations and extension of language, through a "distortive," playfully "monstrous" look at experience and language, reflected in the equally "monstrous" and "unpoetic" disposition of Białoszewski's language. It is all part of a grotesque optics in which cultural and political mythology, high and low art, ordinary discourse and literary language, show an unexpected face. Set perceptions, cultural idealizations, and biases, which form part of everyday milieu, find themselves deformed and put into question through the distortive prism of Białoszewski's writings. Art clearly is not a life saver, a heroic counter to technology, or a special, exotic island among the minutiae of ordinariness. Poetry is as everyday as walking, going to a store, or paying bills, and it has to accompany the everyday at every moment and attend to any of its aspects, no matter how seemingly dull, prosaic, or even ugly they appear. Poetry has to be more "everyday" than everydayness itself in order to trace what the normalcy of experience hides so well behind its routine masks—the moment of wonder at the "untimely" singularity of happening, the unrepeatable burst of experience.

If repetition marks a key feature of technology, Białoszewski's poetry underscores the always specific contours, the unrepeatable of the event. In chapter 1, I suggested that the reproducibility characteristic of the work of art contains the ability to reproduce art's work as always singular, "historical" in its adaptability and refiguration of the circumstances of what Heidegger calls its "preservation." The work of art keeps true to its poietic character precisely by reproducing itself as each time the same and different from itself and from all its former moments of existence. It is this singular reproducibility that is highlighted by avant-garde poetics, brought to the fore in the linguistic experiments. This reproducibility remains different from the repetitiveness implied in technology and mass production. Reinforced by mechanical reproduction, it reserves, paradoxically, the possibility of questioning the mechanical patterns of reproduction and problematizes the technological "essence" of being in modernity. Always ironic about "grand narratives," Białoszewski prefers to probe the corners of the everyday, the micro-events where technology shows its structuring force, but where, equally, the language transformations performed by his writing retain the critical effects of historicity, which keep interrogating the dominant ideologies of experience. As Białoszewski's poem about the stove indicates, such "holes" in representation reveal the "inexhaustible" critical force of the nonsynchronicity of experience, which reproduces itself in the playfully created "monstrosities" of language. This is why his language always keeps us on the edge of words, at the points where words and sentences "pop open like chestnuts," [57] as one of his poems puts it. It is as though Białoszewski wanted the words never to repeat themselves, to signify less by virtue of their ordinary meaning than by their difference from it. This rupturing of words, like the historicity of the event, remains untimely and nonsynchronous with what the event opens up or produces. To be avant-garde in Białoszewski's idiom means to follow, patiently and daily, the contours of these ruptures, to trace them in a language that undermines the idea of essence, and to demystify the myths that "ordinarily" proliferate in everyday life.

In a physical Universe playing with words
—Howe, *Pythagorean Silence*

7. "A Sounding of Uncertainty"

Susan Howe's Poetic Gendering of History

Susan Howe's works are "soundings of uncertainty," or articulations as sounds and words in time of the uncertainty which operates as the subtext of history and reflects the intrinsically unstable and incomplete inscription of experience. If such soundings of historicity constitute a marked feature of twentieth-century avant-garde poetry and, in particular, of the unprecedented examination of writing undertaken by language poetry, Howe's poetic texts and essays stand out for the intensity, precision, and open-endedness they impart to the temporal dimension of experience. As the title of one of her most interesting works, "Articulation of Sound Forms in Time," indicates, experience measures itself out into time, it unfolds into words and materializes its significations already in a historical manner. I argue that the form this articulation of experience into language takes—an open-ended event whose structure inscribes its historicity—opens the possibility of history. Writing both through and against historical and literary texts—from Dickinson, Rowlandson, and Melville's *Billy Budd* and *Marginalia,* to Swift, Shakespeare, and the accounts of Hope Atherton's wanderings—Howe folds the historical distance those texts open back into the sense of the "presentness" of her own writing. This refolding of history intensifies the syntactical and verbal dislocations and transpositions which qualify the possibility of presence in Howe's work, which, to be more precise, mark this "presence" as the presence of possibilities. Open and incomplete, Howe's poetic texts sound the uncertainty of the articulated forms of those experiences, exploring their "collisions or collusions"[1] with violence, control, and mastery, which mark the production of history as an intelligible narrative providing the knowledge of the past. These retracings and relocations which Howe's writings perform with respect to the silences and ruptures interspersing history figure both the problem of gendering experience and the political and ethical effects of this gesture. As Howe remarks in an interview, "If you are a woman, archives hold perpetual ironies. Because the gaps and silences are where you find yourself."[2]

I am interested here specifically in defining the relation between the problem of history and gender in Howe's work in the context of how her poems, inscribing historicity into and against the narrative articulations of experience, revise its legibility. The production of this different legibility becomes intrinsic to the language plays and textuality of Howe's poetry. It motivates the most radical reconfigurations of textual space—semantic, syntactic, and typographical—which have become the benchmarks of her writing. Since experience is always already textual, rethinking its historical character becomes tied to establishing new parameters of legibility. These parameters accentuate the unpredictable and dislocating effects of historicity over and against the articulated forms of experience, making manifest how the articulation of experience as presence depends upon and precipitates the effacement of the event, and with it the alterity and the fracturing, the temporal noncoincidence, of experience. The "paradoxical" discursive inscription of experience through disjunction and noncoincidence, considered in different ways by Benjamin and Heidegger, finds its characteristic shape in Howe's work in the ruptures and refigurations of textual space. In *The Nonconformist's Memorial,* Howe is interested in rewriting historical scenes and texts specifically through the prism of historicity in order to illustrate the revisions that this way of thinking introduces into the narrative scope and ordering of historical space: "Historicity of the scene / Confused narrative complex // Two women with names / followed by two without names // Distance original disobedience."[3] The poem reappraises the scene from John's Gospel of the first sighting of resurrected Jesus by Mary Magdalene in the context of the subsequent exclusion of women and the "ejection" of sexual difference from the universalizing matrix of experience, "accomplished" through the narrative of "original disobedience." Howe's engagement with reworking the place of gender and sexual difference in the (re)writing of history involves both inscribing the "historicity of the scene" into the narrative thread of thought and measuring the linguistic dislocations produced by this inscription.

The Matter of History, the Historicity of Matter

Following Howe's own remark, "My poems always seem to be concerned with history,"[4] almost all critical assessments agree that this refiguration of (literary) history defines the site and, to a large extent, the scope, of Howe's poetry. Remarking upon the importance of Howe's work for feminist critiques, critics as different as DuPlessis, Perloff, Quartermain, and Ma all indicate that the meticulous linguistic and discursive questioning that the patriarchal and phallogocentric vision of history undergoes in Howe's work opens the space for the inscription of gendered experience[5]—both in the form of "women's voices," which supplement and rewrite the text of history, and as a reinvention of language, which reaches down to its most elemental parts: transposed or decomposed words, single letters, (absence of) conjunctions and syntactical markers, (innovative) page layout. As possibly "a different way of knowing things" (*BM,* 165), poetry becomes for Howe a counterdiscourse to history, provided that history is identified with a largely monological, patriarchal narrative rationalization that aims to produce agreement about the past.[6] Through their linguistic transpositions, Howe's poetic texts produce the opportunity to revisit the discursive space of history: its historiographic, political, and literary dimensions.

If poetry is history revisited and rewritten, the historical distance Howe's poems inscribe does more than reconstitute the past or remake and supplement its narrative in order to counter the erasures and to "sound" the silences that make up the constitutive outside of historical accounts. Howe's engagement with the past and its textual circumscription seems to take place primarily for the sake of the "present," or, to be more exact, for what might be called the "contemporaneity" of experience. I want to differentiate contemporaneity of experience from the idea of an instant of full and complete presence, a "now" that, coinciding with itself, remains entirely saturated in its temporal extension. Nothing could be further from this sense of the transparency and immediacy of presence than the sparsely worded, often de-syntaxed, pages of Howe's poems. Contemporaneity, as I propose to use it here, refers to the nonimmediacy of experience, taken as an already dislocated, withdrawn horizon of an event. The event, as I define it in the context of Irigaray, Heidegger, and Benjamin, refers to a dynamic field of forces, whose historicity undermines the closure of experience into lived moments, representational constants, or psychic spaces. Implied in this idea of the event, the notion of contemporaneity questions the possibility of articulating experience in terms of presence, which is already marked by the rupture of historicity. Contemporaneity always bears the stamp of historicity, which keeps the open-ended structure of experience against the flattening into presence and incorporation into the linearity of progress.

The rewriting of history at work in Howe's "The Liberties" or "Articulation of Sound Forms in Time" should be, therefore, kept nuanced, calibrated to the complex effects it produces within the contemporaneity of the textual space. As Howe explains in her "Statement for the New Poetics Colloquium, Vancouver 1985" and reiterates in her interviews, history is "the record of winners. Documents . . . written by the Masters."[7] This refiguring of the "records of winners" eschews the production of a new, better or fuller, record authorized by the inclusion of voices omitted from the "master" account. Howe's texts clearly render problematic, if not suspect, the desire to retrieve and revise history by projecting oneself into the past; that is, they call into question the idea of an empathic recuperation of what has been elided in the hegemonic discourse(s) of history. Just as Howe's remark about documents written by the Masters brings to mind Benjamin's assertion that adherents of historicism identify with the victor, the hesitations and rewritings which abound in Howe's poetry testify to the problematic status of empathy and are, thus, reminiscent of Benjamin's "Theses on the Philosophy of History." Benjamin's VII Thesis pairs the problem of empathy specifically with the recognition of the troubling investment of history writing in the perspective of the winners:

> To historians who wish to relive an era, Fustel de Coulanges recommends that they blot out everything they know about the later course of history. . . . It is a process of empathy whose origin is the indolence of the heart. . . . [O]ne asks with whom the adherents of historicism actually empathize. The answer is inevitable: with the victor.[8]

The problem with empathy is double: empathy has a tendency to identify with one, usually dominant, perspective, and it operates on the metaphysical basis of a plentiful presence, underscoring the possibility of making the past appear in its "full" and "true" identity.

Benjamin suggests that empathy as the foundation of the (re)construction of history presupposes the effacement of the subsequent development of events, rendering the process of retrieval oblivious to the very course of history. What Benjamin detects in this method of restoring the past is a certain blindness to the "historial" character of history, a blindness which collapses the disruptive and incalculable occurrence of experience into the homogeneous space of presence underlying historical narratives. As the project of retrieval and restitution of the past, historicism, for Benjamin, deliberately effaces its own historical singularity and, thus, effectively collapses and cancels "history-making" as the open-endedness and mobility of temporal distancing and dislocation. More important, it both presupposes and relegitimates the concept of experience as the transparency and immediacy of self-presence. Empathy annuls the historicity of experience, rendering the event uniform and one-dimensional, fully conceivable and intelligible in terms of an instant which remains self-transparent and identical within the contours of its temporal site. Empathic historicism, for Benjamin, occludes the event structure of experience, erasing its historicity and closing off contemporaneity as a field of possibilities. As a result, empathy produces the effect contrary to its purported goal: It effaces historicity, effectively sealing off the radically temporal dimension of thought and its structural openness to change.

In Howe's poetry, the moment of breaching language so that it begins to inscribe contemporaneity as a field of linguistically, historically, and politically charged possibilities, constitutes the event of "poetry-in-the-making." Explaining the title *Singularities*, Howe refers to the mathematical notion of singularity as the point of radical instability and change, as the site of the articulation of difference and possibilities: "The singularity (I think Thom is saying) is the point where there is a sudden change to something completely else. It's a chaotic point. It's the point chaos enters cosmos, the instant articulation. Then there is a leap into something else" (*BM*, 173). It could be argued that the linguistic transpositions and decompositions in Howe's poems function like singularities, that is, as sites of radical linguistic, historical, but also ethical and political, instabilities. The singularities of Howe's writings constitute the moments where the uncertainty and possibility that pervade all articulation are inscribed into the linguistic texture of her poems. Such singularities become visible, for example, in the condensed, enigmatic, and polysemic lines like "velc cello viable toil / quench conch uncannunc" (*S*, 10), which signify through semantic instability and underdetermination, verbal decomposition, and the absence of syntactical determination.[9]

The intricacy of Howe's writing consists in the link between the rearticulation of history with the examination of language in view of its "singularities"—that is, its folds of instability and differentiation. Replying to the question "What is in the word?" Howe responds: "It's the singularity. It's a catastrophe of bifurcation. There is a sudden leap into another situation" (*BM*, 177). Howe employs the word "catastrophe" in Thom's sense of a morphology which produces and makes appear a given situation of catastrophe as a *"conflict situation between local regimes"* (*BM,* 174). The "catastrophe of bifurcation" succinctly describes the linguistic morphology of Howe's work, within which significations do not differentiate "evenly" and fail to form determinable configurations of opposites. Instead, they constellate and disperse along unpredictable and unstable vectors of meaning. Tracing this morphology which in the previous chapters I called *poietic,* the "catastrophes" of language in Howe's poetry provide the opportunity for remapping the historical and sexual dimensions of experience. I will return to the issue of this new poietic morphology in the section on gender, but I would like to signal here briefly that the very distinct morphology of Howe's texts calls to mind both Irigaray's remarks on refiguring the sexual morphology of experience and those features of Irigaray's writing which remap the textual morphology of critical and philosophical practice.

Howe's most characteristic practices include: fragmented or broken down syntactical structures, frequent use of words without syntactic modification or relationship—"chaotic architect repudiate line Q confine lie link realm" (*S,* 13–15)—lines and words intersecting or overlaying one another, and the typographical revisions of the horizontal-vertical arrangement of lines,[10] in which pages becomes inverted and transformed into a shifting mosaic of poetic possibilities (*S,* 56–58, 66, 69–70). It is enough to juxtapose these features with Irigaray's strategy of writing in questions, which multiply rather than foreclose possibilities and uncertainty, with her refiguration of being in terms of proximity and indeterminateness of identity, to realize that Howe's poetic morphology reinscribes gender into the articulation of experience. It exposes the correlation between the erasure of historicity and the patriarchal morphology of discourse. Like Irigaray's project, Howe's poetry reclaims sexual difference and inscribes it into the very "matter" of language—into words, syntactical and semantic relationships, morphology of writing—and does so in the context of revising history and experience. I read the "bifurcating morphology" of Howe's work as employing various language "catastrophes" in a concerted effort to question the reliance of the universal claims of history upon the parallel effacement of sexual difference and the event structure of experience.

This morphology of bifurcation underpins the question of identity in Howe's writings, whether it is the matter of American identity constructed out of the colonialist conflicts, the role of poetry in contemporary experience, or the problem of the erasure of sexual identity from language. Whenever identity comes into play in Howe's poetry, it is always contingent upon keeping open the field of possibilities for rearticulating experience. From its initial prose note, "Articulation of Sound Forms in Time" leaves little doubt that the figure of Hope Atherton and the specific historical moment of his "wanderings" are used to multiply linguistic and historical possibilities: relations to the other (the colonists and the natives), historical (narrative) versus poetic text, the constitution and revision of American identity, the reflection on the role of poetry in contemporary culture. The opening section of the poem "The Falls Fight" recounts the historical circumstances that lead to Atherton's "wanderings": "Just after King Philip's War . . . Deerfield was the northernmost colonial settlement in the Connecticut River Valley. In May 1676 several large bands of Indians had camped in the vicinity. The settlers felt threatened by this gathering of the tribes. They appealed to Boston for soldiers. . . . 'The Reverend Hope Atherton, minister of the gospel, at Hatfield, a gentleman of publick spirit, accompanied the army'" (S, 3). Quoting a letter by Stephen Williams, itself a paraphrase of Atherton's own account, Howe contextualizes Atherton's wanderings in the aftermath of the clashes and massacres occasioned by the intervening army: "In the fight, upon their retreat, Mr. Atherton was unhorsed and separated from the company, wandered in the woods some days and then got into Hadley, which is on the east side of the Connecticut River" (S, 5). "The Falls Fight" introduces the circumstances of Atherton's wanderings both to reemphasize the importance of the figures of wilderness and conquest in American consciousness and to question the relation of poetic text to history. Atherton's curiously feminine name "Hope" on the one hand inscribes and ironizes the hope present in the foundational gesture of establishing a New World ("Pre-Revolution Americans viewed America as the land of Hope") and on the other ties the reappraisal of history in Howe's text to the "hope" of a poetic refiguration of experience: "I assume Hope Atherton's excursion for an emblem foreshadowing a Poet's abolished limitations in our demythologized fantasy of Manifest Destiny" (S, 4).

An emblem for the temporal "wanderings" of identity and the linguistic itineraries of Howe's poem, Atherton's name becomes linked from the start to fleshing out the dislocating effects of experience. The introductory narrative frames the series of poems in a way that refolds the historical distance between Atherton's wanderings and Howe's poetic rewriting to render in "sound forms" the elusive marks of historicity. The historical framework of the poem anchors Howe's reflection directly within the revision of the Enlightenment narrative of modernity and its concealed violence: "Theoreticians of the Modern /—emending annotating inventing /

World as rigorously related System / Pagan worlds moving toward destruction" (*S*, 35). Howe explores the exclusionary practices of systemic thinking, which reduces the "singularities" of experience to the homogeneity of historical (and conceptual) narratives, in order to show the futurity inscribed in experience, a futurity irreducible to the horizon of what is (re)presented: "—Hegelian becoming / —Hugolian memory / Patriarchal prophesy at heels of hope / Futurity—" (*S*, 22). There can be little doubt that Howe's (re)construction of Atherton's wanderings questions the idea of an empathic recovery of the past. As much as the poem reconstructs the past, it also underscores the distance opened by writing, the field of possibilities of revisiting and rewriting history. This nonempathic reinscription of history makes possible a rethinking of experience in terms of the inappropriable and multiple folds of historicity, which keep breaching the "illusion" of presence.

American identity, one of Howe's main interests, is thus combined with the question of how to think of history within the double historical fold created by her texts: the reinscription of the past's historical distance into the constitution of the "presence" of the text. Howe's contribution to the contemporary debates about the politics of identity—both vis-à-vis American literary tradition and in the broader context which encompasses Ireland, England, religious conflicts, and postcolonial perspectives—is to emphasize the intrinsic historical instability of such revisions themselves. Howe's text separates the question of identity from empathy and from the idea that experience can be predicated upon the notion of presence. These textual negotiations show the extent to which historicity ruptures the claims of identity based upon immanence, collective essence, or the substantive notions of self and community. In Howe's work, the points of articulation—of identity, history, sexuality—become revised into "catastrophes of language," which take place in the intrinsically unstable and continuously historicized field of differentiation.

In "God's Spies" from "The Liberties," Cordelia responds to Stella's question "Who can tell me who I am?" with the sentence: "Swift, you are swift—" (*ET*, 199), and, this short exchange illustrates how the question of Stella's identity (Stella was a nickname that Swift gave to one of his mistresses, Hester Johnson) entails a difficult negotiation of the layers of textual material, historical distances, and the possibilities opened within the poetic text. The absence of historical material detailing Hester Johnson's life and character and the scarcity of her own texts leave the problem of who Stella is inevitably tied to "Swift," that is, to Swift's portrayal of her and to the patriarchal morphology of language and culture in which this description was created. And yet, as Cordelia remarks, Stella is not only "Swift" but also "swift" — the possibility of critique, rupture, and tension is already inscribed in Stella's question. Who Stella "is" remains a matter of negotiation, the negotiation coded into the play between the capital "S" and the small "s," which must recognize the ambiguity of its own historical status between history and its rewriting.

Both in their structural operations and their cognitive and political implications, Howe's rewritings of historical accounts and literary texts resemble more closely Benjamin's dialectical image than they do, say, the optics of historicism. To flesh out the significance of this parallel for Howe, especially for "Articulation of Sound Forms in Time," let us recall here briefly the dynamic and the effects of the dialectical image as Benjamin presents it in the Arcades project:

> For the historical index of the images not only says that they belong to a particular time; it says, above all, that they attain to legibility only at a particular time. And, indeed, this acceding "to legibility" constitutes a specific critical point in the movement at their interior . . . It is not that what is past casts its light on what is present, or what is present its light on what is past; rather, image is that wherein what has been [*das Gewesene*] comes together in a flash with the now [*der Jetzt*] to form a constellation.[11]

Dialectical images produce the legibility of history; they function as the structural condition of the possibility of reading experience in historical terms. The index of images registers the historicity of being and its effects upon the forms which the articulation of experience takes. The legibility Benjamin has in mind questions the philosophical and political implications of empathic identification, its dependence on the substantialist conception of experience, and takes the form of a constellation whose peculiar "instantaneous" manifestation inscribes the tension and dislocation constitutive of history. This instability and the possibilities it opens constitute the historical dimension of experience. What becomes legible "in a flash" is the heterogeneity inscribed in the unfolding of being, which dislocates experience, pushing it out of balance and, as it were, out of its "time." Perhaps historicity registers as nothing more (or less!) than this impossibility for experience to coincide completely with its own time.

The degree of such noncoincidence evident in Howe's language constitutes probably the most singular feature of her engagement with history, an engagement which produces historical legibility in a way that avoids reproducing the universalist momentum of discourse. The terms of legibility proposed by Howe's work consistently undermine narrative, empathic, and universalizing readings of history. The very difficult, often enigmatic, legibility at work in Howe's writings eschews what Benjamin characterizes as the "additive" method of historicism (*Illuminations,* 262). Instead, it can be regarded in terms of mapping, through linguistic "Tension / Torsion / Traction / Unction / Vection / Version / Vision" (*ET,* 209), the unstable terrain of experience, riddled with possibilities and historical folds. The historical material in Howe's work—whether it is the Dublin of Swift's Stella, the America of the colonial period, or the literary world surrounding Emily Dickinson—allows her to insert a historical perspective and distance right into the very middle of her poetic remapping of experience. The exactness of the representation of the past matters less than the production of the present as a constellation in which, through the interpolation of historical distance, the present becomes redefined by the ruptures of historicity. Perhaps even more complex and unpredictable than the folds and circlings of Benjamin's writing style, the poetic legibility Howe's works produce constitutes one of the most challenging attempts to figure experience in terms of multiple, shifting, and incomplete constellations of historical distances.

Such legibility marked by a double fold of history is at work throughout "Articulation of Sound Forms in Time." Putting in play key motifs in the constitution of American identity, "Articulation" uses the figure of Hope Atherton as an emblem of a poetic rewriting of experience within the context of contemporary life. Signaling the dislocating inscription of the past, the poem brings the force of the historical distance to bear upon the constitution of the "present" in a manner which makes legible the noncoincidence of experience. This noncoincidence operates both on the level of the structure of the entire poem and, particularly intensified, within several discrete sections of the work. Its workings are especially visible on pages 14 to 15, in a complex semantic and visual play that both simulates and undermines the mimetic function of language. Both pages contain the identical number of words and the same lexical items in configurations which represent almost mirror images of each other. In spite of the suggested mirror inversion between the architectures of pages 14 and 15, the opening line ("Posit gaze level diminish lamp and asleep(selv)cannot see") and the two concluding lines are not inverted, except for the final words in the last line which switch places from page to page:

blue glare(essence)cow bed leg extinct draw scribe   upside
    ["sideup" on page 15]
even blue(A)ash-tree fleece comfort(B)draw scribe   sideup
    ["upside" on page 15]

The middle section of each page, consisting of four lines, repeats strings of words in a sort of cross-reverse, except that on page 15 there are no spaces between words, and capital letters replace small ones to mark the junctures between words. For example, "*is* notion most open apparition past Halo view border redden" on page 14 corresponds, in a kind of a mirror cross, to "ReddenBorderViewHaloPastApparitionOpenMostNotion *is*" on page 15. The absence of syntactical determinations and relationships, combined with discrete semantic pieces that resonate within the context of the whole work—"empirical Kantian," "Maori," Mohegan," "shot"—renders reading difficult, at the same time that it also increases, one wants to say almost at a geometric rate, the possibilities of various constellations and articulations. Tracing the relationships at play on pages 14 and 15 within the entire architectonics of "Articulation" would be one way to draw the historical matrix of Howe's work. The "failed" mirror production implies that mirroring or representing the past within the apparently "better" structure of visibility afforded by the present (moment of representation)—a certain version of the dream of symmetry—remains a deceptive and dangerous dream, which denies the temporality of experience.

This sense of temporality and noncoincidence is amplified by the manner in which the prefatory note, "The Falls Fight," frames the subsequent sections in relation to Hope Atherton, the purported focal point of the poem:

Hope's literal attributes. Effaced background dissolves remotest foreground. Putative author, premodern condition, presently present what future clamors for release?
Hope's epicene name draws its predetermined poem in. (*S*, 4)

While the first sentence projects the sense of determinateness and accurateness implied in the phrase "literal attributes," the second one almost immediately undermines it with the mutually reinforcing meaning of "effaced" and "dissolves." The semantic relations opened by those two sentences dramatize the tension between the desire to grasp Hope adequately, to produce a literal representation of him, and the impossibility of such an approach in view of the dislocation intrinsic to experience. The historical background of the poem, the conflicted accounts of Atherton's wanderings in the wilderness of New England, are refracted and blurred, while the foreground—the poetic project structured around and emblematized by these wanderings—is put into question by the disruptive effects of historical distance. In the end, the temporal distance which the text reproduces remains distinct from an interval between stable and defined historical points and works as a changing constellation of proximities and distances between indistinct and incomplete moments, whose contours are "dissolved" and "effaced." Neither the past nor the present can lay claim to distinctness or "literalness," to a fully articulated or stable identity.

A similar set of historical dislocations is again put into play in the next line from the above quote, which scrambles the temporal relations: the past becomes a site which is "presently present," inscribed as past within the textual presence, and which already contains a future which clamors for release. How perspective works in Howe can be seen in the way Hope, because of the inscription of his wanderings into the structure of the text, becomes a putative author. If this gesture of rewriting "discloses" the putative authorship already inscribed, or "predetermined," in the figure of Hope Atherton, and represents his time as "the premodern condition," Howe indicates that such a reflection upon the conditions of reciprocal visibility between the past and the present, upon the moments when their constellations provide the historical legibility for experience, opens up the possibility of a (different) future. It is a future which acquires the ability to read its own experience differently, through the instability and openness implied in the figure of Hope.

Such crossings of the past into the present (and the future), enacted in incomplete, transposed, or decomposed words and images, remind the reader that the focus of Howe's poetry lies precisely on the "singularities" of experience: the moments when time suddenly changes its sign from plus to minus, when the past blows open and "wounds" the present. These points of singularity, of sudden bifurcations and transpositions of meaning, make Howe's works continuously requestion the present. As a result, the present becomes historicized: not simply in the sense that it is related to a historical moment—colonization, eighteenth-century Ireland, the Prague of religious conflict, the America of Melville and Dickinson—but as ruptured by historicity. It is possible to read Howe's poems precisely as attempts to articulate history, to "sound" in words the very opening within experience from which history and the possibility of historical consciousness emerge. As the text of "Articulation" circles constantly around the figure of Hope

Atherton and the various voices that speak through it, the title suggests that its focus falls on the poetic articulation of the "scattering" effects of historicity within experience.

Before I discuss the place of gender in Howe's historical scatterings of experience, let me briefly consider the political implications of her figuration of history. What lies almost on the surface of Howe's works is the political implications of her reinventions of historical past, personages, and events: the reimagining of "the American experience" through historical and literary texts, from Puritan writings through the complexities of the textuality of Melville's and Dickinson's works to reflections on the contemporary tasks of poetry. For instance, Howe's relentless problematization of the effects of the standardization and uniformization of a Melville or a Dickinson text draws attention to the practices of effacing the intrinsic unreadability and open-endedness of these texts, of their plural textualities, for the sake of producing an underlying version of experience as closed and readable. These practices transform experience from an open field of possibilities into a uniform, regulated pattern, into a univocal text which effaces contradictions and conflicts, or singularities, to paraphrase Howe. Howe's poems underscore the fact that the historical legibility which experience affords is that of inarticulation, incompletion, and stuttering. "Scattering as Behavior Toward Risk," which closes *Singularities,* takes its cue from the erasures, corrections, and restoration of words and phrases in the genetic text of *Billy Budd.* In the process of decoding Melville's text, Howe's poem comes to resemble "a text so urgently stumbling almost blindly through a mind-boggling series of tentative and at times almost desperate castings-about for words and phrases that we are caught up in the sheer suspense the *processes* of the telling generate, a stuttering narrative of inarticulation unspoken within the narrative."[12] Although this remark by Peter Quartermain refers to *Billy Budd,* the characterization, especially the last sentence about stuttering and inarticulation within articulation, seems appropriate for describing the textuality of Howe's *Singularities.* As Howe remarks at the end of the *Talisman* interview, "It's the stutter in American literature that interests me. I hear the stutter as a sounding of uncertainty. What is silenced or not quite silenced. . . . History has happened. The narrator is disobedient. A return is necessary, a way for women to go. Because we are in the stutter. We were expelled from the Garden of Mythology of the American Frontier. The drama's done. We are the wilderness. We have come on to the stage stammering" (*BM,* 181).

Demythologizing the American frontier, Howe's work detects or infuses stutter into the Puritan discourse legitimating the colonization and opens the historical spaces to voices "not quite silenced." This revised idea of historical legibility relies on the peculiar "articulateness" of stutter, on corrections and incompletion which render legible the voices and perspectives erased within the homogenous narratives of history. As they destroy the illusory coherence and transparency of the poetic voice, Howe's texts show that history works as a field of unrecognized possibilities, conflicts, and exclusions, to which one must return in order to gain the legibility of experience. The political significance of this gesture—which frees in the spacings and corrections of Howe's texts the effaced perspectives of women, native Americans, or colonized Ireland—appears today, in the atmosphere of multiculturalism, to require almost no commentary. We should remember, though, that Howe's work, keenly aware of its own historical perspective, is more than a "celebration" of multiplicity or the recognition of the innumerable wrongs of history. Howe's is an enterprise of retracing the contours of a different legibility of experience, as much for the sake of history as for the sake of reflecting upon the present moment. Such legibility avoids producing truth or a uniform vision of history, and it prefers to undermine and "scatter" the universalist momentum of language. A sounding of uncertainty rather than a production of knowledge, this legibility renders readable the political and ethical fallout of the immanentist and universalist representations of experience.

Such a reinvention of history touches upon the politics of experience, that is, upon the question of what might be called the political momentum of experience, of rendering legible the unsettled, "singular" character of the space in which action and policy making originate. It is in this sense of the political impetus of experience that Heidegger rethinks the meaning of the Greek *polis* in his lecture series on Hölderlin's hymn "Der Ister." *Polis* is neither the organization of a city nor the political apparatus of the state, and, even less, the conflation of the two in the notion of the city-state, which Heidegger sees as the imposition of the modern perspective upon the Greek understanding of the historical character of experience. Trying to understand the political momentum inscribed in the historicity of experience, Heidegger suggests that "[p]erhaps the πόλις is that realm and locale around which everything that is question-worthy and uncanny turns in an exceptional sense. The πόλις then is πόλος, that is, the pole, the swirl in which and around which everything turns."[13] Experience is *polis* and, therefore, political, to the extent that its occurrence opens the unsettled, "questionable and undomesticated," space of history and representation. I see Howe's texts as an exploration of such a *polis* of experience in terms of the "singularities" of language, of the semantic and syntactical folds in which the unsettled space of experience retains its indetermination. Her *Singularities* moves between the exclusions and silencing of Native American perspectives in the frontier mythology and the question of the political or of the emergence of the political space through the linguistically and historically unsettled inscriptions of experience. These folds produce experience in terms of the unsettling of history, as the political momentum which puts into question the attempts to domesticate experience and represent it in the guise of a historical account. One cannot underestimate here the political resonance of such "unsettlings" in Howe's writings, literally inscribed in the tension between American wilderness and the foundational gesture of its settling, and evoked also in terms of the British colonization of Ireland. Howe's texts induce the rethinking of the political sphere of experience, suggesting the impossibility of detaching politics from the articulation of the contours of experience. It is these contours, their political questionability and unsettling effects, that Howe's works trace down to the elements of language.

The Gender of Legibility, or Reading Sexual Difference

The problem of gender in Howe's poetry can be characterized by two questions: What is the gender of legibility, and how, given that the conditions of legibility have patriarchal origin, can we at all read sexual difference? In other words, how do we need to rewrite the conditions of the legibility of experience so that the new sexual morphology could register in the text of history? Historically, the parameters of readability and understanding have been prescribed by a grid of concepts related to phallogocentric representations of experience: subjectivity, immediacy, presence, immanence, sameness, universality, and so on, all designed to generalize the singularity of experience and, in the process, to efface its sexual markings. Underscoring the masculine gender of such legibility, Howe's poetry rewrites the space of the inscription and alters its morphology to reflect the workings of sexual difference within experience.

This set of questions is reminiscent of Irigaray's project, in which the attempt to refigure the morphology of experience is at all times correlated with the rigorous questioning of the conditions of legibility—of the specular dialectics of thinking—and with the revision of discursive practices. Irigaray suggests that for sexual difference to inscribe itself in cultural practices—from philosophy, technology, and science to law and politics—we need "the production of a new age of thought, art, poetry, and language: the creation of a new *poetics*."[14] The poetics that Irigaray has in mind is a rethinking of experience beyond the discourse governed by the patriarchal erasure of sexual difference. To that extent, the question of the sexual morphology of experience is inseparable from the question of language. As Irigaray is well aware, such a poetics requires more than a reinsertion of other voices, and the voices of others, into a discursive paradigm that will continue to erase their differences because it is determined and regulated by the unifying momentum of the specular logic operative in patriarchal thought. This poetics involves a critico-poetic rethinking of how the basic philosophemes of Western thought produce and regulate linguistic practices. It postulates reinventing the "matrix" of language so that it would inscribe, rather than (ab)use and obliterate, the feminine and sexual difference. Irigaray's rewriting of the sexual morphology of experience entails the recognition of how the specular economy of discourse first sexualizes being, dividing it into matter and spirit, only to cover up this distinction and secure the speculative unity of difference. In spite of the apparently proliferating differences, thought and language continuously reaffirm their universalist momentum, their tendency toward "specularizing" difference and reinscribing it within the "domain of sameness." Irigaray's project consists in diagnosing the degree to which the logic of sameness has been regulating the elements of discourse and in reinscribing (sexual) difference within these discursive elements in ways that undermine the dialectical pull of this logic. Irigaray's gesture is, therefore, always double: The tendency toward sameness is at once recognized and undermined, mimicked and questioned through a new "poetics" which employs fluid syntax, nonassertive and fragmented sentences, questions rather than statements, mixed registers, and empty subject positions.

It is on this discursive level that I propose to approach the question of gender and experience in Howe's poetry. Howe's works suggest that, in order to inscribe sexual difference into language, it is necessary to work often from within the basic structures of language, its elemental parts, even minimal semantic and syntactical units. To discern the significance of sexual difference in rethinking experience, one has to operate on the level of parts of speech, to transpose and decompose words and syntax, to bypass grammatical rules, and to undermine or abandon the conventional connections and junctures of language. In *My Emily Dickinson,* Howe herself outlines the reach and the elemental character of such a questioning in relation to the writings of Dickinson and Stein: "Emily Dickinson and Gertrude Stein also conducted a skillful and ironic investigation of patriarchal authority over literary history. Who polices questions of grammar, parts of speech, connection, and connotation? Whose order is shut inside the structure of a sentence? What inner articulation releases the coils and complications of Saying's assertions? In very different ways the countermovement of these two women's work penetrates to the indefinite limits of written communication."[15] Howe's own poetry modifies and extends the insights of her "critical" writings, operating on the assumption that the workings of language—from sentence structure, punctuation, and the linearity of writing to the horizontal-vertical arrangement of the page—must be involved in refiguring the morphology of experience.

If the legibility of experience and history is gendered, if the patriarchal articulation of being as monological and universal determines the dialectical dynamic of thought and permeates the elements of language, then an attempt to rethink experience along gender lines requires such an "avant-garde" reinvention of language that would affect relations beyond or "below" the play of signification. Already Gertrude Stein, in what I termed her poetics of the event, combines the reimagining of English with the question of gender and lesbianism, and, in the process, "liquefying" English word order and increasing indefinitely the plasticity of syntax and the elasticity of words and meaning. Howe takes her writing in a different direction: She explores the possibilities of an unsettled, and unsettling, arrangement of the page, with multiple possibilities enacted simultaneously (words revised and/or crossed out) and made indeterminate by the absence of conjunctions, the disappearance or minimalization of syntactic relations, the erasure of line definitions (crossing, overlapping, overlaying lines and words), and the decomposition of sentences and words.

Keeping in mind the various discursive levels on which Howe "undetermines" the legibility of experience, I propose to examine three related aspects of how her writings reinscribe gender into the patriarchal morphology of articulation: first, the inside/outside perspective characteristic of the inscription of women's voice (for example, in "The Liberties"); second, the heterogenous space of Howe's most interesting works ("Articulation," "The Liberties"); and third, the ways in which the first two strategies contextualize and amplify her reworking of the elements of poetic language. I will focus my discussion on "The Liberties," in part because this text attempts to refigure the space of history through feminine voices: Stella and Cordelia. The prominence I give to "The Liberties" does not imply that the three aspects of Howe's rethinking of gender cannot be found in her other poems. For example, the opening section of "Articulation of Sound Forms in Time" mixes various modalities of discourse, from letters and narratives to poetry, as part of how it rethinks sexual difference. Linking the narrative development of the poem with the name "Hope," Howe underscores the gender ambivalence inscribed in the name: "Hope's epicene name draws its predetermined poem in" (*S*, 4). The adjective epicene signals the importance of sexual difference to Howe's exploration of the poetic refiguration of experience as "articulation of sound forms in time." According to the *Oxford English Dictionary*, "epicene" refers to: "1. In Lat. and G. grammar, said of nouns which, without changing their grammatical gender, may denote either sex. 2. Partaking of the characteristics of both sexes. 3. Adapted to both sexes; worn or inhabited by both sexes." Indeed, Hope is inhabited, worn as a name, by both the Puritan minister and the poet's voice; in fact, it is inhabited by both, or more, voices, sexes, and genders at once. What resonates in the name Hope, "an emblem foreshadowing a Poet's abolished limitations in our demythologized fantasy of Manifest Destiny," is the problematic of gender difference and sexual morphology of experience: "Archaic presentiment of rupture / Voicing desire no more from here" (*S*, 38). The epicene name designates the place where sexual difference ruptures experience, a peculiar "singularity" where the bifurcation of the feminine and the masculine enfolds history in its significations and where this difference remains problematic, fraught with the possibility of being collapsed and erased within the "manifest destiny" of the sexes: that is, the domain of sameness characteristic of the patriarchal economy of thought. Hope's epicene name becomes an emblem of how the problematic of sexual difference complicates the temporal articulation of experience indicated in the poem's title. If *Singularities* presents experience as a field of (linguistic) singularities where unstable vectors of possibilities keep rewriting the articulation, then this particular morphology is inflected by the figure of Hope, whose name echoes in the openings and lesions of Howe's text.

In "The Liberties," I examine the problematic of gender by looking at Howe's linguistic and typographical inventions in a double context: the recreation of feminine voices and the plural textuality of the work, which comprises multiple quotations, journal entries, prose sections, short and long poems, and plays. The textual map of "The Liberties" — "flags charts maps / to be read by guesswork through obliteration" (*ET*, 163) — is indeed even more complex than the one of "Articulation," as it inscribes the problem of identity into a collage of texts, voices, and personages, ranging from

Swift and "his" Stella and Shakespeare's *King Lear* and *Hamlet* to Howe's own reinvention of Stella and Cordelia as part of the meditation on her Irish heritage. "The Liberties" is a mosaic of texts which allows itself to be broken and spaced by other voices, quotations, and perspectives, even as it continuously rewrites the cited voices and works. Such a writing strategy is reminiscent of DuPlessis's remarks about "female aesthetic" in "For the Etruscans": "A both/and vision born of shifts, contraries, negations, contradictions. . . . A both/and vision that embraces movement, situational."[16] What DuPlessis designates "a both/and vision," a vision which arises out of contradictions, continuous movement and rewriting, produces textuality that is polyphonic, multiperspectival, and nonhegemonic. In "The Liberties," the poetic I—part of the meditation upon the identity of the author and its cultural roots—never dominates the poem or constructs a privileged, hegemonic perspective. Its voice becomes refracted and modified by the other voices in the poem, voices that are both quoted (Swift, Shakespeare) and (re)invented (Stella, Cordelia). Howe's anagramic play on her name—

> I am composed of nine letters.
> 1 is the subject of a proposition in logic.
> 2 is a female sheep, or tree.
> 3 is equal to one.
> 4 is a beginning.
> 5 & 7 are nothing.
> 6 7 & 8 are a question, or salutation.
> 6 7 8 & 9 are deep, a depression
>
> (*ET,* 209)

—contains no traces of personal experiences and desires, and reads "her" identity, like the rest of the voices in "The Liberties," through the condensation of semantic, syntactical, and typographical innovations. The short two word line following Howe's "self-identification"—"THE KEY"—both ironizes the idea that the author holds the key to her identity and text and suggests that it is indeed the alphabet that remains the "linguistic" key to experience.

Even when one reads "The Liberties" through the optics of Howe's exploration of her Irish heritage, it is clear that the problematic of the authorial voice and identity functions as part of the larger negotiation of the possibility of feminine voice, as an element in the articulation of what Irigaray would call the double movement of (de)sexualization of experience within the patriarchal morphology of discourse. This exploration is contingent upon the possibility of securing the legibility of a sexual morphology of experience, that is, on elaborating alternative parameters of legibility which revise the boundaries of the patriarchal order of reason: subject, uniformity, and noncontradiction. The first "key" to Howe's elaboration of this alternate legibility can be found in the discursive and stylistic plurality of her texts, riddled with numerous literary and historical citations and reappropriations. This way of writing with, in DuPlessis's words, "multiple centers of attention" ("FE," 279) undercuts the monological standards of legibility which characterize patriarchal discourse,[17] and does so in a gesture that, like the typographical puzzles of "The Liberties," opens the space for a reading of experience that retains difference. What I see operating here is an inversion of legibility which makes it possible to read the staples of modern rationality—the logic of identity, noncontradiction, or universality—as a "misunderstanding":

> We are
> discovered

> not solid

> the floor

> based

> on misunderstanding. (*ET,* 211)

It is not surprising, then, that the readability of feminine identity (and the identity of the feminine) rewrites the rules of visibility, presence, and truth operative in Western thought. Femininity is "to be read by guesswork through obliteration," that is, through an undecidable play between a "negative" reading of the effacement of sexual difference and a "positive" reading (of femininity) *by means of* undermining the patriarchal structure of discourse. "The Liberties" rewrites the feminine, as it were, onto three voices—Stella, Cordelia, and "Susan Howe" ("I am composed of nine letters")—and makes the identity of each voice contingent upon and inflected by the exchanges with the other two. Interlacing the three voices, "The Liberties" departs from the notion of a homogeneous identity and its roots in the binary schema of speculative mirroring, and presents a heterogeneous and open-ended model of identity as an alternative to the closures operative in the metaphysical concept of the subject. Even though several sections of "The Liberties" invite a "personalizing" reading of the poem in the context of the author's visit to Dublin: "Across the Atlantic, I / inherit myself / semblance / of irish susans / dispersed / and narrowed to / home" (*ET,*

213), such a reading becomes refracted and complicated by the textual labor of reinventing femininity through the voices of Stella and Cordelia. The phrase "I am composed of nine letters" works against the idea of a recognition or recovery of an already existing identity, determined by the double American and Irish context, both spanned and dislocated by the space of the Atlantic. It is more of a rewriting, even a reinvention, which requires as its condition of possibility a different matrix of experience: one that would allow for the articulation of sexual difference. For the nine letters of Susan Howe's name to resonate in language, it is necessary to redo this language, to rewrite its rules, so that a different figuration of the feminine can emerge, and with it, a revised morphology of experience.

As the ironic ending of the "Book of Cordelia" suggests, such a morphology deliberately sidesteps successful articulations, that is, moments of presence and meaning, and negotiates a difficult path of failures and obliterations: "I can re // trac // my steps // Iwho // crawl // between thwarts // Do not come down the ladder // ifor I // haveaten // it a // way" (ET, 179–80). With its lines forming the rungs of a verbal ladder, this fragment plays with the idea of order, progression, and symmetry, as it decomposes words and writes them over one another, in order to form unstable and shifting lines of semantic and syntactical relations, which dismantle the very configuration they build. "ifor I" indicates an exchange of identity, of a de-emphasized and fractured "i" for the model of "strong" identity with capital "I," which seemingly guarantees closure and self-presence. In what may be a parody of Wittgenstein's famous remark from the *Tractatus,* the ladder, instead of being discarded after performing its necessary mediating function, is "eaten a / way" by the "corrosive" and unstable language of Howe's poetry. Such a "corroded" linguistic ladder cannot provide the logical steps of progression, for it signifies the deregulation and, in extreme cases, a total disappearance of conjunctions and syntactical relations. For example, on pages 204 to 208, grammatical relations become reduced to a degree zero and words are left, in a parody of Hamlet's remark, as "words   words   words." Language no longer serves as the mediation in the process of the production of identity but becomes the space where the points of singularity—the decomposing and transposing rungs of the textual ladder—articulate the legibility of experience in terms of fractures and obliterations.

In the overall architectonics of "The Liberties," this issue of legibility is most visible in the play "God's Spies," the longest text in the work, which through a series of parodies of Swift and Shakespeare reinvents Stella and Cordelia as dramatic characters. "The Liberties" begins with a narrative section which recounts briefly the available material on Stella, emphasizing the absence of letters and texts written by Hester Johnson herself ("None of Stella's letters have been saved" [*ET,* 151]) and the fact that what is "known" about her comes almost exclusively from men's accounts and portraits of her. Illustrating the patriarchal framework reflected in Stella's portraits, the opening section sets up the task of a reconstruction, or, to be more precise, a reinvention, of Stella as part of a change in the representational optics which would allow for a different figuration of femininity. This recreation of Stella becomes intertwined with the figure of Cordelia in a dialogue between two female characters which complicates the idea of femininity beyond the roles of mistress and (un)dutiful daughter. In what has become a trademark of Howe's multisectioned and multilayered texts, the "books" of Stella and Cordelia (the second one set up against the well-known quotation from *King Lear* in which Cordelia refuses to embellish upon the praises of her father already delivered by her two sisters) enact, as much visually as semantically, the undoing of the portraits of the two women constructed by Swift's letters and Shakespeare's play. The "Book of Stella" continuously surprises the reader with the changing compositions of the page, ceaselessly redrawing the context in which a "new" Stella emerges. The first page of the section (*ET,* 159) parodies the attempt to contain the text (Stella?) within fixed and equal margins. While the beginnings and endings of each line are arranged in perfect vertical columns, the effort to keep equal line extensions forces an uneven and disrupted distribution of words within lines, occasionally producing split words. Intervals between words range from two or three spaces to wide gaps extending for over half a line. The subsequent pages produce the impression of a text which explodes the narrowly prescribed boundaries and metamorphoses from page to page into unexpected visual constellations, as if to render "visible" the swiftness of Stella's soul:

> moving or capable of moving
> with great speed
> rapidly running   flying   following
>   flight of an arrow
> known for the swiftness of her soul
> (ET, 163)

In their linguistic and textual inventions, the "Book of Stella" and the "Book of Cordelia" problematize the legibility of experience available within the heritage of the cultures "across the Atlantic." It is no surprise, therefore, that when both Stella and Cordelia gain their "own" voices as characters in "God's Spies," the drama consistently parodies *Hamlet* as a pivotal text in the establishment of the parameters of Western (male) subjectivity. It would take too long to list all the allusions to Shakespeare that Howe weaves into the play, from cross-dressing reminiscent of his comedies to the parody of Hamlet's encounter with his father's ghost. What is important for my argument is the fact that "God's Spies," reaching back to the beginnings of modernity in the Renaissance, complicates and rewrites the emergence of the monological, unified subjectivity in *Hamlet* and projects an alternative "stage" of experience where identity becomes fractured, open, and contingent. Howe's play unfolds a continuous parody of Hamlet's tendency to soliloquize: Stella and Cordelia are almost constantly present together on stage, always in dialogue or conversation. If indeed the modern notion of subjectivity as an autonomous, self-enclosed space of interiority has one of its sources in Hamlet's monologues, Howe's rewriting of *Hamlet* into two female voices which keep inflecting and modifying each other suggests that the regendering of subjectivity reaches well beyond the idea of women (re)claiming a separate and autonomous agency of the subject, which, so far, has been accessible only to men. At issue is the refiguration of the very notion of subjectivity: from the monological and self-enclosed space of interiority—the subject of soliloquy—to an open-ended relation, refracted through the unpredictable turns and twists of the exchanges with the other.

"God's Spies" presents a scenario of the gendering of experience which is similar to how Irigaray figures a new morphology of experience through the notion of two lips, which, neither one nor two, escape and inflect the dialectical dynamic of identity. With the exception of the appearance of Swift's ghost who, by contrast with Hamlet's father, fails to even attract Stella's attention, the entire play transpires between Stella and Cordelia in a series of exchanges which keep negotiating the shared and mutually inflected space of identity between the two of them. This ambiguity is reflected in Cordelia's answer to Stella: "Swift, you are swift," which situates Stella between Swift's portrayal and her own ceaselessly metamorphosing (like the pages in the "Book of Stella") "swiftness." The uncertainty opened up by the gendered difference of perspectives begins to suggest the possibility of an alternative, "feminine" articulation of experience: one that is fractured and fluid, operating on the model of proximity ("neither one nor two") which blurs the lines of demarcation and enclosure characteristic of the patriarchal model of identity.

The type of social and communal relations developed in "God's Spies" would also have to be read along the lines of the nonimmanence and the absence of sameness outlined in Irigaray's *This Sex Which Is Not One:* "Neither one nor two. I've never known how to count. Up to you. In their calculations, we make two. Really, two? Doesn't that make you laugh? An odd sort of two. And yet not one. Especially not one. Let's leave *one* to them: their oneness, with its prerogatives, its domination, its solipsism: like the sun's."[18] "God's Spies" uses similar language: "We are at peace—pathless./ Clinging close we come in couples—conversing at landmarks. / Or we rise to the surface at seamark—still—still—far wide—. . ." (*ET,* 199). In "The Liberties" discrete and definable identity is replaced by a more fluid textual motion which keeps articulating itself in couples and in conversation. The notions of identity and sociality we find in Howe's text are a result of a renegotiated matrix of experience; its gendered legibility becomes visible against the structuring concepts of the phallogocentric representation of experience: subject, presence, oneness, sameness, immanence, and so on.

The echoing refrain of "God's Spies"—"They murder each other"— underscores the violence implied in the ideas of sameness and unified experience and captures the sense of exile and estrangement from such society which marks the "community" established in the conversations between Stella and Cordelia. It is important to note that the action of "God's Spies" extends over one week, and, as Perloff suggests, blurs the boundaries between the historical, the mythical, and the poetic ("CC," 520). The action's span suggests, on the one hand, a certain "recreation" of reality at stake in "The Liberties" (an allusion to the biblical story of creation) and, on the other, Howe's interest in the everyday, ordinary dimension of experience. Even though "God's Spies" explicitly invokes and parodies Shakespeare, it also possesses a certain stark Beckettian quality: Nothing much happens in the play except for the conversations between Stella and Cordelia, and even the scene in which Swift's ghost appears is a dramatic anticlimax, an ironic twist on *Hamlet,* as Stella, too engrossed in reading aloud Hamlet's address to his father's ghost: "Speak to me," does not even notice the apparition. The absence of spectacular theatrical events or twists of the plot and the repetition of the same motifs and phrases reinforce the implicit connection to Beckett: both another link to Ireland's history and culture, always in the background of "The Liberties," and a gesture toward everydayness.

Any analysis of "The Liberties" would be incomplete without the consideration of the link between Howe's rethinking of historicity through the singularities of language and the question of freedom implicit in the title. All of Howe's works obsessively return to the problematic of America and its promised freedoms: its founding, history, cultural identity, and literature. "Articulation of Sound Forms in Time" reposes the question of America as "Hope" by demythologizing Manifest Destiny and by inscribing the problematic of otherness, violence, and domination into the reinvented wanderings of Hope Atherton. The massive reconsideration to which Howe submits "America" revolves around the problematic of freedom, or more accurately, of "liberties," for which "America" remains an ambiguous and contested icon. The title of "The Liberties" indicates the multiple meanings this word possesses in Howe's work. It refers, obviously, to a section of Dublin, and illustrates how Howe's writing remains itself dislocated, spanning her transatlantic American-Irish heritage. On an ironic level, "The Liberties" invokes the countless liberties Howe takes with language, molding and reforming it to reflect experience as a "singularity." These linguistic liberties open the space for rethinking the problem of freedom and for conceiving experience in terms of the "folds" of liberties.

To see this undercurrent of Howe's work, freedom has to be rethought beyond the optics of agency and the idea of freedom as an individual's property or possession. I propose, instead, to link the question of freedom in Howe to the idea of historicity. I follow here Jean-Luc Nancy, who, in *The Experience of Freedom,* rethinks Heidegger's approach to freedom as openness to the unknown and the other. For Nancy, freedom extends beyond the idea of civil liberties as defined by the libertarian and communitarian traditions. Freedom is a matter of experience, of a certain "liberality" marked in the singular contours of experience, whose occurrence yields no essence, exceeds representation, and remains inaccessible to cognition. Freedom, then, never belongs to itself, never possesses itself, and, as such, cannot be possessed or become a property of an agent whose liberty would be guaranteed by law and made possible by its status as a "free" subject. Freedom, much like in Heidegger's work, is for Nancy "the being of a bursting of being that delivers being to existence." [19] Freedom thought this way

> is never at first on the order of action, nor is it on the order of volition or representation. It is a bursting or a singularity of existence, which means existence as deprived of essence and delivered to this inessentiality, to its own surprise as well as to its own decision, to its own indecision as well as to its own generosity. But this "own" of freedom is nothing subjective: it is the inappropriable burst from which the very existence of the subject comes to the subject. . . . (*EF,* 57–58)

Traditionally, freedom is thought to be a matter of will and action, or a property arrogated to a subject who is capable of exercising, losing, or regaining it. In Nancy's reading, freedom describes the singular, unpredictable, and inappropriable contours of how existence opens and manifests itself. As the burst(s) of being, freedom gives existence to the subject who at no point is in possession of what lets him be. The singularity of freedom renders the subject forever out of step with itself, inappropriable, because freedom exceeds the subject's powers of representation and cognition and remains outside the scope of "his" will. It is clear that Nancy thinks here of both the experience of freedom and, more important, of experience *as* freedom: In other words, freedom is marked as the singular and unpredictable field of experience, as the temporal contours of the event. Such freedom (re)occurs against and bursts through the thought's inclination to assign an essence to experience, to represent it in terms of a cause, foundation, or substance. Paradoxically, freedom both incites representation and the will to knowledge—it delivers the subject to itself by means of self-representation— and remains free, singular and untraceable, in relation to representational and cognitive powers. To think and to experience freedom means to think experience in a nonfoundational and nonmetaphysical manner, as the explosion—the catastrophe?—which keeps remapping and resingularizing its own contours.

Even though Howe borrows a mathematical conception of singularity, she deploys it in relation to experience, which becomes a map of the catastrophes of bifurcation, bursting through and opening the confines of representation. The reconstellating and metamorphosing pages of the "Book of Stella" are among Howe's most characteristic strategies of "writing" the freedom of experience, of (re)figuring experience as "liberties." Writing experience as freedom means being attentive to the undercurrents of language, to what moves language, crystallizes its semantic and syntactical relations, and (dis)allows the sedimentation of experience into representation. Among various modes of avant-garde writing, Howe's appears especially invested in bringing to (the surface of) the page the undercurrents of language and history, in letting them burst through conventions of language and thought and thus register their singularity against the representational articulations of experience. It is within such a syntactically and semantically open space that identities are formed and reformed, without ever becoming fully articulated and sedimented. In *The Nonconformist's Memorial,* the I of John's Gospel becomes a figure for an open-ended space of textuality, opposed to the idea of the subject as the locus of meaning and intelligibility:

it is I
without any real subject
all that I say is I
A predicate nominative
not subject the I is
the bread the light the door
the way the shepherd the vine
(NM, 10)

Further into the text, this fractured or scattered I is invoked in the context of reinscribing sexual difference into experience: "Pronoun *I* or her name // Or break its boundaries" (*NM,* 20). If the notion of the subject is conditioned by the necessary erasure of sexual difference and the inscription of the feminine in the universal claims of rationality, Howe's decomposition of the subject fissures the "single narrative thread" of history into "immensities" registered, even though only by erasure, in the historicity of experience: "utter immensities whisper" (*NM,* 20).

Such questioning of the cognitive and linguistic mechanisms of appropriation makes Howe's work part of the critique of modernity's reliance on forms of thought and discourse which seek to foreclose the play of possibilities, to cover over the "catastrophic" morphology of experience, in order to provide secure foundations for the regime of representation. It is in this sense that I take the avant-garde to be a questioning of the principles of representation: Producing postaesthetic works, the avant-garde does not become at all disinvested from external or empirical reality, and, hence, from politics, ethics, and culture. On the contrary, it rigorously rethinks the conceptual framework of representation in view of the "inappropriable" contours of experience. I see works like Howe's as emphatically *invested* in experience, as, on some level, "unthinkable" without this idea of refiguring experience. What interests me in the avant-garde is how it figures experience *as* freedom, and to that effect, reinvents language as a continuously opening inscriptional space in which experience can register its singularity. What characterizes such an avant-garde is the play between the bursts of representational and discursive freedom and "unfree," regimented experience. I would like to suggest here that the problem of how modern art is related to politics and ethics should be thought in terms of this "rigorous" play. In other words, it is the specific sense of experience as freedom that contributes to the political significance of avant-garde art.

Attentive to the ruptures which historicity produces in experience,

Howe's writing inaugurates a new kind of legibility, which tries to free experience from the control of the powers of representation. What is most interesting about this legibility is that it takes its cue from the indetermination of the event, from what Nancy describes as the "other thought" within thinking:

> this experience of freedom (which is not experience "in thought," but which is thought, or thinking, *as* experience) is only the knowledge that in every thought there is *an other* thought, a "thought" which is no longer thought by thought, but which thinks thought itself (which gives it, expends it, and *weighs* it—which is what "thinking" means): a thought other than understanding, reason, knowledge, contemplation, philosophy, other finally than thought itself. The *other* thought of all thought . . . is the burst of freedom. (*EF,* 59) [20]

Nancy emphasizes the dislocation at work in thinking, the fact that thought always traces "an other" thought within it, a thought which disrupts the representational pull of thinking and retraces its own contours. This structural dissymmetry of thought has to be differentiated carefully against the sense of the dialectical doubling of thought, a kind of specular mirroring, which reunifies thinking and sublates all its detours through otherness. It is this dissymmetry that unbalances knowledge, understanding, and reason and keeps freedom in play.

This other of thought, which keeps (re)thinking and inflecting thought, and which thought itself can never represent or control, is the historicity with which thought unfolds. Historicity cannot be represented because it itself is never present, because, opening the space of representation, it never obtains in representational terms. Unrepresented and unrepresentable for this specific reason, historicity marks itself as always "new," unexpected, singular. It is in terms of this distinctive sense of new-ness that I approach the problematic of freedom in the avant-garde. This "historical" signification of the new must be distinguished from Pound's idea of "making it new," of recovering a past greatness and redesigning it for the purposes of the present. The "new" also does not signify a remake of the past, a representing anew. Similarly, it is quite different from the narrow interpretation of avant-garde poetry as incessant novelty, as rebellion for the sake of something new. As both Benjamin and Adorno show, this idea of novelty has been quickly appropriated by capitalism and worked into its machinery of production in order to cover over the monotony of technical reproduction and increase the consumer appeal of products. These false appearances generated by capitalism effectively cover over the disappearance of the new from the increasingly repetitive modern experience: "A constant sameness governs the relationship to the past as well. What is new about the phase of mass culture compared with the late liberal stage is the exclusion of the new. The machine rotates on the same spot."[21] The novelty for novelty's sake dissimulates the essentially unchanging conditions of everyday life and preempts any attempt at creating a different relation to the past.

The avant-garde idea of the new requires that we think experience as constantly reinventing itself, without the need of essence and the illusion of stability. The new should be thought of in terms of historicity, which remarks experience in ways which let it happen as singular. Attentive to the ever "new" historicity of experience, avant-garde art focuses on what underlies and moves thought and language, and produces it as a challenge to the practices of representing history within the framework of transparency and immediacy.[22] Its challenge translates into a different understanding of meaning: meaning irreducible to signification, to the play of linguistic signs, but, instead, thought of in terms of opening the space *for* meaning: "Being's difference-in-itself . . . does not make meaning available as *signification,* but is the opening of a new space for meaning, of a spacing, or, we could say, of 'spaciosity': of the spacious element that alone can receive meaning" (*EF,* 18). What manifests itself in experience seen without the subject as its foundation is another legibility, which defines itself in terms of the always "new" singularity of experience.

This particular resetting of experience "at freedom" underlies Howe's typographical experimentations, her "distortions" and reformatting of the page, from the changing pages of the "Book of Stella" to the crisscrossed puzzles of *Singularities* and *The Nonconformist's Memorial.* What Howe's work almost literally lays open on the page is the space, the interval, in which signification begins. The frequent instances of "syntax degree zero"

love	tongue	milk	pasture	words
bare	arm	cause	cube	words

(*ET,* 208)

function as language singularities, as spaces for meaning, in which their reinscription as "new" counteracts signification's pull toward generality. In Howe's texts, this sense of the new is continuously extended into the past, released or "liberated" from the fixed, stationary accounts of history. Howe's work is a rewriting of history, but a more radical one than those which provide new accounts or give new meaning to the past. It is more "radical" because it opens the space of meaning differently, allowing experience to remain singular and new, legible as singularity rather than through the generality of the linguistic sign. One of the most characteristic moments of such a "release" or "scattering" is Howe's invocation in *Singularities* of the genetic text of *Billy Budd*, the text which remains "other" in relation to all the edited, (mis)appropriated versions of Melville's story. For Howe, *Billy Budd* is a text which, because of its manuscript form, remains inappropriable, always "new," in spite of the attempts to impose an "artificial," reasonable readability upon it. Against the readability which operates in terms of sameness, clarity, and understanding, Howe's texts delineate a legibility of the "new," that is, the legibility of the "other," inappropriable, contours of experience. I read Howe's linguistic singularities in terms of those two kinds of legibility, whose difference releases history from the bounds of empathic accounts into the *poietic* possibilities of freedom. As the end of "The Liberties" suggests: "Here set at liberty / Tear pages from a calendar / scatter them into sunshine and snow" (*ET,* 217).

Howe's works, however, also complicate Nancy's portrayal of freedom, indicating, for example, in the title of "The Liberties," that the issue of freedom itself becomes "plural" or differentiated in the context of rethinking difference. Apart from the idea of different freedoms, I mean here the need to bring the question of sexual difference to bear upon the "liberty" of experience, to consider to what extent the idea of freedom may be implicated in the patriarchal genealogy of what has come to count as "experience." A critique of the connection between the idea of freedom and the notion of the unified subject as its foundation has to take into account the disappearance of sexual difference which marks such conceptions of subjectivity. As *The Nonconformist's Memorial* suggests, the uniformity prescribed by logocentric discourse excludes, first and foremost, sexual difference: "The act of Uniformity / ejected her / and informers at her heels" (*NM,* 5). This exclusion becomes reinforced by the erasure of the name—"In Peter she is nameless"—which allows the history to become "A single thread of narrative." Citing the reasons for the unity of historical narrative, Howe's poem begins to undermine them through its radical typography: The lines are arranged in a way similar to those sections of "Articulation of Sound Forms in Time" which "almost" mirror each other. Yet, the symmetry of the mirroring is skewed and asymmetrical, continuously undoing itself in the process of its own construction. These visual "inconsistencies" of the text render legible the erasure which instituted the apparent uniformity of the narrative and call into question the alleged transparency of history. The next two pages (*NM*, 8–9) reinforce this revision of legibility through the gesture of crisscrossing the reversed columns of the same text, which, placed on the opposite pages with additional lines to break the symmetry, undermine the linearity of reading and literally open the textual space into multiple directions, into plural vectors of legibility.

Howe's work offers important possibilities for rethinking the legibility of history in the context of sexual difference, possibilities which she makes manifest in the poetic workings of language, and their "Liberties   unperceived" (*ET*, 159). The blank space between "liberties" and "unperceived" literally breaks open the space for a different articulation of experience. This interval suggests that, in order for sexual difference to become part of how experience is thought, so far unperceived, *poietic* spaces of language have to be opened. Perhaps the most difficult aspect of Howe's work is its insistence that we learn to read these spaces not only in formalist and aesthetic terms but also historically and politically. It is easy by now to assign to such spaces the dubious aesthetic value of formal(ist) experimentation, but it still remains much harder to read them historically, against the conformity of thought and experience worked out discursively and politically within the patriarchal framework of culture. As one of Howe's books makes clear, this setting of language at liberty should be read as "the nonconformist's memorial" against the act of Uniformity—of thought, history, and experience—which ejected sexual difference from the articulation of experience and constructed the representational space on the foreclosure of the "singularizing" effects of this difference.

Beyond the Negative

An Afterword on the Avant-Garde

In this book, I have presented the avant-garde as an event of continuing cultural and philosophical importance, which offers us a radical revision of experience, temporality, and aesthetics. Against Bürger's or Huyssen's contention that the avant-garde is today primarily of historical interest, I rearticulate the catalyzing role of the avant-garde for twentieth-century art and culture in terms of its refiguration of experience beyond empirical, subjectivist, and technological conceptions. I argue that in its critical gesture, the avant-garde aesthetics recasts experience in temporal terms as an event, that is, as intrinsically open to the future and to transformation, and thus irreducible to the categories of consciousness, dialectics, and representation. To elaborate the historical and philosophical importance of this critique of experience, I turn to Heidegger, Benjamin, Irigaray, and Lyotard, a group of diverse thinkers who address issues critical to modernity: technology, everydayness, history, gender, and aesthetics. My readings of four poets — Khlebnikov, Stein, Białoszewski, and Howe — illustrate the revisions which avant-garde poetry introduces into these constitutive elements of modern experience. Stein's "tenderized" syntax, Khlebnikov's corners of events, or Białoszewski's wondering of the mundane are all articulations of the event of experience into a poetic practice. Showing how avant-garde poetry enacts the constitutive role of temporality and history, I counter the assertions about the exhaustion or death of the avant-garde and develop the critical implications of avant-garde aesthetics beyond the idea of negation.

Fundamental to the move beyond these "negative" conceptions of the avant-garde is the rethinking of radical aesthetics beyond the idea of "subversive intent" or linguistic innovations. The chapters on Stein, Howe, Khlebnikov and Białoszewski all center on showing the extent to which such radical "experimentation" with language and aesthetics, without exhausting itself in its subversive impulse, reformulates the constitutive character of temporality and history for modern everydayness. I emphasize this conjunction between innovative aesthetic and critical reformulation of experience by illustrating how, in their different ways, Irigaray, Lyotard, Benjamin, and Heidegger all establish the dependence of the philosophical critique of modernity on a radical critique of aesthetics. Benjamin is one of the first thinkers to show that the rethinking of experience in relation to art, technology, and history is crucial to the critique of modernity. Pivotal to my approach is the juxtaposition of Benjamin's critique of experience with Heidegger's articulation of a postaesthetic notion of the work of art in terms of the temporal event of unconcealment, which breaks with the dominant conceptions of modernist art such as art for art's sake, formalism, and art as commodity. Heidegger hints at this crucial revision of art in his remarks in "The Way to Language" about the necessity of a transformation in our relation to language: "In order to think back to the essence of language, in order to reiterate what is its own, we need a transformation of language, a transformation we can neither compel nor concoct. The transformation does not result from the fabrication of neologisms and novel phrases. The transformation touches on our relation to language."[1] For Heidegger, the radicality of art lies in its ability to transform our relation to language, and thus to history and experience. I take Heidegger's remark as an indication of the need to rethink the linguistic invention characteristic of the avant-garde beyond the idea of negation or subversiveness, and to examine how the avant-garde, situating art beyond the aesthetic framework, stages the event temporality constitutive of experience. I see such a liberation of art from aesthetic categorizations, undertaken in order to stress art's critical links with experience and history, as constitutive of the avant-garde movement. Beyond the rupturing of the representational paradigms and the rejection of aesthetic conventions, which occupy the center stage in such recent studies as Felski's or Suleiman's, the avant-garde's challenge to traditional literary, visual, and musical languages transforms such categorical determinations of modern experience as technology, instrumentalization, commodification, or sexual difference. What changes in the avant-garde transformation of aesthetics and language is the very mode of relationality that forms being and experience in modernity: from commodification and instrumentality to relations which are nonappropriative and intrinsically open to future and otherness.

To see how this critical role of the avant-garde extends beyond the idea of subversion, it is necessary to elaborate the redefinition of the category of experience in the avant-garde. Most studies of modernist and avant-garde aesthetics either leave this concept unexamined or, like Felski, take experience to be a category of consciousness, explainable in terms of representation. While there have been different "theories" of the avant-garde, from Poggioli to Bürger, none of them fleshes out the underlying philosophical stakes of the avant-garde with respect to the problematic of experience and temporality. Pointing out that such a rethinking of the relationship between aesthetics, experience, and historicity lies at the core of how Irigaray, Heidegger, or Benjamin critically engage modernity, I argue that a similar redefinition of experience occurs in avant-garde poetry. The readings in parts II and III show that avant-garde poetry not only refashions experience beyond the optics of subjectivity and consciousness but also critiques the erasure of historicity in the technological formation of being in modernity. The avant-garde's alternative is the idea of experience as a poietic event. This event is not a temporal punctuality but an open-ended, future-oriented field of forces, whose historicity prevents experience from being reduced into representational spaces, commodifiable objects, or aesthetic states. This notion of the event juxtaposes the technological modality of revealing with what I call a "poietic" unfolding. Unlike *technē,* the poietic event constitutes experience in its historicity, underscoring its irreducibility to the orders of representation and consciousness. As long as historicity and temporality continue to be "forgotten" for the sake of the representability of experience, the avant-garde impulse which, in my view, defines the work of art in modernity, will reappear with the force of a ghost in Derrida's sense of the term: as a task and a demand produced by the spectrality of being, by the event-ness of experience. In this specific sense, art in technological modernity is indeed "dead"; it is possible only as a ghost, as an attempt to bring into a figure that which does not, and cannot, exist as a being or object—the temporality of the event. As the "ghost"—hopefully also of Ophelia and not only of Hamlet's father—art haunts modern technologies of power, and, I think, will continue to haunt technological culture, so that it does not play out the patriarchal family scenario in which the still hesitant and questioning Hamlet is replaced by that other son, the triumphant and self-assured Fortinbras. My analyses in *The Historicity of Experience* reconfigure experience in terms of this tension between the poietic and the technic and examine the ways in which this rift marks the question of everydayness, history, and sexual difference. In this context, I suggest that the avant-garde poetics contests the modern practices which constitute the everyday either in terms of instrumentality and commodification or as their apparent opposite: a private sphere of aesthetic experience removed from history.

As my readings of Stein and Howe indicate, crucial to this rethinking of the everyday by the avant-garde is the problem of sexual difference. This is why Irigaray's critique of patriarchy becomes important to my study: On the one hand, Irigaray rewrites experience as an ethics of sexual difference and, on the other, she explicitly cast her ethics in terms of a new, radical poetics of language and thought. Linking poetics and sexual difference in the context of Irigaray's work, I not only show how sexual difference determines the character of experience in modernity but also how it develops an aspect of the avant-garde which offers an alternative to what Suleiman diagnosed as the avant-garde's male aggressivity. The irreducibility of the poetic event to the order of consciousness and representation becomes in Irigaray's work the mark of sexual difference, of the inflections of identity through the fluid proximity to the other (sex). I emphasize the connection between Irigaray's poetic idiom and the nonappropriative, ethical relations to the other (sex) which this discourse figures. Seeing technology and commodification as a desexualization of experience and an effacement of its materiality, Irigaray links historicity with the fluid and "poetic" texturing of sexual difference. In my readings of avant-garde poets, I underscore their revision of experience into a matrix of exchanges that occur in the middle voice, beyond both passivity and activity. Not limited to aesthetic subversion or experimentation, the avant-garde poetic idiom analyzed in *The Historicity of Experience* produces a new configuration of experience which not only does not erase or stereotype sexual difference but makes the proximity characteristic of Irigarayan ethics of sexual difference into a model for the ethical relation to the other.

All these various aspects of the reconceptualization of experience in terms of the event allow us to discern in the avant-garde, beyond the merely negative and even nihilistic readings of avant-garde aesthetics, a critique of the dominant models of experience and history. Moving beyond the negative characterizations is important, because, as I would argue, the avant-garde's revision of experience also provides an alternative to the post-Hegelian and Marxist approaches, so important to contemporary critical and philosophical debates. To see these implications of the avant-garde, however, we need a concept of negativity irreducible to dialectical negation. One venue for such a new understanding of negativity could be Heidegger's critique of Hegelian negativity in his lecture course *Hegel*. Even though the Hegelian dialectics, as Adorno's brilliant reformulation of it in *Negative Dialectics* demonstrates, can offer a way of recognizing and maintaining the nonidentical, the force of difference and otherness it preserves remains circumscribed as negative. Claiming that such negativity remains "questionless" *(fraglosig)*, Heidegger rethinks in *Hegel* the valency of the Hegelian negation in terms of temporality. For Heidegger, Hegel's negativity is no negativity, because it does not really put into practice the nothingness that works in the force of temporality: In Hegel, the nothing is already sublated into the "yes."[2]

Reformulating the negative, Heidegger takes a different route from Adorno's: Rather than emphasizing and privileging the negative over the positive moment of (the impossible) synthesis, Heidegger revises the very notions of temporality and history so that it becomes possible to think historicity nondialectically, in terms of the temporality of the event. The "nothing" manifest in the event refers not to negation but to the groundlessness or the abyss *("Das Nichts der Ab-grund")*, which marks the transformative and futural character of temporality. This revision lets us think the temporal ungrounding of experience beyond lack and negation, as "more critical" than critique through negation. What emerges from Heidegger's questioning is a different sense of otherness beyond lack and the negative, beyond the recuperable or sublatable differences. In a way, it is possible to read Heidegger as a radicalization of Hegelian negativity and critique beyond the dialectical schema. Adorno misses the point when he claims that Heidegger's ontico-ontological difference evacuates the force of the negative. Rather, Heidegger—and Irigaray in her own different way—radicalizes the negative into the futural force of temporality and redescribes it as the transformative opening of the present. This difference could finally be explained in terms of the distinction between dialectical and futural temporalities at play in Hegel (and post-Hegelianism) and Heidegger. The negating force of history in Hegel is not "negative" enough because it sublates, both cancels and elevates, the differences that make up experience. The futural force of temporality in Heidegger, by contrast, does not lead to sublation or abstraction but keeps opening up the ungrounding and transformative occurrence of the event as spatio-temporal differentiation. This force is more radically "negative" in its finitude than any dialectical sense of negation or of the nonidentical, because it locates the negative not in the negating force of an oppositional identity but in the transformative opening of temporality. I can only mention here that in her recent writings, in particular *I Love to You* and *Être deux,* Irigaray similarly reformulates the Hegelian negative to articulate the transformative valency of sexual difference beyond lack or negation.[3]

This Heideggerian and Irigarayan reformulations of the Hegelian *Erfahrung* (experience) open the possibility of rearticulating the transformative, rather than simply destructive or negating, impact of the avant-garde in relation to modern experience. First of all, it allows us to rethink the contestatory movements, like Dada, beyond the idea of negativity and rejection and to tie them to the recognition of the futurity of the event. The avant-garde's critique does not spend itself in the negative or self-destructive impulse but reaches toward an understanding of nondialectical event of experience. This foray of avant-garde art beyond "aesthetics" into the *work* of experience and temporality lets us locate the critical importance of the avant-garde beyond the idea of a promised future utopia. The approach I propose in *The Historicity of Experience* regards the avant-garde as a form of critique more radical than critique based on negation, as a futural and transformative reinvention of experience. As event, experience unfolds beyond the strictures of presence and beyond the poles of the identical and the nonidentical, the fragmentary and the totalizable, which work as parts of the dialectical economy of presence. It occurs as a kind of its own "avant-garde," as experience always in translation, ahead of and differentiating itself from the presence, identity, and signification to which it has always already submitted itself. Reformulating the valency of experience in modernity from technic to poietic, the avant-garde poses the question not only of freedom from aesthetic conventions but of experience as freedom. In this gesture it also calls for the critique of the technicity which determines modern experience in terms of power. Manifested as the general structures of availability, calculation, or commodification, these power relations describe the space where the radical "postaesthetics" of the avant-garde continues to have cultural and political resonance. It is in these resonances that we discern the avant-garde's singular contribution to rethinking modernity with its tangled web of relations between experience, technology, and aesthetics.

Notes

Introduction

1. I articulate such convergences between Benjamin and Heidegger in "After Aesthetics: Heidegger and Benjamin on Art and Experience," where I argue that they allow us to begin thinking about art in a postaesthetic manner; *Philosophy Today* 41, no. 1 (1997): 199–208. It is important to remember in this context that, in his writings from late 1930s, Benjamin's assessment of technology becomes less enthusiastic than, for example, in "The Work of Art in the Age of Mechanical Reproduction." The picture of Benjamin as writing optimistically about the emancipatory effects of technology is, therefore, incomplete. It is in reference to these more critical comments that Benjamin eventually makes about technology that I draw out the similarities between his and Heidegger's critiques of experience.

2. One of the most notable exceptions is Marjorie Perloff's study, *The Futurist Moment*, which, exploring the idea of the "futurist moment" or breakthrough in various avant-gardes, provides an excellent discussion of the writings of Russian futurism and the accompanying developments in the visual arts, in particular, suprematism and constructivism. *The Futurist Moment: Avant-Garde, Avant Guerre, and the Language of Rupture* (Chicago: University of Chicago Press, 1986), 42–79, 116–60. Subsequently cited as *FM*.

3. Jean-François Lyotard, *The Postmodern Condition: A Report on Knowledge*, trans. Geoff Bennington and Brian Massumi (Minneapolis: University of Minnesota Press, 1984), 73 (hereafter cited as *PC*).

4. Two important studies, Bürger's *Theory of the Avant-Garde*, trans. Michael Shaw (Minneapolis: University of Minnesota Press, 1984), and Huyssen's *After the Great Divide: Modernism, Mass Culture, Postmodernism* (Bloomington and Indianapolis: Indiana University Press, 1986), agree on this point: While aspects of the avant-garde aesthetic have trickled down or been adopted by consumer culture, the project of integrating art and transforming social life through art failed.

5. "What is new about the phase of mass culture compared with the late liberal stage is the exclusion of the new. The machine rotates on the same spot. While determining consumption it excludes the untried as a risk. The movie-makers distrust any manuscript which is not reassuringly backed by a bestseller. Yet for this very reason there is never-ending talk of ideas, novelty, and surprise, of what is taken for granted but has never existed." Max Horkheimer and Theodor W. Adorno, *Dialectic of Enlightenment*, trans. John Cumming (New York: Continuum, 1993), 134.

6. Jean-François Lyotard, *The Inhuman: Reflections on Time*, trans. Geoffrey Bennington and Rachel Bowlby (Stanford: Stanford University Press, 1991), 106 (hereafter cited as *IN*).

7. Huyssen argues convincingly for maintaining, despite their frequent inter-sections, a distinction between the avant-garde and modernism: "But even though the boundaries between modernism and avantgardism remained fluid, the distinc-tion I am suggesting permits us to focus on sufficiently discernible trends within the culture of modernity. More specifically, it allows us to distinguish the histori-cal avant-garde from late-nineteenth-century modernism as well as from the high modernism of the interwar years." Andreas Huyssen, *After the Great Divide*, viii.

8. Bürger's theory of the avant-garde as a failed attempt to reintegrate art and *praxis*, placing most emphasis on the institutional character of art in bourgeois society, does not address the aesthetic-philosophical critique of experience which animates the avant-gardes. Adorno's reading of radical modernist art as a "nega-tive imprint" of society and its evisceration of experience, an imprint which allows art to operate its social critique, avoids the oppositional optics of separation and integration (see note 11).

9. "Today the best hopes of the historical avantgarde may not be embodied in art works at all, but in decentered movements which work toward the transformation of everyday life"; *After the Great Divide*, 15.

10. In *The Inhuman*, Lyotard claims that a "study of the avant-gardes is impera-tive"; *IN*, 115.

11. Tristan Tzara, *Seven Dada Manifestoes and Lampisteries*, trans. Barbara Wright (New York: Riverrun Press, 1992), 13.

12. In his reflections on *l'art pour l'art* and on social aesthetic, Adorno sees the opposition between separation and integration of art as a false dilemma. For Adorno, art has to be autonomous to be able to critique the society in which it has been produced. The separation of art, however, does not cut it off from the social sphere; conversely, it allows it to be a determinate negation of the historical situa-tion in which it exists: "Art's asociality is a determinate negation of a determinate society" (226). It is in Beckett's work that modern art becomes the negation of the administered world of technology: "This shabby, damaged world of images is the negative imprint of the administered world" (31). This "negative imprint," though, is never a simple negation but an exposure of the emptiness of modern social life, an evisceration of experience covered over by the continuous novelty of capitalist pro-duction. Through a dialectic of absence and presence, Beckett's negative imprint *in extremis* points to an absence of utopia, leaving as "unspeakable" its difference from the critiqued reality of the present. Art functions as the negative of the social by emphasizing, through a kind of conspicuous absence, what reality lacks. See Theodor W. Adorno, *Aesthetic Theory*, trans. Robert Hullot-Kentor (Minneapolis: University of Minnesota Press, 1997).

13. It would take too long to enumerate all the various readings of Heidegger which Derrida has carried out through many years, from *Of Grammatology* and *Margins of Philosophy* to *Truth in Painting*, *Of Spirit*, or *Specters of Marx*. Let me just agree here with Bernasconi that today, when we read Heidegger, we cannot help

but always find "Derrida's Heidegger," a Heidegger which is often more complex than the Heidegger "critiqued" by many Derridians; see Bernasconi, *Heidegger in Question: The Art of Existing* (Atlantic Highlands, N.J.: Humanities Press, 1993), 208. Bernasconi's book is an excellent contribution to new Heidegger scholarship, as it demonstrates the nuances of both Heidegger's texts and Derrida's readings, which often disappear in the simplified versions of the Heidegger-Derrida opposition (210). I would also like to mention Christopher Fynsk's study *Heidegger: Thought and Historicity,* recently reissued in its second edition (Ithaca, N.Y.: Cornell University Press, 1993), in particular for its careful and illuminating readings of the question of historicity and the work of art.

14. Martin Heidegger, "The Way to Language," *Basic Writings,* 2d ed., ed. David Farrell Krell (New York: Harper Collins, 1993), hereafter cited as *BW.* Bernasconi provides an excellent discussion of Heidegger's transformation of language in his chapter, "The Transformation of Language at Another Beginning," from *Heidegger in Question,* 190–210.

15. "Propriative event" is Krell's translation of *Ereignis* in "The Question Concerning Technology"; it keeps in play the twofold sense of occurring and propriating, suggesting that *Ereignis* is never a "mere" event but a happening in which what is occurs "properly," or, to be more exact, "propriatingly." Martin Heidegger, *BW,* 337.

16. I borrow this phrase from Robert Bernasconi's excellent discussion of Heidegger's displacement of metaphysical concepts, including that of experience, in "The Way to Language." Bernasconi, *Heidegger in Question,* 206.

17. See the chapter "Time and Creation" in Cornelius Castoriadis, *The Imaginary Institution of Society,* trans. Kathleen Blamey (Cambridge, Mass.: MIT Press, 1987), 195–201.

18. This is the reason why Castoriadis identifies only institutional reasons for the frequent occlusion of historicity in various conceptions of history: "[b]orn in, through and as the rupture of time, a manifestation of the self-alteration of society as instituting society, the institution in the profound sense of the term can exist only by posing itself as outside of time, by refusing to be altered by time, by posing the norm of its immutable identity and by posing itself as this norm of immutable identity, without which it would not exist," *The Imaginary Institution of Society,* 214.

19. Writing about technology and Heidegger's thought inevitably brings up the question of the Holocaust and mass extermination during World War II. This is obviously a complicated and vexed issue, to which I can only allude here. For a detailed treatment of this problem, one can consult the recent *Martin Heidegger and the Holocaust,* ed. Milchman and Rosenberg (Atlantic Highlands, N.J.: Humanities Press, 1996), in particular, Manning's "The Cries of Others and Heidegger's Ear" and Milchman and Rosenberg's "Heidegger, Planetary Technics, and the Holocaust." Heidegger's reading of technology as formative of the modern experience

of the world on a fundamental, structural level can explain the framework within which human beings can be regarded as "processable resource," as a segment of being that can be calculated, ordered, and made "available" for extermination on a mass scale. Heidegger shows how technology can reduce knowledge to the terms of efficiency and availability, erasing the historical dimension of experience, the historicity of the event, which accounts for the heterogeneity and singularity of experience. In this way, technology foreshortens experience to the explainable and calculable matrix of efficiency. Heidegger's view does not, obviously, account for the ideological and cultural forces behind the Holocaust, for anti-Semitism and for the propaganda of hatred, determinative of the years of fascism. This moment of silence makes it imperative to read Heidegger critically on those issues. But Heidegger's reflection on technology also makes clear that his reading of the historicity of experience contains "critical" resources for questioning the political formation of national socialism with which he aligned his thought in the 1930s. It is only with the recent publication of two of Heidegger's previously unpublished texts from late 1930s, *Besinnung* (1938–39) and *Die Geschichte des Seyns* (1939–40), published by Vittorio Klostermann as volumes 66 and 69 of the *Gesamtausgabe* in 1997 and 1998, that we can see how Heidegger himself extends his critique of metaphysics, subjectivity, and power into a critique of nationalism, communism, socialism, and race.

20. In his early texts on technology, "Art in the Age of Mechanical Reproduction" or "A Short History of Photography," Benjamin writes optimistically about the aesthetic and political possibilities opened up by the development of the technological means of reproduction. He believes that they can successfully rid the work of art of its aura of uniqueness and change its political effects on mass audiences. His late writings, however, are much more cautious, even skeptical, about the effects of modern technology upon experience. In "Some Motifs in Baudelaire," Benjamin deplores the destruction of experience brought about by information: "The replacement of the older narration by information, of information by sensation, reflects the increasing atrophy of experience"; Walter Benjamin, *Illuminations,* ed. Hannah Arendt (New York: Schocken, 1969), 159. It is this later Benjamin that shows some definite affinities with Heidegger's critique of technology.

21. In his "Afterword" to *Postmodernism Explained,* Godzich writes about Lyotard's argument in *The Postmodern Condition* about the altered status of knowledge in postindustrial societies: "Within such societies, knowledge is treated as the major force of production and is increasingly dissociated from individuals who possess it in order to become a commodity in the marketplace; it is redefined in terms of specifiable bits of information, and its chief function is to ensure the optimal performance of the system"; Wlad Godzich, "Afterword: Reading Against Literacy," in Jean-François Lyotard, *Postmodernism Explained* (Minneapolis: University of Minnesota Press, 1993), 113.

22. In "The Origin of the Work of Art," Heidegger uses the term *Gestalt* (figure)

to indicate that his approach to art is not a matter of form or formalism. It seems to me that Adorno's emphasis in *Aesthetic Theory* on form as the bearer of social critique plays a similar role. Although the term "form" may create a misleading impression that Adorno's theory leans toward formalism, his understanding of how form (re)figures content, points beyond formalist readings of art; see, for example, page 230.

23. I explore those issues in more detail in "The Ethos of Everydayness: Heidegger on Poetry and Language," *Man and World* 28, no. 4 (1995): 377–99.

24. Heidegger's position is here similar to those of Adorno and Horkheimer, who regard modernity as a progressive reduction of being to the formal patterns of unification, systematization, and so on: "In advance, the Enlightenment recognizes as being and occurrence only what can be apprehended in unity: its ideal is the system from which all and everything follows"; *Dialectic of Enlightenment,* trans. John Cumming (New York: Continuum, 1993), 7.

25. Foucault's critique of experience can be found in *The Order of Things: An Archeology of the Human Sciences* (New York: Random House, 1970), 320–21.

26. See Godzich's discussion of Appel's critique of the positivism of social sciences in favor of a hermeneutics of social experience; "Afterword: Reading against Literacy," 118.

27. Renato Poggioli, *Theory of the Avant-Garde,* trans. Gerald Fitzgerald (Cambridge, Mass.: Harvard University Press, 1968), 69.

28. "Thus, the irruption within the order of language of the anteriority of language evokes a later time, that is, a forever. The poem's time frame is some 'future anterior' that will never take place, never come about as such, but only as an upheaval of present place and meaning." Julia Kristeva, *Desire in Language: A Semiotic Approach to Literature and Art,* trans. Thomas Gora, Alice Jardine, and Leon S. Roudiez (New York: Columbia University Press, 1980), 32 (hereafter cited as *DL*).

29. Luc Ferry, *Homo Aestheticus* (Paris: Grasset, 1990), 260. Quoted after Thomas Docherty, "Postmodernism: An Introduction," in *Postmodernism: A Reader* (New York: Columbia University Press, 1993), 16.

30. The event is *made understandable* in terms of being dislocated ahead in relation to its time, in advance of the contemporary. It is dislocated, however, in a way that allows for the recuperation and reappropriation of this distance at some point in the future, the point at which the new standards of comprehension would catch up with what now shocks as the "incomprehensible," futural moment of the avant-garde.

31. Docherty emphasizes Virilio's point that the avant-garde is not only in conflict with the dominant aesthetics of its time but also "in conflict with time itself, being out of its proper moment; it is always necessarily _anachronistic_. This collocation of time and conflict is of the essence of the political for Virilio"; "Postmodernism: An Introduction," 19. I would add that the political moment of the avant-garde lies in the fact that in its art the moment itself cannot ever be "proper,"

belong to itself or to representation. It is not simply that the avant-garde must be anachronistic in relation to its proper moment, that is, the moment in which its aesthetics would become "dominant," but that the recognition that time does not belong to itself is already political.

32. Georg Lukács, "Realism in the Balance," in Ernst Bloch et al., *Aesthetics and Politics* (London: Verso, 1980), 48.

33. The significance of the avant-garde for contemporary French thinking is linked, at least in part, to the influence of *Tel Quel* and the writers associated with it. It marked such diverse approaches as those of Derrida and Kristeva, and provided the context for linking feminist critique to radical writing practice.

34. Luce Irigaray, *L'oubli de l'air: Chez Heidegger* (Paris: Éditions de Minuit, 1983).

35. I find Irigaray's poetic practice, the textuality of her nonpropositional writing, more conducive to rethinking the avant-garde's critique of experience then Kristeva's distinction between the symbolic and the semiotic in *The Revolution in Poetic Language,* trans. Margaret Waller (New York: Columbia University Press, 1984). Irigaray is much more closely engaged with Heidegger's conception of language and *poiēsis,* and links the question of poetics to technology, economic exchange, and commodification. Her rethinking of sexual difference discloses the link between, on the one hand, changing the imaginary and the morphology of language and, on the other, a retexturing of experience.

36. Heidegger discusses the "emergence" of being in the shattering of a word in relation to the concluding lines of George's poem "Words"; "Words," *On the Way to Language,* trans. Peter D. Hertz (San Francisco: Harper and Row, 1971), 139–56.

37. I have given that question more attention in "The Ethos of Everydayness: Heidegger on Poetry and Language," *Man and World* 28, no. 4 (1995): 377–99.

38. I have in mind here terms like *Volk,* German *Dasein,* and *Führung,* which, although equivocal in Heidegger's texts and certainly not coextensive with their ideological use by fascism, implicate Heidegger in the political climate of the 1930s. Recent years have seen a plethora of publications on Heidegger's involvement with national socialism, his silence about the Holocaust, and, finally, the politics implicit in his work, from the "early" books by Derrida, Lyotard, and Lacoue-Labarthe to more recent work on Heidegger and politics (Dallmayr, *The Other Heidegger,* Thiele, *Timely Meditations,* and so on) and studies such as *Martin Heidegger and the Holocaust.* Also illuminating is Bernasconi's discussion of how Heidegger's exploration of art and poetry is tied with politics; see especially chapters 4, 6, and 8 of *Heidegger in Question.* Views differ widely on all those questions, which testifies to the complexity and contested nature of those issues in Heidegger. These divergences also have to do with which specific moments in Heidegger's work various interpretations choose to emphasize. It is impossible to do justice here to all those questions in Heidegger or to their interpretations in relation to ethics and politics—it would require a different study. This wider debate constitutes the con-

text for my specific focus on the radical implications of how Heidegger thinks of the relation between art and technology in modernity, and their importance for contemporary poetry; this is where Heidegger's thought still remains insufficiently explored. My reading of Heidegger, side by side with Benjamin, focuses on the remarks on art and technology which suggest a conception of experience structurally open to otherness and resistant to closure or totalization, that is, a notion which problematizes not only the idea of representation and full cognition, but also exclusion and reduction of or blindness to alterity. The conception of experience which emerges from such a reading of Heidegger does not explain or absolve his writings from involvement with national socialism, but it should be borne in mind in discussions of the ethical and political dimensions of Heidegger's thought. My discussion explores, then, aspects of what Fred Dallmayr calls, in the context of politics, the "other Heidegger," and extends Heidegger's insights beyond the limits of his work on aesthetics and poetry. It focuses on those moments when Heidegger's understanding of experience as event opens up a nexus of relations which link poetic language with the problem of technological determinations of being in modernity and the historicity of the everyday, which is also the site of the avant-garde explorations of art.

39. To my knowledge, there are only two book-length translations of Białoszewski's work into English: a volume of early poems, *The Revolution of Things,* trans. Busza and Czaykowski (Washington, D. C.: Charioteer Press, 1974), and the translation of *Pamiętnik z powstania warszawskiego; A Memoir of the Warsaw Uprising,* ed. and trans. Madeline Levine (Ann Arbor, Mich.: Ardis, 1977).

40. This alternative view of the trends in Polish poetry after World War II is developed in a series of essays published by the Institute of Literary Studies of the Polish Academy of Sciences under the title *Pisanie Białoszewskiego,* ed. Głowiński and Sławiński (Warszawa: Wydawnictwo IBL, 1993). This is the most interesting collection of scholarly essays about Białoszewski's work to appear to date in Polish.

Chapter 1

1. In his discussion of the distinction between *Erlebnis* and *Erfahrung,* Benjamin employs the notion of the technological disciplining of the human sensorium characteristic of modern life: "Baudelaire speaks of a man who plunges into the crowd as into a reservoir of electric energy. Circumscribing the experience of the shock, he calls this man 'a *kaleidoscope* equipped with consciousness.' Whereas Poe's passersby cast glances in all directions which still appeared to be aimless, today's pedestrians are obliged to do so in order to keep abreast of traffic signals. Thus technology has subjected the human sensorium to a complex kind of training." See "On Some Motifs in Baudelaire," *Illuminations,* ed. Hannah Arendt (New York: Schocken Books, 1969), 175 (hereafter cited as *I*).

2. Much of Heidegger's late writing on art is predicated upon disengaging art from its aesthetic classification and thus recognizing art's significance as lying outside of the realm of narrowly understood "cultural activity." See, for example, "The Question Concerning Technology," *Basic Writings*, 2d ed., ed. David Farrell Krell (New York: Harper Collins, 1993), 339–41 (hereafter cited as *BW*).

3. Recent years have seen an increasing number of publications exploring connections between aesthetics and fascism: Alice Yaeger Kaplan, *Reproductions of Banality: Fascism, Literature, and French Intellectual Life* (Minneapolis: University of Minnesota Press, 1986); *Fascism, Aesthetics, and Culture*, ed. Richard Golsan (Hanover, N.H.: University Press of New England, 1992); "Fascism and Culture," *The Stanford Review* 8, nos. 1–2 (1990), special number.

4. Heidegger's reflections on art in the 1950s and 1960s, some time after his own fateful engagement with national socialism, can be used to provide some indications as to how such a meteoric, though effective, aestheticization of politics can at all become historically possible. Heidegger's diagnosis of the complicity between aesthetic definitions of art and the technological regimentation of experience (into aesthetic, everyday, labor, and so on), not unlike Adorno's critique of the Enlightenment, underscores the underlying metaphysical schematization of experience (subject—object or resource) that facilitates the transition between seemingly incompatible orders of aesthetics and technology.

5. The most obvious difference is Benjamin's political and cultural critique of fascism and Heidegger's association of some of his ideas in the 1930s with the "revolution" proposed by the National Socialist party. There is no space here to discuss the implications of Heidegger's involvement (the rapidly growing body of scholarship on the subject as well as on the political implications of Heidegger's thought makes anything less than a sustained study of these issues seem disingenuous). I limit, therefore, my remarks on Heidegger largely to his ideas about art, technology, and history in "The Origin of the Work of Art" and the postwar essays on technology, art, and poetry. For a sketch of the philosophical and political implications of the Heidegger affair, see Fynsk's "Postface" to the second edition of *Heidegger: Thought and Historicity* (Ithaca: Cornell University Press, 1986, 1993), 230–49 (hereafter cited as *HTH*). I am largely in agreement with Fynsk, especially on two points: first, that Heidegger's thought is always "political," not only because of its explicit engagement with the politics in the 1930s and 1940s but because of the way it questions the limits of thinking about politics; second, I do not think that Heidegger's thought is "essentially" or entirely determined by the complicities of some of his ideas and actions. As Fynsk suggests, taking Heidegger's political entanglements seriously does not lead in any simple way to abandoning his texts or to foreclosing the radical critical insights his critique of the metaphysics of subjectivity and of history makes possible. I suggest that Heidegger's ideas about the event and art radically open up the notion of experience and refashion it in view of historicity in ways that render it structurally open and "mindful" of otherness.

These motifs, which predominate in Heidegger's thought from the time of *Bei-träge zur Philosophie,* are clearly at odds with claims that Heidegger's work "supports" the fascist worldview. Acknowledging Heidegger's investment in what he perceived, at least for a while, to be important about national socialism (which he mistakenly saw as the site of a decisive confrontation with planetary technology; see Alan Milchman and Alan Rosenberg, "Heidegger, Planetary Technics, and the Holocaust," in *Martin Heidegger and the Holocaust,* ed. Milchman and Rosenberg [Atlantic Highlands, N.J.: Humanities Press, 1996], 216), we also need to recog- ✓ nize the radicality of his critique of being, which tries to think of the event beyond the fold of technology. I agree with Fynsk that it is Heidegger's confrontation with *Technik* that still needs to be thought. My rethinking of *poiēsis* and event extends this confrontation with technology beyond Heidegger's work. As I indicate, especially in chapter 2, this revision of experience is not without political and ethical implications of its own.

6. Both Fynsk and Bernasconi draw attention to this performative aspect of Heidegger's idea of the work of art. See Christopher Fynsk, *HTH,* 136–38, and Robert Bernasconi, "The Greatness of the Work of Art," *Heidegger in Question: The Art of Existing* (Atlantic Highlands, N.J.: Humanities Press, 1993), 99–116.

7. In *Paraesthetics,* Carroll indicates the necessity of moving beyond the optics of aesthetics in order to flesh out the critical implications of art: "If 'art' is to function critically and indicate a movement 'beyond theory,' it must also move 'beyond art' and function outside of all forms of aestheticism"; David Carroll, *Paraesthetics: Foucault, Lyotard, Derrida* (New York: Methuen, 1987), 4.

8. Such a postaesthetic approach to art, as a critique of the tripartite division into the cognitive, the moral, and the aesthetic, is explored at length in J. M. Bernstein's book, *The Fate of Art: Aesthetic Alienation from Kant to Derrida and Adorno* (University Park: Pennsylvania State University Press, 1992): "If 'aesthetics' in its narrow sense refers to the understanding of art as an object of taste outside truth and morality, then 'post-aesthetic' theories of art are themselves critiques of truth-only cognition insofar as their going beyond aesthetics implies a denial of the rigid distinctions separating the claims of taste from the claims of knowing or right action" (3). Bernstein's insightful book deals with the "postaesthetic" theories of art, without engaging at length this art itself. My own project integrates the post-aesthetic approach to art that is being worked out in Benjamin and Heidegger with the analysis of avant-garde poetry's unworking of the aesthetical framework.

9. Walter Benjamin, *Reflections,* ed. and into. Peter Demetz (New York: Schocken Books, 1986), 179 (hereafter cited as *R*).

10. For a detailed discussion of futurism's involvement in the formation of fascist political culture, see Emilio Gentile, "The Conquest of Modernity: From Modernist Nationalism to Fascism," trans. Lawrence Rainey, Special Issue, "Marinetti and the Italian Futurists," *Modernism/Modernity* 1, no. 3 (1994): 55–87.

11. Gentile argues that aestheticization of politics by fascism functioned side by

side with its politicization of aesthetics. Singling out aestheticization of politics can be misleading "if it obscures fascism's other important feature, its 'politicization of aesthetics,' which not only inspired fascism's attitude toward avant-garde culture, but stood at the very origin of the encounter between Futurism and fascism and of the participation of many modernist intellectuals in fascism"; "Conquest of Modernity," 57. A similar argument can be made about the complex relationship to art and the avant-garde after the 1917 revolution in Russia and the creation of the Soviet Union.

12. "Only a thoughtless observer can deny that correspondences come into play between the world of modern technology and the archaic symbol-world of mythology," Walter Benjamin, *The Arcades Project,* trans. Howard Eiland and Kevin McLaughlin (Cambridge, Mass., and London: Belknap Press of Harvard University Press, 1999), 461.

13. Benjamin's reflections on the role of art and literature in the figuration of modern experience take their cue from the disappearance of lyrical poetry ("On Some Motifs in Baudelaire") and the impact of mechanical reproducibility upon the social function of the work of art ("The Work of Art in the Age of Mechanical Reproduction").

14. In section 273 of *Beiträge zur Philosophie,* entitled *"Geschichte,"* Heidegger expounds the implications of the difference between *Geschichte* and *Historie. Historie* is aligned with historiology, with the historicist determination and description of *Geschichte* in terms of progress, becoming, or understanding, which conceals historicity as the futural force of history. In Heidegger's harsh judgment, historiology *(Historie)* always ends up in anthropological-psychological biographism: *"Alle Historie endet im anthropologisch-psychologischen Biographismus." Geschichte,* on the other hand, is defined by Heidegger in relation to the notion of the event as the modality of being: *"Das Seyn als Er-eignis ist die Geschichte; von hier aus muss deren Wesen, unabhängig von der Werdens- und Entwicklungsvorstellung, unabhängig von der historischen Betrachtung und Erklärung, bestimmt werden"* (494). See *Beiträge zur Philosophie (Vom Ereignis), Gesamtausgabe,* vol. 65 (Frankfurt am Main: Vittorio Klostermann, 1989), 492–94.

15. See "After Aesthetics: Heidegger and Benjamin on Art and Experience," *Philosophy Today* 41, no. 1:199–208. For a discussion of Heidegger's overcoming of aesthetics, see Bernasconi, *Heidegger in Question.* As Heidegger writes in *Beiträge zur Philosophie,* "This question [of the origin of the work of art] is intimately connected with the task of overcoming aesthetics and that means simultaneously with overcoming a certain conception of beings as objectively representable." *Contributions to Philosophy (From Enowning),* trans. Parvis Emad and Kenneth Maly (Bloomington and Indianapolis: Indiana University Press, 1999), 354. In the original, this remark can be found on p. 503. It could be argued that one feature of such art is its "weak" messianic character, to paraphrase Benjamin, its futurity or structural openness to the future and the other. In *Spectres de Marx,* Derrida refers to the

thought of such an opening as *la messianique,* the messianic: *"pensée de l'autre et de l'événement à venir"* (102). Although the term is Benjaminian, one can identify in Derrida's use of the messianic traits of both Levinas (the injunction of the other) and of Heidegger (the thought of the event, of *das Ereignis* underlies Derrida's approach to Marx). The Derridean "messianic" describes the displacement of the subject, its exposition, toward the other. It functions as the injunction of alterity, the dislocation of self-presence, that in advance, "an-archically," forecloses the possibility of self-coincidence and identity. *Spectres de Marx* (Paris: Galilée, 1993).

16. *Periri* recurs in *periculum,* peril or danger. In German, *Erfahrung* plays both on the verb *fahren,* to travel, to be on the way, and on the old high German *fara,* danger, from which stem the modern *Gefahr,* danger, and *gefährden,* to endanger. As Eduardo Cadava suggests, Benjamin's understanding of *Erfahrung* in its strict sense refers to existing "within a permanent state of danger and emergency" ("Words of Light: Theses on the Photography of History," *Diacritics* 22, nos. 3–4: 108; hereafter cited as "WL"). Heidegger's approach indicates in turn that the traversing and the danger implicit in the etymology of *Erfahrung* constitute the very structure of experience, its traversal or transposition from the giving of the event, the excess of *es gibt,* to its always already being given as a fact or instant of experience. For Heidegger, the danger of experience lies in its always already collapsible structure, in the inherent reducibility and reversibility of the giving of the event to the presence of the given.

17. "Just as Derrida has provided a 'deconstructed' reading of certain metaphysical texts and their concepts, Heidegger, in *Hegel's Concept of Experience,* in his reading of Hegel's word 'experience' as a word of Being, has heard its claim from beyond metaphysics," *Heidegger in Question,* 206.

18. See *Unterwegs zur Sprache* (Pfullingen: Neske, 1959), 159–61 and 241 (hereafter cited as *UZS*); *On the Way to Language,* trans. Peter D. Hertz (New York: Harper and Row, 1971), 57–59 (hereafter cited as *OWL*); and *BW,* 397.

19. Martin Heidegger, *Zur Sache des Denkens* (Tübingen: Niemeyer, 1976), 20.

20. Martin Heidegger, *Besinnung, Gesamtausgabe,* vol. 66 (Frankfurt am Main: Vittorio Klostermann, 1997), 307. Hereafter cited as *B.*

21. Martin Heidegger, *Bremen und Freiburger Vorträge* (Frankfurt am Main: Vittorio Klostermann, 1994), 54.

22. For an incisive redefinition of "experience in the context of historicity and interpretation," see Joan W. Scott's essay " 'Experience,' " *Feminists Theorize the Political,* ed. Judith Butler and Joan W. Scott (New York: Routledge, 1992), 22–40.

23. Heidegger employs various figures to describe such modalities of relating: *Entsprechung* (co-respondence), *Stimmung* (tuning), *Dis-position;* see *What Is Philosophy?* trans. and intro. William Kluback and Jean T. Wilde (Twayne Publishers, 1958), 70–89.

24. For a more extensive discussion of Heidegger's views on the philosophy of

life, see David Farrell Krell, *Intimations of Mortality: Time, Truth, Finitude in Heidegger's Thinking of Being* (University Park: Pennsylvania State University Press, 1986), 12–26.

25. For the German text, see Heidegger, "Die Frage nach der Technik," *Vorträge und Aufsätze* (Pfullingen: Neske, 1954), 32.

26. See my discussion of the infold in *Inflected Language: Toward a Hermeneutics of Nearness: Heidegger, Levinas, Stevens, Celan* (Albany: State University of New York Press, 1994), 33–42.

27. Rodolphe Gasché, "Saturnine Vision and the Question of Difference: Reflections on Walter Benjamin's Theory of Language," in *Benjamin's Ground: New Readings of Walter Benjamin,* ed. Rainer Nägele (Detroit: Wayne State University Press, 1988), 92. Throughout the essay, Gasché underscores the disruptive effect of translatability on the unity of form and content of the work of art: "[T]ranslatability represents in the work of art the objective call for overcoming this still natural unity rooted in mythical linguistic relations" (91).

28. Heidegger, *Hölderlins Hymne "Der Ister," Gesamtausgabe,* vol. 55 (Frankfurt am Main: Vittorio Klostermann, 1984), 80; *Hölderlin's Hymn "The Ister,"* trans. William McNeill and Julia Davis (Bloomington and Indianapolis: Indiana University Press, 1996), 65.

29. *"Die Sprache selbst ist in den Dingen selbst nicht vollkommen ausgesprochen"; Gesammelte Schriften,* vol. 2, part 1 (Frankfurt am Main: Suhrkamp, 1991), 147.

30. When we consider Heidegger's statements and lectures from 1933 to 1934 as an integral part of his philosophical enterprise, the situation becomes more complicated. In 1933 in the *Rektorat* speech, Heidegger inscribes the historico-political context, the national socialist "revolution," directly into his work. This political commitment of his thought is intertwined, however, with a change in Heidegger's philosophical terminology, which "compromises" the ontological character of his earlier analysis in *Being and Time,* changes the valency of some of his key terms from ontological to ontic (for example, German *Dasein*), or reintroduces terms (for example, *Geist*), which the earlier thought critiqued. To put it briefly, as many commentators have remarked, Heidegger's thought at this historical moment involves itself explicitly with the metaphysical terminology that the project of *Being and Time* set out to deconstruct (Derrida, Lacoue-Labarthe). Later on in the 1930s, Heidegger's texts attempt to reread the terms of his analysis, to change again their semantic value (for example, *Dasein,* which refers no longer simply to the existential ontology of *Being and Time,* or to the German *Dasein* as in the texts of early 1930s, but describes the attentiveness to the lighting of Being itself) or abandon them (as is the case with resoluteness, *Entschlossenheit*). Heidegger's writings also begin to refer to history in more general terms, projecting themselves against the broad spectrum of metaphysical thought and, in particular, its culmination in the nineteenth and twentieth centuries in technology as the prevalent mode of the revealing of Being. It is in this context that Heidegger's remarks on historicity are

situated, as a form of analysis that sets up the paradigm for the unfolding of history as event *(das Ereignis)*, without engaging explicitly the specifics of the historical circumstances that "constitute" contemporary history.

31. Writing about the continuing need to rethink the aspects of Heidegger's thought which concern political thought, Fynsk suggests that Heidegger's radicality manifests itself in questioning the very legibility of the political and forces us to keep reexamining "the political meaning of an engagement with the very grounds of legibility" *(Heidegger: Thought and Historicity,* 249). In chapter 7, I explore this political meaning of legibility through the work of Susan Howe.

32. For an insightful and comprehensive discussion of the common misreadings of modernist aesthetics and poststructuralism's proximity to it as aesthetic formalism or skepticism, see Ewa Płonowska Ziarek, *Rhetoric of Failure: Deconstruction of Skepticism, Reinvention of Modernism* (Albany: State University of New York Press, 1995).

33. Jürgen Habermas, *The Philosophical Discourse of Modernity,* trans. Frederick G. Lawrence (Cambridge, Mass: MIT Press, 1992), 185.

34. Martin Heidegger, "Hölderlin and the Essence of Poetry," *Existence and Being* (Washington, D.C.: Regnery Gateway, 1988), 273; translation modified (hereafter cited as "EB").

35. The German text is quoted from *Erläuterungen zu Hölderlins Dichtung, Gesamtausgabe,* vol. 4, 37 (hereafter cited as *EHD*).

36. See also my discussion of Heidegger's *"die Sprache spricht"* in *Inflected Language.*

37. Rebecca Comay, "Framing Redemption: Aura, Origin, Technology in Benjamin and Heidegger," in *Ethics and Danger: Essays on Heidegger and Continental Thought* (Albany: State University of New York Press, 1992), 161. Indeed, the proximity of Benjamin's and Heidegger's ideas of history underscores the necessity of keeping in view the interplay of the ontic and the ontological in Heidegger's notion of *Ereignis* and of recognizing the ontic as a "material corrective" to the ontological.

38. Cezary Wodziński, *Heidegger i problem zła* (Warszawa: Państwowy Instytut Wydawniczy, 1994), 537; translation mine.

39. *Besinnung* appeared in 1997 as vol. 66 of *Gesamtausgabe. Die Geschichte des Seyns* (vol. 69) appeared in 1998, while *Metaphysik und Nihilismus* (vol. 67) was published in 1999.

40. I discuss the problematic of power in Heidegger in more detail in "Powers to Be: Art and Technology in Heidegger and Foucault," *Research in Phenomenology* 28 (1998): 162–94, and in "Proximities: Irigaray and Heidegger on Difference," *Continental Philosophy Review* 33, 3:133–58.

41. The Heideggerian way-making of language does not lie far apart from Benjamin's notion of translatability, especially when we realize that for Benjamin the translatability inscribed in each text serves as an index point for a sort of translatability that describes the workings of language as such or, in other terms, the "pure

language." Translatability marks the inner limit of the original and, as a "structural feature that, within the work itself, points beyond it" (Rodolphe Gasché, "Saturnine Vision and the Question of Difference: Reflections on Walter Benjamin's Theory of Language," *Benjamin's Ground,* 90), inscribes otherness within the text. Benjaminian translatability indicates that the "essence" of the work of art is not self-identity but difference, the work's openness to the otherness of translation. Translatability understood as the internal limen of the text functions itself as a mark of a broader translational pattern that, for Benjamin, characterizes language and the work of art, as such. For the purpose of translation is not so much to render a text into another language as to lay open the workings of language: "Translation thus ultimately serves the purpose of expressing the central reciprocal relationship between languages. It cannot possibly reveal or establish this hidden relationship itself; but it can represent it by realizing it in embryonic or intensive form" (*I,* 72). This reciprocal relationship remains hidden *(verborgene Verhältnis)* because of the nature of translation involved in language and its tendency to efface itself once language reaches articulation. A particular instance of translatability can register this internal mechanism of language to the extent precisely that at stake in translation is not the form or the content of a text but rather the linguistic intention that animates the original: "The task of the translator consists in finding that intended effect upon the language [*Intention auf die Sprache*] into which he is translating which produces in it the echo of the original" (*I,* 76).

The intention in question refers to the intention of language itself, specifically to the way in which each text "intends" the workings of its language, the manner in which it points to and marks the "way" of its language. The kinship between languages which translation discloses is not a question of their proximity in origin or history but rather one of the translatability of their intention: the possibility of translating not only the linguistic intention of one text into another but, with it and through it, of revealing the proximity between the intention — the way-making or the translation — of the languages in question. What Benjamin refers to as "pure language" is this supplementing, supplementlike, to paraphrase Derrida, relationship between intentions animating languages. Since translation allows us best to see the intention that underlies a given language by way of contrasting it with that of another, the translatability inscribed in each work functions as the mark of "pure language," that is, the commemoration or remembrance of language's already "hidden" (by words themselves) intention of "translating" itself into words. Translatability works as the marker of pure language because pure language is both inscribed in each language (as its particular mode of translation or way-making into words) and, at the same time, extends beyond the intention of any single language. What is it that exists in language and comes into our view in particular in translations, in the modes of signification particular to each language? It is the fact that there is meaning at all, or, to put it differently, the manner in which languages signify, come into words. Thus, what Benjamin means by pure language is that translatory mechanism that allows for words to signify, that allows us to have words at all. Obviously, each language has its own modes of signification, developed and modified over the course of its history and specific to its society. But what marks the "proximity" of languages is the fact that there are words at all, that there is meaning at all—that is, the proximity of the "intentions" of languages to signify, their "pure language." In this sense, pure language at the same time remains inscribed in and exceeds each single language.

42. As Benjamin writes in "The Task of the Translator," *"Intention auf die Sprache"* "is a feature of translation which basically differentiates it from the poet's work, because the effort of the latter is never directed at the language as such, at its totality, but solely and immediately at specific linguistic contextual aspects" (*I,* 76). This point, however, does not take into consideration the explicit translative effort within the poetic work of Khlebnikov, for example, or the intralinguistic translative movement characteristic of the poetry of Gertrude Stein or Paul Celan, who indicate that "translating" is integral to the workings of poetic language. It is no surprise, therefore, that Menninghaus's study of Celan's poetry, for instance, aligns Benjamin's notion of the *"Intention auf die Sprache"* with Celan's characteristic "undoing" of poetic language; Winfried Menninghaus, *Paul Celan: Magie der Form* (Frankfurt am Main: Suhrkamp, 1980).

43. Khlebnikov's idea of "beyonsense" language as presented in *Zangezi* operates on the principle of a phenomenal saying, the linguistic manifestation of the world, not unlike Heidegger's notion of *die Sage*. See Velimir Khlebnikov, *The King of Time: Selected Writings of the Russian Futurian,* trans. Paul Schmidt (Cambridge, Mass.: Harvard University Press, 1985), 198–205.

44. In his lecture course on Hölderlin's hymn "Der Ister," Heidegger's remarks on translation parallel Benjamin's concluding remarks about translation as a practice of expanding and transforming one's own language: *"Das Übersetzen ist vielmehr eine Erweckung, Klärung, Entfaltung der eigenen Sprache durch die Hilfe der Auseinandersetzung mit der fremdem"* ("Rather translation is more an awakening, clarification, and unfolding of one's own language with the help of an encounter with the foreign language"); *Hölderlins Hymne "Der Ister," Gesamtausgabe,* vol. 53 (Frankfurt am Main: Vittorio Klostermann, 1984), 80. *Hölderlin's Hymn "The Ister,"* trans. William McNeill and Julia Davis (Bloomington and Indianapolis: Indiana University Press, 1996), 65–66. The term *Auseinandersetzung,* a polysemous sheaf of meanings ranging from exposition, analysis, arrangement, and settlement to argument, difference, and conflict, renders well the tension between identification and difference, the same and the other, that Heidegger describes as the dynamics of translation (a most interesting discussion of the Heideggerian *Auseinandersetzung,* in particular in the context of the political involvements of Heidegger's thought, can be found in Cezary Wodziński, *Heidegger i problem zła,* 5–10). Heidegger's remarks about translation are clearly at odds with passages about German *Dasein* and poetry, which commentators sometimes see as unequivocally consonant with the

conception of Germany advanced by national socialism. A similar *Auseinanderset-zung*, a tension that strings the transition of the manifestational saying *(die Sage)* into words, is at work in Heidegger's conception of language. My argument is that in the works of the avant-garde, this tension is inscribed into their very language, constituting a distinctive poetics of intralingual translation.

45. Discussing the latency inherent in the structure of experience itself, Cadava remarks that "[i]t is what is not experienced in an event that paradoxically accounts for the belated and posthumous shock of historical experience" ("Words of Light," 109). Looking at this latency not as a repressed part of the content of an experience, a "forgotten reality," but rather as the peculiarity of the manner of experiencing underscores its historical trajectory, in which forgetting becomes the integral part of experience. To put it differently, experience takes place as the forgetting of itself; it produces itself as its own latency.

46. Heidegger, *BW,* 339.

47. Walter Benjamin, *The Arcades Project,* trans. Howard Eiland and Kevin McLaughlin (Cambridge, Mass., and London: Belknap Press of Harvard University Press, 1999), 462–63 (hereafter cited as *AP*).

48. In a slightly different context, Fynsk draws attention to the double meaning of *Moment* in Benjamin's work. Christopher Fynsk, "The Claim of History," *Diacritics* 22 (Fall–Winter 1992): 118–19 (hereafter cited as "CH").

49. The beginning of N 3.1 rejects Heidegger's notion of *Geschichtlichkeit,* as a failed attempt of reading history "phenomenologically": "What distinguishes images from the 'essences' of phenomenology is their historical index. (Heidegger seeks in vain to rescue history for phenomenology abstractly through 'historicity')," *(AP,* 462). Perhaps Benjamin would have been more receptive to Heidegger's thought if he had recognized that historicity marks an address, a claim *(Anspruch)* to which the present answers, and which, by virtue of being always already "past" — "immemorial" and irrecuperable — dislocates, each time in a singular manner, the recapitulations of the present. See Fynsk, "CH," 116, note 2.

50. "Materialist historiography does not choose its objects arbitrarily. It does not fasten on them but rather springs them loose from the order of succession" *(AP,* 475).

51. I follow here Fynsk's insightful remarks about the historical index as the quasi-transcendental condition of historical experience: "With the dialectical image, Benjamin effectively historicizes the address of truth and draws it into historical experience as its quasi-transcendental condition." Fynsk, "CH," 125.

52. Underscoring the nonaesthetic character of art in Greece, Heidegger is not, however, interested in its historically primary religious function. Instead, by the nonaesthetic he means the historical function of art in terms of opening up a world. As "The Origin of the Work of Art" indicates, gods and religion are part of the historical world inaugurated by art. Only to that extent can art be taken to have

a religious, ritualistic meaning, as part of the world-disclosure at work in art. *BW,* 167–72.

53. Cadava develops this point in more detail; see "WL," 96–97.

54. Samuel Weber, "Theater, Technics, and Writing," *1–800* (Fall 1989): 17.

55. Cadava, "WL," 95.

56. In what follows, I build on Fynsk's benchmark reading of "The Origin of the Work of Art" in *Heidegger: Thought and Historicity,* 131–73. Particularly interesting is his discussion of the work's performative *"Dass es sei,"* "that it be," which inscribes in art its createdness and makes it possible for the work to be "re-performed" in its reception (see, in particular, pages 136–38). Fynsk explains that the demand "that it be" calls on the artist to work it into the work and on the "preservers" to repeat it. In this way, the work both opens and opens *upon* its conditions of enunciation. Where my approach differs from Fynsk's interpretation is with respect to historicity. While he places the emphasis on *Dasein's* finitude as the limit which the work of art makes manifest (154–55), I suggest that the boundary which the work of art (re)produces is historicity as the limit of experience. *Dasein's* finitude becomes manifest through historicity as the limit and the excess figured as art's work.

57. Jacques Derrida, "Shibboleth: For Paul Celan," trans. Joshua Wilner, in *Word Traces: Readings of Paul Celan,* ed. Aris Fioretos (Baltimore and London: Johns Hopkins University Press, 1994), 18.

58. Without developing the point or situating it in the context of art, Timothy Bahti points to the link between transition or translation, on the one hand, and the making of history, on the other. "History as Rhetorical Enactment: Walter Benjamin's Theses 'On the Concept of History,' " *Diacritics* 9 (Fall 1979): 12–13.

59. The use of *gründen* may suggest that Heidegger proposes here a foundationalist approach to art. In fact, we have to remember that for Heidegger this "grounding" characteristic of art is tantamount to an ungrounding, which constantly unworks the historicist model of history by reference to the remainder of historicity. Art "grounds" history in the sense of staging the historicity of the event, the play of the reserve, and the concealment, intrinsic to the historical unfolding of the world.

60. Heidegger's notion of the earth in "The Origin of the Work of Art" can be read as providing this paradoxical "ground," which, though apparently solid, is, in fact, impenetrable, and thus continuously disarticulates the world that it "grounds."

61. Both Fynsk and Bernasconi demonstrate how Heidegger's remarks on history in "The Origin of the Work of Art" are tied to his reflection on the decision which faced a historical people, that is, the German people, in the 1930s, a decision which Heidegger believed had to do with the confrontation with global forces of technology; see Fynsk, *Heidegger: Thought and Historicity,* 238–42, and Bernasconi, *Heidegger in Question,* 135–48. I would argue, though, that the way Heidegger re-

thinks history, even in the texts from the 1930s undercuts, as Fynsk also indicates, the idea of the *mytho-poiēsis* and the kind of national aestheticism sought after by the National Socialist party.

62. For the German text, see *Holzwege, Gesamtausgabe,* vol. 5, 55.

63. For a more detailed discussion of Benjamin's deployment of aesthetic production against fascist aesthetics, see Cadava's "WL," 96–97.

Chapter 2

1. *"Angesichts der heutigen Wirklichkeit, die sich als Industrie- und Lesitungsgesellschaft versteht, die sich selbst und die von ihr benutzten Bestände selber produziert, entleert sich das Wort des Dichters für jedermann leicht zur blossen Phantasterei. Dichtung versteht sich selbst gesellschaftlich als Literaturproduktion"*; Martin Heidegger, *Aus der Erfahrung des Denkens, Gesamtausgabe,* vol. 13 (Frankfurt am Main: Vittorio Klostermann, 1983), 213.

2. Martin Heidegger, "The Origin of the Work of Art," *Basic Writings,* 2d ed., ed. and into. David Farrell Krell (New York: Harper Collins, 1993), 166 (hereafter cited as *BW*).

3. Symbolic hypotyposes "express concepts not by means of a direct intuition but only according to an analogy with one, i.e., a transfer of our reflection on an object of intuition to an entirely different concept, to which perhaps no intuition can ever directly correspond." Immanuel Kant, *Critique of Judgment,* trans. Werner S. Pluhar (Indianapolis: Hackett, 1987), 228.

4. See the translation of *Ereignis* in the Addendum to "The Origin of the Work of Art," *BW,* 210.

✓   5. Hans Richter, *Dada: Art and Anti-Art* (New York: Oxford University Press, 1978), 352. This work is hereafter cited as *DAA*.

6. Francis Picabia, "How New York Looks to Me," *New York American,* March 30, 1913, p. 11. Quoted in "Introduction," *New York Dada,* ed. Rudolph E. Kuenzli (New York: Willis Locker and Owens, 1986), 3.

7. For a detailed discussion of the role of the machine in the formulation of the futurist poetics, see Jeffrey T. Schnapp, "Propeller Talk," Special Issue, "Marinetti and the Italian Futurists," *Modernism/Modernity* 1, no. 3 (1994): 153–78.

8. I quote this passage after Jean-Joseph Goux, "Politics and Modern Art— Heidegger's Dilemma," Special Issue, "Heidegger: Art and Politics," *Diacritics* 19 (Fall–Winter 1989): 22, 23.

9. *"Die in der modernen Technik verborgene Macht bestimmt das Verhältnis des Menschen zu dem, was ist"*; Martin Heidegger, *Gelassenheit* (Pfullingen: Neske, 1959), 20.

10. Martin Heidegger, *Überlieferte Sprache und technische Sprache* (St. Gallen:

Erker, 1989), 18 (hereafter cited as *US*). *Discourse on Thinking,* trans. John M. Anderson and E. Hans Freund (New York: Harper and Row, 1966), 50.

11. See, for example, Heidegger's discussion of technology in "The Question Concerning Technology," *BW,* 320–25.

12. Technology here signifies a certain reading of the differential event of the world in terms of the possibility of a total or complete calculation and ordering—a reading which takes the form of what Heidegger calls "calculative thought" *(rechnendes Denken).* This modality of understanding possesses its own philosophical genealogy and its predominance becomes historically determinable by reference to the theoretical requisites of modernity, which have produced the scientific practices associated with the project of the Enlightenment. This specific deployment of the term "technology" identifies it with the forming of the differential of manifestation into a schema of definable and calculable differences. It links technology with what might be called a "calculus of difference," that is, with the mapping of experience on the basis of an underlying principle, which has the power to schematize difference and render its play representable and calculable in its totality. What produces the sense of quantifiable totality associated with calculative thought is the assumption that the differences which constitute the matter of experience can be defined, made understandable, and, thus, processed, as information. The global scope of the techniques of producing and processing information, continually intensified by the development of computer technology, reflects the degree to which the schematic computation of differences has become the paradigm of modern experience.

13. I want to mention briefly the implications of this notion of technology, which reach beyond the ontological dimension of modern experience to the sphere of political and social practice. Derrida's explicit remarks on politics and political philosophy in *Specters of Marx* owe a lot to Heidegger's critique of technology and render much more concrete what only lies implicit in it with regard to politics. Reacting to the triumphalist proclamations of the victory of liberal capitalism and of the end of history after the Cold War, Derrida warns about the political and ethical dangers of the current attempt to consolidate a worldwide hegemony of liberal capitalism. Under the guise of the "true" solution to the world's problems, such a hegemonic reality would, in fact, foreclose any possibility of a different future, that is, the possibility of emancipation and responsibility. The "new world order" of "democracy" proliferating in the various forms of liberal capitalism becomes possible through technological globalization and technocratic management. In its rhetoric of democracy, it equates the proper management of the world affairs through finance, economy, and trade, with an automatic elimination of oppression and injustice. As a result, politics, ethics, and justice cease to guide social life and become themselves "mere" extensions of economic calculation and technocratic management, with the global institutions erected for their efficient administration.

Derrida's reading tacitly follows Heidegger's interpretation of technology: Technology progresses toward the point when it becomes the exclusive structure and matrix of contemporary reality, reality which it represents as, in essence, calculable—that is, as structured in ways that allow for globalization and total management. Heidegger would say that the very idea of global management would not be possible without the underlying technological schema, in which being becomes conceived in terms of the calculus of resources. Derrida's insightful remarks allow us to distinguish Heidegger's rethinking of technology and *poiēsis* from the aestheticization of experience, to demonstrate how the notion of *poiēsis* preserves the political and ethical significations of experience against their progressive identification with management and control of resources.

14. "[T]he revealing that holds sway throughout modern technology does not unfold into a bringing-forth in the sense of *poiēsis*." *BW,* 320.

15. Martin Heidegger, *Bremen und Freiburger Vorträge, Gesamtausgabe,* vol. 79 (Frankfurt am Main: Vittorio Klostermann, 1994), 20.

16. I presented a detailed discussion of the notions of proximity and inflection in *Inflected Language* (Albany: State University of New York Press, 1994).

17. Tristan Tzara, "Dada Manifesto 1918," *Seven Manifestoes and Lampisteries,* trans. Barbara Wright (London, Paris, New York: Calder Publications and Riverrun Press, 1992), 4 (hereafter cited as *SM*).

18. Tristan Tzara, "Dada Manifesto 1918," 13.

19. In this reading, the dream of immediacy and common knowledge associated with ordinary language and life practices does not produce an antidote to reification but, instead, becomes an extension of the technological vision of complete availability of beings as resources. The discovery of local differences, of various "common knowledges" and the lived differentials of experience, although crucial to the critique of cultural forms of power, may not be radical enough to escape from the increasing calculability of differences on the global scale.

20. Lefebvre criticizes both existentialist philosophies and avant-garde poetry for their apparent disregard for or even a "conspiracy" against the everyday. He takes issue especially with surrealism, which he accuses of fleeing the everyday to the mysterious and the bizarre. See *Critique of Everyday Life,* trans. Moore (London and New York: Verso, 1991), 117–29. Lefebvre's remarks recall and reinforce Benjamin's suspicion that the practice of suffusing the ordinary with the marvelous, seeking redemption from the routine and the mundane, entails the risk of remythologizing reality and its ⌐mbodiment in politics or the state, a risk that affects Heidegger's own reading of Germany and *Volk* in the 1930s. Heidegger's idea of *Volk* and Germany from "The Origin of the Work of Art" and the Hölderlin lectures and essays is markedly different from the fascist ideology of "blood and soil" as the essential characteristics of the *Volk*. Heidegger's anti-essentialism makes clear that a people is not constituted by an essence, certainly not a racial one. However, the invocation of these problematic and politically compromised terms, even if different from the

official politics of 1930s Germany, produces a continuous reassociation of Heidegger's work from that period with the remythologization of German *Dasein* by the National Socialist party.

Chapter 3

1. Judith Butler underscores the strategic importance of the difference from philosophical texts effected by Irigaray's miming: "This miming is, of course, tactical, and her reenactment of philosophical error requires that we learn how to read her for the difference that her reading performs"; *Bodies that Matter: On the Discursive Limits of "Sex"* (New York: Routledge, 1993), 36 (hereafter cited as *BTM*). Mary Ann Doane describes Irigaray's mimicry as enacting "a defamiliarizing version of femininity"; *The Desire to Desire: The Woman's Film of the 1940s* (Bloomington: Indiana University Press, 1987), 182.

2. For Weed, Irigaray's style is never purely formal but functions as a "figurative thematics," which keeps refiguring sexual difference: "In the years since 'Cosi Fan Tutti' was published, in reading after reading, Irigaray has produced an elaborate thematics of sexual difference: a figurative thematics that works against the thematizable, a couple that works against the copula, a sexual difference rich in discursive positivity"; see Elizabeth Weed, "The Question of Style," *Engaging with Irigaray: Feminist Philosophy and Modern European Thought,* ed. Burke, Schor, and Whitford (New York: Columbia University Press, 1994), 102. The different tenor of current discussions of Irigaray owes much to the recent body of scholarship, which has not only relegated to the past the mistaken essentialist/anti-essentialist debate, but has also begun to read Irigaray through her complex involvement with Lacanian psychoanalysis and Continental philosophy. The three most important works to date are: Margaret Whitford, *Luce Irigaray: Philosophy in the Feminine* (London and New York: Routledge, 1991), Tina Chanter, *Ethics of Eros: Irigaray's Rewriting of the Philosophers* (New York: Routledge, 1995), and the already mentioned volume of essays, *Engaging with Irigaray.*

3. Weed, "The Question of Style," 101.

4. Weed, "The Question of Style," 84–85.

5. Chanter, *Ethics of Eros.*

6. Joanna Hodge, "Irigaray Reading Heidegger," and Ellen Mortensen, "Woman's Untruth and *le Féminine:* Reading Luce Irigaray with Nietzsche and Heidegger"; both essays are included in *Engaging with Irigaray,* 191–209 and 211–28, respectively.

7. In *An Ethics of Sexual Difference,* Irigaray casts her critique in terms of a new poetics of language, thought, and culture. Since Irigaray sees language as constitutive of being and experience, this poetics is never just a matter of style or textual strategies but refers to the texture of experience and sexual relations, reworked be-

yond the logocentric and phallomorphic makeup of being; *An Ethics of Sexual Difference,* trans. Burke and Gill (Ithaca: Cornell University Press, 1993), 5 (hereafter cited as *ESD*).

8. In his translation of "The Way to Language," David Krell renders *Ereignis* as "propriation," in order to preserve the sense of "ownness" and the proper inscribed in the German term; see Martin Heidegger, *Basic Writings,* 2d ed., trans. and intro. Krell (New York: Harper Collins, 1993), 396 (hereafter cited as *BW*). In "The Question Concerning Technology," *das Ereignis* is translated as "the propriative event" (*BW,* 337), which keeps the twofold sense of occurring and propriating in play, showing that for Heidegger being is never a "mere" happening but an event in which what is occurs ("propriates") as such. Heidegger's most extensive discussion of *das Ereignis* comes in *Beiträge zur Philosophie: Vom Ereignis* (Frankfurt am Main: Vittorio Klostermann, 1989). Another important discussion of *Ereignis,* crucial for my approach to *poiēsis,* can be found in "The Way to Language," where Heidegger explains the occurring at play in the *Ereignis* in terms of language, as a form of saying *(Sagen).*

9. In 1981, two essays, Christine Fauré's "The Twilight of the Goddesses or the Intellectual Crisis of French Feminism" (*Signs* [1981]: 81–86) and Carolyn Burke, "Irigaray Through the Looking Glass" (*Feminist Studies* 7, no. 2 [1981]: 288–306) initiated the critique of Irigaray's work on the grounds of essentialism and idealism. This criticism has continued through the 1980s and into the 1990s (see, for example, Annamarie Jagose, "Irigaray and the Lesbian Body: Remedy and Poison," *Genders* 13 [1992]: 30–41). Among many responses to this criticism, one should mention Jane Gallop's pioneering revision of Irigaray's reception in "*Quand Nos Lèvres S'Ecrivent:* Irigaray's Body Politic," *The Romanic Review* 74 (1983): 77–83; reprinted in Jane Gallop, *Thinking Through the Body* (New York: Columbia University Press, 1988), 92–100, 117–18, under the title "Lip Service"; Diana Fuss's "Luce Irigaray's Language of Essence" from her *Essentially Speaking* (New York: Routledge, 1989), 55–72; and Maggie Berg, "Escaping the Cave: Luce Irigaray and Her Feminist Critics," in *Literature and Ethics,* ed. Gary Wihl and David Williams (Kingston, Montreal: McGill Queen's University Press, 1988), 62–76. Berg's essay lists the many critical reactions to Irigaray's work that appeared in the early 1980s; see, in particular, page 74, note 3. An excellent discussion of Irigaray's criticism up to the 1990s, especially the essentialism/anti-essentialism debate, can be found in Naomi Schor's "Previous Engagements: The Receptions of Irigaray," which opens the recent collection of essays *Engaging with Irigaray,* 3–14, especially pages 5–8. For an assessment of Irigaray's thought from the perspective of the Frankfurt School and social critique, see Nancy Fraser's "Introduction" to *Revaluing French Feminism: Critical Essays on Difference, Agency, and Culture,* ed. Nancy Fraser and Sandra Lee Bartky (Bloomington: Indiana University Press, 1992), 1–24.

10. Luce Irigaray, *This Sex Which Is Not One,* trans. Catherine Porter (Ithaca: Cornell University Press, 1985), 134 (hereafter cited as *TS*).

11. Irigaray, *Marine Lover: Of Friedrich Nietzsche,* trans. Gillian C. Gill (New York: Columbia University Press, 1991), 105. It is at this point that proximity becomes crucial to Irigaray's rethinking of the economy of the gift through sexual difference. The amorous exchange in proximity allows something to be reserved and withheld, without making it enter the economy of gift exchange. Moreover, it can be argued that what allows that gift economy to work is indeed that which withholds itself from economic exchange: the giving of itself (as) giving, which can never be transposed into the gift, or the object of giving; Luce Irigaray, *L'oubli de l'air: Chez Heidegger* (Paris: Éditions de Minuit, 1983), 86–87; *The Forgetting of Air in Martin Heidegger,* trans. Mary Beth Mader (Austin: University of Texas Press, 1999), 93–94.

12. Irigaray, *The Irigaray Reader,* ed. Margaret Whitford (Oxford: Basil Blackwell), 181 (hereafter cited as *IR*).

13. One could argue that in *Otherwise than Being or Beyond Essence,* trans. Alphonso Lingis (The Hague: Martinus Nijhoff, 1981) Levinas appears to take to heart Irigaray's inscription of the body into the relation of proximity, as he himself refigures his notion of proximity into the new tropes of inverted breath, sensibility, and the-one-for-the-other—all figures of an enfleshed ethical affliction. However, as Chanter argues, this moment of rendering sensibility—the other's touch—ethical coincides in Levinas's thought with the de-eroticization of the feminine and with the flattening of sexual difference into the familiar patriarchal economy of procreation—the feminine becomes equated with the maternal, the "difference" of sexual difference subsumed under the paradigm of maternity (hence another return to the problematic of the future as the son, and so on). In other words, the inflection of ethics through the body—a move most important to Irigaray's own project—for Levinas becomes possible not as an acknowledgment and inscription of sexual difference but as its effective erasure. While for Irigaray ethics needs sexual difference to be "ethical," that is, it has to be thought through the difference of sexes and genders, for Levinas ethics takes priority over sexual difference and even mandates its forgetting. See Tina Chanter's discussion of Irigaray and Levinas in *Ethics of Eros: Irigaray's Rewriting of the Philosophers* (New York: Routledge, 1995).

14. Luce Irigaray, *Speculum of the Other Woman,* trans. Gillian C. Gill (Ithaca, N.Y.: Cornell University Press, 1985), 275.

15. In her remarkable chapter on the double signification of matter in the context of Irigaray's thought, "Bodies that Matter," Butler bases her explanation of materiality on the critique of the presumption of an unposited, unsignified body, an apparent locus of prelinguistic experiential plenitude. Judith Butler, *Bodies that Matter,* 30.

16. See *IR,* 175.

17. It is only recently that Irigaray criticism began exploring the relation of her writings to Heidegger's thought. Tina Chanter's *Ethics of Eros* devotes a separate chapter to Irigaray's critique of the question of being through the question of sexual

difference. Two other essays on Irigaray and Heidegger, Joanna Hodge, "Irigaray Reading Heidegger," and Ellen Mortensen "Woman's Untruth and *le Féminine:* Reading Luce Irigaray with Nietzsche and Heidegger," appeared in *Engaging with Irigaray,* 191–209 and 211–28.

18. Irigaray, *Sexes and Genealogies,* trans. Gillian C. Gill (New York: Columbia University Press, 1993), 107 (hereafter cited as *SG*).

19. As much is suggested in "Questions to Emmanuel Levinas," where one of the most interesting moments reappraises, in fact, Heidegger's thought in the context of the ethics of sexual difference. Responding to Levinas's charge that Heidegger's thought is only an "ethics of the 'fruits of the earth,'" Irigaray remarks:

> The philosophy of Heidegger is more ethical than that [that is, Levinas's] ex- pression conveys, than his philosophy itself says explicitly. To consider the other within the horizon of Being should mean to respect the other. It is true that the definition of Being in terms of mortal destiny rather than in terms of living existence raises a question about the nature of respect. And in addition, this philosophy is more or less silent on man's sexual dimension [*la dimension de l'homme comme sexué*], an irreducible dimension of human existence. Perhaps Heidegger's thought was preparing the way for thinking the sexually identi- fied subject [*sujet comme sexué*], in particular as a possible future for thought. (Irigaray, "Questions to Emmanuel Levinas," in *IR,* 184)

My concern is less with Irigaray's diagnosis of the importance of Heidegger's thought for a future thinking of the human mode of being as sexuate—a diagnosis with which Derrida appears to concur in "*Geschlecht* I"—than with understanding how the problematic of sexual difference intersects with and complicates the issue of experience in modernity, in particular, how it modifies the correlation between experience, technology, and art, which I have explored in the context of Benjamin and Heidegger.

20. "In order to think back to the essence of language, in order to reiterate what is its own, we need a transformation of language, a transformation we can neither compel nor concoct. . . . The transformation touches on our relation to language" (*BW,* 424–25).

Chapter 4

1. Toril Moi, *Sexual/Textual Politics: Feminist Literary Theory* (London and New York: Methuen, 1985), 17.

2. Marianne DeKoven, *A Different Language: Gertrude Stein's Experimental Writing* (Madison: University of Wisconsin Press, 1983).

3. Luce Irigaray, *This Sex Which Is Not One,* trans. Catherine Porter (Ithaca: Cornell University Press, 1985), 214 (hereafter cited as *TS*).

4. Cope engages in an explicit polemic with Stimpson, suggesting that sexual difference is intrinsic to Stein's language; see " 'Moral Deviancy' and Contemporary Feminism: The Judgement of Gertrude Stein," in *Feminism Beside Itself,* ed. Diane Elam and Robyn Wiegman (New York and London: Routledge, 1995), 163–64.

5. Both DeKoven and Stimpson discuss Stein's evolving relation to feminist aspirations. As Stimpson puts it, "[t]hough Stein was never a public feminist, during the 1920s she began to cut the cord she and Western culture had tied between masculinity and towering creativity"; "The Somagrams of Gertrude Stein," *The Lesbian and Gay Studies Reader,* ed. Abelove, Barale, and Halperin (New York and London: Routledge, 1993), 646.

6. The translations of both essays have been published in *The Lyotard Reader,* ed. Andrew Benjamin (Oxford: Basil Blackwell, 1989), 196–211 and 240–49 (hereafter cited as *LR*).

7. This characteristic link between subversive and transformative effects of the event and the questions of justice, judging, and community is visible in many of Lyotard's texts. Perhaps the most well known among them is *The Differend;* see also *Peregrinations. The Differend: Phases in Dispute,* trans. Georges Van Den Abbeele (Minneapolis: University of Minnesota Press, 1988) and *Peregrinations: Law, Form, Event* (New York: Columbia University Press, 1988).

8. Although Heidegger did not express much interest in the avant-garde, and although he certainly never approached avant-garde art the way Lyotard does, his work on the event and its significance for modern art and philosophy provides the background against which the avant-garde's importance for contemporary debates on language and aesthetics can be better appreciated. It is not clear to what extent Heidegger's references to Klee in his later writings and his interest in Cézanne could be taken as signs of his changing attitude toward contemporary and avant-garde art. Even though the term "modern" remains rather vague when Heidegger asks in his 1967 lecture "The Origin of Art and the Destination of Thinking" about the necessity to which modern art responds, it seems probable that Heidegger has in mind a variety of modern artistic and literary works, including those of the avant-garde. What is obvious is that Heidegger's ideas from the 1950s and 1960s about art, poetry, and language reach beyond his intentions and the "canon" of poetic texts and visual arts he expressly discusses in his work. It is this moment that is of particular importance to my argument here, since I am less interested in Heidegger's comments on or commitment to specific works and artistic trends than in the relevance of his thought about art and language for discerning the broader implications of modern art's departure from the canons of aesthetics.

9. Martin Heidegger, *Basic Writings,* 2d ed., ed. David Farrell Krell (New York: Harper Collins, 1993), 326 (hereafter cited as *BW*).

10. Heidegger's thought carefully maintains the critical distinction between the poetic *(Dichtung)* and poetry as a literary genre *(Poesie).* This difference is already

at play in "The Origin of the Work of Art" (1936), where Heidegger claims that the poetic element of language and experience underlies all manifestations of art, including that of poetry (*Poetry, Language, Thought,* trans. Albert Hofstadter [San Francisco: Harper and Row, 1971], 72). In "The Question Concerning Technology" (1953), Heidegger goes even further, suggesting a distinction between the poetic and what might be called the *poietic.* Heidegger, for whom experience transpires always as thinking, that is, as active, embodied, being-in-the-world, employs the *poietic* to refer specifically to the experience of the unfolding of the world suppressed and erased in the calculative and objectifying attitude characteristic of modern rationality. The difference between the poetic and the *poietic,* between poetic forms of literary discourse and *poiēsis* in the broader, "Greek" sense of unfolding and letting come into presence, indicates that poetry itself is in the sphere of influence of technological rationality, and its language needs to be put in question just as much as the conceptual apparatus of metaphysics.

11. Seeking a thinking that would not be monopolized by forms of calculative reasoning, Heidegger delineates the poietic understructure of experience, covered over by its technological rationalization. See, in particular, Heidegger's discussion of *poiēsis* and *technē* in "The Question Concerning Technology," *BW,* 318–41.

12. In his early work on Hölderlin, Heidegger places the emphasis upon the gathering force of art, upon its ability to disclose the world in its being, that is, its nexus of relations, differences, and singularities. Already in "The Origin of the Work of Art," we can see that this "poetic," as Heidegger calls it, character or ability of art (see *BW,* 197) matters to his thought specifically because it puts into question culturally and philosophically dominant schema of experience. If we take seriously Heidegger's suggestion that only few works of art remain attentive to art's "poetic" capacity and disclose the world accordingly, then it becomes clear that Heidegger's admiration for art is coupled with a most severe critique of its traditional system of representation and its codification in aesthetics. Only art that puts in question its metaphysical provenance and its conceptual system that governs our experience counts for Heidegger as one with critical, and perhaps even transformative, artistic and intellectual potential. It is my contention here that this poetic ability to disclose and let be, which Heidegger ascribes to art, is also at work in avant-garde poetry. To that extent, Heidegger's work on thinking and poetry as acts of letting things be in the singularity of their occurrence, as activity that questions both the schematization of being characteristic of the age of technology—objectivity, resource, standing-reserve *(Bestand)*—and art's often unacknowledged conformity with this practice, becomes important to my own argument about the avant-garde and Stein's poetic writings.

13. The question of the relation between experience and representation is one of the defining traits of Benjamin's whole work; his most provocative discussions of this topic can be found in translation in the "Epistemo-Critical Prologue" to *The Origin of German Tragic Drama,* trans. John Osborne (London: NLB, 1977),

27–56, and in his essays on Baudelaire, Proust, the work of art, and history from *Illuminations,* ed. Hannah Arendt (New York: Schocken, 1965). Adorno's conception of modernist art and its significance for the critique of the Enlightenment is presented most extensively in his *Aesthetic Theory,* trans. and ed. Robert Hullot-Kentor (Minneapolis: University of Minnesota Press, 1997).

14. At the beginning of his essay on *Tender Buttons,* William Gass remarks specifically upon this connection between ordinary life and philosophical concerns that I see as characteristic of Stein's work: "Thematically, they are composed of the implements, activities, colors and pleasures of home life, its quiet dangers, its unassertive thrills. . . . The highest metaphysical categories of sameness and difference, permanence and change, are invoked, as are the concerns of epistemology, of clarity and obscurity, certainty and doubt"; "Gertrude Stein and the Geography of the Sentence: *Tender Buttons,*" in *Gertrude Stein,* ed. and into. Harold Bloom (New York: Chelsea House, 1986), 145.

15. Gertrude Stein, *How to Write* (West Glover, Vt.: Something Else Press, 1973), hereafter cited as *HTW.*

16. For an illuminating discussion of Stein's ways of undermining meaning and the act of reading, see Peter Quartermain's chapter on Stein, " 'A Narrative of Undermine': Gertrude Stein's Multiplicity," in his book: *Disjunctive Poetics: From Gertrude Stein and Louis Zukofsky to Susan Howe* (Cambridge: Cambridge University Press, 1992), 21–43.

17. For the question of the performative character of Stein's writing, especially as it relates to her "plays," see Jane Palatini Bowers *"They Watch Me as They Watch This": Gertrude Stein's Metadrama* (Philadelphia: University of Pennsylvania Press, 1991).

18. In his 1957 review of "Stanzas in Meditation," John Ashbery underscores the monotony characteristic of the poem, seeing it as Stein's way of celebrating the minutiae of everyday life. At the same time that the monotony of "Stanzas" frustrates all attempts at extracting a plot or a story line, it also makes Stein's poem "a hymn to possibility; a celebration of the fact that the world exists, that things can happen"; see "The Impossible," in *Critical Essays on Gertrude Stein,* ed. Michael J. Hoffman (Boston: G. K. Hall, 1986), 105.

19. Gertrude Stein, *The Yale Gertrude Stein* (New Haven: Yale University Press, 1980), 342 (hereafter cited as *YGS*).

20. Chessman's study *The Public Is Invited to Dance* draws numerous parallels between Stein's writings and the works of Kristeva and Irigaray. She suggests, however, that for Stein language is an open field, not wholly structured by patriarchy: Stein "recreates language as a field of immense possibility for the articulation of intimacy as well as difference"; Harriet Scott Chessman, *The Public Is Invited to Dance: Representation, the Body, and Dialogue in Gertrude Stein* (Stanford: Stanford University Press, 1989), 73 (hereafter cited as *PID*).

21. Jean-François Lyotard, *The Differend: Phrases in Dispute,* 68.

22. Among the rapidly increasing number of book-length feminist readings of Stein, especially interesting are Marianne DeKoven, *A Different Language,* Lisa Ruddick, *Reading Gertrude Stein: Body, Text, Gnosis* (Ithaca: Cornell University Press, 1990) and Harriet Scott Chessman, *The Public Is Invited to Dance.*

23. It is possible to argue that both the *jouissance* and the frustration associated with Stein's writings are results of her "impossible" attempt to amplify and fore-ground a space that Kristeva identifies as the semiotic, that is, as the prethetic processes and articulations that produce the subject and the symbolic without ever becoming themselves part of the system that they institute. See Julia Kristeva, *Revolution in Poetic Language,* trans. Margaret Waller (New York: Columbia University Press, 1984), 36, in which Kristeva's discussion of the relation between the symbolic and the semiotic constitutes the first part of the English edition of her book, pages 19 to 106. The play of the semiotic within the symbolic inscribes language with plural and heterogenous processes of signification that encompass "the flow of drives, material discontinuity, political struggle, and the pulverization of language" (*Revolution,* 88). Kristeva identifies the ruptures and the refusal of the predominantly thetic signification specifically with poetry and the poetic function of language. Always located within the symbolic as its intra- or infra-text, the semiotic or the poetic irrupts in poetry and thus reactivates the process and the contradiction (the semiotic versus the symbolic/thetic) that instituted the symbolic in the first place (*Revolution,* 69). Exposing the unicity of the thetic, of grammar and narrative as Stein would say, the semiotic continuously allows the symbolic to constitute itself and, at the same time, dismantles its semblance of unity and self-sufficiency. Unlike Kristeva, however, Stein regards language as not completely determined by the patriarchal discourse and attempts to write language before, as it were, the rule of grammar and linguistic conventions. See also note 16 above.

24. In her multivocal essay "For the Etruscans," DuPlessis characterizes feminist revisions of aesthetics as an attempt to translate (compose?) the "Etruscan language": a language for the erased, never understood space of experience associated with sexual difference; "For the Etruscans," *New Feminist Criticism: Essays on Women, Literature, and Theory,* ed. Elaine Showalter (New York: Pantheon Books, 1985).

25. Gertrude Stein, *Lectures in America* (New York: Random House, 1935), 242 (hereafter cited as *LA*).

26. Discussing Stein's strategy of avoiding the traditional practices of naming in *Tender Buttons,* William Gass reads individual entries as discarding "old titles and properties" and rewording the world: "[t]o denoun and undenote, then to rename, and finally to praise the old world's raising of the new word out of the monitoring mind" (148).

27. One of Stein's most characteristic gestures is to turn repetition (itself a prime feature of Patriarchal Poetry as evidenced by the ironic cultural-culinary "menu" — "Patriarchal poetry and venison on Wednesday Patriarchal poetry and fish on Fri-

day Patriarchal poetry and birds on Sunday . . ." [*YGS,* 111]) into a critique of itself by extending it almost *ad absurdum* (see *YGS,* for example, pages 110, 114, 120–21, and 129).

28. Stein's manner of writing certainly differs drastically from that of the poets Heidegger discusses in his essays: Hölderlin, Rilke, and Trakl. As is often the case with Heidegger's thought, though, his insights extend beyond the confines of his "literary taste" and, when situated in the context of texts like Stein's, can in turn reflect back upon Heidegger's work and render problematic its limitations. This is particularly important and fruitful with respect to the question of the everyday, whose significance Heidegger's own idiom, especially in his texts on poetry, tends to underplay, even though everydayness—the event of everyday being—constitutes from the beginning the framework and the goal of his philosophical project. Heidegger's thought is important to my argument about Stein and the avant-garde precisely to the extent to which his reflection about art, aesthetics, and technology can be shown as anchored in the problematic of the everyday.

29. Gertrude Stein, *Tender Buttons* (Los Angeles: Sun & Moon Press, 1991), 23 (hereafter cited as *TB*).

30. When Gass reads this tension characteristic of *Tender Buttons* as the conflict between concealment and expression, his terms are reminiscent of Heidegger's approach to poetry and art (162–63).

31. A more in-depth discussion of indeterminacy in Stein and the work of other avant-garde poets can be found in Marjorie Perloff's study *The Poetics of Indeterminacy: Rimbaud to Cage* (Evanston: Northwestern University Press, 1980).

32. Don Byrd, *The Poetics of the Common Knowledge* (Albany: State University of New York Press, 1994), 181.

33. The implications and new possibilities for feminist politics opened by the critique of the notions of the universal and the common are explored, for example, in a recent volume *Feminists Theorize the Political,* ed. Judith Butler and Joan W. Scott (New York and London: Routledge, 1992). In her "Contingent Foundations: Feminism and the Question of 'Postmodernism,'" Butler discusses the complicity of the substantive notion of the universal in perpetuating the hegemonic relations of power: "To herald that notion then as the philosophical instrument that will negotiate between conflicts of power is precisely to safeguard and reproduce a position of hegemonic power by installing it in the metapolitical site of ultimate normativity" (7–8). See also Scott, " 'Experience' " (22–40), and Chantal Mouffe, "Feminism, Citizenship, and Radical Democratic Politics" (369–84).

34. If one can talk at all about the common in Stein, about a community or a politics, it would have to be along the lines of Jean-Luc Nancy's writings about the community that constantly unworks itself, that recognizes itself only in its strangeness. For Stein's language is a language in the process of exposing itself to otherness, a language continuously rewriting itself not so much into the commonness of meaning as into the inscriptions of its shifting and always singular limits.

See *The Inoperative Community*, in particular the title essay and "Literary Communism," which provide the most sustained discussion of Nancy's notion of *"être-en-commun"* (being-in-common); Jean-Luc Nancy, *The Inoperative Community*, ed. Peter Connor (Minneapolis: University of Minnesota Press, 1991).

35. Judy Grahn, *Really Reading Gertrude Stein: A Selected Anthology with Essays by Judy Grahn* (Freedom, Calif.: Crossing Press, 1989), 11.

36. *The Lesbian and Gay Studies Reader*, 651.

37. Gertrude Stein, *Everybody's Autobiography* (New York: Vintage, 1973), 153.

38. Gertrude Stein, *Many Many Women* (Barton, Vt.: Something Else Press, 1972), 130. As Ellen E. Berry suggests, *"Many Many Women* is an extended meditation on sameness and difference, a compression of the discourse of self and other"; *Curved Thought and Textual Wandering: Gertrude Stein's Postmodernism* (Ann Arbor: University of Michigan Press, 1992), 29.

39. Gertrude Stein, *Ida* (New York: Vintage, 1971), 7.

Chapter 5

1. A notable exception is Marjorie Perloff's discussion of Russian futurism in the context of Western European avant-garde in *The Futurist Moment: Avant-Garde, Avant-Guerre, and the Language of Rupture* (Chicago and London: University of Chicago Press, 1986). The chapter entitled "The Word Set Free: Text and Image in the Russian Futurist Book" analyzes Russian cubo-futurist poets, including Khlebnikov and Kruchonykh; see pages 116–60.

2. Velimir Khlebnikov, "Our Fundamentals," *Collected Works*, vol. I, *Letters and Theoretical Writings*, trans. Paul Schmidt, ed. Charlotte Douglas (Cambridge, Mass.: Harvard University Press, 1987), 377 (hereafter cited as *CW I*).

3. Velimir Khlebnikov, *The King of Time: Selected Writings of the Russian Futurian*, trans. Paul Schmidt (Cambridge, Mass.: Harvard University Press, 1985), 198 (hereafter cited as *KT*).

4. I quote Mayakovsky after Raymond Cooke's book, *Velimir Khlebnikov: A Critical Study* (Cambridge: Cambridge University Press, 1987), 1. For a detailed introduction to Khlebnikov's life and writing, see the first chapter of Cooke's book, "Biography, Discourse," 1–30.

5. A detailed discussion of Russian futurism can be found in Vladimir Markov, *Russian Futurism: A History* (Berkeley: University of California Press, 1968), hereafter cited as *RF*. A short history of Khlebnikov's participation in cubo-futurism and other Russian avant-garde groups is given by Cooke in the first chapter of *Velimir Khlebnikov*. The texts of the two manifestos can be found in *KT*, 119–22.

6. Jean-Claude Lanne, *Velimir Khlebnikov: Poète Futurien*, vol. 1 (Paris: Institut D'Études Slaves, 1983), 58 (hereafter cited as *VK*).

7. Duganov suggests that Khlebnikov locates his favorite number "in the very

basis of all that is imaginable, thinkable, of the 'rational' (умный, also 'speculative') world, including artistic creation"; Rudolf Valentinovich Duganov, Велимир Хлебников: Природа творчества (*Velimir Khlebnikov: Priroda tvorchestva*) (Moscow: Izdatelstvo Sovietskij Pisatel, 1990), 52.

8. Julia Kristeva, *Desire in Language: A Semiotic Approach to Literature and Art,* trans. Gora, Jardine, Roudiez (New York: Columbia University Press, 1980), 32 (hereafter cited as *DL*).

9. Describing the inadequacy of contemporary understanding of language, Khlebnikov complains about the need for a systematic exploration of word creation: "And all because there exists no science of word creation" (*CW I*, 376).

10. Even though the actual authorship of the two texts is still disputed, both Kruchonykh and Khlebnikov signed them. *CW I*, 255–58.

11. Charlotte Douglas, "Introduction" to Khlebnikov, *CW I*, 20.

12. Quoted after Denis Mickiewicz, "Semantic Functions in *Zaum*'," *Russian Literature* 15, no. 4 (1984): 364–65.

13. Denis Mickiewicz, "Semantic Functions in *Zaum*'," 365.

14. Vladimir Markov and Merrill Sparks, eds., *Modern Russian Poetry* (Indianapolis and New York: Bobbs-Merrill Company, 1967), 337.

15. *Modern Russian Poetry,* 337.

16. Martin Heidegger, *Basic Writings,* 2d ed., ed. David Farrell Krell (New York: Harper Collins, 1993), 414 (hereafter cited as *BW*).

17. Martin Heidegger, *Was Heisst Denken?* (Tübingen: Max Niemeyer Verlag, 1961), 89; *What Is Called Thinking?* trans. J. Glenn Gray (San Francisco: Harper and Row, 1968), 130 (hereafter cited as *WCT*).

18. Walter Benjamin, *Reflections,* ed. and into. Peter Demetz (New York: Schocken Books, 1986), 325 (hereafter cited as *R*).

19. For Kristeva, Khlebnikov's extravagant use of alliteration and onomatopoeia, and especially his glossolalia, produces a supplementary meaning to the "normative line of signification," a supplement which is charged with instinctive drives and meaning. Such a linguistic "experimentation" is meaningful in the sense that it forces language to recognize relations in experience which it cannot or does not want to say: "[H]e wants to make language perceive what it doesn't want to say, provide it with its matter independently of the sign, and free it from denotation" (*DL,* 31). Kristeva underscores in this context the subjective sphere of desire and instinctual drives, which "semiotically" disrupt the codified linguistic structures. In Khlebnikov's poetry, the disruptions originate within the shifting contours of experience, in the space prior to the articulation of the split between the subject and the object.

20. Velimir Khlebnikov, *Sobranie sochinenii,* vol. II, reprint of the Moscow Edition 1928–33 (München: W. Fink, 1968–73), 337.

21. I would like to thank Brian Reed for his comments about Plane Ten, his suggestions about the role of magic in Khlebnikov's poetics, and for drawing my

attention to Kristeva's brief but incisive reading of Khlebnikov in *Desire in Language*.

22. Max Horkheimer and Theodor W. Adorno, *Dialectic of Enlightenment*, trans. John Cumming (New York: Continuum, 1993), 12.

23. Adorno and Horkheimer's remarks about myth and the Enlightenment provide probably the best context for discussing the intersection in Khlebnikov's texts of fascination with technology with an extensive use of magic and of pagan and Asian mythologies. Is magic and myth an escape route from the rationalization and disenchantment of life in modernity, or is there a recognition in Khlebnikov, albeit "unconscious" and untheorized, that science as a panacea for modern reality approaches the status of magic? *Dialectic of Enlightenment* argues that the Enlightenment sought in vain to evacuate magic and myth, and that, in the all-inclusive reach of the repetitive formalism of scientific classification and technological and economic efficiency, it "returns to mythology, which it never really knew how to elude" (27). If *zaum* is a "poetic" extension of science to devise "ultimate" laws of history, then Khlebnikov's interest in magic can be seen as integral to that pursuit: Poetry becomes the space in which science fulfills its "myth" of becoming the "true" answer to the riddle of being.

24. Derrida and Nancy have made amply evident the ethical and political implications of thinking experience on the model of a disjunctive event, irreducible to its signification. The notion of "a disjointed or disadjusted now, 'out of joint,'" frames Derrida's discussion of Marx's "spectrology" and the "spectral," disjointed phenomenality of being in *Specters of Marx: The State of the Debt, the Work of Mourning, and the New International,* trans. Peggy Kamuf (New York and London: Routledge, 1994), 3 (hereafter cited as *SM*). This disjunction inscribed in the present opens it to alterity and the future, marking the now with a debt to an otherness it has no way of knowing or predicting. The ethical and political stakes of this conceptualization of the event become evident in Derrida's discussion of Fukuyama's conception of history. Similarly, Nancy casts his description of being as freedom in terms of the inappropriable and singular contour of the event—its "excessive" happening; *The Experience of Freedom,* trans. Bridget McDonald (Stanford: Stanford University Press, 1993).

25. Duganov, *Velimir Khlebnikov,* 10.

26. For a detailed history of various trends and developments in Russian futurism, belying the apparent aesthetic and political unity of the movement, see Markov's *Russian Futurism.* The Hyleans or the cubo-futurist group concentrated around David Burliuk, Mayakovsky, Khlebnikov, and Kruchonykh constitute what is certainly the most interesting among various futurist orientations, one that gave rise to significant poetic and literary work.

27. For a detailed discussion of the context and the personal and artistic conflicts surrounding Marinetti's visit to Russia, see Markov, *Russian Futurism,* 147–63.

28. This fragment comes from the leaflet signed jointly by Khlebnikov and Benedikt Livshits; quoted after Markov, *Russian Futurism,* 151.

29. Markov discusses the role this group played in the developments of futurism in Russia in *Russian Futurism,* 303–5.

30. Duganov characterizes Khlebnikov's notion of *priroda* in terms of the verbs or words of nature *(glagoly prirody); Velimir Khlebnikov,* 10.

31. For Kristeva, the language of futurist poems produces the permeability and alterability of the linguistic and social limits: "[W]hat is implied is that language, and thus sociability, are defined by boundaries admitting of upheaval, dissolution, and transformation"; *DL,* 25.

32. I emphasize this sense of uncontrollable futurity of the beyonsense language, evident especially in *Zangezi,* to juxtapose it with the magisterial streak in Khlebnikov's work, where *zaum* is often spoken by an authority: gods, teachers, prophets. Khlebnikov associates *zaum* with pedagogical authority, capable of controlling and explaining beyonsense through quasi-scientific or poetic formulas. As "King of Time," the poet assumes a whole gamut of magisterial roles: a futurist prophet, a scientist, a historian, and, at times, a magician. Politically, this position resembles the elitism characteristic of many modernist figures, investing the poet with access to truth and cultural, if not directly political, authority. Without playing down the importance of these prophetic roles in Khlebnikov's work, I want to suggest that they coalesce, only to become ironized, in the figure of the prophet/fool Zangezi, in his precarious balancing between *zaum* and *neum*. Zangezi opens the door to the contestation of the pedagogical pose Khlebnikov often assumes by underscoring the futurity marked in the present. The irreducibility of the event in the end precludes the closure of beyonsense even within a revised representational space and questions its compression into a set of rules for history and language. To translate the event into norms and "alphabetic verities"—signs generalized beyond the boundaries of a single language—could be a mark of *neum,* that is, of rendering history "senseless," of emptying it of beyonsense through the hypergeneralization of laws concerning the alternative, nonnormative lines of signification. My thanks here again to Brian Reed for his helpful comments.

33. Khlebnikov invents the terms *budetlyanstvo* and *budetlyanin* (futurian) from the phrase *budet,* "it will be."

Chapter 6

1. To my knowledge, there exist only two book-length translations of Białoszewski's work into English, a volume of early poems, *The Revolution of Things,* trans. Busza and Czaykowski (Washington, D.C.: Charioteer Press, 1974), and the rendering of *A Memoir of Warsaw Uprising,* ed. and trans. Madeline Levine (Ann

Arbor, Mich.: Ardis, 1977), reprinted Evanston: Northwestern University Press, 1991 (hereafter cited as *RT* and *MWU*). Occasional translations of a few poems are dispersed through anthologies of Polish or Eastern European poetry. One could claim as a cause of this absence the extraordinary, both linguistic and cultural difficulty and "resistance" to translation of Białoszewski's work, at least of his poetry if not of the prose pieces, but this argument is quickly countered by the proliferating translations of such "untranslatable" poets as, for example, Mallarmé or Celan.

2. David Antin's talk poetry and some of Stein's texts, with their emphasis on ordinary events and objects or on domesticity, come close, in spite of their very different idioms, to Białoszewski's poetics. Białoszewski goes further than any other writer in inventing words and rewriting the idiom of poetry through ordinary language, colloquialisms, and even grammatically incorrect or nonstandard expressions and inflections.

3. Quoted after Helena Zaworska, *"Spiszę wszystko," Twórczoć* 33, no. 5 (1977): 101.

4. Stanisław Barańczak, *"Człowiek bezbronny (O Pamiętniku z powstania warszawskiego, Mirona Białoszewskiego"* in *Literatura wobec wojny i okupacji,* ed. M. Głowiński and J. Sławiński (Wrocław: Zakład Narodowy im. Ossolińskich, 1976), 300.

5. I treat this problem in Heidegger's work, especially in the context of Habermas's attack on what he envisions as the aestheticist esoterism of Heidegger's poetic thinking, in "The Ethos of Everydayness: Heidegger on Poetry and Language," *Man and World* 28, no. 4 (1995): 377–99.

6. Here Białoszewski succeeds more than Beckett, whose stark and intense prose retains, perhaps intentionally, vestiges of pathos. Białoszewski's fascination with the surprising alterity that breaks through the routine facade of the ordinary has a very different tonality from Blanchot's often obsessive, sometimes rhetorically inflated, tracing of the otherness of things, persons, and events.

7. Madeline G. Levine's essay, "Fragments of Life: Miron Białoszewski's Poetic Vision," provides a good discussion of Białoszewski's writings from 1956 into 1970s; *Slavic and Eastern European Journal* 20 (1976): 40–49. Another English-language publication, a translation of Artur Sandauer's long essay, "Junk Poetry," can be found in Sandauer, *Białoszewski,* trans. Adam Czerniawski (Warsaw: Authors Agency and Czytelnik, 1979), 29–76.

8. See Michał Głowiński, *"Białoszewskiego gatunki codzienne," Pisanie Białoszewskiego,* ed. Głowiński and Sławiński (Warszawa: Wydawnictwo IBL, 1993), 144 (hereafter cited as *PB*).

9. This very important volume of essays on Białoszewski by foremost scholars of contemporary Polish literature appears to be intended precisely as a testimony to an alternative poetic tradition in post-Second World War Polish poetry; *Pisanie Białoszewskiego* (Warszawa: Wydawnictwo IBL, 1993).

10. For a brief discussion of Białoszewski in the context of Polish language poetry, see Tadeusz Nyczek, *"Mówić wprost," Miesięcznik literacki* 17, no. 4: 45–47. The best example of a thorough analysis of the language of Białoszewski's writings is Stanisław Barańczak's study, *Język poetycki Mirona Białoszewskiego* (Wrocław: Zakład Narodowy im. Ossolińskich, 1974). Barańczak focuses on the prenormative, "substandard" level on which Białoszewski's language operates. This is a level of language "below" the criteria of normal linguistic usage, which constitutes the "degree zero" of language and serves as the initial field of poetry. Burkot, on the other hand, suggests that Białoszewski's poetry does not so much register substandard linguistic forms and expressions as it consciously constructs an idiom that deforms and breaks linguistic rules; Burkot, *Miron Białoszewski* (Warszawa: Wydawnictwa Szkolne i Pedagogiczne, 1992), 62 (hereafter cited as *MB*).

11. This connection between banality and deformation of reality, on the one hand, and the experience of the Second World War, on the other, is discussed by Madeline G. Levine in "Fragments of Life," 40–49. Levine provides a little summary of the critical deliberations about the influence of war on Białoszewski's poetic experiments, 45–46.

12. Gilles Deleuze and Félix Guattari, *Kafka: Toward a Minor Literature,* trans. Dana Polan (Minneapolis: University of Minnesota Press, 1986), 16.

13. Deleuze and Guattari discuss the tensors and intensives at length, especially on pages 22 to 23.

14. The term "little narratives," describing Białoszewski's short prosaic forms was introduced by Michał Głowiński in his essay *"Małe narracje Mirona Białoszewskiego," Teksty* 1, no. 2 (1972): 10–28.

15. *"Szacunek dla każdego drobiazgu"* ("Respect for Every Detail"), an interview of Z. Taranienko with Miron Białoszewski, *Argumenty* no. 36 (1971); my translation. Unless otherwise noted, translations of Białoszewski's work are mine. One note of explanation is necessary. Writing about Białoszewski in English entails a conscious "compromise" of the inventiveness of his poetic texts. They depend, often entirely, upon word creation, frequently based upon colloquialisms, grammatical and semantic dislocations, or "mistakes." What makes them even more difficult to translate is their use of substandard regions of everyday language and diverse cultural registers, often strikingly different from normative culture. Unlike Herbert or Zagajewski, who write in a "universal" and "cultured" poetic language, recognizable across cultural divides, Białoszewski descends in his writing into subtle and untranslatable minutiae of cultural and "folk" lore, which provide much of the parodic and iconoclastic energy of his texts.

16. See Martin Heidegger, *Sein und Zeit* (Tübingen: Max Niemeyer Verlag, 1976), 167–68.

17. I quote this story after Martin Heidegger, whose commentary in "Letter on Humanism" on Heraclitus's remark about the connection between the ordinary

and the gods is of particular importance in understanding Białoszewski's poetics of "wondering the ordinary." See Martin Heidegger, *Wegmarken* (Frankfurt am Main: Vittorio Klostermann, 1967), 185, and *Basic Writings*, 2d ed., ed. David Farrell Krell (New York: Harper Collins, 1993), 256 (hereafter cited as *W* and *BW*).

18. The German phrases are quoted from *"Brief über den 'Humanismus'"* as it appeared in *W,* 351–52.

19. Aristotle, *Aristotle's Metaphysics,* intro. and commentary, W. D. Ross (Oxford: Clarendon Press, 1988), English translation from *The Complete Works of Aristotle Vol. 2,* ed. Jonathan Barnes (Princeton: Princeton University Press, 1984), 1554.

20. A little later, *Metaphysics* specifies that the wonder pertains to the manner in which things exist: "For all men begin, as we said, by wondering that the matter is so" (1555). Θαυμάζειν, then, describes the relationship of the human mind to the fact of existence or being: It characterizes the way in which human beings respond to things as they are, to the phenomenon of their being.

21. The fact that the story refers to the visitors as "strangers" or "foreigners" (ξένοι) underscores this precarious relation between wonder and knowledge: It not only means that they come from a foreign land or another πόλις, but that, because of their incomprehension of the wonder of the everyday, they are strangers to thinking as Heraclitus understands it. Expecting from philosophy a systematic inquiry that achieves the "better state" of knowledge, the visitors are foreigners to the thought that wonders about the everyday and the mundane, where "gods are present" even by a stove which becomes worthy of thinking, of φιλοσοφεῖν, even if such thinking does not yield anything that meets the criteria of knowledge.

22. The title is slightly modified from the one given by Busza and Czaykowski in *The Revolution of Things* to correspond exactly to the Polish title: *"'Ach, gdyby, gdyby nawet piec zabrali . . .' Moja niewyczerpana oda do radości."* The translation, unchanged, is quoted from this volume. The text in the original can be found in *Utwory zebrane,* vol. 1, *Obroty rzeczy, Rachunek zachciankowy, Mylne wzruszenia, Było i było* (Warszawa: Państwowy Instytut Wydawniczy, 1987), 116 (hereafter cited as *UZ I*). For a detailed discussion of the poem and its ironic relation to the poetic tradition, see Irena Urbaniak, *"Trwalsze od spiżu," O wierszach Mirona Białoszewskiego: Szkice i interpretacje,* ed. Jacek Brzozowski (Łódz: Oficyna Bibliofilów, 1993), 36–44.

23. The original phrase *"szaranagajama"* is stylized, with a good deal of self-irony about linguistic stereotypes, as "Japanese." Urbaniak argues that this phrase evokes the Eastern wisdom about the necessity of renouncing our attachment to material things, underscored in the poem by the figure of the poet left only with words. *"Trwalsze od spiżu,"* 43–44.

24. Białoszewski's use of the word "ode" in this context turns into "a polemic with the literary and cultural traditions" that see an ode as an elevated, lofty poetic form. Urbaniak, *"Trwalsze od spiżu,"* 39.

25. The Polish text reads as follows:

> *Nie jestem godzien, ściano,*
> *abyś mię ciągle syciła zdumieniem . . .*
> *to samo—ty—widelcze . . .*
> *to samo—wy—kurze . . .*
>
> (*UZ I,* 71)

26. In Polish the passage reads:

> *Tak*
>
> *w mojej pustelni kusi:*
> *samotność*
> *pamięć świata*
> *i to, że mam się za poetę.*
>
> *Dziwię się*
> *i dziwię siebie,*
> *i komentuję wciąż żywoty otoczenia.*
>
> (*UZ I,* 71)

27. The Polish texts reads:

> *Włóż, włóżcie papierowe kwiaty do czajników,*
> *pociągajcie za sznury od bielizny*
> *i za dzwony butów*
> *na odpust poezji*
> *na nieustanne uroczyste zdziwienie . . . !*
>
> (*UZ I,* 72)

28. It is in this specific sense that Heidegger writes about building as related to the thinking that takes the form of letting-dwell: "Building thus characterized is a distinctive letting-dwell." Heidegger, "Building, Dwelling, Thinking," *Poetry, Language, Thought,* trans. Albert Hofstadter (San Francisco: Harper and Row, 1971), 159.

29. Burkot begins his study with a detailed discussion of Białoszewski's ambivalent relationship to the avant-garde, in which he specifies the various points where Białoszewski critiques avant-garde writing; Stanisław Burkot, *Miron Białoszewski,* 21.

30. Jarosław Anders, "Unsentimental Journey," *New Republic,* 12 Dec. 1994, 34.

31. Zbigniew Bauer, *"Powrót czy ucieczka? (W stronę prozy),"* *Poezja* 2 (1976): 46.

32. *"Ballada o zejściu do sklepu," UZ I,* 120.

33. This grotesque optics is discussed by Jacek Brzozowski in *"Budujące zejście do sklepu," O wierszach Mirona Białoszewskiego,* 51 and 57. For Brzozowski, the form of this poem suggests that Białoszewski's poetry assumes this optics as the basis of its textuality.

34. Brzozowski shows that the epilogue of the poem does not lead us back to

the apartment, since that would be stating the obvious, a tautology. The emphatic "And truly, / truly / I returned" carries more weight, as it underscores the perceptual transformation in the poem. See *"Budujące zejście do sklepu,"* 55–56.

35. The text in Polish reads: *"A potem— była słynna późna i piękna Wielkanoc 1943. Aryjczycy— tak zwani jeszcze wtedy my— po kościołach— odświętni— a tam— to piekło —to wiadome, tylko bez nadziei. . . . Tak teraz my byliśmy tymi odciętymi, niepodziwianymi. Przynajmniej z nadzieją frontu,"* Pamiętnik z powstania warszawskiego, Utwory zebrane III (Warszawa: Państwowy Instytut Wydawniczy, 1988), 80–81.

36. In fact, Lewandowski suggests that Białoszewski was a poet of the Holocaust, in the sense that his interest in the intersection of the peripheral and the culturally central was marked by the border between the "Aryan" and the Jewish cultures. Białoszewski's destabilized world without foundations, full of erratic movement and flying around *(latanie)*, reflects the post-Holocaust space-time of experience; Wacław Lewandowski, *"Stacja: żydzi do mnie!"* in *Pisanie Białoszewskiego,* 60–61.

37. There is obviously not enough room here for an exhaustive discussion of Białoszewski's use of language or even for a summary of the existing critical discussions of it. Stanisław Barańczak's *Język poetycki Mirona Białoszewskiego* provides an admirable and comprehensive diagnosis of the peculiarities and innovations of Białoszewski's language, their motivations and their various symptoms, in particular, the prolix coining of new words and idiomatic expressions. Classifying and systematizing the variety of uses to which Białoszewski's texts put language, Barańczak discovers three major matrices of rules that map and govern this linguistic play: children's language, spoken language, and colloquial language. He argues that Białoszewski borrows from the reservoirs of language so far unexplored by poetry in order to compromise poetic conventions, attack the accepted systems of valuation and interpretation of literary texts, and challenge the limits of literature. The first part of Barańczak's careful analysis discerns the mechanism through which Białoszewski uses the logic underlying children's linguistic mistakes to dislodge the "adult" forms of language (40–42), in particular their proclivity toward overgeneralization and displacements in the application of linguistic rules (49), the creation of new words (44–45), and finally the various forms of delexicalization, that is, the segmentation and playful use of words, phrases, proverbs, and sayings, specifically those types of utterances which tend to remain unchanged and precisely resist most strongly any attempts at decomposition or transformation (54–61). In the second part, the book shows how Białoszewski's use of the spoken language and the transfer of its characteristics into writing (for example, intonation, the phonic gesture, emphasis, and so on [122]) allows for a better means of presenting reality in a work of literature (125). The last part explores the influence of colloquial language upon Białoszewski's work and the way it motivates the opposition between the cultural center and its margins and peripheries. While Barańczak's book provides a

concise taxonomy of Białoszewski's linguistic strategies and the way they affect our understanding of the poetic use of language, my reading concerns itself primarily with the motivation and stakes behind Białoszewski's language innovations and "monstrosities." Barańczak's study thus remains constantly in the background, providing some of the guidelines for classifying and interpreting Białoszewski's poetic language.

38. Burkot discusses this problem in greater detail; see *MB*, 60–69.

39. See *Język poetycki Mirona Białoszewskiego*, 140.

40. For a brief discussion of this aspect of Białoszewski's poetry see Barańczak, 165.

41. "—*[B]iałe konie / — bryka/ — czarne konie / — bryka / — rude konie / — bryka / — Magnifikat!*" (*UZ I*, 38).

42. This explains why the proclamation of his own "philosophy" as a critique of high culture takes place in "The Philosophy of Wołomin" from the vantage point of the little town of Wołomin rather than Warsaw, where Białoszewski lived his entire life. I should mention here that both "The Philosophy of Wołomin" and "A Merry-go-round with Madonnas" are included in a cycle of poems symptomatically entitled *"Ballady peryferyjne"*—"Peripheral Ballads."

43. Białoszewski, *Moja świadomość tańczy* (Warszawa: Młodzieżowa Agencja Wydawnicza, 1989), 218 (hereafter cited as *MŚT*).

44. Lewandowski suggests instead that it was the Holocaust, especially the Ghetto uprising of 1943, that had the most important impact upon Białoszewski's sense of reality without foundations; Lewandowski, *"Stacja: żydzi do mnie!" PB,* 54–55.

45. Maria Janion, *"Polska proza cywilna,"* 257.

46. Maria Janion, *"Wojna i forma,"* in *Literatura wobec wojny i okupacji* (Wrocław: Ossolineum, 1976), 232–36. Lewandowski links *latanie* in the *Memoir* with the image of running and hurrying feet observed by Białoszewski in the Paris metro and with the scene, recounted to him by his Paris guide, in which a Polish Jew lost in the Paris metro calls out in Polish for help to his fellow Jews: "Jews, come to me!" *("żydzi do mnie!")* and is immediately helped out by someone who understands his cry. Through these multiple references Lewandowski sees *latanie* as an icon of post-Holocaust modernity, which reflects the fears present in the new archetype of the collective unconscious, that is, the fears of mass relocation and murder, evoked by the image of a mass of shoes, one of the characteristic signs of extermination camps. As Lewandowski observes, in the metro scene the only descriptive element of the "hurrying" masses are the shoes, their soles, visible from below through the rungs: "The entire description of the persons who constitute the crowd in the corridor— in the relocation—has been reduced to shoes" (my translation); Lewandowski, *"Stacja: żydzi do mnie!"* 49.

47. "A chronicler who recites events without distinguishing between major and

minor ones acts in accordance with the following truth: nothing that has ever happened should be regarded as lost for history"; Benjamin, "Theses on the Philosophy of History," *Illuminations* (New York: Schocken, 1969), 254.

48. Białoszewski, *MśT,* 216–17.

49. For Cavell's discussion of Emerson and Thoreau in the "neighborhood" of Heidegger, see especially *In Quest of the Ordinary: Lines of Skepticism and Romanticism* (Chicago: University of Chicago Press, 1988).

50. These moments of "poetic" solemnity explain, for example, Habermas's impatience with Heidegger's writing on poetry, although Habermas, in his rash judgment, fundamentally misreads the role that poetry plays in Heidegger's critique of technology.

51. Miron Białoszewski, *Utwory zebrane,* vol. 7, *"Odczepić się" i inne wiersze* (Warszawa: Państwowy Instytut Wydawniczy, 1994), 102; my translation (hereafter cited as *UZ VII*).

52. Other favorite expressions Białoszewski invents to describe the modern conditions of mass dwelling are *"latarnia"* (lighthouse) and *"ilościowiec"* (multirise). See *UZ VII, 65–66.*

53. *"Moje nowe miejsce"*: *"Miasto się odrąbało. // Ja wywindowany. / Na dziewiąte"* (*UZ VII,* 38).

54. *"Nie zabłądzcie. // Bądzcie. // Mijajcie, mijajmy się, / ale nie ominmy. // Minmy. // My! / Wy! Co latacie / i jesteście popychani!" UZ* VII, 66

55. *"Rozmowa Leszka Elektorowicza z Mironem Białoszewskim,"* in Burkot, *MB,* 140.

56. Głowiński, *"Białoszewskiego gatumki codzienne,"* in *PB,* 144–51.

57. This is a phrase employed by Artur Sandauer to characterize Białoszewski's use of words and its tendency to push words to their limit, to the point of breaking open. Białoszewski mentions the remark in *"Mówienie o pisaniu,"* in Burkot, *MB,* 144.

Chapter 7

1. "Collision or Collusion with history" is a line from one of the poems in "Articulation of Sound Forms in Time," *Singularities* (Hanover and London: Wesleyan University Press, 1990), 33 (hereafter cited as *S*). Marjorie Perloff discusses the linguistic play and the critical operation upon history signaled by it in her " 'Collision or Collusion with History': The Narrative Lyric of Susan Howe," *Contemporary Literature* 30, no. 4 (1989): 518–33 (hereafter cited as "CC"). Perloff suggests that Howe's texts explore "the collisions (and sometimes, it may be, collusions) of three codes—the historical, the mythic, the linguistic—all three, it should be added, as informed by an urgent, if highly individual, feminist perspective" (520).

2. *Talisman* interview, with Edward Foster, in Susan Howe, *The Birth-Mark:*

Unsettling the Wilderness in American Literary History (Hanover and London: Wesleyan University Press, 1993), 158 (*Birth-Mark* is hereafter cited as *BM*).

3. Susan Howe, *The Nonconformist's Memorial* (New York: New Directions, 1993), 15 (hereafter cited as *NM*).

4. "The Difficulties Interview," *Difficulties* 3, no. 2 (1989): 20.

5. Perloff ("Collision or Collusion with History"), DuPlessis (*The Pink Guitar: Writing as Feminist Practice* [New York: Routledge, 1990]), Quartermain (*Disjunctive Poetics: From Gertrude Stein and Louis Zukofsky to Susan Howe* [Cambridge: Cambridge University Press, 1992]), and Ma ("Poetry as History Revised: Susan Howe's 'Scattering as Behavior Toward Risk,'" *American Literary History* 6, no. 4 [1994]: 717–18) all comment on the double optics of Howe's work, its stance both inside the historical space she revisits and outside the hegemonic, patriarchal discourse that has produced it.

6. For Ma Howe's poems "subpoena history for an investigation of its violent crime against women," "Poetry as History Revisited," 718.

7. "Statement for the New Poetics Colloquium, Vancouver 1985," *Jimmy and Lucy's House of "K"* 5 (1985): 15.

8. Walter Benjamin, *Illuminations,* ed. Hannah Arendt (New York: Schocken, 1969), 256.

9. Perloff discusses the section from which those lines come at some length in "'Collision or Collusion with History,'" developing the map of semantic and syntactical allusions suggested by the passage; see pages 525–26.

10. Susan Howe, *The Europe of Trusts* (Los Angeles: Sun & Moon Press, 1990), 90–96 (hereafter cited as *ET*).

11. Walter Benjamin, *The Arcades Project,* trans. Howard Eiland and Kevin McLaughlin (Cambridge, Mass., and London: Belknap Press of Harvard University Press, 1999), 462–63.

12. Quartermain, *Disjunctive Poetics,* 187.

13. Martin Heidegger, *Hölderlins Hymne "Der Ister"* (*Gesamtausgabe,* vol. 53; Frankfurt am Main: Klostermann, 1984), 100–1. *Hölderlin's Hymn "The Ister,"* trans. William McNeill and Julia Davis (Bloomington and Indianapolis: University of Indiana Press, 1996), 81.

14. Luce Irigaray, *An Ethics of Sexual Difference,* trans. Carolyn Burke and Gillian C. Gill (Ithaca: Cornell University Press, 1993), 5.

15. Susan Howe, *My Emily Dickinson* (Berkeley: North Atlantic, 1985), 11–12.

16. Rachel Blau DuPlessis, "For the Etruscans," *The New Feminist Criticism: Essays on Women, Literature, Theory,* ed. Elaine Showalter (New York: Pantheon, 1985), 276 (hereafter cited as "FE").

17. Obviously a departure from the monological criteria of legibility and endorsement of the multiple character of textuality is in itself not equivalent to the reinscription of sexual difference. Patriarchal, "male," modernist avant-garde can be read along such lines and, at the same time, diagnosed as specifically reinforc-

ing the erasure of sexual difference from the "standards" of experience. Misogynist proclamations by many avant-garde artists, reflected in their artistic or literary practice, indeed illustrate well Irigaray's claims about the simultaneous sexualization of experience—designating the unacknowledged or undesirable as "feminine"—and its desexualization as necessary for the production of a generalizable, even universal, economy of experience. They can also be read, as Alice Jardine suggests, as instances of (male) appropriation of the feminine in order to revitalize art in modernism without explicitly critiquing the "sexual" economy of experience.

18. Luce Irigaray, *This Sex Which Is Not One*, trans. Catherine Porter (Ithaca: Cornell University Press, 1985), 207.

19. Jean-Luc Nancy, *The Experience of Freedom*, trans. Bridget McDonald (Stanford: Stanford University Press, 1993), 57 (hereafter cited as *EF*).

20. When Nancy refers to what "weighs" thought, he plays on the similarity in French between *penser* and *peser*, indicating that the other, inappropriable current in thought is what motivates, what "weighs" it; see page 59.

21. Max Horkheimer and Theodor W. Adorno, *Dialectic of Enlightenment*, trans. John Cumming (New York: Continuum, 1993), 134.

22. Lyotard's idea that avant-garde art concerns itself with the "here and now" of the happening of everyday experience, that is, with the insistently reposed question "Is it happening?" underscores precisely the elusive and inappropriable newness of each burst of experience: "Newman's *now* which is no more than *now* is a stranger to consciousness and cannot be constituted by it." The question mark delivered each time as an event or occurrence marks the new of experience. See Lyotard, "The Sublime and the Avant-Garde," in *The Lyotard Reader*, ed. Andrew Benjamin (Oxford: Basil Blackwell, 1989), 197.

Afterword

1. Martin Heidegger, "The Way to Language"; *Basic Writings*, 2d ed., ed., trans., and intro. David Farrell Krell (New York: Harper Collins, 1993), 424–25.

2. "*Hegels Negativität ist keine, weil sie mit dem Nicht und Nichten nie ernst macht,—das Nicht schon im das 'Ja' aufgehoben hat*"; Hegel, *Gesamtausgabe*, vol. 68 (Frankfurt am Main: Vittorio Klostermann, 1993), 47.

3. Irigaray, *I Love to You*, trans. Alison Martin (New York and London: Routledge, 1996); *Être deux* (Paris: Grasset, 1997).

Bibliography

Abelove, Henry, Michèle Aina Barale, and David M. Halperin, eds. *The Lesbian and Gay Studies Reader.* New York and London: Routledge, 1993.

Adorno, Theodor W. *Aesthetic Theory.* Translated by Robert Hullot-Kentor. Minneapolis: University of Minnesota Press, 1997.

Anders, Jarosław. "Unsentimental Journey." *New Republic,* 12 December 1994, 34.

Aristotle. *The Complete Works of Aristotle Vol. 2,* ed. Jonathan Barnes. Princeton: Princeton University Press, 1984.

———. *Aristotle's Metaphysics.* Intro. and commentary W. D. Ross. Oxford: Clarendon Press, 1988.

Ashberry, John. "The Impossible." In *Critical Essays on Gertrude Stein,* edited by Michael Hoffman, 104–7. Boston: G. K. Hall, 1986.

Bahti, Timothy. "History as Rhetorical Enactment: Walter Benjamin's Theses 'On the Concept of History.' " *Diacritics* 9, no. 3 (1979): 217.

Barańczak, Stanisław. *"Człowiek bezbronny: O Pamiętniku z powstania warszawskiego."* In *Literatura wobec wojny i okupacji,* edited by M. Głowiński and J. Sławiński. Wrocław: Zakład Narodowy im. Ossolińskich, 1976.

———. *Język poetycki Mirona Białoszewskiego.* Wrocław: Zakład Narodowy im. Ossolińskich, 1974.

Bauer, Zbigniew. *"Powrót czy ucieczka? (W stronę prozy)."* *Poezja* 2 (1976).

Benjamin, Walter. *Illuminations.* Edited by Hannah Arendt. New York: Schocken, 1969.

———. *The Origin of German Tragic Drama.* Trans. John Osborne. London: NLB, 1977.

———. *Reflections.* Ed. Peter Demetz. New York: Schocken, 1986.

———. *Gesammelte Schriften.* Vol. 2, part 1. Frankfurt am Main: Suhrkamp, 1991.

———. *The Arcades Project,* trans. Howard Eiland and Kevin McLaughlin. Cambridge, Mass., and London: Belknap Press of Harvard University Press, 1999.

Berg, Maggie. "Escaping the Cave: Luce Irigaray and Her Feminist Critics." In *Literature and Ethics,* edited by Gary Wihl and David Williams, 62–76. Kingston, Montreal: McGill Queen's University Press, 1988.

Bernasconi, Robert. *Heidegger in Question: The Art of Existing.* Atlantic Highlands, N.J.: Humanities Press, 1993.

Bernstein, J. M. *The Fate of Art: Aesthetic Alienation from Kant to Derrida and Adorno.* University Park: University of Pennsylvania Press, 1992.

Berry, Ellen E. *Curved Thought and Textual Wandering: Gertrude Stein's Postmodernism.* Ann Arbor: University of Michigan Press, 1992.

Białoszewski, Miron. *"Szacunek dla każdego drobiazgu." Argumenty* 36 (1971).

———. *The Revolution of Things*. Translated by Busza and Czaykowski. Washington, D.C.: Charioteer Press, 1974.

———. *A Memoir of the Warsaw Uprising*. Edited and translated by Madelin Levine. Ann Arbor, Mich.: Ardis, 1977.

———. *Utwory zebrane*. Vol. 1. *Obroty rzeczy, Rachunek zachciankowy, Mylne wzruszenia, Było i byto*. Warszawa: Państwowy Instytut Wydawniczy, 1987.

———. *Utwory zebrane. Pamiętnik z powstania warszawskiego*, Vol. 3. Warszawa: Państwowy Instytut Wydawniczy, 1988.

———. *Moja świadomość tańczy*. Warszawa: Młodzieżowa Agencja Wydawnicza, 1989.

———. *Utwory zebrane. "Odczepić się" i inne wiersze*. Vol. 7. Warszawa: Państwowy Instytut Wydawniczy, 1994.

Bowers, Jane Palatini. *"They Watch Me As They Watch This": Gertrude Stein's Metadrama*. Philadelphia: University of Pennsylvania Press, 1991.

Brzozowski, Jacek, ed. *O wierszach Mirona Białoszewskiego*. Łódź: Oficyna Bibliofilów, 1993.

Bürger, Peter. *Theory of the Avant-Garde*. Translated by Michael Shaw. Minneapolis: University of Minnesota Press, 1984.

Burke, Carolyn. "Irigaray Through the Looking Glass." *Feminist Studies* 7, no. 2 (1981): 288–306.

Burke, Carolyn, Naomi Schor, and Margaret Whitford, eds. *Engaging with Irigaray: Feminist Philosophy and Modern European Thought*. New York: Columbia University Press, 1994.

Burkot, Stanisław. *Miron Białoszewski*. Warszawa: Wydawnictwa Szkolne i Pedagogiczne, 1992.

Butler, Judith. *Bodies that Matter: On the Discursive Limits of "Sex."* New York: Routledge, 1993.

Butler, Judith, and Joan W. Scott. *Feminists Theorize the Political*. New York and London: Routledge, 1992.

Byrd, Don. *The Poetics of the Common Knowledge*. Albany: State University of New York Press, 1994.

Cadava, Eduardo. "Words of Light: Theses on the Photography of History." *Diacritics* 22, nos. 3–4 (1992): 84–114.

Carroll, David. *Paraesthetics: Foucault, Lyotard, and Derrida*. New York: Methuen, 1987.

Castoriadis, Cornelius. *The Imaginary Institution of Society*. Translated by Kathleen Blamey. Cambridge, Mass.: MIT Press, 1987.

Cavell, Stanley. *In Quest of the Ordinary: Lines of Skepticism and Romanticism*. Chicago: University of Chicago Press, 1988.

Chanter, Tina. *Ethics of Eros: Irigaray's Rewriting of the Philosophers*. New York: Routledge, 1995.

Chessman, Harriet Scott. *The Public Is Invited to Dance: Representation, the Body, and Dialogue in Gertrude Stein.* Stanford: Stanford University Press, 1989.

Comay, Rebecca. "Framing Redemption: Aura, Origin, Technology in Benjamin and Heidegger." In *Ethics and Danger: Essays on Heidegger and Continental Thought,* edited by Arleen B. Dallery and Charles E. Scott, 139–67. Albany: State University of New York Press, 1992.

Cooke, Raymond. *Velimir Khlebnikov: A Critical Study.* Cambridge: Cambridge University Press, 1987.

Cope, Karin. "'Moral Deviancy' and Contemporary Feminism: The Judgment of Gertrude Stein." In *Feminism Beside Itself,* edited by Diane Elam and Robyn Wiegman, 155–78. New York and London: Routledge, 1995.

Dallmayr, Fred. *The Other Heidegger.* Ithaca and London: Cornell University Press, 1993.

DeKoven, Marianne. *A Different Language: Gertrude Stein's Experimental Writing.* Madison: University of Wisconsin Press, 1983.

Deleuze, Gilles, and Félix Guattari. *Kafka: Toward a Minor Literature.* Translated by Dana Polan. Minneapolis: University of Minnesota Press, 1986.

Derrida, Jacques. *Spectres de Marx.* Paris: Galilée, 1993.

———. "Shibboleth: For Paul Celan." Translated by Joshua Wilner. In *Word Traces: Readings of Paul Celan,* edited by Aris Fioretos, 3–72. Baltimore and London: Johns Hopkins University Press, 1994.

———. *Specters of Marx: The State of Debt, the Work of Mourning, and the New International.* Translated by Peggy Kamuf. New York and London: Routledge, 1994.

Doane, Mary Ann. *The Desire to Desire: The Woman's Film of the 1940s.* Bloomington: Indiana University Press, 1987.

Docherty, Thomas, ed. *Postmodernism: A Reader.* New York: Columbia University Press, 1993.

Duganov, Rudolf Valentinovich. Велимир Хлебников: Природа творчества [*Velimir Khlebnikov: Priroda tvorchestva*]. Moscow: Izdatelstvo Sovietskij Pisatel, 1990.

DuPlessis, Rachel Blau. "For the Etruscans." In *New Feminist Criticism: Essays on Women, Literature, and Theory,* edited by Elaine Showalter. New York: Pantheon Books, 1985.

———. *The Pink Guitar: Writing as Feminist Practice.* New York: Routledge, 1990.

Fauré, Christine. "The Twilight of the Goddesses or the Intellectual Crisis of French Feminism." *Signs* 7 (1981): 81–86.

Ferry, Luc. *Homo Aestheticus: The Invention of Taste in the Democratic Age.* Chicago: University of Chicago Press, 1993.

Foucault, Michel. *The Order of Things: An Archeology of the Human Sciences,* unidentified collective translation. New York: Random House, 1970.

Fraser, Nancy. "Introduction." In *Revaluing French Feminism: Critical Essays on Difference, Agency, and Culture,* edited by Nancy Fraser and Sandra Lee Bartky, 1–24. Bloomington: Indiana University Press, 1992.

Fuss, Diana. "Luce Irigaray's Language of Essence." *Essentially Speaking.* New York: Routledge, 1989.

Fynsk, Christopher. "The Claim of History." *Diacritics* 22, nos. 3–4 (1992): 115–26.

———. *Heidegger: Thought and Historicity.* Ithaca, N.Y.: Cornell University Press, 1993.

Gallop, Jane. "*Quand Nos Lèvres S'Ecrivent:* Irigaray's Body Politic." *The Romanic Review* 74 (1983): 77–83. Rpt. in *Thinking Through the Body,* 92–100.

———. *Thinking Through the Body.* New York: Columbia University Press, 1988.

Gasché, Rodolphe. "Saturnine Vision and the Question of Difference: Reflections on Walter Benjamin's Theory of Language." *Benjamin's Ground: New Readings of Walter Benjamin,* edited by Rainer Nägele, 83–104. Detroit: Wayne State University Press, 1988.

Gass, William. "Gertrude Stein and the Geography of the Sentence: *Tender Buttons.*" In *Gertrude Stein,* edited by Harold Bloom, 145–63. New York: Chelsea House, 1986.

Gentile, Emilio. "The Conquest of Modernity: From Modernist Nationalism to Fascism." Translated by Lawrence Rainey. *Modernism/Modernity* 1, no. 3 (1994): 55–87.

Głowiński, Michał. "*Małe narracje Mirona Białoszewskiego.*" *Teksty* 1, no. 2 (1972): 10–28.

Głowiński, Michał, and Jamusz Sławiński, eds. *Pisanie Białoszewskiego.* Warszawa: Wydawnictwo IBL, 1993.

Godzich, Wlad. "Afterword: Reading Against Literacy." *Postmodernism Explained,* by Jean-François Lyotard. Minneapolis: University of Minnesota Press, 1993.

Golsan, Richard, ed. *Fascism, Aesthetics, and Culture.* Hanover, N.H.: University Press of New England, 1992.

Goux, Jean-Joseph. "Politics and Modern Art—Heidegger's Dilemma." *Diacritics* 19, nos. 3–4 (1989): 10–24.

Grahn, Judy. *Really Reading Gertrude Stein: A Selected Anthology with Essays by Judy Grahn.* Freedom, Calif.: Crossing Press, 1989.

Habermas, Jürgen. *The Philosophical Discourse of Modernity.* Translated by Frederick G. Lawrence. Cambridge, Mass.: MIT Press, 1992.

Heidegger, Martin. "*Die Frage nach der Technik.*" *Vorträge und Aufsätze.* Pfullingen: Neske, 1954.

———. *Vorträge und Aufsätze.* Pfullingen: Neske, 1954.

———. *What Is Philosophy?* Translated by William Kluback and Jean T. Wilde. New York: Twayne Publishers, 1958.

———. *Gelassenheit.* Pfullingen: Neske, 1959.

———. *Unterwegs zur Sprache.* Pfullingen: Neske, 1959.

———. *Was Heisst Denken?* Tübingen: Max Niemeyer Verlag, 1961.

———. *Being and Time.* Translated by John Macquarrie and Edward Robinson. New York: Harper and Row, 1962.

———. *Discourse on Thinking.* Trans. John M. Anderson and E. Hans Freund. New York: Harper and Row, 1966.

———. *Wegmarken. Gesamtausgabe.* Vol. 9. Frankfurt am Main: Vittorio Klostermann, 1967.

———. *What Is Called Thinking?* Translated by J. Glenn Gray. San Francisco: Harper and Row, 1968.

———. *On the Way to Language.* Translated by Peter D. Hertz. San Francisco: Harper and Row, 1971.

———. *Poetry, Language, Thought.* Translated by Albert Hofstadter. San Francisco: Harper and Row, 1971.

———. *Sein und Zeit.* Tübingen: Max Niemeyer Verlag, 1976.

———. *Zur Sache des Denkens.* Tübingen: Max Niemeyer Verlag, 1976.

———. "Hölderlin and the Essence of Poetry." *Existence and Being.* Washington, D.C.: Regnery Gateway, 1988.

———. *Beiträge zur Philosophie (Vom Ereignis). Gesamtausgabe.* Vol. 65. Frankfurt am Main: Vittorio Klostermann, 1989.

———. *Überlieferte Sprache und technische Sprache.* St. Gallen: Erker, 1989.

———. *Basic Writings,* 2d ed. Edited by David Farrell Krell. New York: Harper Collins, 1993.

———. *Hegel, Gesamtausgabe.* Vol. 68. Frankfurt am Main: Vittorio Klostermann, 1993.

———. *Bremer und Freiburger Vorträge.* Frankfurt am Main: Vittorio Klostermann, 1994.

———. *Hölderlin's Hymn "The Ister."* Translated by William McNeil and Julia Davis. Bloomington and Indianapolis: Indiana University Press, 1996.

———. *Besinnung. Gesamtausgabe.* Vol. 66. Frankfurt am Main: Vittorio Klostermann, 1997.

———. *Die Geschichte des Seyns. Gesamtausgabe.* Vol. 69. Frankfurt am Main: Vittorio Klostermann, 1998.

———. *Contributions to Philosophy (From Enowning).* Trans. Parvis Emad and Kenneth Maly. Bloomington and Indianapolis: Indiana University Press, 1999.

———. *Metaphysik und Nihilismus. Gesamtausgabe.* Vol. 67. Frankfurt am Main: Vittorio Klostermann, 1999.

Horkheimer, Max and Theodor W. Adorno. *Dialectic of Enlightenment.* Translated by John Cumming. New York: Continuum, 1993.

Howe, Susan. *My Emily Dickinson.* Berkeley: North Atlantic, 1985.

———. "Statement for the New Poetics Colloquium, Vancouver 1985." *Jimmy and Lucy's House of "K"* 5 (1985): 13–17.

———. "The Difficulties Interview." *Difficulties* 3, no. 2 (1989): 17–27.

———. *The Europe of Trusts.* Los Angeles: Sun & Moon Press, 1990.

———. *Singularities.* Hanover and London: Wesleyan University Press, 1990.

———. *The Birth-Mark: Unsettling the Wilderness in American Literary History.* Hanover and London: Wesleyan University Press, 1993.

———. *The Non-Conformist's Memorial.* New York: New Directions, 1993.

Huyssen, Andreas. *After the Great Divide: Modernism, Mass Culture, Postmodernism.* Bloomington and Indianapolis: Indiana University Press, 1986.

Irigaray, Luce. *L'oubli de l'air: Chez Heidegger.* Paris: Éditions de Minuit, 1983.

———. *Speculum of the Other Woman.* Translated by Gillian C. Gill. Ithaca: Cornell University Press, 1985.

———. *This Sex Which Is Not One.* Translated by Catherine Porter. Ithaca: Cornell University Press, 1985.

———. *The Irigaray Reader.* Edited by Margaret Whitford. Oxford: Basil Blackwell, 1991.

———. *Marine Lover of Friedrich Nietzsche.* Trans. Gillian C. Gill. New York: Columbia University Press, 1991.

———. *An Ethics of Sexual Difference.* Translated by Carolyn Burke and Gillian C. Gill. Ithaca: Cornell University Press, 1993.

———. *Sexes and Genealogies.* Translated by Gillian C. Gill. New York: Columbia University Press, 1993.

———. *I Love To You.* Translated by Alison Martin. New York and London: Routledge, 1996.

———. *Être deux.* Paris: Grasset, 1997.

———. *The Forgetting of Air in Martin Heidegger.* Translated by Mary Beth Mader. Austin: University of Texas Press, 1999.

Jagose, Annamarie. "Irigaray and the Lesbian Body: Remedy and Poison." *Genders* 13 (1992): 30–41.

Janion, Maria. *"Polska proza cywilna." Teksty* 20 (1975): 15–38.

———. *"Wojna i forma."* In *Literatura wobec wojny i okupacji.* Wrocław: Ossolineum, 1976.

Kant, Immanuel. *Critique of Judgment.* Translated by Werner S. Pluhar. Indianapolis: Hackett, 1987.

Kaplan, Alice Yaeger. *Reproductions of Banality: Fascism, Literature, and French Intellectual Life.* Minneapolis: University of Minnesota Press, 1986.

Khlebnikov, Velmir. *Sobranie sochinenii*. 5 vols. Reprint of the Moscow Edition 1928–33. München: W. Fink, 1968–73.

———. *The King of Time: Selected Writings of the Russian Futurian*. Translated by Paul Schmidt. Cambridge, Mass.: Harvard University Press, 1985.

———. *Collected Works*. Vol. 1. *Letters and Theoretical Writings*. Translated by Paul Schmidt. Edited by Charlotte Douglas. Cambridge, Mass.: Harvard University Press, 1987.

Krell, David Farrell. *Intimations of Mortality: Time, Truth, and Finitude in Heidegger's Thinking of Being*. University Park: Pennsylvania State University Press, 1986.

Kristeva, Julia. *Desire in Language. A Semiotic Approach to Literature and Art*. Translated by Thomas Gora, Alice Jardine, and Leon S. Roudiez. New York: Columbia University Press, 1980.

———. *Revolution in Poetic Language*. Translated by Margaret Waller. New York: Columbia University Press, 1984.

Kuenzli, Rudolph E. *New York Dada*. New York: Willis Locker and Owens, 1986.

Lanne, Jean-Claude. *Velimir Khelbnikov: Poète Futurien*. Vol. 1. Paris: Institut D'Etudes Slaves, 1983.

Lefebvre, Henri. *Critique of Everyday Life*. Translated by John Moore. London and New York: Verso, 1991.

Levine, Madeline G. "Fragments of Life: Miron Białoszewski's Poetic Vision." *Slavic and Eastern European Journal* 20 (1976): 40–49.

Levinas, Emmanuel. *Otherwise than Being or Beyond Essence*. Trans. Alphonso Lingis. The Hague: Martinus Nijhoff, 1981.

Lukács, Georg. "Realism in the Balance." In Ernst Bloch et al., *Aesthetics and Politics*. London: Verso, 1980.

Lyotard, Jean-François. *The Postmodern Condition: A Report on Knowledge*. Translated by Geoff Bennington and Brian Massumi. Minneapolis: University of Minnesota Press, 1984.

———. *The Differend: Phrases in Dispute*. Trans. Georges Van Der Abbele. Minneapolis: Minnesota University Press, 1988.

———. *Peregrinations: Law, Form, Event*. New York: Columbia University Press, 1988.

———. *The Lyotard Reader*. Edited by Andrew Benjamin. Oxford: Basil Blackwell, 1989.

———. *The Inhuman: Reflections on Time*. Trans. Geoffery Bennington and Rachel Bowlby. Stanford: Stanford University Press, 1991.

Ma, Ming Qian. "Poetry as History Revised: Susan Howe's 'Scattering as Behavior Toward Risk.'" *American Literary History* 6, no. 4 (1994): 716–37.

Markov, Vladimir. *Russian Futurism: A History*. Berkeley: University of California Press, 1969.

Markov, Vladimir, and Merrill Sparks, eds. *Modern Russian Poetry.* Indianapolis and New York: Bobbs-Merrill Company, 1967.

Menninghaus, Winfried. *Paul Celan: Magie der Form.* Frankfurt am Main: Suhrkamp, 1980.

Mickiewicz, Denis. "Semantic Functions in *Zaum*.'" *Russian Literature* 15, no. 4 (1984): 363–464.

Milchman, Alan, and Alan Rosenberg, eds. *Martin Heidegger and the Holocaust.* Atlantic Highlands, N.J.: Humanities Press, 1996.

Moi, Toril. *Sexual/Textual Politics: Feminist Literary Theory.* London and New York: Methuen, 1985.

Nancy, Jean-Luc. *The Inoperative Community.* Edited by Peter Connor. Minneapolis: University of Minnesota Press, 1991.

———. *The Experience of Freedom.* Translated by Bridget McDonald. Stanford: Stanford University Press, 1993.

Nyczek, Tadeusz. *"Mówić wprost."* *Miesięcznik literacki* 17, no. 4 (1972): 45–47.

Perloff, Marjorie. *The Poetics of Indeterminacy: Rimbaud to Cage.* Evanston: Northwestern University Press, 1980.

———. *The Futurist Moment: The Avant-Garde, Avant-Guerre, and the Language of Rupture.* Chicago: University of Chicago Press, 1986.

———. " 'Collision or Collusion with History': The Narrative Lyric of Susan Howe." *Contemporary Literature* 30, no. 4 (1989): 518–33.

Poggioli, Renato. *Theory of the Avant-Garde.* Translated by Gerald Fitzgerald. Cambridge, Mass.: Harvard University Press, 1968.

Quartermain, Peter. *Disjunctive Poetics: From Gertrude Stein and Louis Zukofsky to Susan Howe.* Cambridge: Cambridge University Press, 1992.

Richter, Hans. *Dada: Art and Anti-Art.* New York: Oxford University Press, 1978.

Ruddick, Lisa Cole. *Reading Gertrude Stein: Body, Text, Gnosis.* Ithaca: Cornell University Press, 1990.

Sandauer, Artur. "Junk Poetry." *Białoszewski.* Translated by Adam Czerniawski. Warsaw: Authors Agency and Czytelnik, 1979, 29–76.

Schnapp, Jeffrey T. "Propeller Talk." *Modernism/Modernity* 1, no. 3 (1994): 153–78.

Schor, Naomi. "Previous Engagements: The Receptions of Irigaray." In *Engaging with Irigaray: Feminist Philosophy and Modern European Thought,* edited by Carolyn Burke, Naomi Schor, and Margaret Whitford. New York: Columbia University Press, 1994.

Scott, Joan W. "Experience." In *Feminists Theorize the Political,* edited by Judith Butler and Joan W. Scott. New York: Routledge, 1992.

Sobolewska, Anna. *Maksymalnie udana egzystencja: Szkice o życiu i twórczości Mirona Białoszewskiego.* Warszawa: Wydawnictwo IBL, 1997.

Stein, Gertrude. *Lectures in America.* New York: Random House, 1935.

————. *Ida.* New York: Vintage, 1971.

————. "Many Many Women." *Mattise, Picasso and Gertrude Stein with Two Short Stories.* Barton, Vt.: Something Else Press, 1972, 117–98.

————. *Everybody's Autobiography.* New York: Vintage, 1973.

————. *How to Write.* West Glover, Vt.: Something Else Press, 1973.

————. *The Yale Gertrude Stein.* New Haven: Yale University Press, 1980.

————. *Tender Buttons.* Los Angeles: Sun & Moon Press, 1991.

Stimpson, Catherine. "The Somagrams of Gertrude Stein." In *The Lesbian and Gay Studies Reader,* edited by Abelove, Barale, and Halperin, 342–52. New York and London: Routledge, 1993.

Suleiman, Susan Rubin. *Subversive Intent: Gender Politics, and the Avant-Garde.* Cambridge, Mass., and London: Harvard University Press, 1990.

Tzara, Tristan. *Seven Dada Manifestoes and Lampisteries.* Translated by Barbara Wright. New York: Riverrun Press, 1992.

Urbaniak, Irena. *"Trwalsze od spiżu."* In *O wierszach Mirona Białoszewskiego: Szkice i interpretacje,* edited by Jacek Brzozowski, 36–44. Łódź: Oficyna Bibliofilów, 1993.

Weber, Samuel. "Theater, Technics, and Writing." *1–800* (Fall 1989): 15–20.

Weed, Elizabeth. "The Question of Style." In *Engaging with Irigaray: Feminist Philosophy and Modern European Thought,* edited by Burke, Schor, and Whitford. New York: Columbia University Press, 1994.

Whitford, Margaret. *Luce Irigaray: Philosophy in the Feminine.* London and New York: Routledge, 1991.

Wodziński, Cezary. *Heidegger i problem zła.* Warszawa: Państwowy Instytut Wydawniczy, 1994.

Zaworska, Helena. *"Spiszę wszystko." Twórczość* 33, no. 5 (1977): 99–104.

Ziarek, Ewa Płonowska. *The Rhetoric of Failure: Deconstruction of Skepticism, Reinvention of Modernism.* Albany: State University of New York Press, 1995.

Ziarek, Krzysztof. *Inflected Language: Toward a Hermeneutics of Nearness: Heidegger, Levinas, Stevens, Celan.* Albany: State University of New York Press, 1994.

————. "The Ethos of Everydayness: Heidegger on Poetry and Language. *Man and World* 28, no. 4 (1995): 377–99.

————. "After Aesthetics: Heidegger and Benjamin on Art and Experience." *Philosophy Today* 41, no. 1 (1997): 199–208.

————. "Proximities: Irigaray and Heidegger on Difference." *Continental Philosophy Review* 33.2 (1997): 133–58.

————. "Powers to Be: Art and Technology in Heidegger and Foucault." *Research in Phenomenology* 28 (1998): 162–94.

Index of Names